NEAR EASTERN RELIGIOUS TEXTS
RELATING TO THE OLD TESTAMENT

THE OLD TESTAMENT LIBRARY

General Editors

NEAR EASTERN RELIGIOUS TEXTS RELATING TO THE OLD TESTAMENT

Edited by
WALTER BEYERLIN

in collaboration with Hellmut Brunner,
Hartmut Schmökel, Cord Kühne, Karl-Heinz Bernhardt,
and Edward Lipiński

THE WESTMINSTER PRESS
Philadelphia

Translated by John Bowden from the German
Religionsgeschichtliches Textbuch zum Alten Testament,
Volume 1 in *Grundrisse zum Alten Testament,*
supplementary series to *Das Alte Testament Deutsch,*
published 1975 by Vandenhoeck & Ruprecht, Göttingen

Published by The Westminster Press ®
Philadelphia, Pennsylvania

PRINTED IN THE UNITED STATES OF AMERICA

Library of Congress Cataloging in Publication Data

Main entry under title:

Near Eastern religious texts relating to the Old
  Testament.

  (The Old Testament library)
  Translation of Religionsgeschichtliches Textbuch
zum Alten Testament, which is a translation of ancient
Egyptian, Mesopotamian, Hittite, Ugaritic, and North
Semitic texts, with commentary.
  Includes bibliographical references and indexes.
  1. Near East — Religion — History — Sources.
2. Bible. O.T. — History of contemporary events, etc.
— Sources. I. Beyerlin, Walter. II. Series.
BL1060.R4413   291.8′0956   77-28284
ISBN 0-664-21363-4

PREFACE

The present volume, the first in the series *Grundrisse zum Alten Testament* (Old Testament Outlines), represents a co-operative effort by scholars from both ancient Near Eastern and Old Testament studies. Individual contributions were as follows: H. Brunner the Egyptian texts, H. Schmökel the Mesopotamian texts, C. Kühne the Hittite texts, K.-H. Bernhardt the Ugaritic texts and E. Lipiński the North Semitic texts from the first millennium BC. The arrangement of the book and the principles used in selecting and presenting the texts are those of the editor. I have edited the book in accordance with these principles, and where it seemed appropriate have also added a considerable number of references to points of comparison in the Old Testament. My work has been considered and accepted by each contributor concerned. I am most grateful to my colleagues for this fruitful collaboration, not least for all the patience that has been needed over this complicated undertaking. I am also grateful to J. Halbe for his unfailing labour over the final stages and the correction of proofs, and above all for compiling the index. I am also grateful to Vandenhoeck and Ruprecht for being so ready to listen to suggestions for the shaping of this book and for putting them into effect.

Münster   W. Beyerlin
Summer 1975

CONTENTS

Preface   v

List of Illustrations in the Text   xiii

List of Plates   xiv

Abbreviations   xv

Introduction   xxi

A. EGYPTIAN TEXTS (Hellmut Brunner)

Introduction   1

I. Myths   3

The creation of the world   3

1. Creation according to the theology of Memphis   4
2. Re describes his creation   5
3. The world before creation   6
4. The four good deeds of the creator   7

Human disorder   8

5. The annihilation of the human race   8

The end of the world   11

6. Conversation of Osiris with Atum   11

II. Cultic hymns (and literary imitations)   12

7. Hymn to Amun from the Eighteenth Dynasty   12
8. Akhenaten's great hymn to Aten   16
9. The hymn of a thousand strophes   20
10. Hymn of Mer-Sekhmet   25

III. Royal texts   27

11. The founding of a temple in Heliopolis   27
12. Votive inscription of Ramesses II in Abydos   28
13. Short quotations from other texts   29
14. Stele of king Pi (formerly Piankhi) of Gebel Barkal   29
15. The conception and birth of the god-king   29

IV. Personal Prayers and Hymns   30

Vows and Intercessions   32

   16. Votive stele of the painter Neb-Re, dedicated to Amun-Re   32
   17. Votive stele of the worker Nefer-abu for the mountain peak   35
   18. Prayer stele of Nefer-abu to Ptah   36
   19. Prayer of Iit-Noferti, the spouse of Sennodiem
       (Thebes, tomb no. 1)   37
   20. Prayer and dedication of Simut, called Kiki   37

Hymns of praise and thanksgiving   39

   21. Hymn of Nekh-Atum (or Khu-Atum?) to the divinized King
       Amenophis I   39
   22. Amun as shepherd   40
   23. Hymn to Amun in the form of a prayer   40
   24. Religious sentences and maxims   41
   25. The form of letters in the Ramesside period   43

V. Precepts for Life   44

   26. The teaching of Merikare   44
   27. The teaching of a man for his son   47
   28. The teaching of Ani   48
   29. The teaching of Amenemope   49
   30. An inscription in the tomb of Petosiris   62

VI. From the Book of the Dead   63

   31. The negative confession of sin (Book of the Dead, Saying 125)   64

B. MESOPOTAMIAN TEXTS (Hartmut Schmökel)

Introduction   68

I. Myths, Epics and Scattered Saga Material   74

The creation and ordering of the world   74

   1. From the Sumerian epic 'Gilgamesh, Enkidu and the Underworld':
      the separation of heaven and earth   74
   2. Sumerian hymn to the mattock   75
   3. Sumerian myth 'Enki and Ninmah': the creation of man   76
   4. The Babylonian incantation to the 'tooth-worm'   77
   5. Sumerian myth 'Enki and the Ordering of the World'   78
   6. Akkadian myth 'When on high' ('Creation Epic')   80

Creation stories   85

   7. Sumerian myth 'Enki and Ninhursanga': paradise?   85
   8. Sumerian epic 'Enmerkar and the Lord of Aratta': paradise?   86
   9. The Sumerian 'confusion of tongues'   86
   10. The Sumerian kings before the flood   87
   11. Sumerian myth of the flood   89

12. The Akkadian Atrahasis epic: the flood 90
13. Eleventh tablet of the Akkadian epic of Gilgamesh: the flood 93

Scattered saga material 97
14. Sumerian myth 'Inanna and the Gardener': plague of blood 97
15. The Akkadian legend of Sargon: divine protection of the chosen child 98

II. Hymns, Prayers and Laments 99
16. Sumerian hymn to Enlil 99
17. Akkadian hymn to the sun god Shamash 101
18. Sumerian 'raising of the hand' prayer to the moon god Nanna-Suen (Sin) 104
19. Sumerian temple hymn 106
20. Sumerian hymn to the king 107
21. Akkadian invocation to an anonymous god 108
22. Akkadian invocation to Ishtar 109
23. Prayer of Gudea, ruler of Sumer, from his hymn on building a temple 112
24. Lamentation from a hymn of Ashurnasirpal I to Ishtar 113
25. Prayer from a building inscription of Nebuchadnezzar II 115
26. A Sumerian lamentation on the destruction of Ur 116

III. Predictions and Prophetic Sayings 118
27. 'A ruler will come . . .' 118
28. The Shulgi prophecy 119
29. Prophetic speech of Marduk 120
30. Prophetic sayings from Mari 122
    (i) Offering for a dead father (ARM III 40)
    (ii) Warning and encouragement (ARM X 7)
    (iii) Reprimand and promise of help (ARM X 8)
    (iv) Good news from Dagan about the Jaminites and a warning to pay more heed to the god (A 15)
    (v) Warning against warlike adventures (ARM X 50)
    (vi) Good news about Eshnunna (ARM X 80)
    (vii) Prophecy of victory (ARM XIII 23)
    (viii) Good news about the threat from Hammurabi of Babylon (ARM XIII 114)

IV. Curses in Treaties, Catalogues of Sins 129
31. Esarhaddon's vassal-treaty 129
32. Shurpu – the Akkadian series of adjurations 131

V. Wisdom 133
33. An Akkadian dialogue on the unrighteousness of the world 133
34. 'I will praise the Lord of Wisdom' 137
35. 'Man and God' – the 'Sumerian Job' 140
36. Lamentation for Urnammu of Ur 142

C. HITTITE TEXTS (Cord Kühne)

Introduction   146

I. Myths   151

    1. From the Song of Ullikummi, tablet 3: the separation of heaven
        and earth   151
    2. The kingship in heaven   153
    3. The weather god and the dragon Illuyankas   155
    4. The myth of the disappearance of Telipinu   159

II. Prayers   165

    5. From the prayer of Kantuzilis   167
    6. The so-called second plague prayer of Mursilis II   169

III. From Royal Substitutionary Rituals   174

    7. From the nine-day ritual of the substitute king   175
    8. From the ritual of the substitute king *KUB* XXIV 5 + IX 13 178

IV. Instructions   179

    9. Instructions for cultic officials and temple personnel   180

D. UGARITIC TEXTS (Karl-Heinz Bernhardt)

Introduction   185

I. Myths   190

    1. A banquet for Baal   192
    2. Anat's war   193
    3. Baal's plan to build a temple   196
    4. Anat's audience with El   199
    5. The message to Kusharu-hasisu, the master-builder   201
    6. The dispute over the permission for the building   203
    7. The fight between Baal and Yam   203
    8. Ashirat and Baal   206
    9. A temple for Baal!   207
   10. The temple window   209
   11. Who is king?   211
   12. Baal's message to Mut   213
   13. Baal's entry into the underworld   214
   14. Lament over Baal   215
   15. Ashtar's abortive enthronement   216
   16. Anat's conflict with Mut   217
   17. Baal's victory over Mut   218
   18. Baal as weather god   220

II. Prayer   222
    19. Prayer-song to El and the assembly of the gods   222

III. Epics   223
    20. Keret   223
    21. Daniil   225

E. NORTH SEMITIC TEXTS from the first millennium BC
(E. Lipiński)

Introduction   227

I. Votive Inscriptions   228
    1. The Melqart stele of Bar-hadad   228
    2. The Zakkur inscription   229
    3. Votive inscription of a Melqart worshipper from Cyprus   232
    4. Punic votive inscriptions   234

II. Inscriptions on Buildings   237
    5. The Mesha inscription   237
    6. The Karatepe inscriptions   240
    7. The inscription from Pyrgi   243
    8. Inscription of a Chemosh worshipper   244

III. Sepulchral Inscriptions   245
    9. Sepulchral inscription of King Tabnit of Sidon   245
    10. Early Jewish sepulchral inscription   245

IV. Seals   246
    11. Seal of an Edomite king   246
    12. Seal of a prophet of Melqart   246
    13. Seal of a priest of the moon god   247

V. Incantations   247
    14. First amulet from Arslan Tash   247
    15. Second amulet from Arslan Tash   249

VI. Cultic Inscription   250
    16. The incense altar from Lachish   250

VII. Graffiti   251
    17. Hebrew graffiti from a chamber tomb   251

VIII. Administrative Texts   252
    18. The Ophel ostracon   252
    19. Document from Elephantine   252

  IX. Correspondence   253
    20. An Arad ostracon   253
    21. A letter from Tahpanhes   253
    22. The passover letter from Elephantine   254
    23. A letter from Memphis to Aswan   255

  X. Treaty Inscriptions   256
    24. State treaties between Katk and Arpad   256

  XI. Mythography   266
    25. Fragments from Philo of Byblos   266

Index of Names and Subjects   269
Index of Biblical References   279

LIST OF ILLUSTRATIONS IN THE TEXT

1. Akhenaten and his consort sacrificing to the sun god Aten   17
(*ANEP*, fig. 408)

2. Amun begets the successor to the throne by the queen   31
(H. Brunner, *Die Geburt des Gottkönigs*, ÄA 10, 1964, centre of plate 4)

3. Scarab with text A 24 (vi)   42
(*ZÄS* 79, 1954, 4)

4. Weighing the heart at the judgment   63
(*ANEP*, fig. 639)

5. Gods fighting the dragon   81
(*ANEP*, fig. 691)

6. Procession of the gods (Malatya)   100
(*ANEP*, fig. 537)

7. An Assyrian dignitary in prayer before the god Ashur   114
(*AOB*, fig. 334)

8. Procession of the gods (Yazilikaya)   149
(E. Akurgal, *Orient und Okzident*, Kunst der Welt, 1966, 73, fig. 27)

9. The weather god fighting a dragon   156
(E. Akurgal, op. cit., 97, fig. 60)

10. King Tudhaliya (IV) in the embrace of a god   168
(E. Akurgal, op. cit., 96, fig. 59)

11. Anat as goddess of war   194
(U. Cassuto, *The Goddess Anat*, 1950, frontispiece)

12. Baal with a cedar in his left hand   212
(*Syr* 14, 1933, plate XVI, facing p. 122)

13. Melqart, 'Baal of Tyre'   228
(*ANEP*, fig. 499)

14. Mesha Inscription   236
   (M. Lidzbarski, *Handbuch der nordsemitischen Epigraphik*, 1898, [2]1962,
   II, plate 1)
15. Seal of a priest of the moon god   247
   (M. A. Levy, *Siegel und Gemmen*, 1869, plate II, no. 12)

Figures 1, 4-7 and 11-13 were drawn from plates in the above-mentioned sources by
Frau Christel Gorys.

LIST OF PLATES

I   Hieroglyphs chiselled in stone with a praying figure   *facing page* 4
   (Photograph H. Brunner)

II Hieratic script on papyrus: Teaching of Amenemope   36
   (Photograph British Museum: Papyrus no. 10,474)

III Akkadian cuneiform tablet: epic of the creation of the world,
   tablet IV   196
   (Photograph British Museum: Babylonian Tablet no. 93,016)

IV Clay tablet from Ras Shamra: Saga of Aqhat, the son of Daniil   228
   (Photograph Musée du Louvre: AO no. 17324a)

ABBREVIATIONS

ÄA	Ägyptologische Abhandlungen, Wiesbaden
AAeg	Analecta Aegyptiaca, Copenhagen
AcOr	*Acta Orientalia*, Leiden, etc.
ADAW	Abhandlungen der deutschen (until 1944 preussischen) Akademie der Wissenschaften, Berlin
AfO	*Archiv für Orientforschung*, Graz etc.
AfOB	*Archiv für Orientforschung*, Beiheft
AHAW	Abhandlungen der Heidelberger Akademie der Wissenschaften, Heidelberg
AHAW, PH	Abhandlungen der Heidelberger Akademie der Wissenschaften, Heidelberg, philosophisch-historische Klasse
AION	*Annali del'istituto universitario orientale di Napoli*. Pubblicazioni
AJSL	*American Journal of Semitic Languages and Literatures*, Chicago
AnBib	Analecta Biblica, Rome
ANEP	*The Ancient Near East in Pictures Relating to the Old Testament*, ed. J. B. Pritchard, Princeton, NJ 1954, [2]1969
ANET	*Ancient Near Eastern Texts relating to the Old Testament*, ed. J. B. Pritchard, Princeton, NJ 1950, [2]1955, [3]1969
AnOr	Analecta Orientalia, Rome
AnSt	*Anatolian Studies*. Journal of the British Institute of Archaeology at Ankara, London
AO	Der Alte Orient. Gemeinverständliche Darstellungen, Leipzig
AOAT	Alter Orient und Altes Testament, Kevelaer, etc.
AOB	*Altorientalische Bilder zum Alten Testament*, collected and described by H. Gressmann, Berlin etc. [2]1927
AOT	*Altorientalische Texte zum Alten Testament*, ed. H. Gressmann, Tübingen etc, 1909, [2]1926
ArCl	*Archeologica Classica*, Rome
ARM	*Archives Royales de Mari. Textes cunéiformes*, Paris (quoted by volume and number)
ARM.T	*Archives Royales de Mari. Transcriptions et traductions*, Paris
ArOr	*Archiv Orientální*, Prague
AS	Assyriological Studies, Chicago, Ill.

ASAE	*Annales du Service des Antiquités de l'Égypte*, Cairo
ASAW	Abhandlungen der sächsischen Akademie der Wissenschaften, Leipzig
BA	*The Biblical Archaeologist*, New Haven, Conn.
BAr	*Bulletin Archéologique du Comité des Travaux Historiques et Scientifiques*, Paris
BASOR	*Bulletin of the American Schools of Oriental Research*, New Haven, Conn., etc.
BeO	*Bibbia e Oriente*, Milan etc.
BG	A. Heidel, *The Babylonian Genesis. The Story of Creation*, Chicago etc. ²1951
BHS	Biblia Hebraica Stuttgartensia, ed. K. Elliger, W. Rudolph, etc., Stuttgart 1968ff.
Bib	*Biblica*, Rome
BibOr	Biblica et Orientalia, Rome
BIFAO	*Bulletin de l'Institut Français d'Archéologie Orientale*, Cairo
BiOr	*Bibliotheca Orientalis*, Leiden
BMB	*Bulletin du Musée de Beyrouth*, Paris etc.
BRGA	Beiträge zur Religionsgeschichte des Altertums, Halle
BTTK	*Belleten. Türk tarih kurumu. Revue, Société d'Histoire Turque*, Ankara
BSAW, PH	Berichte der sächsischen Akademie der Wissenschaften zu Leipzig, Leipzig, philosophisch-historische Klasse
BZAW	Beihefte zur *Zeitschrift für die alttestamentliche Wissenschaft*, Berlin etc.
CIS	*Corpus Inscriptionum Semiticarum*, Paris
CT	*The Egyptian Coffin Texts*, ed. A. de Buck and A. H. Gardiner, OIP 34ff., Chicago 1935ff.
CTA	A. Herdner, *Corpus des tablettes en cunéiformes alphabétiques découvertes à Ras-Shamra - Ugarit de 1929-1939*, Paris 1963
DOTT	Winton Thomas, *Documents from Old Testament Times*, London 1958
EeC	Études et Commentaires, Paris
EvTh	*Evangelische Theologie*, Munich
FS	Festschrift
FTS	S. N. Kramer, *From the Tablets of Sumer*, Indian Hills, Colorado 1959
GbS	S. N. Kramer, *Geschichte beginnt mit Sumer*, Munich 1959
GCS	Die griechischen christlichen Schriftsteller der ersten drei Jahrhunderte, Berlin
GGA	*Göttingische gelehrte Anzeigen*, Göttingen
Gordon, *UgT*	C. H. Gordon, *Ugaritic Textbook*, AnOr 38, Rome 1965
HAW	Handbuch der Altertumswissenschaft, Munich
Hist	*Historia. Zeitschrift für alte Geschichte*, Wiesbaden
HKL	*Herder's Konversationslexikon*, Freiburg im Breisgau
HO	*Handbuch der Orientalistik*, Leiden, etc.

HRG	*Handbuch der Religionsgeschichte*, Göttingen
HTR	*Harvard Theological Review*, Cambridge, Mass.
IEJ	*Israel Exploration Journal*, Jerusalem
Iraq	*Iraq.* British School of Archaeology in Iraq, London
JA	*Journal Asiatique*, Paris
JAOS	*Journal of the American Oriental Society*, Baltimore, Maryland
JBL	*Journal of Biblical Literature*, Philadelphia, Pa
JCS	*Journal of Cuneiform Studies*, New Haven, Conn.
JEA	*Journal of Egyptian Archaeology*, London
JEOL	*Jaarbericht van het Vooraziatisch-Egyptisch Genootschap (Gezelschap) 'Ex Oriente Lux'*, Leiden
JNES	*Journal of Near Eastern Studies*, Chicago
JSS	*Journal of Semitic Studies*, Manchester
JTS	*Journal of Theological Studies*, Oxford
KAI	*Kanaanäische und aramäische Inschriften*, ed. H. Donner-W. Rollig, Wiesbaden 1962-1964, ^{2}1967-1969
KBo	Keilschrifttexte aus Boghazköi, Leipzig
KUB	Keilschrifturkunden aus Boghazköi, Berlin
LÄ	*Lexikon der Ägyptologie*, Wiesbaden
LÄS	Leipziger Agyptologische Studien, Glückstadt, etc.
LSS	Leipziger semitische Studien, Leipzig
LXX	Septuagint
MÄS	Münchener Ägyptologische Studien, Berlin
MAOG	Mitteilungen der Altorientalischen Gesellschaft, Leipzig
MDAIK	*Mitteilungen des deutschen archäologischen Instituts*, Abteilung Kairo, Munich
MDOG	*Mitteilungen der deutschen Orient-Gesellschaft*, Berlin
MIOF	*Mitteilungen des Instituts für Orientforschung*, Berlin
MUSJ	Mélanges de l'Université Saint-Joseph, Beirut
MVÄG	Mitteilungen der vorderasiatisch-(ägyptisch)en Gesellschaft, Leipzig, etc.
NESE	*Neue Ephemeris für semitische Epigraphik*, Wiesbaden
NR/NS	New series
OIP	Oriental Institute Publications, Chicago, Ill.
OLP	*Orientalia Lovaniensia Periodica*, Louvain
OLZ	*Orientalistische Literaturzeitung*, Berlin etc.
Or	*Orientalia*, Rome
OrAnt	*Oriens Antiquus*, Rome
OT	Old Testament
OTS	*Oudtestamentische Studien*, Leiden
OTSt	Old Testament Studies, Edinburgh
PEFA	*Palestine Exploration Fund Annual*, London
PEQ	*Palestine Exploration Quarterly*, London
PRU	*Le Palais Royal d'Ugarit*, Paris
RA	*Revue d'Assyrologie et d'Archéologie Orientale*, Paris

RB	*Revue Biblique*, Paris
RdE	*Revue d'Égyptologie*, Paris etc.
RES	*Revues des Études Sémitiques*, Paris
RGG	*Die Religion in Geschichte und Gegenwart*, Tübingen 1909–1913, [2]1927–1932, [3]1956–1965
RGL	*Religionsgeschichtliches Lesebuch*, ed. A. Bertholet, Tübingen 1908, [2]1926–1932
RHA	*Revue Hittite et Asianique*, Paris
RHR	*Revue de l'Histoire des Religions*, Paris
RLA	*Reallexikon der Assyriologie*, ed. E. Ebeling–B. Meissner, Berlin etc. 1928ff.
RPOA	R. Labat – A. Caquot – M. Sznycer – M. Vieyra, Les religions du Proche-Orient Asiatique. Textes Babyloniens, Ougaritiques, Hittites (= Le Trésor Spirituel de l'Humanité), Paris 1970
RSF	*Rivista di Studi Fenici*
SAHG	A. Falkenstein – W. von Soden, *Sumerische und akkadische Hymnen und Gebete*, Zürich/Stuttgart 1953
SAOC	Studies in Ancient Oriental Civilization, Chicago
SBFLA	*Studii Biblici Franciscani Liber Annuus*, Jerusalem
SDAW	*Sitzungsberichte der deutschen* (to 1944: *preussischen*) *Akademie der Wissenschaften zu Berlin*, Berlin
Sem	*Semitica*. Cahiers publiés par l'Institut d'Études Sémitiques de l'Université de Paris, Paris
SM	S. N. Kramer, *Sumerian Mythology*, New York 1961
SOr	Sources Orientales, Paris
StBT	Studien zu den Boğazköy-Texten, Wiesbaden
StP	Studia Pohl, Rome
SVT	Supplements to *Vetus Testamentum*
Syr	*Syria*. Revue d'Art Oriental et d'Archéologie, Paris
TCS	Texts from Cuneiform Sources, Locust Valley, NY
TDNT	*Theological Dictionary of the New Testament*, ed. G. Kittel, trans. and ed. G. W. Bromiley, Grand Rapids, Mich., 1964ff.
TGI	*Textbuch zur Geschichte Israels*, ed. K. Galling, Tübingen 1950, [2]1968
ThLZ	*Theologische Literaturzeitung*, Leipzig
ThR	*Theologische Rundschau*, Tübingen
ThSt	Theologische Studien, ed. K. Barth, etc., Zürich
ThZ	*Theologische Zeitschrift*, Basle
UF	*Ugarit-Forschungen*, Neukirchen, etc.
UVB	*Vorläufigen Bericht über die . . . Ausgrabungen in Uruk-Warka*, Berlin
VAB	Vorderasiatische Bibliothek, Leipzig
VIOF	Veröffentlichungen des Instituts für Orientforschung, Berlin
VT	*Vetus Testamentum*, Leiden

WM	*Wörterbuch der Mythologie*, ed. H. W. Haussig, Stuttgart
WMANT	Wissenschaftliche Monographien zum Alten und Neuen Testament, Neukirchen
WO	*Die Welt des Orients*. Wissenschaftliche Beiträge zur Kunde des Morgenlandes, Göttingen etc.
WVDOG	Wissenschaftliche Veröffentlichungen der deutschen Orientgesellschaft, Leipzig etc.
WZ(J)	*Wissenschaftliche Zeitschrift der Friedrich-Schiller-Universität Jena*, Jena
WZKM	*Wiener Zeitschrift für die Kunde des Morgenlandes*, Vienna
ZA	*Zeitschrift für Assyriologie und vorderasiatische Archäologie*, Leipzig etc.
ZAW	*Zeitschrift für die alttestamentliche Wissenschaft und Kunde des nachbiblischen Judentums*, Berlin
ZÄS	*Zeitschrift für ägyptische Sprache und Altertumskunde*, Berlin etc.
ZDMG	*Zeitschrift der deutschen morgenländischen Gesellschaft*, Wiesbaden etc.
ZDPV	*Zeitschrift des deutschen Palästina-Vereins*, Wiesbaden etc.

INTRODUCTION

Before the middle of the last century, no really significant traditions were known from the world of the Old Testament, the ancient Near East. The texts of the Old Testament had to be interpreted in their own terms, unless they were interpreted in terms of their connection with the New Testament. Since then, over a period of little more than a century, this situation has changed fundamentally. All over the 'fertile crescent' and beyond, in Egypt and Mesopotamia, in Asia Minor and Syria, in Lebanon and in Palestine, which is the more immediate setting of the Old Testament, archaeology and Near Eastern studies have salvaged an almost immeasurable wealth of texts which invite comparison with the biblical traditions. It is unthinkable now that the Old Testament could really be understood without taking this comparative material into account. Nor should anyone suppose that the religious convictions expressed in Old Testament texts can be grasped satisfactorily regardless of the religious evidence from the world of the ancient Near East. Anyone concerned to understand the Old Testament and the religion to which it bears witness faces the task of making good use of the possibilities of comparing the material within the Old Testament with that outside it.

This volume is concerned with that task. First, it brings into prominence a limited selection of important comparative texts from the vast number of ancient Near Eastern writings which have been discovered, in a form that is easy to grasp. Secondly, it collects in a single volume material which hitherto has been scattered and isolated, often published in specialist journals which are difficult to get hold of. Thirdly, it presents the texts from the ancient Near East in translations which take into account the present state of our knowledge. Fourthly, it provides introductions and notes which will help to make the texts comprehensible and will put them in context. And lastly, it aims to prompt comparative study by cross-references and suggestions, as well as by an extensive index.

The title, *Near Eastern Religious Texts relating to the Old Testament*, indicates the essential criteria of selection. One important requirement is that the texts should relate to the Old Testament. 'Relationship' is understood in wider terms than those of direct dependence or influence. It also includes parallels – where an ancient Near Eastern text may be thought to explain an Old Testament tradition without there being any direct connection; when it 'corresponds' to the Old Testament in a substantial way despite some difference or other; when there are close similarities in intention, theme or in other respects; when there are more than peripheral points of contact; when a comparison sheds light or, in some circumstances, provides a significant contrast. The other criterion indicated in the title of the book is that texts should be relevant to the religion of the ancient Near East. It therefore leaves aside texts which might serve to illuminate the history of Israel, the geography of Palestine, the history of Old Testament literature or other cultural aspects, but which are of little or no help towards a better understanding of the religious testimony of the Old Testament.

Unlike the more comprehensive collections to be mentioned later, a selection made on this special basis cannot fulfil all expectations. For example, it does not represent fully all the literary forms which are attested in the various areas of the Near East. True, because the comparative material assembled here is also classified by genres within the various divisions of the book, an impression of this kind might arise. However, it is impossible to give a complete picture, because it is quite impossible to take into account here literary forms which are essentially insignificant in terms of the religious testimony of the Old Testament.

There is a further important limitation. Only those dimensions of the religions of the ancient Near East which have points of comparison with the Old Testament evidence are illustrated by the texts included here. That means that comprehensive and self-contained accounts of Near Eastern religions cannot be given. This is impossible in a book of texts whose selection is determined by their relationship to the Old Testament and its religion. All that can be done by way of compensation is to give bibliographical references to accounts which are concerned with the religions of the ancient Near East, individually and as a whole. The editors of the texts were well aware that those which were selected could only be understood in the context from which they had been taken. Accordingly, the introductions and notes to the individual texts seek to provide what is needed in the context, especially of the religion concerned.

Not least, lack of space has meant that numerous texts which could have been related to the religious evidence in the Old Testament have had to be omitted. In particular, ancient inscriptions from southern Arabia have been left out of account completely. This has been done for various reasons, including the fact that they belong to the more distant background. In order to make the best possible use of the space available, only extracts from some texts have been given; in that case, appropriate explanations have been added. Where possible, the passages have been arranged so that they shed light on one another; this should also make it easier to understand them.

This volume is not without its predecessors. There is little point in giving a more or less complete list of them here. For the sake of brevity, reference may be made to the survey given in K.-H. Bernhardt, *Die Umwelt des Alten Testaments* I, 1967, 2f. It is, however, worth showing how the collection here differs from similar works which are readily available. The *Textbuch zur Geschichte Israels*, ²1968, edited by K. Galling, covers texts which shed more light on the history of Israel than on its religion. None of the texts which it contains are included here, with the one important exception of the Moabite stone, which is also of religious significance. The two volumes thus supplement each other and are meant to be used side by side. Nor does the *Altorientalische Kommentar zum Alten Testament* edited by A. Jirku offer any real competition. Because the comparative material is arranged in the same order as the books in the canon of the Old Testament, its connection with the Old Testament is made particularly striking. However, since the collection is limited to the texts discovered up to the date of its publication in 1923 and to the state of scholarship at that time, it is in many ways out of date. The same can be said of the collection *Altorientalische Texte zum Alten Testament* edited by Hugo Gressmann. Significant though the book is, it is nevertheless rooted in the state of scholarship and knowledge of the year 1926, in which the second edition appeared; the 1970 edition is just an unaltered reprint. A selection of the texts discovered since 1926 was first published in J. B. Pritchard, *Ancient Near Eastern Texts Relating to the Old Testament*; the selection given was progressively enlarged over the course of three editions (1950, ²1955, ³1969). This voluminous work, like that of Gressmann, contains Near Eastern texts relating to all dimensions of the Old Testament, and not only to the religion to which it bears witness. It therefore covers a wider range than the present book of texts, including the specialist area represented here. The two may thus be seen as parallel works, though supplementary material of many kinds will be found here – in the most favourable instances material which has been made available after 1969. This is not so much the case with the considerably briefer selection edited by D. Winton Thomas, *Documents from Old Testament Times*, on behalf of the Society for Old Testament Study. True, it too relates ancient Near Eastern texts (reflecting the state of scholarship in 1958, the year in which it was published) to various aspects of the Old Testament, and not only to its religious testimony; its range of comparisons is thus wider. However, because of the brevity of the volume, the documents in the collection which have a religious significance hardly ever go beyond the range of texts encompassed by the present volume.

It goes without saying that texts have to be included here which have long been available in earlier collections: a selection which aims to give a convenient summary of material which is of special importance for Old Testament religion must obviously contain well-known and even 'classic' texts from its environment. But it can also prove necessary to provide new editions of these texts, because new insights, from philology or other studies, may be applied. On the other hand, it is to be hoped that the way in which this new collection makes available texts discovered in most recent years will be equally obvious.

The indications of possible parallels with the Old Testament have been made with deliberate restraint, and more should not be read out of them than they in fact say. The word 'compare' is used a great deal, but it is not to be understood as indicating that the item to be compared is exactly the same, identical; there will be differences as well. Where 'correspondence' or 'parallelism' is indicated, even if a *mutatis mutandis* has not been added explicitly, the possibility should certainly not be ruled out that there are also peculiar differences at one point or another. Where these are noted, the fact can only be indicated in an allusive way; no thorough discussion is possible. Any attempt here not only to suggest points of comparison but to develop the comparisons exhaustively would take us beyond the limits of this book and beyond the bounds of what seem to be present possibilities. Furthermore, the comparative passages within the Old Testament are not always listed exhaustively; we have often had to be content with a selection of examples. The fact that in this respect, too, lines have only been sketched out and not drawn in full detail must be kept in mind, particularly when using the index of biblical references. When 'parallels' are mentioned, no indication is necessarily given of how they came about. Sometimes it remains an open question from beginning to end whether they are caused by some direct connection between the traditions and texts being compared or whether there is simply a parallel development based on the identity or similarity of conditions and circumstances. Often there is just not enough evidence to make a decision possible. Often, too, there are impenetrable barriers. And often the case is that more thorough detailed investigation is necessary to make matters clearer. In view of all this it is obvious how many issues must necessarily remain unresolved in a comparison between ancient Near Eastern texts and the religious witness of the Old Testament.

Indeed, the situation is so open that we even have limited possibilities in using parallels to elucidate such important questions as whether and how far the religion is to be found in the Old Testament traditions is a stranger to the world of the religions of the ancient Near East, or whether it is a part of that world, rooted in it, shaped by it, and incomprehensible without it. The present volume can only be of limited help towards progress over these questions. It can, however, provide material which promises to supply further information relating to them. It can prompt new consideration of whether one feature of Old Testament religion or another seems to be alien to the religious world in which it is set, or rather is common and familiar. Perhaps, too, it can counter the all too familiar tendencies (outlined most recently by H. Graf Reventlow in *Kerygma und Dogma* 20, 1974, 199ff.) to be biased in one direction or another. But in view of its particular plan and aim it cannot do much more than that.

The material for comparison is grouped according to the different areas of the ancient Near East. This best suits the concern of the book with the history of religions. For the most part, it also leads to a grouping by languages. The material has deliberately been divided into literary genres only within the sections relating to particular regions. The distinction between the penultimate part of the book (D) and the last part (E) is only in part regional: E not only takes the evidence further, but also goes beyond the area with which D is exclusively concerned. In this case the two sections are also distinguished by a considerable difference in time: the writings grouped together in E come from the first millennium BC, whereas those collected in D are earlier. References to the contents of the book are abbreviated, as above, using the letters attached to the main sections and the numbers which relate to the individual texts within them.

The following details are important in the presentation of the texts. Insertions aimed at making the text more understandable are distinguished from the text itself by being printed in smaller type. To give some examples, this is the case with inserted notes which clarify the structure of the text (cf. e.g. A 31), with mutilated texts, with gaps (cf. e.g. B 16), with the indication of different versions (cf. e.g. C 3), with notes which form connecting links over omissions in the texts (cf. D throughout) or even with notes about the siting of one inscription or another (cf. e.g. E 14). Superior Arabic numbers generally give the numbering of lines. On the whole, the translations reproduce the lines as they are in the original texts. Where necessary, details are given in the introductions to individual texts about the particular original and the edition by which the lines are numbered. Following widespread usage, numbers are given only for each fifth line, but the first and last lines are always numbered to indicate the extent of a particular passage. (Superior Arabic numerals occasionally

also denote the pages of a papyrus manuscript; in that case, they precede
the numbering of the lines, and are followed by a comma; see A 29).
Roman numerals are used to indicate larger units: tablets, columns etc.
The abbreviations will make it clear which one is meant. Superior letters
indicate the corresponding footnotes. The use of *italics* in translations
serves only one purpose in the present book: it indicates words which
have been left untranslated (including names); it does not indicate doubtful translations, as is the practice elsewhere. The latter are marked by
question-marks in brackets (?). Three points . . . indicate that the complete text has not been cited. This may happen for a number of reasons.
First, it may seem desirable to reproduce only part of a text, the whole
of which can in fact be translated. Points at the beginning and end of a
passage indicate that only an excerpt has been quoted. The same is true
of points which coincide with a jump in the numbering of lines; these
replace the portion of text which has been omitted. On the other hand,
points can also be used quite apart from this to indicate passages which
present translation difficulties or are incomprehensible. They are used
in a similar way to show gaps in the transmission of the text. In this
capacity they indicate an unwillingness to fill gaps by means of conjecture. Gaps in the texts are indicated by square brackets. The words within
the brackets have been inferred by the translator; they are attempts to
restore the text. Material within round brackets is of quite a different
kind: it has been added to make the translation more comprehensible.

Where untranslated words and phrases or even the transcriptions of
names appear in the context of the translations – and also in the accompanying commentary and the explanatory footnotes – diacritical marks
have been avoided as far as possible. Exceptions have only been made
where exact details seem essential. On the whole, the conventional spelling
of familiar names has been retained. This has inevitably led to inconsis-
tencies, but these are not of any significance.

In connection with the problem of transcription, it has been borne in
mind that many readers are unfamiliar with the original languages in
which the texts were written; such readers are considered even more in the
explanations which are to be found in the various introductions and footnotes (distinguished from the translations by being printed in small type).
The original text is only cited when this is unavoidable, for example in
explanations of how texts have been deciphered or supplemented, or
where a translation needs some philological explanation. Where dis-
cussions of this kind have been published separately, reference has been
made to the relevant publication. In one way or another an attempt has
been made to give some indication of the scholarly basis both to profes-
sionals and to interested laymen. However, with a view to those readers

who are not concerned with such information, this part of the apparatus has been kept as unobtrusive as possible. Any other explanations have been directed to a readership which extends beyond theologians and scholars, and indeed beyond teachers and doctoral students.

With a view to this wider readership, and at the same time because of the limited space available in the book, only a select bibliography has been given. As a rule older works which have been superseded by more recent publications have been omitted. Titles listed are primarily in German, then in English. Publications in other languages have been listed much less frequently. However, they are mentioned where they are fundamental works, or the only ones available. Where bibliographical references have been abbreviated, it is for reasons of space; titles of books and articles are not given where publications can easily be indicated by the abbreviations of series and scholarly journals in regular use. A list of abbreviations is given on pp. xv–xix, following the suggestions worked out by S. Schwertner in his *Internationales Abkürzungsverzeichnis für Theologie und Grenzgebiete*, 1974.

Finally, a word on the function of the various sections of the commentary which accompanies the text. First of all, the introductions which open the main sections of the book give a general indication of the points worth noting as a whole in each particular group of texts, including the relationship of the texts selected to the body of writing still extant. Where footnotes are needed, they indicate the readings presupposed and the basis for them, the way in which translations have been made and what their significance is. They can also indicate where features of the text translated are reminiscent of the Old Testament tradition. The notes in small type which precede the individual texts serve four separate purposes (as far as possible, they are divided into four sections):

1. The original text on which the translation is based is indicated. Additional information given can be when and where it was found, what condition it is in, where it is kept, where it was first published or its definitive edition. Where necessary, there is also a note of the edition on which the numbering of the lines (or other features) is based.

2. An outline is given of its historical and literary context: the time and the occasion, the presuppositions on which the text is based and the circumstances in which it was composed. Where such details are meaningful, there is an indication of its authorship, and often of aspects of its form and genre. If only an extract of a text is translated, a summary of the rest is given.

3. Details are given of points of comparison with the Old Testament. As has been indicated above, only an introduction to the comparison is given and it is not carried out in detail.

4. A selection of relevant literature is cited: books and articles are mentioned which take the discussion further and to a deeper level; not least, they indicate what is fundamental for the elucidation of the text in question.

Not all these points can be attended to in each case; sometimes it seems appropriate to summarize the information. However, it will prove helpful to read the introductions to the individual texts with these aspects in mind.

The present volume has a certain amount of pictorial material from the ancient Near East. The principle behind its choice is that the pictures should supplement the texts where this is necessary (cf. especially the introduction to the Egyptian texts, p. 2). However, a book of texts can only include samples: on the one hand pictures which illustrate conceptions expressed in written terms in the passages which have been translated, and on the other hand tablets which give an idea of methods of writing and writing materials through which the texts have come down to us. This volume does not try to compete with the relevant collections of illustrations; rather, they will prove a valuable supplement. Special reference should be made to *Altorientalische Bilder zum Alten Testament*, [3]1927, edited by H. Gressmann, and also to *The Ancient Near East in Pictures Relating to the Old Testament*, 1954, edited by J. B. Pritchard, to which a supplement was added in 1969.

Finally, the indices at the end of the book are intended for two principal purposes; first, they list significant items for a comparison with the evidence for Old Testament religion, and secondly, they list those passages of the Old Testament which are relevant for purposes of comparison. Those who begin from Old Testament situations or texts will find their way to comparable Near Eastern texts collected here by means of the index of biblical references.

EGYPTIAN TEXTS

INTRODUCTION

Egypt and Israel became great in the same area of the ancient Near East, with similar conceptions and similar thought-forms. So it is hardly surprising that similar experiences in similar circumstances have led to similar linguistic forms. But do these similarities amount to parallels? Is it not important to realize that each of the two religions inhabits a self-contained world of its own? We cannot even begin to touch on the question how far we have the effect of common human dispositions or the common ancient Near Eastern setting (whether these common features are determined by somatic affinity, similar conditions of life or even by the dubious idea of a 'spirit of the time'), or how far the influence was direct. (In any case, for many centuries Egypt ruled Palestine or influenced it culturally – with interruptions, over a period lasting for two millennia.) A warning has to be given against over-hasty conclusions from real or apparent consonances. The only certain instance of a work from Egypt being taken over in Palestine is that of the Teaching of Amenemope (no. 29), and here there have been marked internal changes; that is why the work occupies a relatively large part of this collection. All other instances of proximity in content or language can only be clarified by an extensive and careful investigation, which is not the purpose of the present volume.

True, there are some individual investigations of the relationship of Egyptian religious conceptions to those of Israel. However, there are only a few surveys. Reference may be made to two lexicon articles: in *RGG*[3] I, 1957, cols. 119ff., S. Morenz has enumerated the 'literary connections' between Egypt and Israel, dealing thoroughly with external forms which often also have some affinity in content. In 1973, an article by R. Grieshammer on the Old Testament, 'Altes Testament', appeared in the *Lexikon der Ägyptologie*, ed. W. Helck and E. Otto, with a section on the connections between the two civilizations, and in particular the literary ones (I, cols. 163-6). Many questions, indeed almost all of them, still remain open.

Those who wish to investigate the considerably more certain subject of Egyptian religion should refer to the three standard works written in German: H. Bonnet, *Reallexikon der ägyptischen Religionsgeschichte*, 1952, where the results of the state of knowledge of the time are given under key words; S. Morenz, *Ägyptische Religion*, 1960, and finally E. Hornung, *Der Eine und die Vielen*, 1971. All three accounts attempt to give the spiritual connections between the facts and begin from the fact that for three thousand years people ventured to live by this faith.

The number of question-marks in the text has been limited so as not to disfigure the presentation of the writings too much, but the translations are by no means all certain. The most dubious passages have been omitted. Those who want to build constructions on often striking similarities should remember how carefully strands of tradition and cultural links must be disentangled, both in Egypt and in Israel.

The greatest problem posed to the translator is not the fact that the sources for Egyptian religion are so abundant and that as a result of the restricted space in this book, important material has to be omitted. Even stronger than the fear that notable parallels to Old Testament conceptions have been passed over is the fear that by taking these passages out of context, the religion of ancient Egypt may have been distorted, and that the fragments presented may be incomprehensible or even misleading. For the most part their content only becomes plain in the context of the larger formal units, and even more when they are seen alongside other texts of the same, or a similar, genre. The widespread absence of pictures is at least as serious a problem. One of the great advantages of Egyptian culture is that it has handed down pictures which illustrate ideas transmitted in writing, even religious ideas; indeed, many metaphors can only be understood as renderings of pictorial art. Language and picture belong together in Egypt, and supplement and explain each other.

Proximity to statements in Old Testament texts has been the chief determining factor in the selection. This has meant the omission of whole areas of Egyptian religion: the wide area of beliefs about the dead, and also the Osiris myth, which is a strong influence on Egyptian religious thought, or the numerous rituals on which scholars are increasingly focusing their attention. It is a great pity that it has proved impossible to include the Admonitions of Ipuwer, and above all the reproach they make against God; however, they have no close Old Testament parallels. True, Job also argues with God over questions of justice, but he does so because of his personal fate, while Ipuwer laments the fate of mankind and reproaches his creator for the imperfection of creation and the existence of evil. So this work, which is of the essence of Egyptian religious thought, has had to be omitted.

The same is true of the conversation between a man weary of life and his soul (the interpretation of which is still, of course, very much a matter of dispute). This also deals with a problem alien to the Israelites, though it had central significance for the Egyptians: the significance of ritual burial and the service of the dead.

Finally, it has been impossible to consider purely literary parallels like love songs or the theme of Potiphar's unfaithful wife. To include literary genres like the royal *Novelle*, which Israel seems most likely to have taken over from Egypt, would have proved too much for the framework of the book because of their length. In accordance with the aim of the book, the selection has had to be limited to similar religious material. Another factor has been the desire to include not only indispensable texts which have often been translated, but also others which so far have not been included in similar works (like *AOT* or *ANET*). This latter category consists primarily of contributions on personal religion (Section IV), a hitherto neglected sphere in Egyptology.

It would be welcome if these texts succeeded on the one hand in highlighting the Old Testament by showing both its proximity to and its remoteness from Egyptian belief, and on the other in arousing new interest in Egypt, the religion of which is not so remote from us as some apparently abstruse forms might suggest at first sight. It is to be hoped that many readers will feel drawn to give them a second glance.

I. MYTHS

The creation of the world

It was generally the Egyptian view that creation did not come about out of nothingness, but out of the primal sea, the Nun, which was unbounded, unmoved and full of potential fertility without being creative. In it and from it the god created a first piece of firm land, the 'primal hill', which was his starting-point for creation. According to another notion he flew over the water in the form of a bird and laid the primal egg upon it. The four pairs of gods who embody the world before creation, unboundedness, lightlessness, timelessness and nothingness (the names vary), all took part in creation.

No continuous creation story has been preserved. All that has come down to us is in the form of fragments, most of which have been incorporated into the alien setting of the texts of the dead, being reworked in the process. The fragments which are given below do not present a complete picture of the numerous and varied Egyptian conceptions of creation.[a] Very little is said about the creation of man, mostly only that he arose out of the creator's tears.[b] More detailed and more substantial information about Egyptian ideas of creation and anthropology can be inferred from hymns and similar texts (Section II).

1. *Creation according to the theology of Memphis*

The text is written in hieroglyphs on a basalt stone which is now in the British Museum. It was recorded by Shabaka (716–701 BC) from an ancient papyrus. It is published in H. Junker, *Die Götterlehre von Memphis*, ADAW 1939, no. 23.

There is some dispute over the date of the composition of the original text on which the copy made on the Shabaka stone is based. Conjectures vary from a dating early in the Old Kingdom to the suggestion of a 'forgery' by the Ethiopian king Shabaka. The text presents a polemically shaded theology directed against the claims of Heliopolis, and presents Ptah as the creator. References are continually made to the common structure of all living beings, to the 'laws' of all that lives. A few extracts have been chosen here which describe creation by knowledge and a word of command.[c]

Creation by the word can be found in the OT in the Priestly account of creation, Gen. 1, esp. vv. 3, 6, 14; in Deutero-Isaiah, esp. Isa. 41.4; 44.26f.; 48.13; 50.2; 55.10f.; also in Job 37.5f. and not least in Pss. 33.6, 9; 148.5. For the creative action of bestowing a name cf. also e.g. Ps. 147.4 (Isa. 40.26), and for the deity resting after creation (line 59) see Gen. 2.2f.

The text has often been translated, most recently by M. Lichtheim, *Ancient Egyptian Literature* I, 1973, 51ff.

[55] ... The nineness of the gods[d] is the teeth and the lips in this mouth which named the name of all things from which Shu and Tefnut came forth,[56] who created the nineness. The sight of the eyes, the hearing of

---

[a] See S. Sauneron and J. Yoyotte, *La naissance du monde selon l'Égypte Ancienne*, SOr 1, 1959, 18–91.

[b] *LÄ* I, col. 303.

[c] There is a collection of a number of Egyptian passages relating to creation by the word in J. Zandee, 'Das Schöpferwort im Alten Ägypten', *Verbum*, FS H. E. Obbink, 1964, 33–66.

[d] This is to be understood as the group of subordinate gods to be found alongside the creator god.

Plate I Hieroglyphics carved in stone: below a supplicant
addresset a goddess with a gesture of surrender

the ears, the sniffing of the air by the nose, they report to the heart. It is
the heart which makes all knowledge arise, and it is the tongue which
repeats what the heart devises.[e] [57] So all the gods were made and his
nineness was completed. Indeed each word of god came about through
what was devised by the heart and commanded by the tongue ....[58] Thus
were made all work and all craft, the action of the hands and the walking
of the feet and the movement of all limbs in accordance with this command which is devised by the heart and which proceeds through the
tongue ....[59] So Ptah rested after he had made all things and all the words
of god.

2. *Re describes his creation*

The text is on two hieratic papyri which are in the Egyptian Museum in
Turin and the British Museum in London. Both come from the time of the
Ramessides. The text is published in A. H. Gardiner, *Hieratic Papyri in the
British Museum*, 3rd Series, 1935, plates 64-65 (numbering of lines follows the
Turin papyrus).

The description is given in the context of a mythical narrative according to
which Isis seeks to learn the secret name of the sun god by making a magic
creature which bites him; she only relieves his torment when he has revealed
his secret name to her. Before he makes known this last name he gives other
'names', those of his work of creation.

The context in the narrative from which the following passage comes has
some similarity to the refusal in the OT to answer questions about the name of
God, Gen. 32.29 (Judg. 13.17f.); however, as a whole the passage contrasts
with the sovereign introduction of himself by the God of the OT through the
giving of his name, Ex. 3.14; 6.2; 20.2(, 7) etc. There are individual points of
contact in this passage with OT creation sagas (e.g. Pss. 65.6ff.; 136.5ff.).

The text is also translated in *ANET*[3], 12ff., and in E. Brunner-Traut,
Altägyptische Märchen, [3]1973, 115ff.

[6]. . . I am he who made the earth and knotted the mountains
and created what is on them.
[7]I am he who made the waters, so that the heavenly cow came into
    being.[f]
I am he who made the bull for the cow,
so that the joy of love might come into the world.
I am he who made the heaven and the mysteries of the two horizons,[g]

[e] The heart is the organ which lies behind the will (as in the OT, Ex. 35.5; 36.2; I
Kings 8.17; Jer. 23.20 etc.), the tongue (or the mouth) is the instrument of the accom-
plishment of the will by the creative word.
[f] The cow rises from the primal water and forms the heaven. See no. 5 below.
[g] The places where the sun touches the earth on rising and setting; they were extremely
significant for the Egyptian because of the contact between the two worlds.

so that the souls of the gods might dwell in them.

[8]I am he who opens his eyes, so that it may be light,
and closes his eyes, so that it may be dark,
at whose bidding the floods of the Nile flow down,
but whose [9]name the gods do not know.
I am he who makes the hours, so that days come into being.
I am he who makes the new year festivals and creates the water of
   inundation . . .

3. *The world before creation*

The fragments reproduced here have been taken from various texts: (i) Pyr.
1040; (ii) Pyr. 1466; (iii) *CT* II, 396b and III, 383a; (iv) Pap. Berlin 3055,
16.3f. (i), (ii) and (iv) have been published in H. Grapow, 'Die Welt vor der
Schöpfung', *ZÄS* 67, 1931, 34–38.

All the passages belong to texts which stress the solitude of the creator god
at the act of creation, since this attests his independence from the created world,
his omnipotence and his wisdom. Non-being can only be described with language which rests on the experience of existing entities. Thus the state of the
world before creation is necessarily described in negative expressions. The statements about creation given here have been preserved in texts of the dead, in
which the dead man identifies himself magically with the creator god, or in the
temple ritual of the daily liturgy (no. 4 below).

There are OT parallels at the beginning of the Yahwistic creation narrative
in Gen. 2.4b–5 and in Ps. 90.2, and the same theme is presented in terms of
wisdom in Prov. 8.24–26.

For cultural connections cf. E. Hornung, *Der Eine und die Vielen*, 1971,
169–71, and H. Grapow, op. cit.

(i) . . . when the heaven had not yet come into being, when the earth
had not yet come into being, when the two river banks had not yet come
into being, when disruption had not yet come into being, when there had
not yet come into being that fear which arose because of the eye of
Horus.[h]

(ii) . . . when the heaven had not yet come into being, when the earth
had not yet come into being, when men had not yet come into being,
when the gods had not yet been born, when death had not yet come into
being.

(iii) . . . when two things in this land had not yet come into being.[i]

[h] The first evil deed upon earth came about as a result of the injury to Horus' eye by
Seth, and is thus brought about by gods (unlike Gen.4). From that time onwards, fear
is dominant. According to the Egyptian picture of the world, conflict is an essential
element in creation.

[i] Creation also means differentiation (cf. the acts of 'dividing' in Gen.1.4, 6, 7, 14, 18).
Only the state of things before creation is undivided.

(iv) (Amun is the god) who was in the very beginning, when no god had yet come into being, when no name of anything had yet been named.

4. The four good deeds of the creator

The text has been preserved on seven coffins dating from the Middle Kingdom. It has been published in *CT* VII, OIP 87, 461ff.

In the context of a text of the dead, words of the creator god have been preserved which he utters in order to refute wild human reproaches against him because of the disorder in the world. He addresses them to his followers, who fight against all the powers which threaten the order in creation, both cosmic forces (clouds) and human rebellion. Cf. also no. 5 below.

The point made in the portion of the text presented here, that evil, disruption of creation, stems exclusively from the heart of men, is paralleled in the OT above all in the aetiologically orientated account given by the Yahwist in Gen. 3-11. Cf. esp. Gen. 6.5; 8.21; on the other hand see also Jer. 2.21ff.; 5.23ff.

The passage has often been translated and discussed: cf. E. Otto, *Der Vorwurf an Gott*, 1951; *ANET*[3], 7; L. H. Lesko, The *Ancient Egyptian Book of Two Ways*, 1972, 130f.; G. Fecht, *Der Vorwurf an Gott in den Mahnworten des Ipu-wer*, AHAW 1972.1, 122ff.; M. Lichtheim, *Ancient Egyptian Literature* I, 1973, 131f.

[461]The Lord of all says to those who bring silence out of tumult on the journey of the court:[j] [462]'Go in peace! In order to bring silence out of evil, I repeat to you the good deeds[k] which my own heart did for me in the midst of the serpent coil.[l] I did four good deeds in the gate of the horizon:[m] I created the four winds, [463]so that every man might breathe in his place;[n] that is one of the deeds. I created the great flood (the inundation of the Nile), so that the poor might have rights (over it) like the rich; that is one of the deeds. I created every man like his neighbour [464]and did not command them to do evil: it was their hearts[o] which disturbed what I had made;[p] that is one of the deeds. I made their hearts so that they could not forget the West (the kingdom of the dead), so that offerings

[j] The reference is to the court of the sun god. Thus he is addressing those who accompany him in the ship of the sun.

[k] Four manuscripts seem to have 'the two good deeds'; the tradition is uncertain.

[l] The symbol of the primal sea (the *tehom*), in which the creator god formed his plan for the world before he brought it about by means of the word. In no. 6 below the god himself is a serpent in the primal sea.

[m] The gate through which the sun appears for the first time at creation and then every day in the east.

'[n] Evidently a reference to the four quarters of the world and the great variety of the works of creation (human races, conditions of life).

[o] The heart as the seat of human reason, and therefore of the freedom of the will and of responsibility (see p. 5 n. e above).

[p] Literally, 'said', that is, creation by means of the word.

might be brought to the gods of the land ;[q] that is one of the deeds.'

Human disorder

5. The annihilation of the human race

The text has been preserved in hieroglyphs in the tombs of Sethos I, Ramesses II, III and VI, but there are errors and lacunae. It has been published in a synoptic edition: C. Maystre, *BIFAO* 40, 1941, 53ff. (the numbering of the lines follows the text of Sethos I).

The present version of the text probably comes from the Eighteenth Dynasty (sixteenth to fourteenth century BC), as the Middle Egyptian text is similar in many ways to the language of this period. The material is certainly earlier (cf. the allusion to the first part of the Teaching for Merikare, no. 27 below, and to the remoteness of God in *CT* II 25 and 34). The form is largely popular. Aetiological interpretations of many episodes depend on word-plays ('and thus there came about'). They have been omitted here.

In some respects, *mutatis mutandis*, the text corresponds to the story of the flood in Gen. 6–8. In Egypt, where the inundation of the Nile is a symbol of blessing, the means by which men are destroyed is not of course the flood, but the burning heat of the desert. Similarly, the survivors are saved not by a floating chest, the ark, but by an intoxicating drink which deceives the vengeful goddess. There is a parallel to the way in which the deity saves a remnant of mankind, who have forfeited their lives through their disorder, in the story of Noah (Gen. 6.8ff.). Finally there is some similarity to the way in which the god becomes more remote from men after their disorder in the expulsion of man from the Garden of Eden, which is mentioned as early as Gen. 3.23f.

The text has often been translated and interpreted: cf. *ANET*[3], 10; E. Brunner-Traut, *Altägyptische Märchen*, [3]1973, no. 69; S. Donadoni, *Testi religiosi egizi*, 1970, 365ff.

[1]Now it came about that [old age] had descended on Re, the god who came into being by himself, when he was king of men and gods altogether. And men planned [2]something against Re.[r] Now his majesty had grown old, his bones were of silver, his flesh of gold and his hair of real lapis lazuli. Then [3]his majesty learned of the things which were being planned against him by men, and his majesty said to his followers: 'Call to me my eye and Shu, [4]Tefnut, Geb, Nut and all the fathers and mothers who were with me when I was in Nun, as well as the god, Nun himself.[s] He

[q] Literally 'the gods of the district', probably as distinct from the dead, who are also often called 'gods'.

[r] The end of the close communion of God with men on earth is brought about by the machinations of men which become possible through the extreme age and the weakness of the god.

[s] 'Nun' is the primal sea before the creation, the potentially fertile but inactive creative flood, corresponding to the OT *tehom*.

is to bring his court [5]with him. But bring them here secretly: mankind shall not see it and their hearts shall not escape.[t] You are to come with them (the gods) to the palace, so that they may present their plans. In the end [6]I shall go back to Nun,[u] to the place where I came into being.

Then these gods were brought in, and these gods (ranged themselves) on both sides, putting their heads to the ground [7]before his majesty, so that he (Re) might make his speech before his father (Nun), the oldest, the creator of men, the king of the people. They said to his majesty, 'Speak [8]to us, that we may hear.' And Re said to Nun: 'O oldest god, from whom I came into being, and you primal gods! Behold, mankind, which [9]came into being from my eye,[v] has devised plans against me. Tell me what you would do about it. Behold, I am seeking (the right solution) and will not kill them until I have heard what you have [10]to say on the matter.'

Then spoke the majesty of Nun, 'My son Re, god greater than the one who begat him, older (i.e. more honourable) than his creator, sit again on your throne![w] [11]Fear of you is great since your eye[x] is directed against those who have moved away from you.'[y]

Then spoke the majesty of Re: 'See, they have fled into the desert. Their hearts are afraid because of what they have devised.' [12]Then they said to his majesty, 'Let your eye go out and smite for you those who have (now) moved away in evil.[z] But there is no eye which is sufficient to smite them for you. [13]Let it come down as Hathor.'[a]

Then this goddess came back after she had slain the men in the desert. And the majesty of this god said: 'Welcome in peace, Hathor, who have done for the creator the deed for which you have come.'

[14]'Then this goddess said, 'As you live for me, I have prevailed over mankind, and it was a refreshment for my heart.'

Then said the majesty of Re, 'Now I will be able to have power over them as king (?), [15]since I have lessened their numbers' . . .

[t] The thought is probably of impotence.

[u] The end is the same as the beginning. See no. 6 below.

[v] An Egyptian myth about the creation of man has it that he is formed from the god's tears. See *LÄ* I, col. 303 (s.v. 'Anthropologie, religiöse').

[w] Re had risen before his father; he addresses only him.

[x] The eye of the sun, which is at the same time the god's daughter (*pupilla*), has fatal force, especially in the desert.

[y] There is a double meaning here: men have departed – outwardly – from the creator at creation, since they stem from his eye; now, however, they have departed from him yet again through their rebelliousness, and have fallen away from him.

[z] See the previous note.

[a] On earth the eye has to assume the form of a goddess. Hathor is the goddess of intoxication: the intoxication of killing as well as that caused by alcohol (and the intoxication of love).

Then said Re: [16]'Summon me swift messengers to rush here, so that they may speed like the shadow of a body.' These messengers were immediately brought to him. [17]Then said the majesty of this god: 'Run to Elephantine and bring me much red ochre.' Then this ochre was brought to him. Then the majesty of this God had [18]the one with a side lock, who is in Heliopolis, to grind up this ochre.[b] In the meantime slave girls had ground barley for (brewing) beer, and now this red ochre was added to the mash, and it looked like [19]human blood. It filled seven thousand jars of beer.

Then came the majesty of the king of Upper and Lower Egypt, Re, together with these gods, to see this beer.

In the meantime the morrow had come [20]on which the men were to be slain by this goddess at the time of their going south. Then spoke the majesty of Re: 'How good it is (the beer)! I shall [21]protect mankind from her (the goddess).' Then Re said, 'Take it to the place where she said, "I will slay mankind there".' The majesty of the king of Upper and Lower Egypt, Re, got up very early, [22]at dead of night, to have this sleep-maker poured out. And the fields were now filled with liquid for three palms, according to the will of the majesty of this god.

Then [23]this goddess came in the morning and found these (fields) inundated. Her countenance became gentle at the sight.[c] Then she drank, and it was good in her heart. She came back drunken without having [24]perceived mankind. Then said the majesty of Re to this goddess: 'Welcome in peace, O gracious one!'

[27] . . . Then said the majesty of Re: 'As truly as I live, my heart is much too weary to be with them (men). Had I annihilated them down to the last remnant, then the [28]length of my arm would not have been too short.' But the gods in his following said: 'Do not revert to your weariness. You have power over what you will.' But the majesty [29]of this god said to the majesty of Nun: 'My limbs are slack as in primal times. I can no longer defend myself (?) against another who attacks me.'

Then said the majesty of Nun: 'My son Shu,[d] have an eye for [30]your father and protect him. My daughter Nut, set him (on your back)!' Then said Nut: 'What do you mean, my father Nun?' Thus spoke Nut. [31] . . . Then Nut changed (into a cow) and the majesty of Re sat on her back . . . men [32] . . . were amazed when they saw him on the back of the

[b] Occasionally the high priest of Heliopolis has a side lock. Only other officials of the New Kingdom are represented as grinding grain. Still, this will be the aetiology for a cultic usage.

[c] The sight of the (supposed) blood delights the goddess and leads her to drink it immediately.

[d] Shu, a son of Re, is the god of the space between earth and heaven.

cow. Then said [33]mankind: '. . . us, then shall we smite your enemies who have devised plans against the one who has made it (?).' [34]But his majesty went (on high) into the palace on the back of the cow and was no longer with them. Then the earth lay in darkness.[e] When the morning dawned, the men went [35]out with their bows.[f]

The end of the world

6. *Conversation of Osiris with Atum*

The text has been preserved in three manuscripts of the Book of the Dead as 'Saying 175'. The best version is in the papyrus of Cha in Turin: E. Schiaparelli, *La tomba intatta dell'architetto Cha*, 1927, 60, Eighteenth Dynasty. Also papyri Leiden T 5 and Brit. Mus. 10, 470 (Ani), both from the Eighteenth and Nineteenth Dynasties (1450–1200). A fragment can already be found in the Coffin Texts of the Twelfth Dynasty (1991–1785), probably as a quotation: *CT* III, 82f. (numbering of lines follows Cha).

This fragment of myth has found its way into the texts of the dead because it speaks of survival and long life.

The fragment has a number of points of contact with OT thought, as when the kingdom of the dead is understood as 'desert'. There are comparable associations in Jer. 2.31 and Job 12.24f.[g] There are even more marked parallels to the mention of the 'deep', in Ex. 15.5 and Ps. 88.6. As in the OT, conditions in the realm of the dead are presented in negative terms: if light is a feature of earthly life, then the dead are in gloom and darkness. For this cf. e.g. Job 10.21f.; 15.22; 17.13; 18.18; 38.17 and above all Ps. 88.6, 12, 18. The fear that death will bring separation from God is also real in the OT: cf. Isa. 38.18; Pss. 6.5; 88.10–12. On the other hand, in ancient Egypt there are quite different, brighter and more friendly notions of life beyond as well as the sceptical, pessimistic thoughts presented here.

The text has often been translated, cf. e.g. E. Otto, *Der Vorwurf an Gott*, 1951; H. Kees, 'Ägypten', *RGL* 10, 1928, 27f.; *ANET*³, 9; S. Donadoni, *Testi religiosi egizi*, 1970, 327f.

[11]What Osiris said to Atum: 'What does it mean that I must go to the desert of the kingdom of the dead? [12]It has no water, it has no air, it is so deep, so dark, so endless!'[h] (Atum:) 'You will live there in peace of mind.' [13](Osiris) 'But no sexual pleasure can be had there.' 'I have given

---

[e] As the god departs from the earth, the earth is wrapped again in the primal darkness from the time before creation – for some of the time, at night.

[f] The passage which follows contains a very mutilated text of a myth of the origin and valuation of war. There are parallel texts in J. Yoyotte, *École Pratique des Hautes Études*, V[e] Section, Annuaire 1971–72, vol. 79, 164f.

[g] See N. J. Tromp, 'Primitive Conceptions of Death and the Nether World' in the OT', *BibOr* 21, 1969, 130–3.

[h] The Beyond has the qualities of chaos: it is lightless, boundless and deep, cf. Gen. 1.2.

a state of transfiguration instead of sexual pleasure, water [14]and air, peace of mind instead of bread and beer,'[i] said Atum. (Osiris) 'But [15]how painful it is for me not to see your face.'[j] 'I will not allow you [16]to suffer want . . .' [19]. . . 'What is (my) duration of life?' [20]asked Osiris. 'You will (live) millions of millions (of years). Life there lasts for millions. [21]But I will destroy everything that I have created. This earth will return to the Nun, to the flood (?), [22]as in its primal state. I alone am a survivor – together with Osiris – when I have changed my form [23]again into a serpent,[k] which no man knows and which no god has seen.'

II. CULTIC HYMNS (AND LITERARY IMITATIONS)

Numerous hymns have been preserved from three millennia of Egyptian history. Of course we barely know the hymns from earlier times sung in the daily worship of the temple; often only to the degree that they have found expression in personal songs, above all those written in tombs and on tombstones. Another indirect source consists in the hymns translated here, which have been written down on papyri and must be evaluated as literary productions, although they reflect at least notions and probably also formulations from the hymns used in temple worship. Cf. J. Assmann, *Liturgische Lieder an den Sonnengott, Untersuchungen zur altägyptischen Hymnik* I, MÄSt 19, 1969.

7. *Hymn to Amun from the Eighteenth Dynasty*

The text is taken from Pap. Boulaq 17, one of a collection of manuscripts now in the Cairo Museum. Its publication was supervised by A. Mariette, *Les papyri égyptiens du Musée de Boulaq*, 1871-76, II, plates XI-XIII (there are extracts and allusions on other monuments).

The hymn was composed in the Eighteenth Dynasty before the reign of

---

Osiris is the god who has experienced the human plight of death and now laments his lot to Atum, the most ancient god and creator of the world. Mankind laments through his mouth.

[i] The variants in the fragment from the Middle Kingdom are better from the literary point of view: 'I have given a state of transfiguration instead of sexual pleasure, greatness of heart instead of narrowness of heart, peace of mind instead of the eating of bread.' As to greatness of heart or narrowness of heart: care constricts the heart and joy makes it great. The imagery is frequent in Egypt.

[j] Atum is also the sun god.

[k] The serpent can live in the primal water; therefore the primal god takes its form (or that of an eel) before and after the period of the created world. Cf. also no. 4 above and p. 7 n. l.

Akhenaten (i.e. before 1365 BC). The manuscript referred to contains four hymns to Amun. Parts of the second and third hymns are given below. The sections omitted contain predominantly mythological descriptions of the power of Amun. At the moment it remains an open question how far this is a literary or a cultic hymn.

The genre of the hymn (descriptive praise) also appears in the OT, there too especially in connection with the acts of God at creation (Job 26.7ff.; 37.2ff.; Pss. 19.1-6; 33.6f., 9; 65.6; 104; 136.5-9; 146.6 etc.). As in the Egyptian text (IV 2, 5; VI 3) there can be references to the mouth of God, who controls the creative word (Pss. 33.6; 148.5). The perspective of God's providence is also connected with the theme of creation in Ps. 104.10ff., 27f. In Ps. 146.6-8 the theme of legal help for the oppressed, a hearing for the captives and the setting upright of those who have been bowed down is incorporated in a way comparable to the Amun hymns (IV 3, 4). The OT community also understands itself to be at the same time both God's creation and his flock (cf. Ps. 95.4-7 with VII 1), and it also addresses the creator as king (cf. Ps. 95.3 with III 5). Even the idea that the creator god created other gods and must accordingly be praised by them (III 6; IV 2; V 1; VII 4ff.) has distant echoes in biblical hymns (Pss. 29.1f.; 148.1ff.; Job 38.7). On the other hand it is an important and unmistakable fact that the praise in the OT cannot be addressed to a sun god (Ps. 148.3). The hymn to the sun in Ps. 19.4b-6 leaves us in no doubt that even the sun is only God's creature. For further references see p. 15 n. u below.

The only edition is that of E. Grébaut, *Hymne à Ammon-Ra*, 1874. There is a complete translation in *ANET*[3], 365-7.

[III 5] . . . Good shepherd, who appears in the white crown,
Lord of the rays, who [6]makes brilliance,
to whom the gods offer hymns,
who extends his arms to the one whom he loves,[1]
whereas his enemy is [7]consumed by a flame:
it is his eye[m] which brings the enemy down.
. . . [IV 1]Hail to you, Re, lord of order,[n]
whose shrine is hidden,[o] the lord of the gods,
[2]Khepri in his barque,[p] who spoke the word and the gods came into
    being,
Atum, who made the people,
who [3]distinguished their natures and made them able to live,
who separated the chief colours one from another;

[1] The translation 'to whom he wills' is also possible.
[m] The eye of the sun also has an evil, consuming force, see no. 5 above.
[n] Maat, 'order', also embraces truth, justice and order in nature and society.
[o] There is no cultic representation of the sun god in a sanctuary as there is of other gods.
[p] Khepri is the form of the youthful sun god in the morning. The sun god journeys in a boat.

who hears the prayer of him who [4]is in captivity (?),
merciful to the one who appeals to him,
who delivers the fearful from the man of violence,
who judges the weak [5]and the injured.
Lord of perception, whose mouth controls the word of creation,
for love of whom the inundation of the Nile comes.
[6]Lord of gentleness, with great love,
who comes to give life to the people (?),
who gives free course [7]to every being,
which is made out of the Nun,[q]
whose gentleness has created the light,
at whose perfection the gods [V1]rejoice,
at whose glance hearts live. The end.

O Re, adored in Karnak!
. . . [4]We hail you. You are at peace.
Lord of joy, powerful at your appearing,
[5]Lord of the primal serpent, with lofty plumes,
with a beautiful diadem and a lofty white crown.
The gods love to see you.
[6]The double crown is fixed on your brow. Your love is spread abroad
    throughout Egypt,
when your rays shine forth in the eyes.
The [7]perfection of the nobility is your arising.
The cattle become tired when you shine.
Your love is in the southern sky,
[VI1]your gentleness in the northern sky.
Your perfection seizes men's hearts,
your love makes arms fall.
[2]Your beautiful form relaxes the hands,
and hearts are forgetful when they see you.[r]
You are the sole one, who made all [3]that is,
the solitary and only one who made what exists.
From whose eyes men came forth,[s]
and from whose mouth the gods came into being.
Who creates the herbs [4]that give life to the cattle,
and the fruit trees for mankind.
Who makes that on which the fishes [5]in the river may live,
and the birds under the heaven.

    [q] As the creation is not complete, God can also create beings as yet unknown, in the future, from the primal sea, the Nun. Cf. Deut. 8.3.
    [r] The consequence of security is a complete relaxation of tension.
    [s] Cf. p. 9 n. v above.

Who gives air to what is in the egg
and nourishes the young of the serpent.
Who makes that on which [6]gnats may live
and worms and flies likewise.
Who supplies the needs of the mice in their holes
[7]and nourishes those things that fly, in every tree.
Hail, you who did all this,
solitary sole one, with many hands,[t]
[VII 1]who spends the night wakeful, when all the world sleeps,
and seeks what is useful for his flock,[u]
Amun, who endures in all things,[v]
[2]Atum and Harakhti,[w]
praise is yours when they all say:
'Jubilation for you, because you [3]weary yourself with us,
honour to you, because you created us!'

Hail to you, because of all cattle,[x]
jubilation to you, because of [4]all foreign lands,[y]
to the height of the heaven and the width of earth, and to the depth of
    the sea!
The gods are bowing down [5]to your majesty
and exalting the power of the one who created them;
they rejoice at the approach of the one who begat them.
They [6]say to you, 'Welcome, father of the fathers of all the gods,
who raised the heaven and laid out the earth,
who [7]made what is and created what will be,
sovereign – life, salvation, health! – and chief of the gods!
We praise your power, [VIII 1]as you have created us.
We sacrifice to you (?) because you have brought us forth.
We offer hymns to you because you have wearied yourself with us.

---

[t] The many hands correspond in the first place to the manifold activity of the creator
and then to his continuing action in the *creatio continua*. The Amarna period gave
pictorial representation to this many-handedness of God: a great many rays go out
from the disc of Aten, the sun, all of them culminating in hands. See fig. 1, p. 17.
    [u] God's flock consists of the people whom he pastures (cf. e.g. Ps. 95.7). For god's
unsleeping care cf. Ps. 121.3. For the image of god or the king as a good shepherd and
of men as a flock cf. D. Muller, *ZÄS* 86, 1961, 126ff.
    [v] This significant statement about Amun is at the same time 'confirmed' by an allu-
sion; *mn*, 'remain', sounds like the name of Amun.
    [w] Atum and Harakhti are manifestations of the sun god during the course of the day.
    [x] This perhaps means wild animals, especially those in the desert, or perhaps also men
as God's flock, and perhaps even both.
    [y] An allusion to the manifold character of creation, which shows a characteristic and
appropriate providence for every country. See no. 8 below.

Hail to you, [2]who made all that is!
Lord of order, father of the gods,
who made mankind and the beasts,
Lord of the grain, [3]who also takes care that the beasts of the
   wilderness can live . . .

8. *Akhenaten's great hymn to Aten*

The text is engraved in hieroglyphs on the tomb of Ay in Tell el-Amarna.
(There are shorter versions on the opposite wall and elsewhere.) Publication
was supervised by N. de G. Davies, *The Rock Tombs of El Amarna* VI, 1908,
plates XXVII and XLI.

The hymn is an original composition by king Akhenaten (Amenophis IV,
1365-1348), but following the old form of the hymn to the rising sun and using
traditional notions and formulae. A significant feature of his new theology is
that he consistently leaves out particular notions, above all those which relate
to survival after death or to myths. Cf. the point of contact with nos. 7 above
and 9 below.

There are parts of Akhenaten's hymn which have striking parallels with Ps.
104 in the OT: cf. e.g. lines 3f. with Ps. 104.20f., line 6 with Ps. 104.25f., line
7 (end) with Ps. 104.24, line 10 with Ps. 104.10ff. The descriptions of the onset
of night show that parallelism does not exclude fundamentally different evalua-
tions (cf. lines 3f. with Ps. 104.20f.). The parallelism has often been discussed,
cf. e.g. G. Nagel, *Bertholet Festschrift*, 1950, 395ff.; S. Morenz, *HO* I. 1. 2,
1970[2], 231ff. For individual points of contact see also p. 18 n. e, p. 19 nn. f, h
and l below.

The text has often been translated, see K. Sethe in H. Schäfer, *Amarna in
Religion und Kunst*, [2]1931, 63ff.; H. Kees, 'Ägypten', *RGL* 10, 1928, 6ff.;
R. J. Williams, in *DOTT*, 142ff., and not least by J. A. Wilson, *ANET*[3],
369ff.

[2]You shine out in beauty on the horizon of heaven,[z] O living Aten,[a]
the beginning of life. When you have appeared on the eastern horizon,
you have filled every land with your perfection. You are beautiful and
great, bright and high above every land; your rays encompass the lands
to the very limit of all that you have made. [3]You are Re and reach to their
limit and restrain them for your beloved son (Akhenaten). Although you
are far away, your rays are on earth; although you are in man's countenance, no one knows your going. When you set on the western horizon,
the earth lies in darkness as in death. The sleepers are in their rooms,

---

   [z] See p. 5 n. g above.
   [a] Aten is the name and manifestation of the god exclusively worshipped by Akhenaten;
of course he is also called Re or Re-Harakhti. The epithet 'living' has been an attribute
of the deity in Egypt from ancient times.

1. King Akhenaten with his consort and daughter sacrificing to
Aten, whose rays end in hands (cf. p. 15 n. t above).

their heads veiled, and no eye beholds another. All that they have under their heads may be stolen – but they do not notice. [4]Every lion has come forth from its den, and all the snakes bite. The darkness is . . . , the earth lies in silence, (for) the one who created it has gone to rest on his horizon. – The earth becomes bright: you have arisen on the horizon. As Aten you shine by day and have driven away the darkness. You shed your rays, and the two lands[b] are in festive mood. The men of the sun are awakened and stand upon their feet; you have raised them up. They wash their bodies and take their [5]clothing, their arms are bent in worship, because you appear. The whole land goes to work. All beasts are satisfied with their pasture, the trees and plants become green. The birds flutter in their nests, raising their wings in worship before your spirit.[c] All the lambs skip around, the birds and everything that flutters [6]live because you have risen for them. The ships sail upstream and down, every way is open because you appear. The fish in the river dart before your face, for your rays penetrate into the depths of the sea.

You make the seed grow in women, make fluid into mankind; you keep the child alive in its mother's womb and soothe it so that it does not weep, you are the nurse even in [7]the mother's womb. You are the one who gives breath to all that he has made, to preserve life. When he descends from the womb to breathe on the day of his birth, you open his mouth completely to speak and supply his needs. When the chick in the egg already speaks in the shell,[d] you give him breath within to keep him alive. You have given him strength to break it (the egg). He comes forth from the egg to speak with all his power, and walks on his legs as soon as he emerges.

How manifold are your works! They are hidden from the face (of man), [8]O sole God, apart from whom there is no other! You have made the earth according to your desire, while you were alone, with men, cattle and all beasts, everything that is on earth going on its feet, everything that is on high flying with its wings, the foreign lands of Syria and Nubia and the land of Egypt. You set every man in his place and see to his needs; each one has his food and his time of life is reckoned. Their tongues are separate in speech,[e] and their nature [9]is likewise; the colour of their skin is different: you distinguish the peoples. You create the Nile

[b] I.e., Egypt.

[c] The Egyptian word Ka, 'spirit', denotes the power of life emanating from God, and passively also that of men.

[d] The difference between men and young birds is stressed. The former only make sounds after their birth, while the latter cheep before they are hatched and can fly as soon as they leave their nests. The poet is concerned with the manifold variety of creation.

[e] Compare Gen. 11.1-9 as an OT counterpart.

in the underworld[f] and bring it up at your pleasure,[g] to sustain the people of Egypt as you have made them, the Lord of all of them, wearying himself with them, the Lord of the whole land, rising for them, Aten of the day, great in majesty. All the distant hill countries, you also make them so that they can live, for you have set a Nile in heaven, and it comes down for them; [10]it makes waves on the mountains like a sea, to water their fields by their settlements. How generous are your plans, Lord of eternity! The Nile in heaven is there for the foreign peoples and for all the wild beasts of the desert which go on their feet. But the (true) Nile comes from the underworld for Egypt.

Your rays make all plants grow tall: when you rise, they live and grow for you. You created the seasons,[h] in order to make all your creation thrive: [11]the winter to cool them, the heat that they may taste you. You made the sky distant in order to rise in it and to see all that you have made, while you were alone, rising in your changeable forms as the living Aten,[i] appearing, shining, far and yet near.

You make millions of forms from yourself, the one, cities and towns, fields, roads and the river. Every eye beholds you over against them, for you are the Aten of the day, high over the earth. [12]. . . There is no other who knows you, but your son Nefer-kheperu-Re Wa-en-Re (= Akhenaten), for you have made him to know your plans and your strength.[j]

The world is in your hand, as you have made it. When you have risen, they live, and when you set, they die, for you are lifetime yourself; men live in you. Eyes [13]look on perfection until you set. All work is laid aside when you set on the right hand.[k] When you rise again, you make every arm stir for the king, and haste is in every limb, since you have founded the earth. You raise them (creatures) for your son who came forth from your body,[l] the king of Upper and Lower Egypt, who lives from order, Akhenaten, and the great royal consort Nefertiti.[m]

[f] It was the view in Egypt that the Nile flows out of the primal sea, which continues to underlie the dry land even after the latter has been created (cf. the 'springs of the deep' Gen. 7.11; 8.2), see also p. 26 n. a below.

[g] It is impossible to calculate when inundations of the Nile will be great and when they will be small.   [h] See Gen. 8.22.

[i] The sun changes form many times from its youthful rising, through midday, to its setting in old age; this is a favourite theme in hymns to the sun.

[j] While every Pharaoh is mediator between the world of gods and the world of men and as such has a greater share in the world of the gods than do other men, there is no other period during which a king makes such a claim as does Akhenaten to exclusive knowledge of God's will and thus to worship.

[k] I.e., in the west.   [l] It is interesting to compare II Sam. 7.14; Pss. 2.7; 89.26f.

[m] At this point the detailed titles of the royal couple are given; they have been abbreviated in the translation.

9. *The hymn of a thousand strophes*

The text has been preserved only in a single manuscript: Pap. Leiden I 350. Its beginning and end are lost. The best published version of it is by J. Zandee, *De Hymnen aan Amon van Papyrus Leiden I 350*. Oudheidkundige Mededelingen uit het Rijksmuseum van Oudheden te Leiden, NR XXVIII, 1947 (with translation and commentary). This is not a cultic hymn, but a literary theological work. The strophes are numbered, first from one to ten, then every tenth strophe; from a hundred they are numbered only every hundred, so that (if the last strophe bore the figure 1000) the complete text contained 28 strophes (of different lengths). The first and last words of each strophe echo the number of the strophe. The text comes from the time after Amarna and depicts Amun as the embodiment of all that is divine, without denying or losing sight of the existence of other gods.

In several respects the work invites comparison with OT hymns, above all in that it celebrates the universal scope of divine action (cf. II 6ff.; III 6ff. with Pss. 8; 29; 47; 103.19; 113) and explicitly includes 'sea and ocean' (cf. I 3 with Pss. 29; 65.7; 93) in so far as it considers both God's all-embracing beneficence (cf. II 3-10, 20; III 11ff. with Pss. 65; 145; 146; 147) and the fear of God which seizes upon all (cf. I 2f.; II 3 with Pss. 33.8; 66.3, 5), not least in that it depicts the obeisance in which all the world, Egypt and foreign lands, gods and men, along with nature, offer the praise of God which is due (cf. I 4ff.; II 6ff., 20; III 12f. with Pss. 47.1, 9; 65.8, 12f.; 66.8; 96.11f.; 98.7f.; 148; 150). The following individual points should be noted: the glorification of the sun (cf. especially II 18f. with the revised, Israelite version of the 'hymn to the sun' in Ps. 19.4b-6); the predication of the exalted and powerful name of God (cf. I 3 with Pss. 8.1a, 9; 29.2; 96.8; 99.3; 111.9; 148.13); the evaluation of the creative word of God (cf. IV 6ff. with Ps. 33); the address 'Lord of Lords' (cf. II 3 with Ps. 136.3); the praise of the kingship of God (cf. III 6ff., p. 22 n. c below, with Ex. 15.18; Pss. 29.10; 47.2; 93; 96.10; 98.6; 99.4; 145.11ff.; 146.10); the celebration of the God who hears prayers (cf. III 16f. with Ps. 65.2), who himself brings about deliverance from the underworld (cf. III 15 with Pss. 33.19 [30.3; 116.8]) who is unfathomable and incomprehensible (cf. IV 17ff. with Ps. 145.3; Isa. 40.8; Job 5.9).

The first editing of the hymn was done by A. H. Gardiner, *ZÄS* 42, 1905, 12-42; there is also a German translation by A. Erman, 'Des Leidener Amonshymnus', *SDAW*, 1923, 62-81. For the sixtieth strophe see also G. Fecht, *ZÄS* 91, 1964, 46ff.

[1 2] . . . Sixth strophe.

Every place stands in fear of you.
The inhabitants of [3] . . . your fear.[n]

[n] The Egyptian word *šfšfyt* embraces the meaning of the two Hebrew words *kabod* and *'ema*.

Your name is high, powerful and strong,[o]
sea and ocean[p] stand in fear of you.
. . . [4]Foreign lands and the hill country come down to you.
. . . The dwellers in Punt come to you.[q]
. . . [5]The land of God grows green for you, for love of you.
[Your ships] row [6]for you, laden with resin,
to make your temple glad with a fragrant aroma.
The incense-bearing trees drop [7]myrrh for you.
The aroma of your dew (= incense) reaches your nostrils,
and (the bees) work on their honey . . .
[9]For you, cedars are planted.[r]
[10]. . . The hills bring you stones
to make great the gate (of your temple).
[11]Merchant ships are at sea, boats at the quay,
loaded down and rowing before your countenance.
[12]. . . The river flows north,
but the wind blows south
and brings you offerings from all that is[s] . . .

[II] [2]Ninth strophe.

The nineness,[t] which has come from the primal water,
assembles itself, [3]when it sees you, great in fear,[u]
Lord of Lords,[v] who has created himself,
he is the Lord.
Those who were blind,[w] he [4]illuminates,
to lighten their countenance in another (new) form.
Their eyes shine, their ears are opened,
every body is clothed, [5]as soon as he (the sun god) shines.
The heaven is made of gold and the Nun from lapis lazuli,
the earth is sprinkled with malachite when he rises in the heaven.
The gods can see and [6]their temples are opened.
Men begin to look and to see through him.

[o] Cf. also Deut. 28.58.
[p] The reference is to specific stretches of water, but these cannot be identified on our maps (Red Sea and Mediterranean?).
[q] A land producing incense on the southern coast of the Red Sea.
[r] Cf. Wen-Amon II 24, *TGI*[2], 45.
[s] These are the conditions in Egypt.
[t] A gathering of an indeterminate number of gods (nine = three times three, i.e. many).
[u] See p. 20 n. n above.
[v] See also Deut. 10.17.
[w] Here and in the following passage there is a mention of sleeping men whom the sun god awakens to new life out of the Nun, into which they have sunk back in sleep.

All the trees rise before his countenance,
they turn towards [7]his eye,
and their leaves unfold.
The scaly creatures leap in the water,
they come out from their pools, [8]for love of him.
The sheep and cattle skip before his presence.
The birds dance with their wings.[x]
They (all) observe that he [9]is in his good time.
They live by seeing him as their daily need.
They are in his hand, sealed with his seal,
and no god can open them but his majesty.
[10]There is no one who acts apart from him,
the great God, life for the nineness.

[II 15]Twentieth strophe.

How you cross over, [16]Harakhti,[y]
daily accomplishing your custom from the day before.
You make the years and bring together the months,
days, nights and [17]hours accord with your course.
Today you are newer than the day before.[z]
. . . You alone are wakeful, for you abhor sleep.[a]
[18]While all men sleep, his eyes keep watch,
he divides eternity with his perfect countenance,[b]
no way on earth . . . is void of him.
With speedy course [19]he leaps up;
he crosses the earth in a moment, and finds no resistance;
he traverses the heaven and passes through the underworld,
the sun on every way, travelling in full view.
[20]All have turned their faces towards him,
both men and gods, and they say, 'Be welcome.'

[III 6]Sixtieth strophe.

Upper and Lower Egypt alike are his;
he alone has taken it [7]by his power.[c]

[x] Nature joins in the praise of God: see Ps. 96.11ff. (I Chron. 16.31ff.) and also e.g. Isa. 43.20.

[y] The sun, which is here designated Horus of the places of rising and setting ('the horizons'), crosses heaven in a boat.

[z] The sun grows old in the evening but is born anew every morning.

[a] See p. 15 n. u above.

[b] The sun marks out divisions in eternity, which is itself undivided, cf. Gen. 1.14.

[c] This strophe deals with the kingship of God, which is also discussed very often in Egypt. For the most part the expressions are taken from the language developed in connection with the earthly kingdom of Pharaoh.

His bounds were strong while he dwelt on earth,[d]
extending across the whole earth and to the height of heaven.
[8]The gods ask of him what they need,
and it is he who gives them sacrificial bread from his possessions,[e]
he, the lord of the ploughland, the river bank and the fields.
To him belongs [9]every act of his land register,
the measuring line from beginning to end.[f]
He measures the whole land with his primal serpents.
[10]The foundation ceremony (?) is carried out for him.
His is the royal cubit which tests the building stones;
he spreads out his measuring line over . . . the earth;
he has founded the [11]two lands in their place,
the temples and the sanctuaries.
Every city is under his shadow,[g]
so that his heart can move in that which he has loved.
People sing to him under every roof,[h]
[12]every foundation stands firm under his love.
They brew for him on festival days,
they pass the night still wakeful [13]at midnight.
His name is passed around above the roofs,[i]
song is made to him at night, when it is dark.
The gods receive sacrificial bread through his life-giving power,
[14]the power of the strong god who protects what is theirs.

III [14]Seventieth strophe.

He who frees from evil and drives away suffering,
a doctor who makes the eye healthy without medicine;
[15]who opens the eyes and cures squinting.[j]
Who saves whom he will, even though he were already in the
    underworld,[k]

---

[d] After creation, the creator god to begin with ruled on earth (in a state of paradise).

[e] Creation and all its produce belongs to the creator, and man simply returns to him what is his. This theme appears often in Egyptian literature. In the OT cf. esp. I Chron. 29.14.

[f] Cf. Job 38.4f.

[g] Shadow as a protection, as in the OT; cf. e.g. Judg. 9.15; Isa. 25.4; 30.2; Pss. 17.8; 36.7; 57.1; 63.7; 91.1f.

[h] Literally: at every resting place.

[i] The priests sing hymns by night on the temple roofs; cf. II Kings 23.12; Jer. 19.13; Zeph. 1.5.

[j] For God as healer cf. e.g. Ps. 103.3, also Ex. 15.26; Jer. 33.6. There are numerous instances of the divinity as healer in Egypt.

[k] This is as frequent an expression in Egypt as it is in Israel. The 'underworld' is the

[16]Who can bring deliverance from destiny according to his wish.[1]
He has eyes and ears,
wherever he is, for the one whom he holds dear.[m]
Who hears the [17]prayers of the one who calls on him,
who comes in a moment from afar to the one who cries out to him.
Who lengthens the span of life and [18]shortens it
and gives over and above what is allotted by fate[n] to the one whom he
    holds dear.
Amun is magic over water when his name is above the deep,
[19]and the crocodile has no power when a man calls his name.[o]
The winds change and the headwind moves round,
it . . . grows still, when one remembers him.
[20]A useful word in a time of tumult,[p]
a gentle breeze for the one who calls on him.
Who saves those who have come to grief,
a gentle god with [21]efficacious counsels.[q]
He belongs to the one who rests his back on him,
when he is in his hour (of grace).
He is more useful than millions to the one who sets him in his heart,
a man [22]is stronger than myriads through his name;[r]
the truly gracious protector,
the benefactor, the infallible, whom man cannot ward off.

III 27 . . . Ninetie[th] strophe.

. . .[s] IV [6]He began to speak in the midst of silence;
he opened every eye [7]and made it see.
He began to call,[t] when the earth (was) still (struck) with amazement.
His call went around when there was still not his like.
He created [8]what is and made it live.

---

isolation of the individual from his surroundings, and above all sickness or living in a
foreign land.
  [1] An Egyptian's destiny is determined from the moment of his birth, but as the gods
stand above these powers of destiny, they can alter this determination. See S. Morenz,
Untersuchungen zur Rolle des Schicksals in der ägyptischen Religion, ASAW 52, 1, 1960.
Cf. II Kings 20.6, and by contrast Isa. 38.10ff.; Ps. 102.23f.
  [m] Comparable formulations are I Kings 8.52; II Kings 19.16; Ps. 33.18; 34.15.
  [n] See n. l above.
  [o] But see the prohibition in the Decalogue, Ex. 20.7 (Deut. 5.11).
  [p] A spontaneous prayer.
  [q] The thought here is of an oracle.
  [r] It is interesting to compare Pss. 54.1; 44.5.
  [s] This chapter sings the praises of creation.
  [t] These calls are the words of creation through which all nature is 'called' to life.

He showed all men the way to go,[u]
and their hearts live when they see him.

[IV 12]Two hundredth strophe.[v]

. . .[17]. . . One is Amun who conceals himself before them,[w]
who keeps himself secret before the gods whose being man does not
    know.
[18]He is further than the heaven and deeper than the underworld –
no god knows his true form.
His being is not unfolded in writings,
one cannot give reliable [19]teaching about him.
He is too mysterious for man to be able to disclose his worth,
he is too great for man to be able to search him out,
too strong to know him.
[20]Sudden death from fear is the destiny of the one
who utters his secret names, knowingly or unknowingly.
Nor is there even any god who could call him by them, the mighty one.
[21]'The hidden one' (= Amun) matches his name, just as he is
    mysterious.

Three hundredth strophe.

Three are all the gods:
Amun, Re and Ptah, and there is none like to them.
He conceals his name as [22]Amun,
he is Re in his countenance and his body is Ptah.[x] . . .

10. Hymn of Mer-Sekhmet

The text comes from a collection of similar hymns on the Ramesside Papyrus
Beatty IV, now in the British Museum (no. 10,684). There is a facsimile,
transcription and translation in A. H. Gardiner, *Hieratic Papyri in the British
Museum*, third series, 1935. The present passage is recto 7.5–8.9. It was composed after the Amarna period. The hymns in the collection were presumably
not cultic hymns, but were composed and sung by individuals to God's glory
(though they do make use of elements from cultic hymns). However, in contrast

---

[u] Illuminating the earth as the sun.
    [v] The theme of this chapter is God's hiddenness and the impossibility of searching
him out.   [w] I.e., before the gods.
    [x] Here all the gods of the Egyptian pantheon are subsumed under a trinity, one of
whose members (Amun) is hidden; the second is visible to all (as the sun) and the third
is corporeal. There are also representations of this trinity during the Ramesside period
(e.g. at Abu Simbel). Cf. J. G. Griffiths, 'Triune Conceptions of Deity in Ancient
Egypt', *ZÄS* 100, 1973, 28ff. (p. 30 has a somewhat different and less probable interpretation of the present passage).

to the hymns collected in section IV, the note of praise in these hymns goes beyond the individual element; there is no reference to the person of the singer.

The parallels between the text and the OT are largely the same as those cited in the introduction to nos. 7 and 9: praise of creation (Job 26.7ff.; Pss. 8.3ff.; 19.1ff.; 24.1f.; 33.6f., 9; 89.11ff.; 95.4f.; 104; 136.5ff., etc.); the creative word of God (Pss. 33.6, 9; 148.5; in addition to the hymns cf. Gen. 1); everything without exception is made by the deity who is praised (Pss. 8; 24.1f.; 104; 146.6; 148; Isa. 37.16; 44.24 etc.); at the same time there is also praise for God's providence (Ps. 104.10ff., 27f.); fear of him on all sides (Pss. 33.8; 66.3, 5), but also a turning towards him (Pss. 47; 148; 150 etc.) and an acknowledgment of belonging to him (Pss. 44.4; 74.12; above all Judg. 5.3b); in the context of the hymn, in addition to the theme of creation there is also that of those in need of special protection and help (Ps. 146, especially vv. 6-9); finally there is praise for 'the one who hears prayer' (Ps. 65.2), the metaphor of shepherd and sheep (Ps. 95.4-7; cf. also Ps. 23.1ff. etc.) and stress on the name of God (Pss. 8.1a, 9; 148.5, 13 etc.).

There is a partial translation in *ANET*[3], 371. The first words of each paragraph are written in red in the papyrus.

[7,5]Praise to you, Amun-Re-Atum-Harakhti,[y] who spoke with [7,6]his mouth and there came into being men, gods, cattle great and small, everything that flies and alights, [7,7]all of them.

You created the banks of the Hanebu,[z] who settle in their cities, and also the fruitful meadows, [7,8]fertilized by the Nun[a] and bearing fruit thereafter,[b] and good things without number, [7,9]to support all that lives.

You are mighty as a herdsman, tending them for all eternity. Bodies are [7,10]filled with your beauty, and eyes see through you. Fear of you is for everyone, but their hearts turn [7,11]to you: You are good at all times. All the world lives from your countenance.

Everyone says, 'We are yours!', [7,12]the strong and the weak together, the rich and the poor with one mouth, and all others likewise. [7,13]You are lovely in all their hearts. No body is free from your beauty.

Do not the widows say, [8,1]'You are our husband', and the small children, 'You are our father and our mother'? The rich boast with your beauty [8,2]and the poor revere your countenance. The prisoner turns to you[c] and the sick man calls [8,3]to you.

Your name will be a protection for the body of anyone who is solitary,

[y] The four names which denote the aspects of the sun god are here combined in one, in order to express the omnipotence of the deity.

[z] The Hanebu are the inhabitants of the islands and coasts of the Eastern Mediterranean.

[a] By virtue of the Nile, which flows out of it, the Nun, the primal flood, guarantees the fertility which is needful for life, cf. p. 9 n. f above.

[b] Literally 'giving birth'.

[c] See also Ps. 79.11.

salvation and health for those who are on the water, salvation from the crocodile. [8,4]It is good to remember him at a time of tumult; (he is) deliverance from the mouth of the hot one.[d] Anyone can turn to you and lay their petitions before you.

Your ears are open to hear them,[e] and you fulfil their wishes, [8,6]you our Ptah who loves his likeness,[f] you shepherd, who loves his flock.[g]

III. ROYAL TEXTS

A very large number of Egyptian texts contain the idea that, as the one who brings salvation to the country, the Pharaoh is chosen by the deity. Usually he has been elected even before his birth ('in the egg') and is given special protection in his youth; the myth, told of virtually all the Pharaohs, that the successor to the throne is fathered by a god gives concrete form to talk of God as the 'father' of the king. We can give only a brief selection from the abundant evidence. Attention must also be drawn at least to the narrative of the conception and birth of the first kings of the fifth dynasty in the Westcar papyrus.[h]

11. *The founding of a temple in Heliopolis*

The text from which excerpts are given here has been preserved only in a hieratic transcription of the original, which was written in hieroglyphs, on a leather scroll in the Berlin Museum (P 3029); the best transcription in hieroglyphs and a translation are to be found in A. de Buck, 'The Building Inscription of the Berlin Leather Roll', AnOr 17, 1938, 48ff. There is also a translation in M. Lichtheim, *Ancient Egyptian Literature* I, 1973, 115ff.

Context: In a declaration from the throne (corresponding to a theme in the genre of the royal *Novelle*), Sesostris I declares his will to build a temple and asserts both his legitimacy and the legitimacy of his knowledge of God's will. Only the relevant words are quoted in the following passage.

OT parallels to the context of this extract are II Sam. 7 (I Chron. 17) and I Kings 3.4–15 (II Chron. 1.1–12): the former text is particularly relevant, since it deals with the theme of building the temple. The latter is relevant

---

[d] The 'hot' one is someone who is aggressive, see p. 51 n. b below.

[e] See p. 24 n. m above; also Ps. 22.24.

[f] Ptah is god of the craftsman. The sun god, who is worshipped here, is compared with him in terms of his creative properties: men are his creation. In a comparable way, in the OT a word meaning 'shape, form' (*ysr*) is used for the making of men (and animals): Gen. 2.7f.(19); Isa. 43.7; 45.9; Jer. 1.5.

[g] See e.g. Deut. 33.3.

[h] There is a translation e.g. in E. Brunner-Traut, *Altägyptische Märchen*, [3]1973, no. 3.

because it places the election of the king by God at the first beginnings of physical growth (I Kings 3.7). OT instances of the idea of an election before birth are to be found in e.g. Judg. 13.5, 7 and Jer. 1.5, but these do not relate to a king. Prov. 21.1 is relevant to the idea that the king is destined to accomplish God's will, and II Sam. 5.2 (I Chron. 11.2); Jer. 3.15; Ezek. 34.2, 23 and Ps. 78.71f. parallels the mention of him as 'shepherd'.

Literature: in general see S. Morenz, 'Die Erwählung zwischen Gott und König in Ägypten', in *Sino-Japonica*, FS A. Wedemeyer, 1956, 118-37 (with numerous but still very incomplete examples, since M. limits himself to the occurrence of the word *mry*, 'love', whereas there are many different ways of putting the idea). Cf. however, S. Herrmann, 'Die Königsnovelle in Ägypten und in Israel', in *Geschichte und Altes Testament*, FS A. Alt, 1953-54, 33-44.

5. . . . He (Re-Harakhti) formed me [6]to do what he has done, and to bring into being what he has commanded to be done. He named me shepherd of this land,[i] for he knew who would hold it together for him. [7]He brought to me what is under his protection and what is illuminated by the eye that is in him,[j] he, who creates all things according to his will and has endowed me with the knowledge[k] of what [8]he has determined. I am a king after his nature, a ruler to whom (rule) did not have to be given. Even as a suckling (lit. nestling) did I conquer; I was [9]mighty in the egg; I already ruled as a young man; he appointed me Lord of the two parts of the land while (I was still) a child, [10]whose foreskin had not yet been cut.[l] He named me lord of my subjects, created (for that purpose) [11]before men. Even as an embryo he set me aside (?) to be in the palace, before I had come from my mother's loins . . .

12. *Votive inscription of Ramesses II in Abydos*

The text is written in hieroglyphs on the outside wall at the east of the great hall of pillars in the temple of Sethos I in Abydos. There is a useful edition of the text in K. A. Kitchen, *Ramesside Inscriptions* II, 323ff. The numbering of lines given here follows Kitchen (the older versions differ).

Context: the king reports his plans to build several new temples and to complete others begun by his father Sethos. He addresses his court and indicates his legitimation.

The OT texts listed in connection with no. 11 are also relevant here: II Sam. 7 (I Chron. 17); I Kings 3.4-15 (II Chron. 1.1-12), and especially I Kings 3.7.

Several translations have been made of the votive inscription, e.g. by G. Roeder, *Kulte und Orakel in Ägypten* (Bibliothek der Alten Welt), 1960, 37ff.

---

[i] Both the king and the deity are very often designated 'shepherd' or 'good shepherd', see D. Müller, 'Der gute Hirte', *ZÄS* 86, 1961, 126ff. (who also gives OT parallels).

[j] The disc of the sun.

[k] Read '*pr*, see *JEA* 32, 1946, 1 n. 1.

[l] In Egypt, circumcision was performed at the beginning of puberty.

. . . [43]I came forth from Re, and you say, 'The order of Re remains.'[m] The one who waited for me and brought me up was [44]the almighty lord himself, when I was still a child, until I took up the rule. He had given me the land when I was still an embryo . . .

13. Short quotations from other texts[n]

(i) King Amosis: 'Possessor of greater popularity than all other kings.'[o]

(ii) The victory of Tuthmosis II came about 'because his father Amun loved him more than any (other) king who has lived since the primal time of the land'.[p]

(iii) It is said of Tuthmosis III that 'he works as a king in this land as if he will not live again in eternity.'[q]

14. Stele of king Pi (formerly Piankhi) of Gebel Barkal

The portion of text given here is on the limestone stele of Gebel Barkal in Nubia. The text of the stele has been published in G. Reisner, ZÄS 66, 1931, 90ff. Only the introductory sentences of the god's speech are given here.

Again, the OT texts cited in connection with no. 11 are relevant for comparison, especially II Sam. 7.14 (I Chron. 17.13) and I Kings 3.7; also Pss. 2.7; 89.26f.; 110.3 and of course Jer. 1.4f., though this is no longer connected with the king (on this see M. Gilula, VT 17, 1967, 114).

[1]It is Amun Re who is speaking, the lord of Napata,[r] who designates one pure one, to [2]his beloved son, king Pi,[s] 'I said of you when [3]you were still in your mother's body, that you would be ruler of Egypt, [4]for I already knew you in the seed, when you were still [5]in the egg, that you would become [6]Lord . . .'

15. The conception and birth of the god-king

The most detailed version of the account of the election by God of the bringer of salvation is to be found in a cycle of fifteen pictures, between which is dis-

[m] I.e. the first name of the king, to which an allusion is made.

[n] These texts stress the elevation of a particular king above all before him and after him; cf. I Kings 3.12f. (II Chron. 1.12) and Ps. 89.27.

[o] Urk. IV 20.

[p] Urk. IV 141.

[q] Urk. IV 199. There are further instances and variations down to the time of Ramesses IV in S. Morenz, 'Die Erwählung zwischen Gott und König in Ägypten', Sino-Japonica, FS A. Wedemeyer, 1956, 123-7.

[r] The residence of the kings of Nubia at Gebel Barkal, Napata, bears the same name in Egyptian as Karnak.

[s] A new reading of the king of the Twenty-Fifth Dynasty (c. 740-713 BC) known under the name of Piankhi.

tributed the text of a myth which was originally independent of them. It is
complete in the temple of Hatshepsut in Deir el-bahri and the temple of
Amenophis III in Luxor. There is a critical edition with a German translation
in H. Brunner, *Die Geburt des Gottkönigs*, ÄA 10, 1964. It is probable that this
myth was recorded of each Egyptian king. The version may go back, at least in
part, to the third millennium. Only part of the fourth scene is given here,
relating to the encounter and conversation of Amun and the queen mother
(see fig. 2).

Once again, II Sam. 7.14 (I Chron. 17.13); Pss. 2.7; 89.26f.; 110.3 are to be
cited as relevant OT parallels. (Marginal reference may be made to points of
contact with the birth narratives in the gospel of Luke.)

The queen mother Mut-em-Uya speaks before the majesty of this
glorious god, the lord of Karnak: 'How great is your power! How perfect
is your . . . ! How hidden are the plans which you make! How contented
is your heart at my majesty! Your breath is in all my limbs', after the
majesty of this god has done with me all that he willed. – Then spoke
Amun Re, the lord of Karnak, before her majesty: 'Amenophis, lord of
Thebes, is the name of this child,[1] which I have given in your body,
corresponding to this binding of the word which has come from your
mouth. He will exercise this benevolent kingship in this land . . .'

IV. PERSONAL PRAYERS AND HYMNS

After the temple cult and the service of the dead and belief in them,
'personal piety' is the third important area for Egyptian religion. In this
life, too, the individual Egyptian felt a direct link with the deity, and
indeed that his life was governed by a deity, quite apart from the cult
which was maintained in the temple on behalf of the state. Often he
dedicates his life to an individual god or goddess, or puts himself under
their protection (e.g. no. 20 below); but the name of the deity can vary
depending on the situation. The relationship is governed on man's side
by devotion, trust, love, obedience, prayer and sacrifice, or taking part
in processions and feasts, and on the divine side by secure guidance,
protection from dangers and similarly by love. Vows, prayers, the hearing of prayers and thanksgiving are the forms in which this relationship
is developed – that is, as far as it can be expressed in any kind of document.

We still need a comprehensive account of this side of Egyptian religion.
But see S. Morenz, *Ägyptische Religion*, 1960, esp. III, IV, VII, and id.,
Gott und Mensch im alten Ägypten, 1964.

[1] The name is formed from elements of the queen's speech.

2. Amun begets the successor to the throne by the queen; he
is holding a symbol of life to her nose. Text 15 is beside them.

Vows and intercessions

Egyptian prayers usually follow a very strict form and draw extensively on hymns. A personal note is most evident at the time of the Ramessides; it is to be found especially among those who worked on the royal tombs at Thebes and lived in the settlement of Deir el-Medina. In the prayer texts on their small votive stelae they refer to individual crises and to their personal relationship with the deity (a local form of the imperial god Amun, the 'summit' of Western Thebes in the form of a snake, Ptah as god of the craftsmen, and others as well). Of course these texts, which have been shaped by immediate experience, quickly become the norm for later texts. Some of the expressions which are typical in this genre, like 'hand' for protection and 'underworld' for isolation in society, also recall the general tone of the Psalms.

16. *Votive stele of the painter Neb-Re, dedicated to Amun-Re*

Text: East Berlin, Inv. no. 20 377. Transcription and translation in A. Erman, 'Denksteine der thebanischen Gräberstadt', *SDAW* 1911, 1087ff. and plate 1, also E. Brunner-Traut, *Die alten Ägypter*, 1974, plate 45.

Background for understanding the text: the painter Neb-Re has vowed to Amun that he will compose a hymn to him and display it in public on a stele if Amun saves his son Nakht-Amun, who is sick. His prayer has been heard, so he sets up the memorial.

Both as a whole and also in many details, the text of the stele has points of contact with 'individual thanksgivings' in the OT (in which the individual praises God and records what he has done): Pss. 18; 22.22ff.; 30; 32; 34; 40.1-4 (,5-11); 41; (92;) 116; 138; Isa. 38.10ff.; Jonah 2.2ff. etc. Comparisons are possible with the 'narrative' reference back to the distress which has been survived (line 8; Pss. 18.3ff.; 30.7; 32.3f.; 116.3; Isa. 38.10ff.) and the description of the way in which God has heard the prayer and come to the rescue (lines 9, 14ff.; Pss. 18.6ff.; 22.24; 30.2f.; 34.4; 40.1f.; 116.1f., 8; 138.3; Isa. 38.17; Jonah 2.2, 6). Compare too, the 'forensic' element, the giving of testimony before others (line 2; Pss. 18.49; 22.22; 34.2, 11; 40.3, 10; 116.13ff.); the all-embracing breadth of the testimony (lines 2f., 8; Pss. 18.49; 22.27ff.; 40.9f.; 116.14, 18; 138.1, 4), the change towards a generalized confession (lines 4ff.; Ps. 18.25ff.; 32.10; 34.9ff.; 116.5f.; 138.6), the inclusion of words of instruction and admonition (lines 2, 4; Pss. 32.6, 10; 34.8ff.) and not least the elements of making and fulfilling vows (lines 13ff.; Pss. 22.25; 116.14ff.; Isa. 38.20; Jonah 2.9). In addition to this it is possible to compare all kinds of details, e.g. praising the name of the deity (lines 1, 7; Pss. 22.22; 34.3; 92.1; 138.2), the predicates 'merciful' and 'gracious' (line 6; Ps. 116.5), confidence that the divine anger will be short-lived (lines 10f.; Ps. 30.5), use of the word 'poor' (line 4, Pss. 22.24; 34.6 . . .), etc. Possibly the custom of erecting a memorial itself has analogies in the OT (see the translation of the superscription *mktm* as applied to the Psalms in the Septuagint and Targum). Of course there is no analogy to the fact that the inscription on the Egyptian stele gives the name of the person who has dedicated it.

The inscription has often been translated before, as in *ANET*³, 380ff. and E. Brunner-Traut, *Die alten Ägypter*, 136-8.

Above the figure of Amun enthroned.

Amun-Re, Lord of Karnak, the great God, the first one of Thebes, the holy God who hears prayers, who comes at the voice of the poor and the troubled, who gives breath to the one who is weak.

¹Giving praise to Amun

I make hymns to his name,
I give him praise to the heights of heaven
   and to the breadth of the earth,
I tell ²of his might to the one who goes downstream
   and the one who goes upstream.
Beware of him!
Repeat it to son and daughter,
   to the great and to the small,
tell it to generation upon ³generation
   which have not yet come into being;
tell it to the fishes in the deep
   and the birds in the heaven,
repeat it to him who does not yet know it
   and to him who knows it:
⁴Beware of him . . .
You, Amun, are the lord of the humble man,
you come at the voice of the poor.
I call to you when I am oppressed,
and you ⁵come quickly, to save me in my wretchedness,
to save me, who am imprisoned (?).ᵘ
You, Amun-Re, Lord of Thebes, are the one
who rescues the one who is already in the underworld,ᵛ
for you are one ⁶who has mercy.ʷ
If a man calls to you,

ᵘ If the translation is correct, we may have here a metaphor like the metaphorical use of 'poor'; in religious language 'poor' does not refer exclusively to material need. Prayer is called *šnmḥ*, i.e. 'making oneself poor', in other words, humbling oneself before God (see also p. 38 n. t below). For the use of the word 'bind' cf. also Ps. 22.17, BHS.

ᵛ See pp. 23f. n. k above.

ʷ Literally: one who is gracious.

you come from afar.

Neb-Re, painter of Amun in the necropolis of Thebes, son of Pay, painter of Amun in the necropolis of Thebes, has made this [7]in the name of his Lord Amun, Lord of Thebes, who comes at the voice of the poor.

What he made for him were hymns to his name,
because his power is so great.
What he made for him were [8]prayers to him,
in the presence of the whole land,[x]
on behalf of the painter Nakht-Amun,
when he was lying sick and likely to die,
under the power of Amun because of his cow.[y]

I [9]found that the Lord of the gods came as the north wind, and that sweet breezes went before him; he rescued Nakht-Amun, the painter of Amun.

[10]He says:
If it is the nature of the servant to commit sin,
it is the nature of the Lord to be gracious.[z]
The Lord of Thebes does not spend a whole [11]day angry.
When he is angry, it is only for a moment,
and nothing is left behind.
The wind has turned for us in grace,
[12]and Amun returns with his breezes.
By your spirit! You will be gracious,
and what has once been turned away will not come back to us.

[13]He says:[a]

'I will make this[b] stele in your name and I shall immortalize [14]this hymn on it as an inscription, if you save the scribe Nakht-Amun for me.' [15]So I said to you, and you heard me. Now see, I am doing what I said. You are the Lord for the one [16]who calls to him and acknowledges the truth,[c] you, the Lord of Thebes.

---

[x] Public praise and confession are of the nature of this kind of religious expression.

[y] There is an obscure allusion here to the reason for the sickness which has been recognized by the man afflicted (theft of temple property?); cf. p. 37 n. o below.

[z] This almost Pauline phrase also appears on the stele of a woman called Ta-kha from about the same time and coming from the same city: B. Bruyère, *Rapport sur les fouilles de Deir el Médinéh*, 1945–47, plate 8.

[a] I.e., 'At that time he said'. There follows a vow made during sickness.

[b] 'This' has been inserted from a present perspective.

[c] The reference here is to the fulfilling of the vow. Cf. Num. 30.3; Deut. 23.23, etc.

17. *Votive stele of the worker Nefer-abu for the mountain peak*

Text: Turin, Cat. Gen. 50 058. The text is published in M. Tosi and A. Roccati, *Stele e altri epigrafi di Deir el Medina*, 1972, 286 and 94ff. Time of composition: Nineteenth Dynasty (about thirteenth century BC). Meret-seger is depicted receiving the text in the form of a serpent with the heads of a vulture, a man and a serpent.

The texts mentioned in connection with no. 16 are to be considered as comparative material.

The inscription has been translated often, e.g. by A. Erman, 'Denksteine der thebanischen Gräberstadt', *SDAW* 1911, 1098ff., and in *ANET*[3], 381. The most recent German translation is in E. Brunner-Traut, *Die alten Ägypter*, 1974, 134.

[1]Giving praise to the peak of the West, honouring her Ka.[d] I give praise, hear (my) call, (for) I was [2]a righteous man on earth. Made by Nefer-abu, worker in the necropolis.

An ignorant man, a [3]fool, does not know good from evil.[e] I did the deed of [4]wickedness against the peak and she punished me. I was in her hand [5]by night and by day. I sat upon the bricks like a pregnant woman, [6]I called out to the air, but she did not come to me.[f] I [7]praised (?) the mighty peak of the West and every god and every goddess: [8]'See, I shall say to great and small among the workers, "Beware of [9]the peak! For a lion is in her. The [10]peak strikes with the blow of a wild lion [11] and pursues the one who transgresses against her." '

So I called to my [12]mistress, and found that (straight away) she came to me as a refreshing breeze. She showed [13]mercy to me. She let me see her hand and now she turned back [14]to me in grace. She let me forget the sickness [15]which had been in my heart. Indeed, the peak of the West is gracious when one [16]calls upon her – says Nefer-abu. He says: 'See, and let all the ears (of those?) [17]who live on earth, hear it: "Beware of the peak of the West!" '

[d] Ka can roughly be translated 'spirit'; here it appears in parallelism as a synonym of the goddess. She dwells on the distinctive mountain peak which towers above the settlement of the workers, the valley with the royal tombs and the whole of the west side of Thebes.

[e] Not only the legal writing but also the style of this hymn composed by Nefer-abu himself (obviously using stereotyped expressions) is clumsy. The translation attempts to reproduce this characteristic.

[f] Nefer-abu seems to understand a snake-bite, which has affected his breathing, as a punishment from the goddess – the snake is one of the forms in which she appears. His lack of breath is compared with that of a woman in labour (for the brick see the Hebrew text of Ex. 1.16).

18. *Prayer stele of Nefer-abu to Ptah*

Text: London, British Museum 589. The text is published in T. G. H. James, *Hieroglyphic Texts*, Part 9, 1970, plate 31. Ptah is depicted on his throne receiving the prayer; above him are two eyes and four ears.

Comparative OT material is as follows: for the confession of sins (v., 2f.) cf. Pss. 32.3ff.; 38.18; 51.3ff. For the nature of the sin committed (v., 2) cf. Lev. 19.12; also Jer. 5.2; 7.9; Hos. 10.4; Zech. 5.3; Ps. 24.4. For the understanding of sickness as a punishment (v., 3 and n. k) cf. Pss. 38.1ff.; 41.4 etc. For the mention of God's 'hand' (v., 7) cf. Pss. 32.4; 38.2. For the inclusion of an admonition to others (v., 3ff.) cf. Pss. 32 (;51.13; 130.7). For the connection with petitionary prayers (r., 3ff., v., 9) cf. Pss. 38.1, 21f.; 51.1f., 7ff. For the association with praise in the form of a doxology (i.e. for the association of confession and doxology) (r., 1ff., v., 8) cf. Josh. 7.19; Job 5.6ff., 9ff., and in some respects also Ps. 7.9b-11.

This inscription, too, has been translated many times, among others by A. Erman, 'Denksteine der thebanischen Gräberstadt', *SDAW* 1911, 1100ff.; E. Brunner-Traut, *Die Alten Ägypter*, 1974, pl. 44 and p. 134.

Recto:

[1]Give praise to Ptah, the Lord of Maat, the king of the two lands, the gracious one[g] on [2]his throne, the one god in nineness,[h] [3]the beloved as king of the two lands; may he give life, salvation and health, insight, [4]praise and love, and may my eyes see Amun daily,[i] [5]thus may it be granted to a righteous one who holds Amun [6]in his heart – from Nefer-abu, the worker in the necropolis.

Verso:

[1]The beginning of the saying of the power of Ptah, south of his wall,[j] through the one who works in the necropolis in western Thebes, [2]Nefer-abu. He says: 'I am a man who has sworn wickedly by Ptah, the [3]Lord of truth, and he has made me see darkness by day.[k] Now I will tell of his power to the one who does not [4]know it, and to the one who does know it, the small and the great. Beware of Ptah, the Lord of truth. He leaves [5]no man's action unnoticed. Keep from mentioning the name of Ptah falsely. See, the one who mentions his name [6]falsely comes to ruin.[l] He made me

---

[g] Literally: 'with beautiful (i.e. imposing, polished) face'.

[h] Any group of gods is called a 'nineness', no matter how many it may be in number. The reference here is to the gods worshipped in Deir el-Medina.

[i] Either looking daily on the sun (the opposite of blindness or death) or visiting the temple daily.

[j] The cult name of Ptah of Memphis.

[k] Nefer-abu feels that his blindness is a punishment for an oath sworn falsely by Ptah.

[l] Literally 'collapses', like an old wall.

Plate II Hieratic papyrus: the Teaching of Amenemope

like the dogs in [7]the houses[m] in that I was in his hand. He made men and gods look upon me, in that I was [8]like a man who has done forbidden things against his Lord. Truly (righteous) is Ptah, the Lord of truth, against me: he has punished me. [9](Now) be gracious to me, look upon me, you are gracious!'

19. *Prayer of Iit-Noferti, the spouse of Sennodiem (Thebes, tomb no. 1)*

Text: Bankes Collection, Kingston Lacy, Dorset, England. The text is published in J. Černý, *Egyptian Stelae in the Bankes Collection*, 1958, no. 6. Period of composition: Nineteenth Dynasty (*c.* thirteenth century BC). For OT comparative material see no. 18 above.

Give praise to Iah-Thoth,[n] the supreme god, who hears prayers; worship Shu, the great god. Be gracious. You have made me see darkness by day because of those words of the women.[o] Be gracious, that I may see your grace!

20. *Prayer and dedication of Simut, called Kiki*

Text: Inscription in the tomb of the person concerned, no. 409, in Thebes. The text is published in an edition by M. Abdul-Qader Muhammed, *ASAE* 59, 1966, 159ff.
Translation: A. Wilson, *JNES* 20, 1970, 190ff.
The idea that restoration should be made to the deity, since all possessions come from her (lines 1off.), has parallels, *mutatis mutandis*, in texts like Deut. 26.1-11 and Ex. 34.19, which in their own way articulate an acknowledgment that God is the real 'owner'. The nearest comparative material elsewhere is to be found in the declarations of trust in individual laments and other OT psalms, including Pss. 27.1ff.; 31.3; 56.3f., 11; 140.7; 142.5, and not least Ps. 91. The detail of the renunciation of 'protectors among men' (lines 17f.) corresponds to Pss. 60.11; (108.12;) 118.8f.; 146.3f. Ps. 16.11 resembles line 3 in speaking of a 'way of life'. But see also Prov. 2.19; 5.6; 10.17; 15.24.
Explanatory comment: After a biographical introduction, Kiki himself speaks. In a first discourse he dedicates his belongings to the goddess Mut of Thebes and gives the reason for his action; in a second discourse he prays to her. The third part of his discourse is a hymn to the goddess. The text is in fragments; a second one with similar content is even more badly damaged: it seems to have given details about the gift.

---

[m] Perhaps watchdog, cf. *RdE* 19, 1967, 136 n. 6.
[n] Iah is a word for 'moon' borrowed from the Semitic. Thoth is the moon god. Shu is the god of daylight. Thus the blind man calls on the gods of light.
[o] An allusion to the reason for his blindness, which is now obscure to us; cf. p. 34 n. y above.

[1]There was a man of southern Heliopolis (= Thebes), a true scribe in Thebes, whose name from his mother was Simut, [2]called Kiki. His deity recognized him and instructed him in his wisdom. [3]He set him on the way of life, to protect his body. [4]The god recognized him even as a child, and special food was arranged for him. Then he took counsel [5]with himself to find a guardian deity, and he found Mut at the head of the gods. Shai and [6]Renenet[p] are with her, length of life and breath are under her control, and everything that happens is at her bidding.[q] [7]Then he spoke:

'Hereby I surrender to her my possessions and all their increase. I know [8]that she is useful for me, that she alone is good and that she can make a space for me in the tumult [9]of battle.[r] She offers protection (?) in an evil moment. She has already come – with the north wind before her[s] – when [10]I call on her name. I was needy in her city, a poor man and [11]a beggar in her city.[t] I came into my possessions through her power alone, because of the breath of life.[u] (Therefore) no [12]member of the household is to have a share in them; they are only to go to her in peace ... [13]I say of a minister at the peak of his power,[v] "He is strong, but he does not [14]equal[w] those who keep to Sekhmet, the great." It is impossible to measure the length of her stride.[x] [15]None of her servants is threatened with incurring wrath[y] for ever and ever.'

'O Mut, ruler [16]of the gods, hear my prayers. A servant bears witness to the good deeds of his Lord (?) ... [17]I look for no protector among men, nor among ... [18]the great, and even my son is (no protector?) ...'

'If Mut [69]takes someone into (her) protection, then no God can come near (to harm them); he is a favourite of the king throughout his life, [70]and dies in grace.

[p] Shai is the destiny given to man at birth, especially his span of life; Renenet is what he acquires in childhood, 'environmental influences'.
[q] See p. 24 n. l above.
[r] Used in a metaphorical sense of all acute threats to life.
[s] The cool north wind, blowing from the Mediterranean up the Nile valley, is felt to be beneficial.
[t] Deprecatory remarks as a sign of helpless surrender to the deity; not necessarily to be understood literally. See p. 33 n. u above.
[u] Sc. through whom she communicated her power. The translation is not completely certain. I have taken the preposition translated 'because of' to have the meaning which it acquired in Coptic.
[v] Literally: 'at his right moment', i.e. at the height of his power.
[w] *tkn*.
[x] I.e. the sphere of her power.
[y] Probably meaning the wrath of the ruler, which has unpleasant consequences, or even the wrath of the goddess.

If Mut takes someone into (her) protection, then no [71]evil can befall him; he is protected every day until he enters the cemetery. If [72]Mut takes someone into (her) protection, how fair is the course of his life! The gracious actions of the king which befall his person belong [73]to the one who takes her to his heart.

If Mut takes someone into (her) protection, he is assured of praise and [74](good) fortune, and good things are written on his birth-brick;[z] he comes into favour.

If Mut takes someone into (her) protection, [75]- how does the one whom she loves prosper! No god can cast him down, as he does not know death.'

Hymns of praise and thanksgiving

The hymns included here differ from those in Section II in that they are hymns of individuals, in which it is possible to see a personal relationship between the god and the singer. Of course they draw on the cultic hymns for their vocabulary and ideas. Too sharp a division would obliterate common features.

21. *Hymn of Nekh-Atum (or Khu-Atum?)[a] to the divinized King Amenophis I*

Text: Turin, Cat. Gen. 50 049. The text is published in M. Tosi and A. Roccati, *Stele e altri epigrafi di Deir el Medina*, 1972, 281, 83f.

Like most documents of its kind, this text comes from the workers' city in the valley of the royal tombs. As the authors are uneducated people, the inscription teems with orthographic errors. The time of composition is the Nineteenth Dynasty (thirteenth century BC). The hymn is addressed to King Amenophis I, who died two to three hundred years earlier and who is depicted on a cultic statue. It is worth noting that the ancient Egyptians could apply basically the same predicates to a dead king as to a god.

There is no evidence of the divinization - apotheosis - of a human king in the OT.[b] However, some of the individual phrases in the Egyptian text find echoes in the OT. For details see the footnotes.

---

[z] For the birth-bricks, cf. again Ex. 1.16. The seven Hathors, who established a child's fate at his birth, wrote his destiny on this brick. See also p. 24 n. 1 above.

[a] A mistake in the writing. Both readings need to be corrected.

[b] Features of Ps. 45 offer only remote parallels: on the one hand the kind of praise which is offered to the human ruler, and on the other the form of address 'God', or 'divine', which is applied to him (Ps. 45.6). The latter is the case only if the Hebrew text can be relied on. On the whole the OT texts only use expressions which approximate to God: thus II Sam. 14.17, 20; Zech. 12.8. But cf. also the passages mentioned under no. 15.

There are translations of the hymn in Tosi and Roccati, loc. cit., and A. Erman, 'Denksteine der thebanischen Gräberstadt', *SDAW* 1911, 1105f.

[1]Give praise to the Lord of the Two Lands, Amenophis I, may he give life, and Tuthmosis IV, [2]the great living God who loves Maat, who saves the one who is in the underworld,[c] and [3]gives breath to the one whom he loves.[d] Anyone who comes to you with a troubled heart, [4]will soon[e] emerge rejoicing. The great come [5]to you because of your name, since they have heard that your name [6]is strong. The one who trusts you[f] rejoices, but woe to anyone who [7]attacks you[g] . . . [8]of a wild lion, [9]puts his hand into a hole with a great snake in it; so you will [10]see the power of Amenophis when he works wonders for his city.[h]

22. Amun as shepherd

A prayer in hieratic script on a limestone ostrakon from the Ramesside period, in the British Museum, no. 5656a. The text is published in A. Gardiner and J. Černý, *Hieratic Ostraca* I, 1957, plate 89.

The text has not been preserved complete. The ostrakon contains several strophes of a prayer to Amun in the form of a hymn. Only the fourth strophe is given here. Others contained allusions to the fate of Akhenaten, so the text must have been written not long after his fall (after 1348).

Ps. 23.1ff. comes closest to it in the OT. Isa. 40.11; Jer. 31.10; Pss. 28.9; 74.1; 79.13; 80.1; 95.7 speak of God as the shepherd of his people.

Individual prayers in the forms of hymns after the style of this text are very frequent in the Ramesside period; cf. nos. 16–20. The ideas and formulations may draw on the temple hymns. For the picture of the good shepherd in Egypt see D. Müller, 'Der gute Hirte', *ZÄS* 86, 1961, 126–44. The following strophe is quoted there, p. 139.

[6]Amun, shepherd, early in the morning you care for your flock and drive the hungry to pasture. The shepherd drives the cattle to the grass; Amun, you drive [7]me, the hungry one, to food, for Amun is indeed a shepherd, a shepherd who is not idle.

23. Hymn to Amun in the form of a prayer

From the hieroglyphic inscription on the reverse of a wooden group of

[c] Probably to be emended thus on the basis of numerous parallels. Another possibility is 'He saves the one who honours you (*sic*!)', thus Tosi and Roccati. For saving from the underworld cf. e.g. Pss. 9.13; 30.3; 49.15; 71.20; 86.13; 116.8.
[d] With the nuance 'preferred, favoured', see E. Otto, *MDAIK* 25, 1969, 98ff.
[e] Miswriting of *nhy*, i.e. after a short time.
[f] Literally, 'his heart filled with you'.
[g] Cf. the antithetical expression of trust in Ps. 25.3.
[h] Trust in God is a protection against lions and snakes.

Amenemopet and his wife Hathor, Berlin 6910. The text is published in *Ägyptische Inschriften aus den Staatlichen Museen zu Berlin* II, 1924, 70f. The following translation is based on a photograph.

The text was composed soon after the Amarna period. As well as having elements from the hymn, it also shows clear signs of personal piety.

In combining prayers in distress (H 6) with elements of praise, it has formal parallels in individual laments and petitions like Pss. 71 and 86, which are composed as hymns. The following details are comparable: the benediction (H 5) with Pss. 40.4; 84.12; the phrase 'who delivers the poor' (H 5) with Jer. 20.13; Pss. 22.24; 69.33; the epithet 'who hears . . . prayers . . .' (H 7) with Ps. 65.2; the theme 'deliverance from the hand of the violent' (H 7) with Jer. 15.21; Pss. 71.4; (86.14); 140.1, 4 etc.

There is also a translation of the prayer in A. Scharff, *Ägyptische Sonnenlieder*, 1921, 73f.

$^{H\,5}$Hail to him who sits on the hand of Amun, who directs the timid, who rescues the poor, who gives the breath of life to the one whom he loves and assigns him a fine old age in the west of Thebes . . . $^{H\,6}$O my god, Lord of the gods, Amon-Re, Lord of Karnak: Give me your hand and save me! Arise for me and help me to stay alive! You are the only God, and there is none $^{H\,7}$like you. You are Re who arises in the heaven, Atum, who created men. Who hears the prayers of the one who calls on him, who saves a man from the hand of the violent, who brings up the Nile for those who are in him,^{i} the perfect guide $^{H\,8}$for everyman. When he rises, men live and their hearts are lifted up when they see the one who gives the breath of life to those who are in the egg,^{j} who keeps men and birds alive, who makes food for mice in their holes $^{H\,9}$and even for worms and fleas. – May he grant a fair burial after old age, so that I am safe in his hand . . .

24. *Religious sentences and maxims*

Numerous scarabs are inscribed with sentences and maxims. The notes give details of where the texts have been published. In most cases the translation follows that of É. Drioton. All the texts come from the Nineteenth and Twentieth Dynasties (fourteenth to twelfth centuries).

Rings worn on the finger or scarabs worn round the neck contain short, pregnant texts, usually in cipher, probably to attract the curiosity of onlookers

---

^{i} Unclear: it can hardly mean fishes. Is the meaning 'who live from him' (literally 'eat')? The text is in some disorder.

^{j} This is also said of unborn men. Here both unborn children and unhatched chickens are meant. The next verse then makes a differentiation in order to show the manifold variety of creation.

by striking, unknown signs and combinations of signs which invited a 'solution'. It is less probable that the wearers wanted to keep their knowledge half-secret – in that case why would they have worn the sentences so that they could be seen at all? Many hundreds of scarabs bear dozens of different texts, many of them with larger or smaller variants. The interpretation is often questionable; only certain instances are given here.

This testimony to personal association with a god and the manner of this association, or the principles of life selected, have close similarities to OT statements, especially in Psalms and Proverbs. Parallels are given in each case in the notes, along with references to relevant literature.

(i) God[k] loves the one who loves him.[l]
(ii) Ptah loves all those who love him and pray to him.[m]
(iii) Ptah recompenses every good deed generously.[n]
(iv) God is the protection of my life.[o]
(v) Amun is behind me (i.e. is my protection); I fear nothing, for Amun is strong.[p]
(vi) There is no real refuge for my heart outside Amun.[q]

3. Scarab. Text 24 (vi) is engraved on its lower side.

(vii) It is the protection of my life to serve Amun.[r]

[k] Most texts also contain divine names instead of the general expression 'God' or 'the god', above all Amun, Ptah, Osiris, and also goddesses. The names change in the same maxims, certainly not at random (e.g. no. 3 is said only of Ptah), but with some frequency.

[l] There are many Egyptian instances of these maxims in É. Drioton, AnBib 12, 1959, 57ff. In the OT, in addition to I Sam. 2.30; Ps. 145.20, cf. above all Prov. 8.17a (where there is an exactly parallel saying from the mouth of the primal 'wisdom'). But cf. also the end of the Song of Deborah, Judg. 5.31 and (mutatis mutandis) the reciprocal formulations in Gen. 12.3.

[m] Drioton, Kêmi 14, 1957, 21ff.

[n] Drioton, op. cit., 9f. – Cf. I Sam. 24.20; Prov. 19.17; Ruth 2.12; also Neh. 5.19; 13.31.

[o] Drioton, Pages d'Égyptologie, 1957, 117. Cf. Pss. 46.7, 11; 59.9, 16f.; 144.2, etc.

[p] Drioton, op. cit., 118. – Cf. e.g. Pss. 3.3-6; 23.4; 27.1ff.; 118.6; also Gen. 15.1; 26.24; Deut. 31.6ff.; Josh. 1.5; Isa. 41.10, 13; and also Micah 3.11.

[q] Drioton, ZÄS 79, 1954, 4. Cf. e.g. II Sam. 22.3, 32; Pss. 11.1; 16.1f.(BHS); 18.31; 62.5-8; also Isa. 30.1ff.; 43.11; 44.8; Hos. 13.4.

[r] Drioton, Pages d'Égyptologie, 118. For the subject see e.g. Ex. 34.10-26; Deut 6.11; Josh. 24; I Sam. 7.3; Mal. 3.13-21.

(viii) It is my boast to serve Amun.[s]
(ix) My good fortune is in the temple of the living.[t]
(x) Your temple, Onnophris, is my delight.[u]
(xi) Amun is the strength of the lonely.[v]
(xii) It is God who leads men on the way of life.[w]
(xiii) The one who loves righteousness is elect of God.[x]
(xiv) Happy the one who sees Amun each day.[y]
(xv) Contentment is better than wrath.[z]

25. The form of letters in the Ramesside period

Egyptian letters from the time around 1000 BC begin with a religious formula which is essentially stereotyped, though details may vary. The first has been translated from Pap. Leiden I 369 (transcription in J. Černý, *Late Ramesside Letters*, 1939, no. 1); the second from Pap. Brit. Mus. 10,417 (no. 14 in Černý).

The first is written from a father living abroad to members of his family and fellow-workers who have remained at home in Thebes. The second on the other hand is a letter from one of his people to him.

In (i) the assurances at the beginning of the letter are worth noting in connection with the intercessions which the Israelites made for one another (Ps. 35.13f.), for their king (Pss. 20.1–5; 61.6f.; 72 etc.), for Jerusalem (Ps. 122.6–9) and for the whole people of God (Ps. 28.9), and also for those who do not believe in Yahweh (Jer. 29.7). In (ii) the conception of the king above the gods is to be compared with Ps. 95.3 and the relationship between him and the individual with Ps. 5.2. See also e.g. Gen. 28.15, 20.

A translation of the two letters can also be found in E. F. Wente, *Late Ramesside Letters*, SAOC 33, 1967, 18, 46f.

(i) A to B. [3]I say to Harsaphes, the Lord of Heracleopolis, to Thoth, the Lord of Hermopolis, and to every god and goddess [4]among whom I

---

[s] Drioton, op. cit., 125. Cf. Jer. 9.23f.; Ps. 34.2.
[t] Drioton, op. cit., 129. Numerous sentences praise the temple as the place of the nearness of God. The 'Zion hymns' in particular are comparable with this (Pss. 46; 48; 76; 84; 87; 122), e.g. Ps. 84.2–5, 10; also Pss. 27.4; 65.4; 137. 'The living one' is frequent as an epithet for the deity. Cf. inter alia Josh. 3.10; I Sam. 17.26; Jer. 10.10; Pss. 42.2; 84.2.
[u] Drioton, op. cit. Cf. also the previous note.
[v] Drioton, *ZÄS* 79, 1954, 10. - Cf. Pss. 27.10 and 25.16, and also Pss. 38.11, 15; 102.1ff., 6f.; also Pss. 3; 31; 62, and in addition Lam. 3.25ff.
[w] Drioton, *Pages* . . ., 126. Cf. e.g. Ps. 23.2ff.
[x] Drioton, *Pages*, 120. Cf. e.g. Ps. 15; 24.3–6; 119; Prov. 14.34; 21.21.
[y] See p. 36 n. i above. Drioton, op. cit., 128. - Cf. Pss. 27.4; 42.2; 63.2f.
[z] Variants: love is better than anger. Drioton, *Hommage à W. Deonna*, 1957, 200. - Cf. Ps. 37.1–11; Prov. 29.8, possibly 19.19.

have come,[a] that they should grant you life, salvation and health, a long life and a fine old age; and that they should give you favour [5]before gods and men.[b] How are things with you? How are things with your people? I still live; [6]tomorrow is in God's hand.[c] I long daily to see you and to hear how you are. How is it [7]that I have sent you these various letters without your sending even one to me? What have I done [8]to you? And if I have done wrong a million times, have I not on some occasion done something good, to bring it into forgetfulness? I am indeed good [9]to you, and not at all evil to you. Please say to Amun of the throne of the Two Lands and to Meresger,[d] that he may bring me back alive [10]from the Yar of Na-mekhai . . .[e]

(ii) . . . I [3]say to Amun, the king of the gods, that he should give you favour before the general, your lord. [Verso.1]May Amun bring you back well that I may embrace you, [Verso 2]when all danger is past and Amun of the throne of the two lands has saved you. You are his servant. . . .

V. PRECEPTS FOR LIFE

26. The teaching of Merikare

This teaching is preserved in three papyrus manuscripts from the New Kingdom. The basic manuscript, according to which the lines have been numbered, is in Leningrad and is almost complete. Two further fragmentary manuscripts have been preserved in Moscow and Copenhagen. All three have been published in a hieroglyphic transcription and have been translated by A. Volten, Zwei altägyptische politische Schriften, AAeg 4, 1945, 3-103. Only three brief extracts are given here.

The discourse is put on the lips of King Achthoes(?) who has just died. He is speaking to his son and successor Merikare (Tenth Dynasty, end of the twenty-second century). In practice it is a kind of governmental decree made by the latter. The text contains a whole series of specific political instructions, general maxims (the first section given here) and finally hymnic sections. It comes to a climax in the cosmological hymn to the power of the sun god, which is the third passage that we include here.

[a] The correspondent is in Middle Egypt and names the gods of the place where he is living.
[b] Cf. Prov. 3.4.
[c] Cf. Ps. 31.15; Prov. 27.1. J. G. Griffiths gives numerous Egyptian, Graeco-Latin and Hebrew parallels in HTR 53, 1960, 219ff.
[d] Theban deities.
[e] Evidently a name for the place where the correspondent is staying.

The most notable parallel is the 'Words to Lemuel' in Prov. 31.1-9, which is also a piece of admonition addressed to a son destined for royal office and which has nevertheless been handed down by the son himself. This gives comparable duties. For the latter see especially II Sam. 23.3ff.; Pss. 72.1-4, 12-14; 101, and also Jer. 21.11f.; 22.1ff.; 23.5. A similar connection of admonition with hymnic discourse (lines 46ff. or 131ff.) can also be found in Job 4.1-5.27 (see especially 5.9-11). For praise of the providence of God (lines 131ff.) cf. Pss. 104.14f., 21, 27f.; 145.15f.; (147.9; Job 38.39-41); for the idea that no one can ward off the invisible attack of the deity (lines 124f.) see especially Job 9.11f.; for the theologoumenon of the hiddenness of God see e.g. Isa. 8.17; 45.15; Ps. 89.46. For all other details see the notes.

Further literature: *ANET*³, 414-8; more recently also M. Lichtheim, *Ancient Egyptian Literature* I, 1973, 97ff.

Do ⁴⁶right and you will live long on earth.ᶠ Calm the weeper, do not oppress the widow,ᵍ ⁴⁷drive no man from his father's possessions,ʰ do not diminish ⁴⁸the property of the great. Be on guard against punishing unjustly. Do not kill,ⁱ that is of no advantage to you; punish, rather, with beatings ⁴⁹and imprisonment, by this the land will be firmly grounded ...
¹²³Among men one generation succeeds another, ¹²⁴and the god, who knows men's characters, has hidden himself.ʲ No one can ward off the blow of the Lord of the hand.ᵏ (Invisible himself) he wards off what the eyes ¹²⁵see (the visible). The god is revered on his processional way,ˡ made of precious stones and fashioned from metal, as one wave can be superseded ¹²⁶by another wave. No river can be concealed (for ever): it leaves the channel in which it had been hidden.ᵐ So too the soul comes to the place ¹²⁷that it knows and does not deviate from its way of yesterday.

ᶠ For a connection with this promise cf. Ex. 20.12; Deut. 5.16.
ᵍ Cardinal issues in social attitudes, in Egypt as in the OT. Cf. e.g. Ex. 22.22ff.; Deut. 24.17; 27.19; Isa. 1.17; Mal. 3.5.
ʰ On this see I Kings 21.1-4; Micah 2.2b.
ⁱ Here probably = punish with the death penalty.
ʲ The biblical expulsion from paradise (Gen. 3.24) corresponds to the second part of the myth given as no. 5 above: a description of God's withdrawal from proximity to man. Since then God keeps himself aloof, remains invisible, but intervenes in the visible world.
ᵏ The 'hand of God' as an image of God's intervention in the fate of the individual or the course of the world (to inflict punishment) is an image to be found often in the Bible. Cf. e.g. Ex. 9.3; Deut. 2.15; I Sam. 6.5; Ezek. 25.13, 16; Amos 1.8.
ˡ It was customary for a man to revere a cultic image, visible but not identical with the god, as a substitute for the invisible god. The majority of people would only encounter this in processions. But cf. Ex. 32.1ff.; I Kings 12.28ff.; Hos. 8.4ff. and on the other hand Ex. 20.4ff.; Deut. 5.8ff.
ᵐ God's hiddenness will one day come to an end: it breaks forth in judgment and encounters men. Cf. the Hebrew text of Pss. 34.16 and 76.7ff.

Make your house in the West glorious and embellish your place in the
[128]necropolis[n] by being upright and doing the justice on which men's
hearts build. The [129]virtue of the man with an honest disposition is
accepted in preference to the sinner's ox.[o] . . .
Well [131]directed are men, the cattle of the god.[p]
He has made heaven and earth for their sake.
He has driven away the water monster.[q]
He made the air for their nostrils [132]to live.
They are his images, who have come forth from his body.[r]
He arises in heaven for their sake,
he has made [133]plants for them,
beasts, fish and birds, to nourish them.
He has killed his adversary,
diminished his own children,
[134]because they planned to rebel against him.[s]
He creates the light for their sake
and goes (in the heaven) to see them.
He has made a [135]shrine to protect them,
and when they weep there, he hears them.[t]
He has made rulers for them in the egg,
governors, [136]to support the back of the weak.[u]
He has made magic for them as a weapon
to ward off the blow of [137]disaster,[v]
and keeps watch over day and night.[w]
He has slain the rebels among them,

[n] This double sentence is a quotation from the teaching of Djedef-Hor, which is
many centuries earlier. What was intended there in a material sense, referring to the
building and equipping of the tomb and to sacrifices, is given a spiritual and moral
meaning here through the addition 'by being upright . . .'.
   [o] Cf. possibly I Sam. 15.22; Isa. 1.10-17; Hos. 6.6; Amos 5.21-24; Ps. 40.6; Prov.
21.3. But perhaps the word translated here as 'virtue' is to be read rather differently,
and translated 'bread'.
   [p] See p. 15 n. u above. Cf. also Isa. 40.11; Jer. 31.10; Pss. 28.9; 74.1; 79.13; 80.1;
95.7.
   [q] Cf. Isa. 51.9f.; Pss. 74.13f.; 89.9f.; Job 9.13; 26.12f.
   [r] For the question of man as God's image in Egypt see E. Hornung, 'Der Mensch als
"Bild Gottes" in Ägypten', in O. Loretz, *Die Gottebenbildlichkeit des Menschen*, 1968,
123ff. Cf. in the OT Gen. 1.26f.; (5.3; 9.6); Ps. 8.5.
   [s] An allusion to the myth of the annihilation of the human race, no. 5 above.
   [t] This is the only purpose of the temple named in our text. Cf. I Kings 8.29ff., and
also I Sam. 1.9-18.
   [u] This is the only purpose of rule named here (cf. Prov. 29.14).
   [v] Cf. by contrast Ex. 22.18; Deut. 18.9ff.; Jer. 27.9.
   [w] Cf. Ps. 121.3ff.

as a [138]man chastises his son for the sake of his brother.[x]
God knows every name.[y]

27. The teaching of a man for his son

Preserved on two papyri and about ten ostraca, all from the New Kingdom. There is a hieroglyphic transcription, a Latin transcription and a translation by K. A. Kitchen, *OrAnt* 8, 1969, 189-208, see now no. 1266 in G. Posener, *Catalogue des ostraca hiératiques littéraires de Deir el Medineh* II, Documents de fouilles 18, 1972. The division into paragraphs follows that of Kitchen. The teaching comes from the Twelfth Dynasty (1991-1785 BC). Strikingly, teacher and pupil ('son') both remain anonymous. The instruction seems to be intended for the general populace (cf. G. Posener, *Littérature et politique dans l'Égypte de la XIIᵉ dynastie*, 1956, 124ff.).

In being framed as a father's instruction of his 'son' the teaching has points of contact with OT wisdom texts: cf. Prov. 1.10, 15; 2.1; 3.1, 21; 4.1, 10, 20; 5.1, etc.; 23.12-24.22. There are further points of contact: with §2 cf. Prov. 4.1f., 10, 20 etc.; with §3 on the one hand Prov. 25.6f., and on the other Prov. 6.6; 24.30ff. etc.; with §4, Prov. 10.19; 12.19; 21.23; with §§13-16 Prov. 16.15. Otherwise see the notes.

§1   The beginning of the teaching which a man has made for his son.
He says,

§2   Hearken to my voice, do not neglect my words,
and do not despise what I want to say to you.

§3   Earn respect for yourself, but do not go too far in this.
Laziness is not seemly for a wise man.

§4   Be reliable and silent, bend your arm[z]
and be benevolent . . .

§13a   He[a] makes the ignorant a wise man,
and the one who is hated becomes beloved.

§13b   He makes the humble surpass the great,
and the last is the first.[b]

§14   The one who did not possess it, has treasure for himself,
and the one who had only a little land now has dependents . . .

§16   He teaches the dumb (?) to speak,
he opens the ears of the deaf . . .[c]

[x] Even rebels are still loved by the divine father; when he punishes them, it is for the sake of other children.

[y] The name as a sign of individuality, cf. Isa. 43.1.

[z] In greeting.

[a] Probably the king.

[b] Marginal mention may be made of a New Testament passage, Matt. 19.30.

[c] Cf. Isa. 35.5, which is related to God's appearing, and has been taken up again in Matt. 11.5 and Luke 7.22.

28. The teaching of Ani

Preserved on four papyri (one of them unpublished) and a number of ostraka.
The basic manuscript is Pap. Boulaq 4, now in the Cairo Museum. The
numbering of the lines is based on this. There is a hieroglyphic transcription
and translation in E. Suys, *La Sagesse d'Ani*, AnOr 11, 1935.

Although the earliest manuscript comes from the time of the Ramessides,
the teaching may have come into being in the second half of the Eighteenth
Dynasty (fifteenth/fourteenth century). The author is a scribe in the temple of
Ahmes Nefertari in Thebes.[d]

The first extract may be compared with Prov. 7.5-23, the second with Hab.
2.20; Zeph. 1.7; Zech 2.13; Ps. 37.7, and also with Prov. 10.19. For the third
extract see the footnotes. It is improbable that the teaching of Ani has any
direct influence on the OT; on the other hand, we should reckon with the
possibility of its influence on the teaching of Amenemope (no. 29) or its model.

There is no recent edition. For questions of textual criticism and individual
sections cf. A. Volten, *Studien zum Weisheitsbuch des Anii*, Hist.-Fil. Meddelel-
ser, Kgl. Danske Videnskabernes Selskab, XXIII 3; cf. also *ANET*³, 420f.

[III 13]Be on your guard against a woman from abroad,[e]
whom no one knows in her city.
Do not gaze at her when she goes [14]past,
and do not know her carnally.
She is a deep water,[f] the extent of which (?) no one knows.
A woman whose husband is far away, says daily to you:[g]
'I am polished (= pretty)!',[h] when she has no witnesses.
She waits[i] and sets her trap.[j] A great crime - and death,[k]
when it is known . . .

[VI 1]Do not make great speeches, but keep quiet. Then it will go well with
you. Do not gossip: [2]the resting-place of God (temple), its prohibition
is tumult. Pray with a loving heart, all the words of which [3]are hidden,
and then he will do what you need.[l] He hears what you say and accepts
your sacrifice . . .

---

[d] Cf. G. Posener, *RdE* 6, 1951, 42 n. 2.
[e] Warnings against a 'strange' woman (the wife of another man or a woman who is
unknown in the city) occur in Egypt from the Old Kingdom down to the Ptolemaic
period. Cf. Prov. 2.16-19; 5.1-14; 6.20-35; 7.1-27.
[f] See also Prov. 18.4a.
[g] Prov. 7.19.
[h] Cf. Prov. 7.5 or 7.21?
[i] Prov. 7.12.
[j] As when catching birds, cf. Prov. 7.23a; Eccles. 7.26f.; Sirach 9.3.
[k] Prov. 7.23b.
[l] In Israel, silent prayer is unusual, cf. I Sam. 1.13. See, by contrast, Matt. 6.5-7.

VIII 3You should not eat 4while another is standing by,
and you do not stretch out your hand for food for him.m
Will it (bread) be here for ever?
Man is 5indeed nothing.
One is rich and another is poor.n
Is food then something permanent?
6Can it not sometimes pass by?
The rich man of last year
is a vagabond this year.
Do not be greedy 7to fill your belly.
Someone will be able to make you ill in the same way.o
You too can come into the position
where another gives you crumbs.
8The course of last year's water has shifted,
it forms a different watercourse this year.
Great lakes 9will dry up,
and river-banks become abysses.
Does this not also happen among men?
Their plan is 10one thing, and that of the Lord of Life is another.p

29. The teaching of Amenemope

The basic text is Pap. Brit. Mus. 10,474, published by E. A. W. Budge, *Hieratic Papyri in the British Museum*, Second Series, 1923, plates 1-14. The numbering of chapters in the text, pages and lines follows the main papyrus.

The teaching may have been composed in the Twentieth Dynasty (1186-1070). It shows clear dependence on the teaching of Ani (no. 28). The author is a tax official, and therefore this sphere is dominant.

There are close and sometimes literal agreements with parts of Proverbs, especially with 22.17-23.11. In detail, the submissive piety of Amenemope has parallels in the OT, e.g. in Pss. 37; 38.13ff. or in Jer. 11.20, and not least in Prov. 20.22.

The teaching has often been translated and discussed. See *ANET*3, 421. There is a complete revision by I. Grumach, *Untersuchungen zur Lebenslehre des Amenope*, MÄS 23, 1972, in which further manuscripts are listed and used.

Introduction

1,1The beginning of the teaching of life,
the instruction for salvation,
all precepts for converse with the great,

m Prov. 14.21.
n Prov. 22.2.
o By leaving you standing there hungry while he is eating.
p Cf. Isa. 55.8; Prov. 16.1; 16.9; 19.21 etc.

the rules for courtiers,
[1,5]to know how to return[q] a (verbal) answer to the one who says it,
to give a (written) message to the one who sends it,[r]
to direct a man rightly on the ways of life,[s]
to make him prosper on earth,
to let his heart go down into his shrine,[t]
[1,10]by steering him from evil,
to rescue him from the mouth of the crowd,
because he is revered in the mouth of men . . .

[3,8]First chapter

Give your ears, hear what is said,[u]
[3,10]Give your heart to understand it.
It is useful to put it (what is heard) in your heart,
but woe to the one who neglects it.
Let it abide in your breast,[v]
that it may be a key in your heart.
[3,15]Then when there is a whirlwind of words,
it will be a peg for your tongue.[w]
If you spend your life-span with this at heart,
you will find that it brings success.
[4,1]You will find my words a treasury of life,
and your body will prosper on earth.[x]

Second chapter

Guard yourself against robbing the wretched and driving away [4,5]a

[q] Along with I. Grumach, I simply read r ḫsf.

[r] Cf. Prov. 22.21.

[s] Cf. Prov. 22.19, and also Ps. 25.4 and Prov. 2.19; 10.17; 15.24.

[t] The heart is the organ through which God's instructions are received. For it to be 'in the body' signifies a reasonable action that is pleasing to God. Amenemope seeks to guide his reader in this direction. ('Shrine' is a metaphor for body.)

[u] Not only the present teaching, but traditional teaching in general; cf. Grumach, op. cit., 25. – Cf. Prov. 22.17a and LXX. In what follows there are correspondences between 3.10 and Prov. 22.17b; 3.13 and Prov. 22.18a; 3.16 and Prov. 22.18b.

[v] Literally 'chest of your body', a further expression for the seat of the heart, cf. n. t above.

[w] That is, to learn the teachings off by heart will give a man a firm position, a point of orientation in cases where his feelings are confused or there is a variety of possible opinions. 'The way of teaching leads from the ear – to the heart [where it is "incorporated"] – to the tongue [which it protects from rashness] – to life [which it makes to prosper, in both the religious and the secular sense]': Grumach, op. cit., 29.

[x] The man who makes this teaching his inner possession will have success before God and man.

weak man.[y]
Do not stretch out your hand against an old man,   .
and do not speak first to a great man (?).
Do not allow yourself to be sent with a rough message
nor love the one who has commissioned you.
[4,10]Do not cry out against the one who wrongs you
and do not go against him on your own account.[z]
The one who does evil, the river-bank rejects him,
and its (the dam's) mire takes hold of him.[a]
The north wind comes and ends his (the wicked man's) hour,
[4,15]it is joined to the storm;
the thunderclouds are high and the crocodiles are wicked.
You hot man, what are you now?[b]
He cries out, and his voice reaches to heaven.
O moon, who establishes his crime,[c]
[5,1]steer, bring the wicked man across to us,
for we have not acted as he has![d]
Lift him up, give him your hand,
leave him in the arms of the god,
[5,5]fill his body with bread of yours,
so that he may be full and ashamed.
Another good deed in the heart of the god
is to pause before speaking.

Third chapter

[5,10]Do not begin any dispute with the hot-mouthed
and do not attack him with words.
Delay before an opponent, bow down before an assailant,
sleep before speaking.

---

[y] This obviously envisages a situation before a court, especially in cases of disputes over legacies. Cf. Prov. 22.22.

[z] Instead, leave defence or vengeance to God. The idea is developed in more detail in the sequel, and is one of the main themes of the teaching (ʿn mšḥ, 'intercede for someone'; frequent in the New Kingdom).

[a] The wicked man who has raised a storm cannot now bring his ship safely to land: he is stranded.

[b] The 'hot man' is the ungovernable man who gives unrestrained expression to his feelings. The contrast between this negative picture of man and the positive picture of the 'truly silent man' is one of the main themes of this teaching.

[c] The moon god Thoth is the guardian of justice. The prayers of those who are not stranded by false conduct are addressed to him.

[d] Not meant 'hypocritically', but in actual fact. Metaphorically, those who have come safely to land pray that even the shipwrecked may still be saved.

Like a storm which arises as fire in the straw,
[5,15]so is the hot man in his time.
Withdraw from him, take no notice (?) –
the god will know how to answer him.
If you spend your span of life with this in your heart,
your children will see it.[e]

[5,20]Fourth chapter[f]

[6,1]As for the hot man in the temple,
he is like a tree growing inside.[g]
Only for a moment does it bring forth young greenery.[h]
It finds its end in the channel,[i]
[6,5]it goes far from its home,
or the flames become its pyre.
But the truly silent man[j] holds himself apart.
He is like a tree which grows in the sunlight.
It grows green and doubles its fruits,
[6,10]it stands before its Lord,[k]
its fruits are sweet, its shade is pleasant,
and it finds its end as a statue.[l]

Fifth chapter

Do not take to yourself portions of the temple;
[6,15]do not be greedy, and you will find an abundance.[m]

[e] Sc. the blessing which rests on the one who takes the teaching to heart. Perhaps the meaning is also that a life led in this way has an exemplary influence.
[f] My interpretation of this much-discussed strophe follows G. Posener, *ZÄS* 99, 1973, 129-35. For the fourth chapter as a whole cf. Jer. 17.5-8 and Ps. 1.
[g] A man can also be compared with a tree in the OT: cf. Jer. 11.16ff.; 17.8; Ezek. 17.5ff.; Pss. 1.3; 52.8; 92.12ff. etc. Here there is a warning against coming too close to God: the tree cannot flourish in the 'temple'; its proper place is 'outside', i.e. in the open air, where it has sunlight.
[h] As it is in the shade, it has only 'rank' growth, which cannot flourish.
[i] The word translated 'channel' is unknown elsewhere. The tree growing in the dark has produced worthless wood which can only be thrown in the water or burnt. For the Egyptian of this period death in the water, in a foreign land or even in fire was a terrible thought.
[j] The 'truly silent man', literally 'the man who keeps silent in the right way, who keeps silent in accordance with Maat' (*gr m3ʿ*), is the ideal picture of the one who is silent over God's ordinance, the 'tranquil' man who accepts his lot, who is modest in everyday matters and does not harry God. He is the positive counterpart to the 'hot man'.
[k] Before the sun god who shines on him.
[l] Because it is so good, its wood is even fashioned into a divine effigy – an apotheosis for the tree, an image of the blessedness of the faithful silent man.
[m] Cf. Prov. 21.26.

Do not cast away a servant of the god,
in order to show good to another.[n]
Do not say, 'Today is like tomorrow,'
[6,19]how will it end?
[7,1]When the morning has come and today is past,
then the flood finds itself the edge of a wave.[o]
The crocodiles lie bare, the hippopotamus is on dry land,
the fish are forced together.[p]
[7,5]The wolves are full and the birds have a feast:
the nets are empty of fish.
But all those who are silent in the temple,
say, 'Re is great in favour!'[q]
Keep to a silent man, and then you will find life,
[7,10]and your body will prosper on earth.

Sixth chapter

Do not carry off the marker at the boundaries of the field[r]
and do not shift the measuring rod from its right place.
Do not be greedy for a cubit of land,
[7,15]and do not disturb the boundaries of a widow.[s]
To step on the furrow: it shortens his time of life
who takes it away from the field.[t]
If a man has appropriated something to himself with a false oath,
he will be fettered by the power of the moon.[u]
[8,1]You recognize the one who does such things (already) upon earth:
he is an enemy of the weak,
he is an opponent who tears down in your body,
in his eye is something which plunders life,
[8,5]his house is an enemy of the city,
his barns are destroyed,
his possessions will be taken away from his children,
what he has will be given to another.

---

[n] Do not attempt, when filling posts, to give preferential treatment to your favourite at the expense of another.
[o] The Nile often shifts its bed quite unpredictably. An image for a change of fortune.
[p] In a pool, where they become an easy prey for their enemies.
[q] Probably the first words of a hymn of thanksgiving, cf. B. Gunn, *JEA* 41, 1955, 92.
[r] Cf. Prov. 22.28; also Deut. 19.14; 27.17; I Kings 21.1–4; Hos. 5.10; Job 24.2.
[s] Prov. 23.10.
[t] A furrow between two fields tempts a man to incorporate it into his own territory.
[u] The moon god Thoth changed from being the one who calculated the phases of the moon and the calendar to being the god of calculation and the guardian of geometers.

(So) refrain from damaging the boundaries of the arable land,
[8,10]so that fear does not seize you.
A man satisfies God with the power of the lord,
determining the boundaries of the arable land.[v]
Strive for your body to prosper,
take guard against the lord of all.
[8,15]Do not enter another's furrow:
it is good for you if it is well kept (?).
Plough the fields, and you will find what you need,
you will receive bread-from your own threshing floor.
Better a bushel if the god give it to you,
[8,20]than five thousand with injustice.[w]
[9,1]They do not spend a day in the granary and the barn,
they make no provisions for the jar.[x]
Their time in the storehouse is only short,
at daybreak they are sunk.
[9,5]Better is poverty from the hand of God
than riches in the storehouse;[y]
better is bread, when the heart is satisfied,
than riches with sorrow.[z]

Seventh chapter

[9,10]Do not set your heart on riches,[a]
for there is no one who knows fate and fortune![b]
Do not set your heart on external things:
for everyone has the hour (appointed for him).
Do not concern yourself to seek more,[c]
[9,15]then your need will remain assured.
If riches are brought to you through robbery,
they will not spend the night with you.[d]
At daybreak they are no longer in your house:
their place can still be seen, but they are no longer there.[e]

[v] 'The lord' is Pharaoh, and his officials have to fix the boundaries fairly; this was especially necessary after the annual inundation of the Nile.

[w] Cf. Prov. 15.16; 16.8.

[x] Beer was brewed from barley and was a basic form of nourishment.

[y] Cf. Prov. 19.1, 22.

[z] Cf. Prov. 17.1; 15.17.

[a] Cf. Ps. 62.10, also Pss. 39.6; 49.5ff.; 52.7; Eccles. 5.9ff.

[b] The position and environmental influences given at birth.

[c] Cf. Prov. 23.4a and also Eccles. 3.1ff.

[d] Cf. Ps. 62.10.

[e] Prov. 23.5a, also 21.6.

9, 20The ground has opened its gorge and done justice to them,
it has swallowed them up,
10,1and they are submerged in the underworld.[f]
They have made themselves a hole as big as they are,
and they are submerged in the realm of the dead.
Or they have made themselves wings like geese
10, 5and have flown to heaven.[g]
Do not delight in riches which have been won by robbery,
and do not sigh about poverty.
If a standard bearer ventures (too far) forward,
then his troop leaves him in the lurch.
10,10The ship of the covetous remains in the mud,[h]
whereas the boat of the silent man voyages with good winds.
Pray to the sun (Aten) when he rises,
and say, 'Give me health and wholeness,'
then he will give you what you need for this life,
10,15and you will be safe from fear . . .

11,12Ninth Chapter

Do not make the hot man your companion,[i]
and do not seek a conversation with him.
11,15Keep your tongue safe (i.e. speak safely), to answer your superior,
and be careful not to agitate against him.
Do not make him cast out his speech to catch you,
and do not let yourself go with your answer.
Discuss the answer with a man of your rank,
11,20and guard against uttering it over-hastily.
12,1The speech of one whose heart is hurt is more hasty than wind and
   rain.[j]
He is destroyed and built up by his tongue,[k]
his discourse is inadequate.

---

[f] See J. Ruffle, *JEA* 50, 1964, 178.
[g] Cf. Prov. 23.5b.
[h] Because it is too heavily laden and therefore lies too low in the water.
[i] Prov. 22.24.
[j] Conjecture following Grumach. What is meant is not someone who has suffered traumas and deserves sympathy, but a man with imperfect insight, whose words are unconsidered and dangerous, for others as for himself.
[k] I.e., he damages himself, but also occasionally benefits himself, as it may happen. It is also possible to translate the phrase in the active, 'He destroys and builds up', but against this must be noted e.g. that in 24.15 such activity is assigned to the deity. Cf. also Prov. 18.21a.

^{12,5}He gives an answer which merits blows
because its burden is damage.^{l}
He goes to all the world,
but has taken on false talk.^{m}
He is like a ferryman who weaves words:
^{12,10}he comes and goes with strife.^{n}
Whether he eats or drinks at home,
his answer is outside.
The day which establishes his misdeeds
is a sorrow for his children.
^{12,15}May Khnum come,
the potter^{o} of the hot-mouthed,
that he may knead the insufficiency of his heart!^{p}
He is like a young wolf in the herd of cattle.
He turns an eye against the other,^{q}
^{13,1}he makes brothers quarrel.
He is driven before every wind like the clouds,
he darkens the colour of the sun.
He catches his own tail like a young crocodile,
^{13,5}his aim is not adequate.
Although his lips are sweet, his tongue is sour,
for the fire burns in his body.^{r}
Do not fly to attach yourself to such a one,
^{13,9}so that fear does not seize hold of you.^{s}

^{13,10}Tenth chapter

Do not greet the hot one in doing violence to yourself,
and do not hurt your own heart:
do not say 'Hail to you' falsely,

---

^{l} Through his answers the 'hot-mouthed' man damages his fellow men.

^{m} He deals unrestrainedly with everyone, but only causes damage through his unconsidered clumsiness (cf. 13.4f.). What is meant here is not the wicked man, but the uneducated, undisciplined man.

^{n} The ferryman goes to and fro between the banks like a shuttle. The hot man is compared to a ferryman who causes disputes while both loading and unloading.

^{o} Cf. Isa. 29.16; 45.9; 64.8; Jer. 18.1ff.; Job 10.9; 33.6 and also Gen. 2.7f., etc.

^{p} Khnum, the god with the head of a ram, creates men from clay on the potter's wheel. The prayer here is that he should remedy the inadequacies of the hot-mouthed man by reshaping him and thus making him capable of receiving proper instruction.

^{q} Either: he has an unattractive look, he squints, or (more probable in view of the content) he makes those around him fall out with one another.

^{r} Even when he takes trouble his words are hurtful, because he is 'hot' within.

^{s} Cf. Prov. 22.24f.

when terror is within you.[t]
[13,15]Do not deal falsely with people,
that is an abomination to the god.[u]
Do not cut off your heart from your tongue,[v]
then all your plans will be successful.
Then you will be important before people,
[14,1]because you are safe in the hand of the god.
God hates the falsifying of words,
his great abomination is the one who is sick within.[w]

Eleventh chapter

[14,5]Do not covet the possessions of a dependant[x]
nor hunger for his bread.
The possession of a dependant remains stuck in one's throat,[y]
it is an emetic (?) for the gullet.
He acquires it[z] by false oaths,
[14,10]whereby his heart is twisted in his body.
Success is weakened through perverseness (?),[a]
and bad and good alike have failure.
You will have failure before your superior,
because you are unsuccessful with your speaking.
[14,15]Your flatteries will be countered with curses,
and your courtesies with blows.
The huge piece of bread which you swallow you vomit up again,
and so are emptied of your good.
You recognize the overseer in dependence
[15,1]in that blows fall on him,
that all his people are shut up in the block,

[t] The instruction is not that one should not greet the hot man at all, but rather that one should not have any 'inner terror' at a casual encounter with him (so I. Grumach).
[u] Abomination: literally something taboo, prohibited. Cf. Prov. 6.16f.
[v] On this see H. Brunner, ' "Eure Rede sei ja ja, nein nein" im Ägyptischen', *Festschrift für S. Schott*, 1968, 7ff.
[w] Anyone who suffers from inadequacy of heart, a character defect, and as a result causes unrest around him, is remote from God.
[x] With 14.5–8; 14.17f. compare Prov. 23.6–8; but Amenemope does not seem to warn against the plundering or exploitation of dependants; on the contrary, he warns against taking on the status of such a client for material advantages (so I. Grumach).
[y] Literally 'is a stopping of the throat'.
[z] I.e., the dependant acquires his apparently secure material position. As a result of this, however, the heart is 'turned round', so that its attitude to God and to his fellow men is perverted.
[a] The 'perverted' heart necessarily leads to 'rebellion' against God's commandments, so that even the good man must fail if he finds himself a dependant.

and the overseer will be led to the place of judgment.(?)
If you let yourself go before your superior,
[15,5]you are worthy of blame for your subordinate.
So go away from the dependent on the way,
only look at him: keep away from his possessions.

Thirteenth chapter

[15,20]Do not diminish a man with a pen upon papyrus:
that is an abomination[b] for the god.
[16,1]Do not bear witness with false words,
nor shift any other (from the list?) with your tongue.
Do not take a (tax) accounting for the one who has nothing,
and do not falsify with your pen.
[16,5]If you find a large debt with a poor man,
divide it into three parts.
Throw away two of them[c] and let only one stand.
You will find it like the way of life:
in darkness you lie down and sleep,
and in the [16,10]morning you will find it like a good message.
It is better to be praised as one who loves men,
than riches in a storehouse.
Better is bread with a contented heart,
than riches with sorrow[d]
. . .[e]

[19,10]Eighteenth chapter

Do not go to sleep if you are fearful of the morrow.
At daybreak, what is the morrow like?
Man does not know what the morrow will be,[f]
God will always be in his success,
[19,15]whereas man will be always in his failure.
One thing are the words (= thoughts) which man says,
and another thing is what God does.[g]
Do not say, 'I have no sin',
nor strive after disorder.[h]

  [b] See p. 57 n. u above.
  [c] Release the debtor from them.
  [d] Cf. Prov. 17.1.
  [e] The chapters which have been omitted give another warning against dependence
(ch. 14) and against the particular professional faults of an administrative official
(ch. 15).
  [f] Cf. Ps. 31.15; Prov. 27.1. See further p. 44 n. c above.   [g] Cf. Prov. 16.9; 19.21.
  [h] Obscure. Is self-mortification, the opposite of self-righteousness, envisaged here?

[19,20]Sin belongs to God,
it is sealed with his finger.[i]
There is nothing perfect in the hand of God,
but there is no failure before him.[j]
[20,1]If a man strains to seek perfection,
he damages himself[k] in a moment.
Restrain your heart[l] and strengthen your heart,
do not make yourself the steersman of your tongue;
[20,5]man's tongue is (indeed) the rudder of the ship,
(but) the all-lord is its pilot.[m]

[20,20]Twentieth chapter

Do not diminish a man in the judgment,
nor push righteousness aside.
[21,1]Do not give your attention to shining garments,
(but) do not spare the one who goes about in rags.[n]
Do not accept a bribe from a strong man,
and do not oppress a weak man for the sake of it.
[21,5]Maat, a great burden of God,[o]
which he gives to whom he will.[p]
The power of the one who is like him
frees the wretched from his blows.
Do not falsify any documents,
[21,10]that is a great treachery worthy of death.
[21,15]Do not appropriate to yourself the power of God,
as though there were no fate and fortune.[q]

---

[i] One can also translate 'seal' instead of 'finger'. The meaning is that God has control over sin as over his property. Cf. the hymn of the thousand strophes (no. 9 above), II.9.
[j] Anyone who puts himself in 'the hand of God' ceases to take any note of success or failure as standards. They are no longer the externals of actions which are in accordance with Maat or contrary to it, but God's free grace (Grumach, 127f.). Cf. also H. Brunner, 'Der freie Wille Gottes in der ägyptischen Weisheit', in Les Sagesses du Proche-Orient ancien, Travaux du centre d'études supérieures spécialisé d'histoire des religions de Strasbourg, 1963, 103-20.
[k] Or 'who damages (his success)'?
[l] Keep yourself under control and be recollected.
[m] Cf. H. Brunner, 'Der freie Wille Gottes', above.
[n] Cf. e.g. Lev. 19.15; Deut. 16.19; Prov. 18.5; 24.23; 28.21.
[o] On this see J. Bergmann, Ich bin Isis, 1968, 208.
[p] See H. Brunner, op cit. The connection between action and result in earlier teaching has been abandoned here. God determines justice and injustice, the distribution of good and evil. They are fundamentally removed from human control.
[q] In this context a warning against falsifying divine oracles or even giving them oneself.

Hand over property to its (rightful) owners,
and seek life for yourself.
Do not let your heart be built in their houses,
[21, 20]while your body falls to the place of judgment.[r]

Twenty-first chapter
[22, 1]Do not say, 'I have found a strong superior,
and now I can attack a man in your city.'
Do not say, 'I have found a protector (?),
and now I can attack the one whom I hate.'
[22, 5]For truly, you do not know God's plans,
and tomorrow you must not be ashamed.
Put yourself in God's hands,
and then your silence will bring about their (the opponents') downfall.
The crocodile, who is robbed of his tongue,[s]
[22, 10]of him fear is deep-rooted.
Do not pour out your innermost thoughts before all the world
and do not damage your reputation (thereby).[t]
Do not let your discourse go round among the people
and do not associate yourself with a passionate man.[u]
[22, 15]Better is a man whose news lies (hidden) in his body
than one who speaks it out injuriously.
A man does not run to reach success,
he does not run to his own damage.

Twenty-second chapter
[22, 20]Do not irritate your opponent in an argument
and do not make him utter his innermost thoughts.
Do not be over-hasty to go before him,
[23, 1]if you do not see what he does.
(Rather) you should first discover tidings from his answer,
and if you can behave quietly, then you will obtain your goal.
Take no notice (?) if he empties out his innermost thoughts.
[23, 5]He finds the one who knows how to sleep.[v]

[r] One should not turn one's heart enviously towards the property of others, cf. 9.1. As far as the 'place of judgment' is concerned, it remains uncertain whether the one who sets his heart on external matters and so forfeits the way of life incurs earthly justice or justice in the beyond.
[s] For the observations of nature and the myths which underlie this statement cf. G. Posener in *Festschrift für S. Schott*, 1968, 106ff.
[t] For these two verses see Prov. 23.9.
[u] Cf. Prov. 22.24.
[v] 'He' is God. He remembers the tranquil man who has control of himself and indeed sleeps during attacks on him.

Grasp his feet,[w] and do not damage him,
show him reverence and do not slight him.
For truly, you do not know God's plans,
and tomorrow you must not be ashamed.
[23,10]Put yourself in the hands of God,
and then your silence will bring about their (the opponents') downfall.

Twenty-third chapter

Do not eat bread before a noble[x]
and do not make yourself eat first (?).
[23,15]If you are satisfied with false biting,
that is only a pleasure for your spittle.
Look at the bowl which stands before you,[y]
and let it satisfy your needs.

[24,8]Twenty-fifth chapter

Do not laugh at a blind man and do not mock a cripple,
[24,10]do not make difficult the fortunes of a lame man.[z]
Do not mock a man who is in the hand of God,[a]
and do not be angry against him if he has erred.
Man is clay and straw,
and God is his builder.[b]
[24,15]He tears down and builds up every day,
he makes a thousand poor as he wishes,
and makes a thousand people overseers,
when he is in his hour of life.
How joyful is he who reaches the West,
[24,20]when he will be safe in the hand of God.[c]

Twenty-eighth chapter

Do not pick out a widow, by marking her down in the field (at the time
    of taxation?),
[26,10]nor fail to be favourable to her reply.

[w] Looking for protection? Or as a gesture of reverence?
[x] Probably a warning against domestic dealings with a superior. 'Bread' is a general term for eating. For ch. 23 cf. Prov. 23.1–3.
[y] Be content with your lot, both with simple eating and with your position generally.
[z] Not quite certain. Perhaps 'do not hurt the feelings'?
[a] An epileptic or someone who is mentally ill.
[b] For the general train of thought cf. Ps. 103.14. For the old mythical theme of God as potter or mason cf. Isa. 29.16; 45.9; 64.8; Jer. 18.1ff.; Job 10.9; 33.6; also Sirach 33.13 and Wisdom 15.7, continued in Rom. 9.21. See S. Morenz, *ZÄS* 84, 1959, 79f. For what follows see Prov. 29.13 and above all I Sam. 2.6f.
[c] With earthly death, physical deficiencies disappear as do differences of social status;

Do not go past a stranger with your beer jar,
but rather give him double before your equals.[d]
God loves the one who respects the poor,
more than the one who honours the exalted.[e]

[27,6]Thirtieth chapter

See these thirty chapters,[f]
they entertain and instruct,
they are at the head of all books,
[27,10]they give knowledge to the ignorant.
Anyone who reads them out to the ignorant
makes him clean (pleasing to God) with their help.[g]
Fill yourself with them, put them in your heart,[h]
and be a man who can explain them,
[27,15]in that he explains them as a teacher.
A scribe who is experienced in his office,
he will be found worthy to be a courtier.[i]
[27,18]End.

30. An inscription in the tomb of Petosiris

This has been published in G. Lefebvre, *Le tombeau de Petosiris*, 1924, vol. III, inscr. 127.

It comes from the end of the fourth century. The tomb lies in the wilderness of Tuna el-Gebel near Hermopolis magna, whose high priest Petosiris was. The section comes from the part of the tomb which belongs to his father, Sia Shu.

The idea that earthly treasures cannot free anyone from death or go with him after death can also be found in the OT: cf. e.g. Pss. 39.6; 49.7ff., 17, and *mutatis mutandis* also Zeph. 1.18; Prov. 11.4.

There is a translation of the inscription in Lefebvre, op. cit. I, 161, and a partial translation in E. Otto, *Die biographischen Inschriften der ägyptischen Spätzeit*, 1954, 48f.

[2]. . . I guide you (those who live later and will read this inscription) on

---

before God men are whole, and even on earth a man is to look on his fellow human beings as God sees them.
[d] See e.g. Ex. 22.21ff.; 23.9; Lev. 19.33f.; Deut. 24.17, 19ff.; 27.19.
[e] Cf. e.g. Job 34.19.
[f] Prov. 22.20.
[g] For 'purify' in the sense of 'educate' see H. Brunner, *Altägyptische Erziehung*, 1957, 112.
[h] Seek to penetrate it and to learn it off by heart.
[i] Prov. 22.29. The notion is already attested in Egypt at the end of the third millennium.

the way of life,[j] and I will tell you your (right) way of life which leads to the city of rejuvenation (happiness in the beyond); keep to my words and you will find them useful and thank me for them. Drink and be drunken and do not cease to celebrate. Follow your heart during the time on earth ... [4]When a man perishes, his possessions also perish, and one who will share in them will then be there, whose turn it now is to fulfil his heart's desire. Then there will be no more sun for the rich. There is no messenger of death[k] who would accept a gift to leave unaccomplished the mission on which he [5]had been sent.[l] He goes suddenly like a dream,[m] and no one knows the day when he comes. It is the work of God to make the heart forget the day (of death). The one who is taken away as a child is like an uprooted plant, even if his house is rich in all things [6] ... It is God who puts it in the heart of the one he hates, so that his possessions will be given to another whom he loves.[n] For he (God) is lord of his possession, and he assigns it to its (respective) possessors. Blessed is the one who sacrifices to his God, in order to keep this in his heart.

VI. FROM THE BOOK OF THE DEAD

4. The dead man makes his confession (text 31 below) before the judges of the other world; the balance shows that what he says accords with the reality of his life.

[j] As has already been indicated elsewhere, this expression is also well known from the OT; cf. Ps. 16.11; Prov. 2.19; 5.6; 10.17; 15.24. In Egypt, as in Israel, the 'way of God' is identical with it.

[k] According to Egyptian views, the gods, and especially Osiris, send messengers to summon men to death.

[l] I.e. no messenger of death can be bribed.

[m] Cf. Pss. 39.6; 73.20 and also Isa. 29.7f.; Job 20.8.

[n] For hardening of the heart cf. e.g. Ex. 7.3; Isa. 6.9-13, etc.

31. *The negative confession of sin (Book of the Dead, Saying 125)*

The text is attested by countless manuscripts which are either unpublished or published only in inadequate editions. As there is no critical edition, the following translation is based on the texts in E. Naville, *Das ägyptische Todtenbuch der XVIII. bis XX. Dynastie*, 1886, and E. A. W. Budge, *The Book of the Dead*, 1898. The numbering of lines follows Naville.

Saying 125, which is evidently composed from various individual passages, is attested for the first time early in the New Kingdom. Although there are numerous textual variants on points of detail, the composition as a whole seems to be canonical. Like most of the Egyptian texts of the dead, this saying is meant to be magical in its present version: the one who speaks it 'is separated from his sins'. However, the enumeration of the sins is evidence of Egyptian ethics and is closely connected with autobiographies and precepts for living. The negative confession of sin could be oriented on formulae asserting purity which priests (or other suppliants?) had to utter when they entered the temple (cf. here Pss. 15; 24.3–6; Isa. 33.14–16). In the present version from the New Kingdom part I is to be spoken by the dead man on entering the hall of judgment, and part II at the point in the examination when the heart of the dead person is weighed against Maat: the balance on which the two scales hang remains steady if the utterance is true and the sin mentioned has therefore not been committed. Finally, as the introduction indicates, part III was probably to be spoken on leaving the hall.

If we leave on one side the special context in which the saying was to be used, the confession in part II has parallels with OT confessions of innocence, and most of all with Deut. 26.13f., with Ps. 26.4f., and also with I Sam. 12.3 and Job 31, though of course the style is different. Individual statements in the confession have substantial points of contact with OT commands and prohibitions, and with related prophetic criticism; cf. e.g. the assertion that measures and weights have not been altered (II 16f.) with Lev. 19.35f.; Deut. 25.13ff.; Ezek. 45.10ff.; Hos. 12.8; Amos 8.5; Micah 6.10f.; Prov. 11.1, etc. The idea of God weighing man appears in Job 31.6, though there it has been detached from the context of judgment after death. It also underlies Isa. 40.15; Ps. 62.9 and Dan. 5.27. Not least, it appears in the iconography of the Christian Last Judgment. The conception of the gods in the train of the great god, who report on men's life (I 3; III 12), recalls (*mutatis mutandis*) Job 1.6ff. Finally, the characterization of the realm of the dead as the 'land of silence' (III 16) has an exact parallel in Pss. 94.17 and 115.17.

The whole of the Book of the Dead has been translated by P. Barguet, *Le livre des morts des anciens Égyptiens*, 1967, and Saying 125 by J. Yoyotte in *Le jugement des morts*, SOr 4, 1961, 15ff.; on this see J. Spiegel, *Die Idee vom Totengericht in der ägyptischen Religion* LÄS 2, 1935.

Introduction

[1]What is to be said on entering the hall of the two truths,° at the separa-

° In Egyptian the number two is often a symbol of perfection, so that it could be

tion of N N from all the [2]evil which he has done, on seeing the faces of the gods:[P] N N speaks:

I. Greeting

Hail to you, great God, lord of the two truths. I have come to you, [3]my lord, I have been brought to see your perfection. I know you, I know the names of the forty-two gods who are with you in [4]the hall of the two truths, who live on those who have preserved evil,[q] who gulp up their blood on that day of [5]the reckoning of the characters before Unnenofer (i.e. Osiris). The one whose two eyes are daughters,[r] lord of Maat is your name. I am come to you, [6]after I have brought Maat to you and have expelled injustice from you.

II. Negative 'penance'

I have committed no injustice against men. I have not mistreated the cattle (of God).[s] I have not committed any unchastity[t] [7]in the place of truth.[u] I do not know what does not exist.[v] I have not done [8]evil . . . [9]My name has not reached the barque of the one who guides the people.[w] I have not [10]blasphemed God. I have not done violence to a poor man.[x] I have not broken the taboo of a God. [11]I have not defamed a servant to his superiors. I have not made (anyone) [12]sick.[y] I have not made (anyone) weep. I have not killed. I have not given orders to kill . . .[z] I have not caused anyone suffering. I have not diminished the food in the [14]temples. I have not damaged the sacrificial bread of the gods. I have not plundered

---

understood to mean 'the unbroken truth'. In Egyptian, 'truth' is called Maat, see p. 13 n. n above.

[P] Variant: 'god, the lord of countenances', i.e. the sun god.

[q] And who therefore were not separated from it, who have not been able to utter the present saying or who have not been acquitted. Less probable: 'who live from watching over sinners (or sins)'.

[r] The god of the sun and the heavens; sun and moon could thus be regarded as his 'daughters'.

[s] Men, see p. 15 n. u above.

[t] Translation uncertain. I am thinking of the word ywyt, which can certainly mean 'brothel' in addition to its general meaning 'house' (Pap. Anast. IV 12, 3 with variants).

[u] I.e. probably in the necropolis, whose rock tombs offered appropriate refuge for lovers.

[v] See E. Hornung, Der Eine und die Vielen, 1971, 166ff.

[w] There is a variant 'office' for 'barque'. What is meant is either the leader of the corvée of forced labour or a detachment of prisoners, probably the former, with whom the speaker got on well.

[x] Variant: the possessions of a poor man.

[y] Probably through sympathetic magic.

[z] In the text of Ramesses IV, who by virtue of his office had to impose the death penalty, there is the addition 'unlawfully'.

the sacrificial cakes [15]of the dead. I have not had sexual relations with a boy, and I have not satisfied myself.[a] [16]I have neither increased nor diminished the bushel. I have not diminished the arable land. I have not taken away any arable land. I have not added anything to the weight of the [17]balance. I have not diminished anything in the plummet of the scales. I have not taken milk from the mouth of babies. I have not deprived [18]cattle of their fodder. I have not caught birds in the reeds of the gods, I have not fished [19]in their lagoons.[b] I have not held up the water in its season.[c] I have not built a dam against running water. I have not quenched the fire in its time (i.e. when it should be burning). [20]I have not gone past the time for the sacrifice. I have not driven away the cattle of the god's property (i.e. the temple). I have not gone against a god in his procession.[d] [21]I am pure (to be said four times)! My purity is the purity of the great phoenix, which is in Heracleopolis, for I am the nose of the [22]lord of the breath of life, who keeps all Egypt alive . . .[e]

III. Closing speech

[2]Hail to you, gods. [3]I know you, I know your names, I will not fall to your [4]slaughter, for you will not report any ill of me to that great god whom you follow. [5]Through you my name will not come (before him), rather you will speak 'truth'[f] of me before the all-Lord, for I have done truth in the [6]land of Egypt. I have not conjured up any god,[g] and I was not

[a] The exact meaning of the two last sentences is obscure. Homosexuality was strictly taboo; an action of this kind is known as the action of a conqueror to humiliate his victim. Cf. Pap. Bremner-Rhind, 22, 19.

[b] In the temple property.

[c] During the period of the inundation of the Nile. What is probably referred to is illegitimate appropriation of water by drawing it off on to one's own fields.

[d] In some processions mythical plays were staged in which people had to engage in armed combat with the god and his followers. Although such performances demanded opponents of the deity, this role seems to have been regarded as a sin.

[e] There follow references to myths of Heliopolis, to whose knowledge and indeed survival the dead man bears witness. According to this, forty-two judges of the dead are called on by name (in cipher) and an assurance is given before each that the sinner has not committed a particular sin (second negative 'penance'). Only in a few cases is it possible to connect the sin with the person who is addressed. Before the judges report the result of this investigation to the god who speaks this judgment, the dead man turns to them once again.

[f] The judges themselves do not give the verdict, but rather report to the 'great god' (Osiris or the sun god), who then pronounces the verdict. The dead man asks that they should pronounce the word 'truth' over him, i.e. confirm that what he has said in his negative confession accords with the facts.

[g] As in the OT, witchcraft towards a god is sin. Cf. Ex. 20.7; Deut. 5.11; Ezek. 13.19. – Variants have read 'blasphemed'; blasphemy would make a pair along with the 'lèse-majesté' which follows.

required because of a ruling king.[h] Hail to you, gods in the hall of the two [7]truths, in whose body there is no injustice, who live from Maat and who drink from Maat [8]before Horus in his sun disc. Save me from Babi,[i] who lives on the entrails of the great on that day of the great reckoning. [9]See, I have come to you without sin, without guilt, without evil, without there being any evil in me, without there being a witness against me, without one against whom I might have done anything (evil). Rather, [10]I live off Maat and drink of the truth. I have done what men have said[j] and with what the gods are always content. I have made the god satisfied with what he loves: [11]I have given bread to the hungry and water to the thirsty, clothes to the naked and a ferry to the one without a boat.[k] [12]I have provided sacrifices for the gods and dead-offerings for the dead. So save me, protect me, do not make any report about me to the great god. [13]I am one with a pure mouth and pure hands, one to whom those who see him say 'Welcome!', for I have investigated that great dispute which the ass and the cat carried on [14]in the house of the one with gaping jaws.[l] The ferryman was witness and let out a loud cry. I have seen the splitting of the Ished tree in the western necropolis.[m] [15]I am the mummifier of the nineness of the gods and know what is in their bodies.[n]

I have come here [16]to keep the scales in balance in the land of silence[o] . . .

[h] What is meant may be giving offence or swearing an oath or other misuse of the name.

[i] An uncanny god in the form of an ape (Babi > Babuin > Pavian).

[j] The reference is to the teachings of Egyptian wise men who, like wisdom (hokmah) in the OT, set up rules (not laws!) for a way of life which is pleasing to God and men.

[k] As the fields often lie on the other side of the Nile or a canal, the poorer people, who do not have a boat of their own, are often open to exploitation by those who do have boats. It is regarded as a social action to ferry over the poor without charge. Cf. III 11 as a whole with Deut. 15.7f.; Isa. 58.7; Ezek. 18.7, 16; Prov. 22.9 and Prov. 11.24ff.

[l] Hippopotamus? An allusion to a myth which is unknown to us.

[m] After a battle against the enemies of the gods the Ished tree (sycamore?) is split so that the sun can rise again (be reborn).

[n] This passage is also concerned with the knowledge of secret things, presented in concrete terms as the content of the body of the gods, which comes to light as the body is opened up for mummifying.

[o] The beyond.

B

MESOPOTAMIAN TEXTS

INTRODUCTION

Scattered individual finds make it increasingly clear that the great works of literature from Sumer and Akkad in Mesopotamia were read throughout the ancient Near Eastern world, evidently even in Egypt. Scholars of this period were therefore well versed in cuneiform and Babylonian. The influence on Canaanite culture in Syria and Palestine was also predominantly Mesopotamian, especially in the second millennium and at the beginning of the first millennium BC.

To begin with, Israel, a comparatively young intruder with an even briefer tradition of its own, seems to have appropriated the heritage presented to it quite quickly. It is impossible to trace this process in detail, but it is clear that assimilation in the cultic and religious spheres was increasingly restrained by strict upholders of belief in Yahweh. Finally, the process was halted and indeed reversed. Israelite religious literature has come down to us only within the narrow limits which were thus marked out. Since the Old Testament is the only surviving source, it therefore offers small scope for comparison with evidence from cuneiform literature.[a]

Any religious comparisons must keep two fundamental facts in view. The evidence from Sumer and Akkad is on the whole considerably older than the corresponding texts in the Old Testament (sometimes by 1500 years and more). (Sumerian continued as an element in 'ecclesiastical' and literary language in Mesopotamia and is therefore difficult to date.)

[a] For detailed comparison, A. Jirku, *Altorientalischer Kommentar zum Alten Testament*, 1923, reprinted 1972, remains indispensable; cf. also S. N. Kramer, *Sumerian Literature and the Bible*, AnOr 12, 1959, 185ff.; K. H. Bernhardt, *Die Umwelt des Alten Testaments*, 1967.

Secondly, in their present form the Old Testament texts have a marked
religious colouring, even in wisdom literature, which is much less the
case with cuneiform documents. The development of Israelite belief in Yahweh eliminated certain
aspects of religion, and above all magic, so that the abundant material of
this kind from ancient Mesopotamia is excluded from any comparison.
On the other hand, in Mesopotamia codified law played a subordinate
role, and so the wealth of Israelite law is also irrelevant. In religious
documents, comparisons or contrasts between the polytheism of Sumer
and Akkad and the monotheism of Israel can be made in five areas: in
myths, epics and other kinds of saga material (I); in cultic poetry (II);
in 'prophetic' texts (III); in the specific content of treaties and catalogues
of sins (IV); and in 'wisdom' (V). The so-called 'cultic love poetry' of
ancient Mesopotamia[b] will be left out of account here, as there is still
considerable dispute over the mythological and cultic interpretation of
the Song of Songs, and at least the more recent relevant Sumerian texts
have so far been edited by only one scholar, and therefore need critical
control.

I. Since the documents mention more than three thousand deities and
there was smouldering rivalry between the priesthoods of the most
significant among them, Mesopotamian myth and epic poetry were
incapable of forming a unitary conception of creation, the ordering of the
world and primal history. One of the earliest lists of gods from Shuruppak
(shortly before 2500) still gives seven pairs of father and mother deities;
towards the end of the Sumerian period, about 2000, the most significant
deities involved in creation are An,[c] the god of heaven and father of the
gods – who is already beginning to fade – , Enlil[d] of Nippur,[e] the wise
and gracious Enki-Ea[f] of Eridu[g] and the mother goddess, who is most
frequently called Ninhursanga.[h] The fiercest fight for the primacy is
between Enki and Enlil; it was probably a kind of 'imperial theology'
from the third dynasty of Ur (2065–1955) which ultimately depicted

[b] Cf. S. N. Kramer, *ANET*[3], 496, 637ff.; id., *The Sacred Marriage Rite*, 1969;
A. Falkenstein, *SAHG*, 119f. (no. 25) and 370; W. G. Lambert, *JSS* 4, 1959, 1ff.; id.,
MIOF 12, 1966, 41ff.
[c] Akkadian Anu, especially worshipped in Uruk, even before Inanna-Ishtar.
[d] Lord of the air (wind), the storm god and the ruler over the surface of the earth.
[e] Present-day Niffer, ninety miles south-east of Baghdad.
[f] 'Lord of the underworld', i.e. the primaeval ocean Apsu, which was thought of as
being under the earth, and god of wisdom.
[g] Abu Shahrain, about eighteen miles south-east of Nasiriye.
[h] A number of goddesses of this type coalesce with her, like Nintu, Ninmah, Nammu,
Mama and Aruru; finally Inanna-Ishtar herself enters upon her heritage. For the
figures of the gods see D. O. Edzard, *WM* I.

both of them at work together, with Ninhursanga to help them. After that, the Babylonian Marduk took some time to achieve the status of creator and orderer of the world, and this development was finally sealed by the 'epic of the creation of the world' (see text 6 below). In contrast to this complete but late poem, we have only fragments of Sumerian traditions on the themes indicated or mythological introductions to texts with a different content.[i] Similarly, in Mesopotamia there is no primal history of the kind to be found in the Bible. Rather, we find only certain ideas reminiscent of the Old Testament notions of paradise, and in addition the 'kings before the flood', the flood story itself and (as has been discovered only recently) an account of the 'confusion of tongues'. Two individual themes which were incorporated into the saga of Moses can also be added.

II. Thus in the circumstances we have not inconsiderable parallels between the mythical epic poetry of ancient Mesopotamia and the biblical creation stories in particular. When it comes to cultic poetry (in the widest sense), however, the situation is different. Israel's Psalms (the hymn book and prayer book of Yahwistic religion) and its Lamentations represent a most carefully chosen selection. There could be only the most limited features in common between it and the corresponding poetry of Mesopotamia, between unique monotheism and extreme poly-theism. That is the case even in view of the fact that we find Sumerian and Akkadian cultic poetry at a stage of untroubled egalitarianism (which was evidently not felt to be contradictory). The divine epithets, for the most part given in lists of exaggerated length, seem to change at random, and therefore in both hymns and prayers we seldom find real religious emotion and committed trust in God through faith. Of course the best of these resonant cultic poems are capable of bearing impressive testimony to the power and glory of the deity who is celebrated. And in the liturgical and 'personal' prayers it seems possible to trace through the texts, most of which have a tone of lamentation, a striving towards the deity that comes from the heart, an honest confession of guilt and true petition. (The deity is usually a personal guardian deity, the 'holy one', male or female, of ancient Mesopotamian faith.) Finally, the lamentations which describe the fall and the end of great and famous cities in many respects under-standably recall the Jewish lamentations over the fall of Jerusalem. As this cultic poetry, for all its monotony and formality, shows us most clearly the pulse of Sumerian-Akkadian worship and its underlying religion, we have given a good deal of space to hymns and prayers.[j]

---

[i] J. J. van Dijk, *AcOr* 28, 1964, 1ff., provides an instructive survey.
[j] There is an extensive collection of Sumerian and Akkadian cultic poetry in *AOT²*,

III. Before the discovery and deciphering of the archive of letters at Mari from the eighteenth century BC, cuneiform literature did not seem to contain any prophetic texts like those in the Old Testament. Those predictions about the future that were known belonged clearly in the sphere of Akkadian omens and were associated with the genres and practices of divination (astrology and the inspection of incense, oil, intestines – especially the liver – and many other items). Yahwistic Israel offers nothing comparable here. Those Babylonian texts which have recently been designated apocalypses,[k] which seem to have treated the course of history as a fixed cycle[l] and so believe that it is possible to read off future events from observation of the past, have parallels of a kind in the Old Testament only with the prophecies of the book of Daniel, since this schematic perspective is unknown to the Old Testament. The famous prophetic sayings from ancient Mari in Babylonia were the first to provide more closely related material.[m] These comprise about two dozen texts, addressed to King Zimrilim, containing admonitions, warnings and messages of good news which are pronounced by cultic prophets from various temples, and even by lay people, on the basis of visions, auditions or dreams. Events of this kind were regarded as being so significant in Mari at that time that in each case they had to be reported to the ruler and verified. Peculiarly enough, this phenomenon, which is a closer parallel to the cultic prophecy attacked by the great prophets of Israel than to the proclamations of the writing prophets, is as far as we now know limited to the time of Zimrilim, the confederate or rival of Hammurabi (1728–1686), and to Mari and some neighbouring areas; as is indicated by the story of Wen-amon (about 1070 BC)[n] and the phenomenon of the Old Testament 'lying prophets',[o] its origin may lie in Syria rather than Mesopotamia.

241ff., which is still instructive, despite the progress made in philology since then. Compare further *ANET*[3], 383ff., and the new specialist publications: A. Falkenstein and W. von Soden, *SAHG*, 1953; A Falkenstein, *Sumerische Götterlieder* I; J. J. van Dijk, *Sumerische Götterlieder* II, both AHAW, PH, 1959 and 1960; A. Sjöberg, *Der Mondgott Nanna-Sin* I, 1960; id. et al., *The Collection of Sumerian Temple Hymns*, TCS III, 1969; J. Krecher, *Sumerische Kultlyrik*, 1966; A. Falkenstein and W. von Soden, 'Gebet' I and II, *RLA* III, fascicles 2, 1959, and 3, 1964.

[k] Cf. W. W. Hallo, *IEJ* 16, 1966, 235ff.
[l] A. K. Grayson and W. G. Lambert, *JCS* 18, 1964, 9f.
[m] See now the basic monograph by F. Ellermeier, *Prophetie in Mari und Israel*, 1968; see no. 30 below.
[n] Cf. K. Galling, *TGI*[2], 1968, 41ff., esp. 43, lines 38ff.
[o] By way of example cf. I Kings 18.20ff. and the relevant polemic from the writing prophets, cf. p. 123, n. u below.

IV. Whereas the appearance of the first cuneiform laws[p] made it clear that there were significant parallels between ancient Near Eastern law and that of Israel (even if they were unimportant from a religious point of view), new cuneiform discoveries and careful stylistic investigations have demonstrated another area of law in which the Old Testament and the ancient Near East have points of contact which also coincide in time. These are the cursing formulae of Assyrian state treaties, containing threats against transgressions of the agreement which had been reached. They are vividly reminiscent of the threats made by the prophets of Israel, whether against their own 'apostate' people or against hostile nations, and still more of the words of condemnation which Deuteronomy and the Priestly Writing hold before Israel if the Israelites transgress against the treaty that Yahweh has made with them. The most extensive and best-known Assyrian document of this kind is the 'vassal-treaty' of Esarhaddon, and since we can take it as certain that Manasseh of Judah (686–649) had to subscribe to a similar document,[q] despite the understandable silence of the Old Testament historians on this point, we are even justified in assuming that in this case the Old Testament texts have been influenced by Assyrian models. The literary pattern was utilized when Josiah refused obedience to the Assyrians and replaced the vassal treaty with Nineveh by the 'new covenant' of Deuteronomy – now between God and his elected people. Of course Yahweh alone took the place of the countless Assyrian gods associated with oaths and curses.

V. Despite unmistakable secularization, wisdom literature is part of the religious foundation of the Old Testament; indeed it seems to have been particularly close to the hearts of the redactors involved in canonization, as is shown by the acceptance of so many sections with virtually no religious significance. It is thus all the more understandable that here Sumer and Babylon offer abundant comparative material. There are poems covering the period from the end of the third millennium to the end of the second which bear witness to a predominantly pessimistic view of the world and are especially concerned with the problem of theodicy. They are 'academic' in character, even down to their artificial acrostics. The two recently-discovered works with which this selection of texts ends (nos. 35 and 36 below) show us that Mesopotamian wisdom literature had ancient traditions and that in particular the question of the reason for the suffering of the innocent was already a legacy of the original

---

[p] Especially the Codex Hammurabi in Susa, 1901/2.
[q] Manasseh's 'sins' (cf. II Kings 21.2ff.; 23.26; 24.3; Jer. 15.4; II Chron. 33.2ff.) probably included the erection of Assyrian altars and the institution in the Jerusalem temple of the cult that went with them.

spiritual culture of Sumer. The gripping and immortal figure of Job in the Bible came from Sumer.

I would ask for the reader's sympathy over the difficult problem of the selection of texts. In fact, most of the ancient Mesopotamian cuneiform documents collected here have already appeared edited by E. Ebeling in Gressmann's AOT^2 of 1926 (though in some respects its philology is now out of date), and some of them also in D. W. Thomas, $DOTT$, 1958, and above all in J. B. Pritchard's $ANET$, already in a third edition which has been considerably expanded. Their documentary value makes it impossible, however, to leave them aside. I am all the more pleased to be able to make at least a few new contributions.

In reproducing the text I have followed the well-tried principle of making the translation as literal as possible while keeping it free enough for the present-day reader to be able to understand. However, in view of the utter strangeness of the Sumerian language, a rather freer translation than usual has sometimes proved necessary.

Ongoing discovery of documents - which sometimes appear with a cuneiform text, sometimes transcribed and translated, sometimes only in translation - means that establishing the text is often a precarious business. For many of the documents selected here we have an increasing number of fragments of varying length - sometimes amounting to only a few lines. To demonstrate them would often occupy whole pages at a time (and would also prove enigmatic to the reader). Since it is necessary to assume that the majority of readers will not be able to read cuneiform, in the comments preceding individual texts I have not cited the cuneiform originals where these are too difficult and too extensive, and instead have contented myself with indicating where an interested reader can find the necessary information. As editions of texts, translations and commentaries have been published together in many cases, it has not always been possible to make a neat distinction between 'text', 'text and commentary' and 'literature'. Here again it is necessary to ask for the reader's understanding. Those wishing to extend their study further will find R. Borger, *Handbuch der Keilschriftliteratur* I, 1967, II/III, 1975, a key work; it contains all the cuneiform documents so far edited, arranged according to editors as well as according to content (vol. III). I am grateful to Dr Borger for much advice and helpful information. The editor is responsible for a large number of references to possible comparative material from the Old Testament; I am grateful to him too for enriching the collection in this way.

I. MYTHS, EPICS AND SCATTERED
SAGA MATERIAL

The creation and ordering of the world

1. *From the Sumerian epic 'Gilgamesh, Enkidu and the Underworld':*
the separation of heaven and earth

Text: J. van Dijk, *AcOr* 28, 1964/65, 16ff.; S. N. Kramer, *SM*, 30ff. and
113 n. 32; id., *FTS*, 77 (= *GbS*, 71); id., *Sumerians*, 199ff.
    Literature: T. Jacobsen, *JNES* 5, 1946, 138ff.; A. Falkenstein, *BiOr* 5, 1948,
164; id., *BiOr* 22, 1965, 282; M. Lambert, *RA* 55, 1961, 184 no. 8; L. Matouš,
ArOr 35, 1967, 20ff.; D. O. Edzard, *WM* I, 70f.; W. von Soden, in: A. Schott
and W. von Soden, *Das Gilgamesch-Epos*, 1970, 112f. The (Akkadian) second
part of the poem appears as a kind of appendix on the twelfth tablet of the
Gilgamesh epic.
    So far there is no complete scholarly edition of the poem, which amounts to
about three hundred lines; some of the translation and interpretation is still
disputed. The text, which was certainly fixed before 2000, gives one of the five
Sumerian (partial) epics, three of which form the basis for the later Akkadian
epic of Gilgamesh. (The first part, which has been preserved in Sumerian,
is also known under the name 'Gilgamesh and the Ḫaluppu tree'.)[r] According
to Sumerian practice the beginning of the poem provides a mythology, here
important acts of creation, and above all the separation of heaven and earth
as in the Priestly Writing, Gen. 1.6ff. (the text follows the new rendering by
J. van Dijk, op. cit.):

On that day, that distant day,
in that night, that night long past,
in that year, that distant year,
when the flowers were blossoming as the gods commanded,
when the flowers were planted in the earth as the gods commanded,
when everything was taken up into the storehouses of the land of
    Sumer,
when the fire was kindled in the oven of the land of Sumer,
when the heaven had been separated from the earth,
when the earth had come down[s] from heaven,
when the seed[t] of man was established,
when An chose heaven for himself,
when Enlil had chosen earth for himself,
when the underworld had been delivered up to Ereshkigal . . .[u]

[r] Cf. S. N. Kramer, AS 10, 1938 (the section of the text included here is to be found
on p. 3).
[s] So van Dijk ('descendit'); Falkenstein (*BiOr* 5, 1964), 'dropped down (herabgetropft)'.
[t] So van Dijk.
[u] Goddess of the underworld, regarded as an older sister of Inanna-Ishtar.

2. Sumerian hymn to the mattock

Translation and commentary: S. N. Kramer, *SM*, 51ff. and 115 n. 52;
T. Jacobsen, *JNES* 5, 1946, 128ff., esp. 137 (partial translation).
Literature: A. Falkenstein, *BiOr* 5, 1948, 164; D. O. Edzard, *WM* I, 77;
M. Civil, *JNES* 28, 1969, 70.
The text has not yet been completely edited and parts of it are still disputed.
It is 108 lines long and is described less precisely as the 'myth of the making
of the mattock'. It celebrates the creation by Enlil of the mattock, which is
indispensable for the countryman and the agricultural worker (especially in
building work); the creation of the human race follows at its initiation. When
Enlil originally struck the earth with the mattock, the first men sprang out of
the opening which this created.[v] The poem continues with praise of the unique
implement and its many uses. The quotation here reproduces lines 1–20,
following Jacobsen (op. cit.); interpretation and translation still present many
problems.

The Lord truly created the right order,
the Lord, whose decisions are unalterable,
Enlil hastened to divide the heaven from the earth,[w]
so that the seed from which the people (grew) could sprout from the
    field.[x]
[5]Yes, he accomplished the division between earth and heaven,
(but) tied together the split for it (the earth) in the 'union of heaven
    and earth',
so that from the *Uzu-e*[y] the first men[z] could (then) come forth.
When the daylight appeared, he brought the mattock into being,
established the duties – the action of the mattock swinger,
[10]so that he stretched forth (his) arm to mattock and basket.
(Then) Enlil began the praise of the mattock.
His mattock was of gold, its blade[a] from lapis lazuli . . .

(Five lines follow which are difficult to interpret)

[17]He struck his mattock into the *Uzu-e*,
then in the hollow (which thus was made) there were the first men.

---

[v] Presumably the place where this once happened was pointed out in Enlil's sanctuary
of Ekur in Nippur; the names in lines 6f. could be an allusion to it, cf. Jacobsen, op cit.,
134ff.
[w] Cf. Gen. 1.6ff.
[x] There are traces of comparable conceptions in Ps. 139.15 and possibly in Job 1.21.
[y] Literally 'bringer forth of the flesh', namely man.
[z] Literally perhaps 'the foreskin'.
[a] Literally, 'head'.

Now when his land[b] came forth through the earth before Enlil,
²⁰he looked upon the black-headed ones[c] in abiding form . . .

3. Sumerian myth 'Enki and Ninmah':[d] the creation of man

Translation and commentary: S. N. Kramer, *SM*, 68ff.; id., *Sumerians*, 149ff.; T. Jacobsen, *JNES* 5, 1946, 143; A. Falkenstein, *BiOr* 5, 1948, 164f.; J. J. van Dijk, *AcOr* 28, 1964/65, 1ff., esp. 24ff.; C. A. Benito, '*Enki and Ninmah*' and '*Enki and the World Order*', 1972, 9ff.
Literature: T. Jacobsen, in Frankfort et al., *Before Philosophy*, 1949, 175f.; M. Lambert, *RA* 55, 1961, 186f.; D. O. Edzard, *WM* I, 58; W. G. Lambert, *JSS* 14, 1969, 264f.; G. Pettinato, *Das altorientalische Menschenbild*, etc., 1971; H. M. Kümmel, *WO* 7, 1973, 25ff.

This poem is only a fragment and the text is difficult (as far as we know it amounts to about 150 lines); nor is its modern title very satisfactory. It has preserved another tradition about the creation of man which is immediately reminiscent of the Yahwistic account in Gen. 2.7, though it is about a thousand years older. A figure was shaped like a clay model from 'clay above the primal ocean (Apsu)' and life was given to it. To begin with we hear of the gods' reluctance to earn their daily bread for themselves, and of their complaints on the subject. (These are evidently meant for the ear of the wise Enki, who is sunk in deep sleep.) Enki, aroused by his mother Nammu,[e] shows her how, with the help of Ninmah, the experienced goddess of creation, she may make from the same clay other beings – men – and further helpers to look after the gods. However, unfortunately the text breaks off at the point where there might have been a mention of the carrying out of these instructions, and all we hear afterwards is a report of a fatal competition in creation between Enki and Ninmah, who in the intoxication of a feast bring into being only defective creatures. The passage may have been intended as an explanation of the existence of abnormal, sick and useless men in Sumerian society (in quite disrespectful terms). In the end the contest seems to end to Enki's advantage (though again the text leaves us in the lurch here).[f] The lines relating to Enki's

[b] The men of Sumer. The idea that the first men grew up through the surface of the earth can also be found in the Sumerian hymn to Eridu, *SAHG* 133, lines 1-3. According to Falkenstein, this runs:
'When the destiny of all who are begotten was determined,
when, in a year of superfluity which An had created,
the men had broken through the earth like grass . . .'
Cf. further van Dijk, *Or*, NS 41, 1972, 342; 42, 1973, 502ff.
[c] The inhabitants of Mesopotamia.
[d] Ninmah, 'exalted mistress', is one of the names of the mother goddess (see p. 69 n. h above), identified with Ninhursanga.
[e] Nammu occasionally has the name 'mother who has borne heaven and earth', or 'who has borne all the gods'. She is perhaps to be regarded as a 'personification of the subterranean deeps' (D. O. Edzard, *WM* I, 107).
[f] Thus Falkenstein, *BiOr* 5, 1948, 165.

instructions to Nammu (30–37) run as follows:[g]

O my mother, the being whom you named is there:[h]
associate the image (?) of the gods with him,
mix the nucleus[i] of clay above the primal ocean.
The gods and princely figures (?) will thicken the clay,
but you must give life to the limbs.
Ninmah will help you here,
the deities . . .[j] will help you as you shape it . . .
O my mother, determine its fate (the fate of the new being)![k]

4. The Babylonian incantation to the 'tooth-worm'

Text, literature: F. Thureau-Dangin, *RA* 36, 1939, 3f.; A. Heidel, *BG²*, 72f.; R. Labat, *RPOA* I, 78f.; E. A. Speiser, *ANET³*, 100f.
The colophon makes it quite clear that this copy, which comes from the neo-Babylonian period, goes back to an ancient Babylonian original from the nineteenth-eighteenth century BC; this is also confirmed by a Hurrian recension which was found in Mari.[l] The incantation is intended as a cure for toothache (of course it is meant to be accompanied by the relevant dental treatment), by driving away the 'tooth-worm' which from the very beginning has been settled in the teeth, through the help of Ea.[m] Again we are interested only in the mythological introduction, lines 1–7:

[g] According to Kramer, *Sumerians*, 150, cf. now Benito, op cit., 36 f.
[h] What is probably meant is that the being already exists as Enki's conception.
[i] Literally 'the heart'.
[j] There follow the names of further divine helpers.
[k] As in Gen. 2.7 (J), so for the ancient Mesopotamian writers of myths, potter's clay is a favourite material for making man. The association of ideas is obvious. In the Atrahasis epic seven pairs of men are made from clay (and the flesh and blood of a rebellious god), cf. W. G. Lambert and A. R. Millard, *Atra-ḫasis*, 1969, 61, lines 249ff. and 63, lines 8ff. The 'beast-man' Enkidu is also made by the goddess Aruru from 'kneaded clay', cf. Schott and von Soden, *Das Gilgamesch-Epos* (see no. 13 below), 19, tablet 1, lines 33ff. A Seleucid building ritual from Babylon still has Ea making gods and men from clay in its mythological introduction, cf. F. Thureau-Dangin, *Rituels accadiens*, 1921, 45ff.; A. Heidel, *BG²*, 65f., lines 24–38. We have already come across the idea that men sprouted from the earth like plants (see above, no. 2), and also find another idea, that man was formed in the depths of the earth, cf. van Dijk, *Or* NS 42, 1973, 502ff., which points towards Ps. 139.15f. In spiritualized forms creation generally is represented as taking place simply by the utterance of the name - as happens in P in Gen. 1.6ff.; or the verbs 'make', 'bring into being', etc., are used. Thus e.g. in the Sumerian flood story (cf. Lambert and Millard, op cit., 140f., lines 47–50): 'When An, Enlil and Ninhursanga had created the black-headed ones, had made the beasts numerous everywhere, and appointed living beings of all sizes, four-footed ones, as a fitting adornment for the steppe . . .' As the following text shows, a further development towards the abstract can be recognized, extending even towards a kind of progressive 'self-creation'.
[l] Cf. F. Thureau-Dangin, *RA* 36, 1939, 4f.   [m] Another name of the god Enki.

When Anu [had created heaven],
when heaven had created [earth],
when the earth had created the rivers,
when the rivers had created the canals,
when the canals had created the marsh,
(and) when the marsh had created the worm,
the worm came weeping before Shamash . . .[n]

5. *Sumerian myth 'Enki and the Ordering of the World'*

Text and translation, Inez Bernhardt and S. N. Kramer, *WZ(J)* 9, 1959/60, 231ff.;[o] A. Falkenstein, *ZA* 56, 1964, 44f.; C. A. Benito (cf. literature on no. 3), 77f.

Literature: S. N. Kramer, *SM*, 59ff.; id., *FTS*, 89ff. (= *GbS*, 8off.); id., *Sumerians*, 171f.; M. Lambert, *RA* 55, 1961, 186, no. 16; D. O. Edzard, *WM* I, 58f.

This poem is a very long one (over 450 lines). It has been preserved predominantly in ancient Babylonian copies from Nippur, but was probably composed in its present form around 2000 BC at the time of the third dynasty of Ur with a harmonizing tendency, being made up of a number of originally independent units. It puts Enki in a central position as the organizer of nature, civilization and worship. However, Enlil is also given his due as ruler and creator god. It was he who bestowed the *me*, the mysterious 'divine powers' which Enki possesses, so that he could now create freely and fully and organize the world. In a closing section which is to be regarded as a later addition, Inanna, later Ishtar, also receives satisfaction through a speech of Enki's which is addressed particularly to her. The previous text has made no reference to her at all and she complains about her neglect. The text is damaged at the beginning and the end. In the main part, to begin with we find a hymn to Enki, the lord of general well-being, prosperity and wisdom, which is followed by a twofold hymn of self-praise by the great lord of the gods, heightened by the assent which is given by the rest of the gods – this is a remarkable characteristic of the hymn-writing of Sumer. In union with his father An and his 'older brother' Enlil, Enki is said to guide the destiny of the world, write down what happens in the cosmos, irrigate the land and make possible rich catches of fish and good harvests. Next rites in Enki's honour are mentioned, and we are told how Enki takes ship on a journey through the lands in order to determine their fortunes. He comes first to Sumer and gives his blessing to it and especially to Ur.[p] Bestowing his grace on all sides, he then visits Melucca[q] and the island of Tilmun

[n] Sun god and god of judgment.
[o] Note 1 (p. 251) of the edition cited is a good illustration of the difficulties presented by the cuneiform text.
[p] The capital of Sumer at the time the poem was composed, which is probably why it is the only city mentioned.
[q] The land of the culture of the Indus, which then had trade relationships with Sumer.

in the Persian Gulf.[r] A curse on the hostile lands of Elam is followed by new blessings on the land of Martu,[s] the lands on the Euphrates and Tigris, and the marshes[t] at the mouth of the rivers. We then hear of the founding of a sanctuary 'in the sea', i.e. probably in a lagoon at the north-west end of the Persian Gulf - the reference may be to the temple of Eengurra in Eridu. Now there begins Enki's ordering of the world - a great construction of human civilization. Its individual institutions - agricultural work, the cultivation of corn, work with the mattock, house building, the domestication of animals, the fixing of boundaries, weaving - are founded, blessed and each put under the responsibility of a particular god. Inanna's lament, Enki's answer and perhaps a short hymn to Enki bring the composition to an end. Although many details of the text are hard to elucidate, it is distantly reminiscent of the Deuteronomic paraenesis in Deut. 7-11 (especially the promises of blessing which are given there) and of Ps. 104. Only a few lines are appropriate for inclusion here.

[189-193]Enki determined its (i.e. Sumer's) destiny:
[190]Sumer, 'great mountain',[u] land of heaven and earth,
filled with a fearful gleam which has given the (whole) land
'divine powers' from dawn to dusk,
your 'divine powers' are supreme, unassailable.
Your purpose is deep, impossible to fathom . . .

[307-323]He summoned the two winds (and) the water of the heaven,[v]
he made them approach like two clouds,
made their life-giving (?) breath go to the horizon,
[310]changed the (barren?) hills into fields.
The one who ushers in the heavy weather, who strikes with lightning,[w]
who puts the sacred bolt in the midst of heaven (?) -
the son of An, the water-master of heaven and earth,
Ishkur,[x] the good, the son of An,
[315]was put in charge of this by Enki.

He instituted plough, yoke (and) span,
the exalted prince Enki made the . . . oxen go in straight lines (when
    ploughing),
opened (?) the holy furrows,

[r] Its identification is still disputed. It is most probably Bahrein (though others make the improbable suggestion that it is Faylakah) in the Persian Gulf.
[s] The homeland of the West Semitic 'Amurru people'.
[t] Probably because it provided reeds which were indispensable for utensils, light structures and fuel in Mesopotamia, a region with little wood.
[u] Perhaps 'elevated land' - except for its (artificial) tell, Sumer is a plain.
[v] For this idea cf. e.g. Ps. 148.4b.
[w] Cf. Ps. 104.3f.; also Ps. 68.33; Deut. 33.26 etc.
[x] The Sumerian weather god.

so that the good ground could make barley shoot.[y]
[320]The lord who wears the diadem(?), the adornment of the high
steppe,
the strong-armed, Enlil's countryman,
Enkimdu,[z] the lord of digging and canals,
[323]was put in charge of this by Enki . . .

[339-346]He drew the line, arranged the foundations,
[340]he built the house beside the council and arranged the rites of
purification,
the great ruler laid the foundation walls (and) set the bricks on them.
The one whose foundation walls set in the earth will never shift,[a]
whose well-built house will never totter,
whose well-established roof reaches like the rainbow to heaven –
[345]Mushdama,[b] Enlil's great master-builder,
was put in charge of this by Enki . . .

[356-365]He set up the hurdles, accomplished the rites of purification,
erected sheepfolds, made fat and milk to be at their best,
bestowed luxuriance on the place where the gods feed,
made the steppe flourish, where grass and herbs grow.
The king, the just protector of Eanna,[c] the friend of An,
the beloved son-in-law of the strong Suen,[d] the holy consort of Inanna,
the queen of heaven, the mistress of the majestic 'divine powers',
the one who brings about meetings . . . on the streets of Kullaba,[e]
Dumuzi,[f] the 'dragon of heaven', the friend of An,
[365]was put in charge of this by Enki . . .

6. Akkadian myth 'When on high' ('Creation Epic')

Text: W. G. Lambert and S. B. Parker, *Enuma eliš*, 1966 (complete cuneiform text); S. Langdon, *The Babylonian Epic of Creation*, 1923; R. Labat, *Le
poème babylonien de la création*, 1935; id., *RPOA* I, 36ff.; A. Deimel, *Enuma
eliš²*, 1936; A. Heidel, *BG²*; E. A. Speiser, *ANET³*, 6off.; A. K. Grayson,
ibid., 501ff.; for the fifth tablet, B. Landsberger and J. V. K. Wilson, *JNES* 20,
1961, 154ff.

[y] Cf. Ps. 104.14f.
[z] God of agriculture and irrigation.
[a] Cf. Ps. 104.5.
[b] God of the master-builder.
[c] The 'house of heaven', the temple of Inanna Ishtar in Uruk.
[d] The moon god.
[e] Another name for, or a part of, Uruk.
[f] The Sumerian name of Tammuz.

Literature: W. von Soden, *ZA* 40, 1931, 163ff.; 41, 1933, 90ff.; A. L. Oppenheim, *Or*, NS 16, 1947, 207ff.; D. O. Edzard, *WM* I, 121ff.; L. Matouš, *ArOr* 29, 1961, 30ff.; W. G. Lambert, *JTS* NS 16, 1965, 290ff.; T. Jacobsen, *JAOS* 88, 1968, 104ff.

This text, which consists of almost 900 lines on seven tablets, is called *Enuma elish* ('When on high'), taking its title according to ancient Near Eastern custom from its opening words. It was recited regularly on the fourth day of the New Year Festival (the great cultic state ceremony) in Esangila, the temple of Marduk in Babylon, from the seventh century BC onwards and perhaps from even earlier, and served to glorify the 'national god' Marduk. Emphasis was laid less on creation or the creation of man than on Marduk's victory over Tiamat, his ordering of the world and his exaltation to be lord of the gods. The poem was also held in great regard by the Assyrians, though they replaced the name of Marduk with that of the state god of Assyria, Ashur. Both the Yahwist and the author of the Priestly Writing, and also the author of Job and many of the composers of psalms, may have known this classic Babylonian

5. Gods fighting the dragon. Impression of an
Akkadian seal (about 2300 BC).

cosmogony, of which there are still echoes in Berossus.[8] The date of its composition is now usually put in the twelfth-eleventh century BC. In a verbose way, with lengthy repetitions, it first reports the creation of the gods by the primal couple Apsu (primaeval ocean) and Tiamat ('the one who gives birth'?) and the creation of further generations of gods. The uproar among the younger gods robs aged Apsu of his repose (as the uproar among men disturbs Enlil in the Atrahasis epic); he decides to destroy them, but at first encounters the opposition of Tiamat. Despite this, a battle takes place in which Apsu is killed, thanks to the magic spell of Ea. Now, of course, Tiamat seeks to take vengeance for her consort, and no god dares to go against her, except for Ea's son Marduk, who as the reward for his victory is made lord over the gods and the cosmos,

[8] P. Schnabel, *Berossos*, 1923, 255. Berossus, a priest of Marduk in Babylon, who later taught in Cos, wrote three volumes of *Babyloniaca* about 300 BC. Unfortunately, we have only fragments of this in later extracts.

as he has been promised. In a fearful battle[h] he kills Tiamat and her helpers, divides Tiamat's body, making heaven and earth out of it,[i] organizes the heavens, setting stars and moon in them, inaugurates the 'sabbath'[j] (among other institutions), and from the blood of Kingu, Tiamat's most powerful helper, makes men to be the servants of the gods. In gratitude the gods build him the temple Esangila and its ziggurat, and celebrate the victor by giving him fifty honorific names. Enlil, the former ruler of the gods, finally bestows on him lordship over the universe. The text then enumerates Marduk's fifty names and ends with the warning that these, like the whole of the poem, are to be kept holy and to be handed on.[k] For comparative material in the OT see the footnotes.

Tablet I[1-10] Opening

When on high the heaven had not (yet) been named,[l]
and below the firm ground had not (yet) been given a name,
when primaeval Apsu, their begetter,
(and) Mummu[m]-Tiamat[n] who gave them all birth,
[5](still) mingled their waters,
the reed had not yet sprung forth nor had the marsh appeared,
none of the gods had been brought into being,
they were (still) unnamed and their fortunes were not determined,[o]
then the gods were created in their[p] midst.
[10](When) Lahmu (and) Lahamu (first) appeared and were called by
   name . . .

[h] The 'fight with the dragon' which is described in detail here, obviously had less direct influence on the corresponding notions in the OT (Isa. 27.1; Ps. 74.14; Job 3.8, though we have no more than allusions to them in the tradition) than the Canaanite-Ugaritic stories from the Baal cycle; cf. O. Kaiser, *Die mythische Bedeutung des Meeres*, BZAW 78, 1962, 74f. S. N. Kramer's theory of the presence of a *Sumerian* saga of the fight with the dragon (the so-called myth of KUR) has proved to be mistaken, cf. T. Jacobsen, *JNES* 5, 1946, 131, 143ff. For the present state of the controversy over the Bible, Babylon and creation cf. W. G. Lambert, *JTS*, op. cit.
[i] The formation of the earth may have been described in a portion of the text which is no longer extant.
[j] *shapattu*, the fifteenth day of the lunar month and at the same time the full moon; cf. Gen. 2.2f.
[k] The numbering of lines follows Speiser and Labat, op cit.
[l] Creation is brought about by giving the name. Cf. Isa. 40.26; Ps. 147.4.
[m] Here probably only in the sense of 'mother', not to be confused with the vizier, who makes an appearance later.
[n] *tehom* in Gen. 1.2.
[o] In Gen. 2.5 the Yahwist also describes the 'world before the creation' with a series of comparable negations.
[p] Namely Apsu and Tiamat.

Tablet IV[129-140] The killing of conquered Tiamat and the creation of heaven

The lord[q] trod on the legs of Tiamat,
[130]with his unsparing mace he crushed her skull,[r]
(and) when he had severed the arteries of her blood,
the north wind bore it[s] to unknown fields.
When his fathers saw this, they were joyful and rejoiced,[t]
they brought him gifts of homage.
[135]Then the lord rested and contemplated her corpse,
intent on dividing the form[u] and doing skilful works,
he split it like a dried fish,
set up one half and made it the firmament,[v]
drew a skin over it, posted guards
[140]and instructed them not to let its water escape . . .[w]

Tablet V[1-18] Creation of the stars and moon[x]

He created the heavenly residence[y] for the great gods,
the stars, their (astral) manifestations, the 'likenesses', he fixed in it,
he determined the year and gave (it) its zones,
he assigned three stars to each of the twelve months.
[5]When he had set up the marks for the year
he determined the station of the pole star, in order to establish their[z]
    spheres
and so that there should be no deviation and no falling short.
With it (the pole) he set up stations for Ea and Enlil,[a]
he opened doors on both sides (of heaven),
[10](and) strengthened the doors on the left and the right.
In her (Tiamat's) body he established the heights of heaven,
he caused the moon god to shine and entrusted the night to him,
he chose him as the emblem of night, to signify the days (of the
    month),
and marked off every month without ceasing by means of his crown:[b]

---

[q] I.e., Marduk.   [r] Cf. Ps. 74.14; also Job 26.12f.
[s] The blood.   [t] Cf. Job 38.7.
[u] Literally 'foetus', cf. Labat, *RPOA* I, 54 n. 2.
[v] In comparison see Gen. 1.7 (P) (Ps. 19.1).
[w] Cf. Gen. 7. 11; 8.2a (P), and most strikingly Job 7.12; 38.8.
[x] Text following B. Landsberger, op. cit., 156f. Cf. Gen. 1.14ff. (P).
[y] Literally 'station'. Pss. 8.3; 148.6 speak similarly of 'setting in place'.
[z] The stars.   [a] Variant: Anu (the ancient god of heaven).
[b] The disc of the moon in its various phases is regarded as the crown of the moon god
Sin.

[15]'When the new moon appears over the land,
you shall shine in the form of growing horns to signify six days,
and then on the seventh day as the half of a crown;
so shall the fifteen-day periods be like one another - two halves for
each month.'

Tablet V[49-51] The determination of the weather[c]

He joined the clouds together and made them overflow with water.
[50]To unleash the wind, to make the rain, to bring cold,
to draw the clouds (and) to put their vapour in layers,
all this he planned himself and took it in hand.

Tablet VI[31-40] The creation of men as servants of the gods

They bound him (Kingu), brought him before Ea,
imposed punishment on him (and) severed his arteries.[d]
From his blood he[e] formed mankind.
He imposed on him service for the gods and (thus) freed them.[f]
[35]After Ea, the wise, had created men (thus)
and imposed on them the service of the gods
- the work went beyond all understanding.
According to Marduk's skilful plan, Nudimmud[g] accomplished it -
Marduk, the king of the gods,[h] divided
[40]all the Anunnaki[i] into those above and those in the depths . . .

Tablet VII[151-155] Closing apotheosis

Abiding is his[j] command and unchangeable his word,
what his mouth spoke no god will change.
If he looks (in anger), he does not turn his neck,[k]
when he is provoked, no god can withstand his anger.
His heart is unfathomable and his purpose is broad.[l]

---

[c] See p. 83 n. x above. Cf. Job 38.22-30.   [d] Literally 'the blood'.
   [e] Marduk's father as the traditional creator god: in this instance the 'Marduk recension' is not complete, but it is harmonized through line 138.
   [f] Gen. 2.15 (J) is significantly different.
   [g] A nickname of Ea.
   [h] Cf. Ps. 95.3, and for the subject-matter Ex. 15.11; Pss. 96.4; 97.9, etc.
   [i] Here it simply means 'the great gods'.
   [j] I.e., Marduk's.
   [k] He is not to be persuaded otherwise.
   [l] The interpretation of the following verses is disputed, but cf. Grayson, *ANET*[3], 503.

Creation stories

7. Sumerian myth 'Enki and Ninhursanga': paradise?

Text: S. N. Kramer, *Enki and Ninḫursag*, *BASOR* Supplementary Studies 1, 1945; id., *ANET*[3], 37ff.; M. Witzel, *Or* NS 15, 1946, 239ff.
Literature: S. N. Kramer, *SM*, 54ff.; id., *Sumerians*, 147ff.; A. Falkenstein, *BiOr* 5, 1948, 164; M. Lambert and R. Tournay, *RA* 43, 1949, 105ff.; T. Jacobsen, *Before Philosophy*, 1949, 170ff.; M. Lambert, *RA* 55, 1961, 185 no. 14; D. O. Edzard, *WM* I, 57f.

This difficult text of about 280 lines depicts Enki's intercourse (which puts Zeus's lackadaisical affairs in the shade) with the mother goddess Ninhursanga,[m] with her two daughters, grand-daughter and great-granddaughter, and celebrates him as the giver of sweet water. The poem, which is perhaps meant to be a mythical interpretation of natural phenomena – thus Jacobsen, op. cit. – is significant for us only in that the setting in which it takes place, Tilmun, is described in possibly paradisal terms,[n] similar to those to be found in the OT (see n. q and p. 86 n. s below). In the land of Tilmun there is peace between men and animals; sorrow and grief are unknown, or at least are not felt as such. To this praise of Tilmun as a 'land of the blessed' it should be added that according to the Sumerian flood saga,[o] the surviving hero Ziusudra is thought to be immortal and is transported there. After introductory praise of the 'pure' Tilmun, lines 12-25 run:

This place is pure, (is radiant).
In Tilmun the raven does not crow,
the . . . bird does not utter the . . . cry,[p]
[15]the lion does not kill,
the wolf does not plunder the lamb,[q]
the dog[r] which snatches the kid is unknown,
the pig which devours the grain is unknown,
(and) unknown is the bird which

[m] This goddess is identified with Ninsikil, who was worshipped in Tilmun (cf. p. 79 n. i above).
[n] This is a subsidiary feature of the account , which does not justify talk of a 'paradise myth' here (so Kramer). That is even less the case since there is no agreement over the interpretation of the lines in question; indeed some scholars question that there was any conception of paradise in Sumer at all; cf. van Dijk, *Or* NS 39, 1970, 302, and B. Alster, *RA* 67, 1973, 101ff., esp. 104 n. 4.
[o] M. Civil in W. G. Lambert and A. R. Millard, *Atra-ḫasis*, 1969, 138ff., esp. 145, lines 256-60, see nos. 10-12 below.
[p] Is this a reference to a bird whose cry meant death?
[q] Cf. the expectation in Isa. 11.6-9 which is directed towards an eschatological restoration of the original peace of paradise (Gen. 1.30). Cf. also Isa. 29.17-21; 32.15-20; 35.9; 65.25; Ezek. 34.25, 28; Hos. 2.18.
[r] Obviously referring to the half-wild Near Eastern pariah dog.

[20]eats the widow's malt spread out on the roof(?).
The dove does not droop its head (?).
The one with a sore eye does not say, 'My eye is sick',
the one with a sore head does not say, 'My head is sick',[s]
its[t] old women do not say, 'I am an old woman',
[26]its old men do not say, 'I am an old man'.[u]

8. *Sumerian epic 'Enmerkar and the Lord of Aratta' : paradise?*

Text: S. N. Kramer, *Enmerkar and the Lord of Aratta*, 1952; id., *FTS*, 14ff. (= *GbS*, 26).
Literature: M. Lambert, *RA* 50, 1956, 37ff.; id., *RA* 55, 1961, 182 no. 1; id., *Syr* 32, 1955, 212ff.; T. Jacobsen, *ZA* 52, 1957, 91ff.; especially 112f., nn. 43-45; R. R. Jestin, *RHR* 151, 1957, 145ff.; S. N. Kramer, *Sumerians*, 269ff.; C. Wilcke, *Das Lugalbanda-Epos*, 1969, passim; B. Alster (cf. p. 85 n. n above).
This text is more than 230 lines long and has been preserved in good condition. It belongs to the cycle of the Uruk epics, whose heroes are Enmerkar, Lugalbanda and Gilgamesh, and describes a quarrel between Enmerkar and the ruler of Aratta (who is not named). Aratta is a land rich in gold, silver and precious stones in Iran, 'beyond the seven hills'. It is perhaps to be identified with Aspadana-Esfahan. A messenger from Enmerkar is to recite verbatim the spell of Nudimmud (= the god Enki) in Aratta in order to bring its king into subjection and to make him pay tribute. In this message we find both the description of a golden future (if the ruler of Aratta yields) and an instance of the Sumerian version of the 'confusion of tongues' (cf. no. 9 below and in the OT Gen. 11.1-9). In lines 136-40 we read:

On this day there is no snake, no scorpion,
no hyena, no lion,[v]
no (wild) dog,[w] no wolf,
no anxiety, no fear,
(and) men will have no (more) enemies.[x]

9. *The Sumerian 'confusion of tongues'*

Text: S. N. Kramer, *JAOS* 88, 1968, 108ff.; id., *Or* NS 39, 1970, 108f. (cf. also the details of the text given in connection with no. 8 above); J. J. van

[s] Cf. Isa. 35.10; 51.11; also Isa. 25.8 and Ps. 126.5f.
[t] I.e. those of Tilmun.
[u] After three incomprehensible verses it is then said that the singers strike up no lamentations in Tilmun.
[v] See Isa. 35.9; Ezek. 34.25.
[w] See p. 85 n. r above.
[x] See e.g. Isa. 29.20f.

Dijk, *Or* NS 39, 1970, 302ff.; B. Alster (cf. p. 85 n. n above).

The section following immediately after the passage quoted above was in fact legible for a further ten lines, but these lines seemed to make no sense in the context of the story. Now, however, a newly identified supplementary fragment offers a meaningful text (it was first interpreted by S. N. Kramer, not altogether aptly, and has been corrected by B. Alster). This follows on from the preceding picture of a possibly imminent golden age. At the dawn of the time of peace which is proclaimed, the great god Enlil will end the 'confusion of tongues' among the nations, so that all the peoples will then be able to praise the gods unanimously in the language of Sumer. Thus we find with another motivation, and in reverse order, several centuries before the Yahwist's story in Gen. 11.1-9, the idea of mankind speaking with one tongue, which is here described as a 'clarification of tongues'. Isa. 19.18 is perhaps intended as a reference to it. We follow Kramer and Alster in reading lines 141ff. as follows:

On this day the lands of Shubur[y] and Hamasi,
whose tongue is opposed to that of Sumer – Sumer the land with a
    noble culture –
Uri,[z] the famous land,
and the lands of the nomads,[a] who sleep on the broad steppe,
the whole inhabited world,
will speak to Enlil in one language.
Enki . . . the lord . . . the prince . ·. . the king[b] . . .
Enki, the lord of over-abundance, whose words are reliable,
the lord of wisdom, who knows the land,
the ruler of the gods,
endowed with wisdom, the lord of Eridu,
will change all existing languages in their mouth,
and then the language of mankind will be one.

10. *The Sumerian kings before the flood*

Text: T. Jacobsen, *The Sumerian King List*, AS 11, 1939, especially 70ff.; A. L. Oppenheim, *ANET*[3], 265f.; information on the text in R. Borger, *HKL* 1, 201.

Literature: F. R. Kraus, *ZA* 50, 1952, 29ff.; M. B. Rowton, *JNES* 19, 1960, 156ff.; J. J. van Dijk, *UVB* 18, 1962, 43ff.; S. N. Kramer, *Sumerians*, 328ff.; J. J. Finkelstein, *JCS* 17, 1963, 39ff.; W. W. Hallo, ibid., 52ff.; W. G. Lambert, *JTS* NS 16, 1965, 292f.; id. and A. R. Millard, *Atra-ḫasīs*, 1969,

---

[y] Subartu = Assyrians.
[z] Akkad.
[a] The West inhabited by the Semites.
[b] In a double verse given each time the title *ada*.

25; W. W. Hallo, *JCS* 23, 1970, 57ff.; W. G. Lambert, in *Symbolae . . . F. M. T. de L. Böhl*, 1973, 271ff.

The famous 'Sumerian king list', containing the names of 140 rulers who are all alleged to have ruled over Mesopotamia and to have followed one another chronologically, was created by learned historians on the basis of earlier dynastic catalogues from individual cities. This they did perhaps under the impact of their liberation from the foreign rule of the Gutians and the unification of the kingdom, which was begun by Utuhengal of Uruk about 2060 (and completed by Urnammu of Ur) – according to others under the usurper Urninurta of Isin (about 1850 BC). Several versions of the list have been handed down; it reached its final form under Sinmagir of Isin (about 1760). In the sequence of rulers, the flood understandably appears as a marked dividing line; the first rulers after the flood also reign for superhuman periods, but these are far exceeded by the number of years in the reigns of the kings before the flood. Eight[c] rulers from five cities reigned 241,200[d] years in all. These Sumerian 'kings before the flood' have rightly been compared with the ten biblical patriarchs from Adam to Noah (Gen. 5.1ff.; cf. 4.17ff.). Here we quote the main version of the list, which names eight rulers (col. I, 1–39):

[1-10]When the kingship came down from heaven, the kingship was in Eridu. In Eridu Alulim became king and reigned for 28,800 years. Alalgar reigned for 36,000 years. Thus two kings reigned for 64,800 years. I (thus) leave Eridu on one side; its kingship was brought to Bad-tibira. [11-19]In Bad-tibira Enmenluanna reigned for 43,200 years. Enmengalanna reigned for 28,800 years. The divine Dumuzi, a shepherd, reigned for 36,000 years. (Thus) three kings reigned for 108,000 years. I (thus) leave Bad-tibira on one side; its kingship was brought to Larak. [20-25]In Larak, Ensipazianna reigned for 28,800 years. (Thus) one king reigned for 28,800 years. I (thus) leave Larak on one side; its kingship was brought to Sippar. [26-35]In Sippar Enmeduranna[e] became king and reigned for 21,000 years. (Thus) one king reigned for 21,000 years. I (thus) leave Sippar

[c] In subsidiary recensions there are also ten kings and once – in an Assyrian fragment from Ashurbanipal's library – nine, cf. W. G. Lambert, *JTS* NS 16, 1965, 292. For there being ten earlier kings in the Sumerian tradition cf. Finkelstein, op. cit., esp. 45; it appears lastly in Berossus (Schnabel, 261f.). – Ten primal kings or heroes also appear in Egyptian, Indian and Chinese tradition.

[d] All the numbers are divisible by the highest sum of the Sumerian duodecimal system, 1 sar = 3600 (60 × 60), or by its sixth. Berossus gives only complete sar numbers.

[e] Enmeduranna (or Enmeduranki), the seventh king of Sumer before the flood, is the counterpart of the biblical Enoch. The mythological feature of Enoch's 'translation' (Gen. 5.24) also comes from Mesopotamia. While Enmeduranna himself is not said to have ascended to heaven, this is said of the wise man called Utuabzu who accompanies him, cf. R. Borger, *JNES* 33, 1974, 183ff.

on one side; its kingship was brought to Shuruppak.[f]

In Shuruppak, Urbatutu[g] became king and reigned for 18,600 years. (Thus) one king reigned for 18,600 years.
[36-40]These are five cities; eight kings reigned for 241,000 years. (Then) the flood streamed over (the earth) . . .

11. Sumerian myth of the flood

Text: M. Civil, in: W. G. Lambert and A. R. Millard, Atra-ḫasis, 1969, 138ff.
Literature: S. N. Kramer, FTS, 176ff. (= GbS, 115ff.); id., Sumerians, 163f. and (with translation) ANET³, 42ff.; A. Schott and W. von Soden, Das Gilgamesch Epos, 1970, 114f.; cf. further the bibliography on the Atrahasis epic (no. 12 below).

At present we know three cuneiform flood myths,[h] the Sumerian myth, the one preserved in the Akkadian Atrahasis epic and the eleventh tablet of the Akkadian epic of Gilgamesh, which has the best tradition. They are evidently dependent on one another, in this sequence; further research is needed to discover how far the dependence extends. At least the two latter poems were read in one of their various redactions by learned men throughout the Near East during the second millennium BC and probably also in the first; the Yahwist also knows the story, and it is now undisputed that the Mesopotamian version served as a model for the OT narrative in Gen. 6-8. As in the creation stories, however, the difference in religious and ethical levels is clear; here the biblical account is superior. The Sumerian myth of the flood was only copied in the post-Sumerian period (nineteenth/eighteenth centuries), but it probably contains earlier material and makes use of earlier models. Because of numerous gaps in the text only about a third of it can be restored, and consequently the course of the action is still obscure. The main part of it takes place in the period before the flood; we hear of the creation of men and animals,[i] of the establishment of civilization through the gods and the origin of the kingship – as in the Sumerian king lists[j] there is mention of royal residences before the flood. On the analogy of the Atrahasis epic we may perhaps assume that increasing tumult among men disturbed the gods – at any rate the majority of the gods resolve to exterminate the human race by a great flood. Ziusudra, the Sumerian Noah (and Berossus' Xisuthros), is told of the danger which threatens by a god who is friendly to mankind (almost certainly to be identified as Enki); this is done through a device which recurs in Atrahasis and Ut-napishtim[k] of a

---

[f] The flood city of the eleventh tablet of the Gilgamesh epic, there called Shurippak.
[g] The father of Ut-napishtim, the hero of the Babylonian flood story.
[h] A fourth flood saga of a different kind, the chief figure in which seems to be Inanna, has just been discovered, cf. C. Wilcke, Das Lugalbandaepos, 1969, 72, lines 564-577.
[i] See above, p. 77 n. k.
[j] See no. 10 above.
[k] Resolutions of the gods might not be made known to men.

warning spoken to the wall of a house. Thereupon Ziusudra builds the ark (this part of the text is no longer extant). By the end of the lacuna in the text the flood has already come, and here we have lines 201 to 211:[1]

All the devastating winds (and) storms came,
the flood storm swept over the great cities.
When the flood had inundated the land for seven days and seven
    nights
and the destructive hurricane had tossed the great ship around in the
    deep floods,
the sun broke through and gave light to earth and heaven.
Ziusudra opened a hatch in the great ship
and the sun shone into the great ship with its rays.
Then King Ziusudra cast himself
down before Utu[m]
(and) the king brought a large number of oxen and sheep as an
    offering.

12. The Akkadian Atrahasis epic: the flood

Text: W. G. Lambert and A. R. Millard, *Atra-ḥasīs*, 1969, which also gives the earlier literature; E. A. Speiser, *ANET*[3], 104ff.; A. K. Grayson, ibid., 512ff.

Literature: J. Laessøe, *BiOr* 13, 1956, 90ff.; W. G. Lambert, *JSS* 5, 1960, 113ff.; L. Matouš, *ArOr* 35, 1967, 1ff.; ibid., 37, 1969, 1ff., 148; ibid., 38, 1970, 74ff.; G. Pettinato, *Or* NS 37, 1968, 165ff.; W. von Soden, ibid., 38, 1969, 415ff.; ibid., 39, 1970, 311ff.; ibid., 40, 1971, 99ff.; W. G. Lambert, ibid., 38, 533ff.; ibid., 40, 95ff.; R. Labat, *RPOA* I, 26ff.; J. Siegelová, *ArOr* 38, 1970, 135ff.; W. L. Moran, *BASOR* 200, 1970, 48ff.; ibid., *Bib* 52, 1971, 51ff.

In its time this poem was known throughout the world. It is composed in short lines, mostly joined together as couplets, but is no poetic masterpiece. It has been preserved in two closely related versions, neither of them complete: one is early Babylonian, composed or at least copied at the time of king Ammisaduqa (1582-1562) by the 'young scribe' Kuaya in Sippar and comprising three tablets; the other is a neo-Assyrian work on two tablets from Ashurbanipal's library in Nineveh. In addition there are further fragments of various dates. The work has only become comprehensible after the identification of new fragments in the British Museum and a complete rearrangement of about twenty-five passages by W. G. Lambert. It now appears as the classical Babylonian text about the creation and the flood, though it is evidently closely related to the Sumerian text on the flood.[n] First of all we hear about the trouble

[1] Cf. Civil, op. cit., 142ff.
[m] The Sumerian sun god.
[n] According to Moran, op. cit., 'a cosmogonic myth' (58f.).

to which the gods were exposed in earning their daily bread in a world still unpeopled by man, of the appointment of 'younger gods' to the work, of their rebellion against Enlil, lord of the gods, and the final expedient of making men as servants for the heavenly ones.[o] However, as mankind increases, its tumult becomes intolerable to the gods,[p] and especially to their lord Enlil, so that the latter seeks to decimate men at intervals of about 1200 years, first by a plague and then by a drought. In both cases Atrahasis, the pious king of men (his name means all-wise), is aided by the gracious Ea, to whom he cries for help. Finally, however, Enlil brings a great flood upon the earth – and only Atrahasis with all his family and what he takes with him into the ark escape it, again thanks to Ea's warning. The flood story, which is later to be adopted by the Gilgamesh epic, though in a slightly altered form,[q] begins on the third tablet of the Kuaya recension with Enki's warning of the flood (he has been forbidden to give this warning, and it is therefore addressed to the wall of Atrahasis' reed hut) and his advice to build the ship. The action then continues, in the third person, in the same way as the well-known fable on the eleventh tablet of the Gilgamesh epic.[r] As the text is often damaged and is full of gaps, some passages have been restored from the third tablet of the early Babylonian redaction.[s]

Col. I[11-48] Enki's warning

Atrahasis opened his mouth
and spoke to his lord:
'Declare to me the meaning [of the dream].
I would like to know [. . .], to learn its outcome(?)!'[t]
[15][Enki] opened his mouth
and replied to his servant:
'You said, "I will seek information in the bedchamber!"'[u]
Hearken to the message that I shall make known to you.

---

[o] See above, p. 77 n. k.

[p] The cities of the ancient Near East, densely populated and built with the houses very close together, were evidently already familiar with the problem of noise endangering health. See on the other hand the suggestion made by W. von Soden ('Der Mensch bescheidet sich nicht . . .', *Symbolae F. M. T. de L. Böhl*, 1973, 353f.) that what might be envisaged could be the uproarious activities of men going beyond their original commission.

[q] Thus in the Gilgamesh epic, the hero of the flood, there called Ut-napishtim, tells his story in the first person. This also happens in the fragment from the thirteenth century BC recently discovered in Ugarit (J. Nougayrol, *Ugaritica* 5, 1966, 300ff.); W. G. Lambert and A. R. Millard, *Atra-ḫasis*, 1969, 131ff.; R. Borger, *RA* 64, 1970, 189.

[r] See no. 13 below.

[s] Lambert and Millard, op. cit., 88f.; cf. also the contents of the Assyrian fragments, 122–9. Compare again from the OT Gen. 6–8.

[t] Literally 'its tail'.

[u] So according to W. von Soden.

[20]Wall, hear me,
reed-wall,[v] pay attention to all my words.
Tear the house down, build a boat;
renounce possessions – save life!
The boat that you build
is . . . to be like . . .

two verses destroyed

Let it be roofed over like the Apsu,[w]
[30]so that the sun does not shine into it,
let it be roofed over above and below.[x]
Its equipment must be very secure,
make the pitch tough and thus (the ship) strong.
I will soon send down
[35]a mass of birds (and) fish in abundance(?)!'
He opened the water clock[y] and filled it,
he proclaimed the coming of the flood to him for the seventh night.
Atrahasis received the instructions,
he made the elders come to his door.
[40]Then Atrahasis opened his mouth
and said to the elders:
'My god is no longer in accord with yours,
Enki and Enlil are at war with one another.
They have told me to go [from my house].
[45]As (?) I reverence [Enki],
he told me that.
So I can [no] longer live in . . .
I cannot [abide] on the soil of Enlil.'[z]

Col. II[42-53] The outbreak of the flood

(While) he (Atrahasis) was sending his family on board,
they were eating[a] and drinking,
but he went in and out, could neither sit nor crouch,

[v] Reed huts, sometimes of considerable height and length, are still built in ancient Near Eastern fashion by the Ma'dan in the Tigris marshes north-west of Basra, cf. S. Westphal-Hellbusch and H. Westphal, *Die Ma'dan*, 1962.
[w] The subterranean primaeval ocean, above which are the vaults of the earth.
[x] The poet is probably thinking of two decks; in the eleventh tablet of the Gilgamesh epic there are even six or seven.
[y] Used for measuring time in the ancient East.
[z] A necessary lie so that he could leave unhindered.
[a] The builders and elders, at a macabre farewell feast.

⁴⁵for his heart was broken and he vomited gall.ᵇ
The appearance of the weather changed,
Adadᶜ rumbled(?) in the clouds.
As soon as (?) he heard Adad's voice,
they brought him clay to seal his door.
⁵⁰When he had shut his door,
Adad (again) rumbled(?) in the clouds.
When the storm began to rage,
he cast off the hawsers and let the boat ride . . .

Col. IV²⁴ᶠ· The duration of the flood

For seven days and seven nights,
there came the flood, the storm . . .ᵈ

13. Eleventh tablet of the Akkadian epic of Gilgamesh: the flood

Text: R. C. Thompson, *The Epic of Gilgamish*, 1930; cf. further P. Garelli
(ed.), *Gilgameš et sa légende*, 1960; A. Heidel, *The Gilgamesh Epic and Old
Testament Parallels*, ²1949, esp. 8off.; E. A. Speiser, *ANET*³, 72ff., esp. 93ff.;
R. Labat, *RPOA* I, 145ff., esp. 212ff.
Literature (only the more recent material can be mentioned): A. L. Oppen-
heim, *Or* NS 17, 1948, 51ff.; L. Matouš, *Das Altertum* 4, 1958, 195ff.; W. von
Soden, *ZA* 53, 1959, 209ff., esp. 232ff.; E. Sollberger, *The Babylonian Legend
of the Flood*, 1962; D. O. Edzard, *WM* I, 72ff.; article 'Gilgamesh', *RLA* III,
fasc. 5, 1968, 357ff.
Whereas in the Atrahasis epic the saga of the flood is organically connected
with the course of events and forms its climax, on the twelve tablets of the
Akkadian epic of Gilgamesh it is clearly an addition. If it were missing, there
would be no perceptible gap. The author of this greatest and most famous
work of cuneiform literature, Sin-leqe-unninni, lived in the twelfth century
BC; he inserted what was already a classic story (which has, however, only
been preserved in fragments in what is so far known of the Atrahasis text, as
we have seen) at an appropriate place and in so doing presumably reshaped it
in some ways.ᵉ When Gilgamesh, shattered by the death of his friend Enkidu,
goes in search of eternal life and in so doing reaches his ancestor Ut-napishtim

---

ᵇ In fear.
ᶜ The god of the weather.
ᵈ Further description and the end of the flood are not contained in the text; we hear
only of the lament of the gods, the sacrifice offered by Atrahasis after the water has gone
down, the appearance of the gods and their dispute, and perhaps a new order for mankind.
ᵉ In addition to this Akkadian poem, which was preserved in the library of Ashurbanipal in Nineveh, but which has unfortunately not come down to us complete, there is also
an early Babylonian version, also in fragments; both go back to episodes from Sumerian
epics.

at the end of the world, Ut-napishtim tells him how he and his wife were saved from the great flood and how afterwards they gained immortality (tablet 11, lines 8-157). The narrative is in the first person and composed in epic verse metre (2:2 stresses). The nucleus of this text is clearly the 'model' for the OT story of the flood in Gen. 6.5-8.22. No reason is given here for the planned extermination of men - in the Atrahasis epic it is their uproar, which disturbs the sleep of the gods, and in J and P their sinfulness.

8-43Then Ut-napishtim spoke to Gilgamesh:
I will say hidden things to you, Gilgamesh,
10I will make known to you a secret of the gods:
Shurippak, a city which you know,
which lies on the banks of the Euphrates –
that city was (already) ancient, the gods lived in it.
To make a flood was the resolve of the great gods.
15Their father Anu took counsel,
the hero Enlil, their adviser,
17/18their vizier Ninurta (and) Ennugi, the 'guardian of their canals'.
Below them sat Ninshiku-Ea;f
20he repeated their words to a reed hut:
'Reed-hut, reed-hut! Wall, wall!
Reed-hut, listen! Wall, perceive!
Mang of Shurippak, son of Ubartutu,
tear down the house (and) build a ship,
25let go your possessions, and concern yourself with existing,
give up what you have and ensure life,
take all kinds of living beings into the ship.
(Concerning) the ship you are to build,
its measurements shall be carefully calculated,
30breadth and length are to be equal,
(and) you are to provide it with a roof like the Apsu.'h
I understood this and spoke to Ea, my lord:
'The instruction, lord, that you have given me,
I shall obey exactly and act accordingly.
35(But) what shall I say to the city, the people, the elders?'
Ea opened his mouth
and said to me, his servant:
'Thus you are to speak to them:
"It is certain that Enlil is hostile to me.

f Another name for Enki.
g I.e. king.
h The primal ocean, which is thought of as being under the vaults formed by the earth and ruled over by Enki-Ea.

[40]So I can no (longer) live in your city
(and) can no (longer) set my feet on Enlil's ground.
I will go down to the Apsu,
and there remain with Ea, my lord!" '

Lines 44-79 describe the building of the ark, its provisioning and the feast for the workers.

[80-161]All that I had I took on board,
all the silver I had I took on board,
all the gold I had I took on board,
all the living beings that I had, I took on board.
I made all my family and kinsmen go into the ship.
[85]The beasts of the field, the wild creatures and all the craftsmen I
        took on board.
Shamash[i] had made an appointed time for me:
'In the morning I will rain down date bread(?), and in the evening
        wheat,[j]
then go into the ship and shut the door.'
This appointed time came,
[90]in the morning he rained down date bread(?), and in the evening
        wheat.
I watched the appearance of the weather,
the weather was fearful to look upon –
then I entered the ship and shut my door,
to the boatman Puzuramurri, who had put pitch on the ship,
[95]I handed over the 'palace'[k] and its contents.
With the first glow of dawn
a black cloud came up from the horizon.
Adad[l] thundered in it,
Shullat and Hanish[m] go before it,
[100]as heralds they hasten over mountain and plain.
Eragal[n] tears out the posts,
Ninurta goes and makes the dikes overflow,
the Anunnaki[o] raise the torches,
setting the land ablaze with their glow.

[i] The sun god – perhaps at the command of Ea.
[j] Unexplained.
[k] The 'palace' ('great house') will mean the mighty ark which Ut-napishtim puts in
the charge of his captain (who has already been mentioned once beforehand).
[l] The god of the weather.
[m] Storm demons? But cf. I. J. Gelb, *ArOr* 18.1-2, 1950, 189ff.
[n] God of the underworld.   [o] The great gods.

[105]Consternation reached the heavens because of Adad,
all that was bright they turned to darkness.
They shattered the broad land like an earthen vessel.
The south storm [raged] for a whole day,
it blew violently, [to submerge(?)] the mountains,
[110]as in battle with [. . .]
No one can see his fellow,
men could not be recognized from heaven.
The gods were in fear of this flood,
they fled up to the heaven of Anu,
[115]crouched like dogs, they lay outside.
Ishtar cried out like a woman in travail,
the mistress of the gods lamented with a loud voice:
'Would that that day[p] were turned to clay[q]
when I counselled evil in the assembly of the gods!
[120]How could I have commanded evil in the council of the gods,
ordered battle for the destruction of my people?
I spoke as follows: "My people are indeed born,
but they will fill the sea like the spawn of fishes." '[r]
The Anunna gods lament with her.

The meaning of lines 125f. is still disputed.

Six days (?) and seven nights
the hurricane, the flood, persists and the south-storm makes the land
    level.
(Only) when the seventh day arrived, the south-storm held the flood,
    the tempest,
[130]which had struck out around like a woman in labour(?).
The sea became quiet, the storm subsided, the flood ceased.
I looked at the weather; stillness had set in,
and all mankind had become clay,
and land lay levelled out like a (flat) roof.
[135]I opened a hatch and light fell on my face,
I sat bowed down and wept,
tears flowed down over my face.
Then I looked for the coastline of the sea:
in twelve . . . an island arose,
[140]the ship settled on Mount Nisir.

[p] The day on which the flood was resolved upon.
[q] I.e. would it had never taken place.
[r] Thus according to R. Borger, *Babylonisch-Assyrische Lesestücke*, 1963, 118 (fasc. III) ad loc.

Mount Nisir held the ship and did not let it move,
a first day, a second day Nisir held the ship and did not let it move,
a third day, a fourth day Nisir held the ship and did not let it move.
A fifth day, a sixth day Nisir held the ship and did not let it move.
[145]When the seventh day arrivèd,
I sent forth a dove, let her free –
the dove flew away, but came again,
because no resting place caught her eye, she returned again.
I sent forth a swallow, let her free –
[150]the swallow flew away, but came again,
because no resting place caught her eye, she returned again.
Then I sent forth a raven, let it free –
the raven flew away, saw that the waters had (now) run away,
found food, fluttered around(?), cawed(?) and did not return.
[155]Then I let out (all) to the four winds, offered a sacrifice
(and) poured a drink offering on the summit of the mountain.
Seven and seven vessels of incense I set up
(and) filled them with cane, cedarwood and myrtle.
The gods smelled the savour,
[160]the gods smelled the sweet savour,
like flies the gods crowded round the sacrificer . . .

The narrative ends with the accusation of the gods against Enlil and the gift of immortality to the hero of the flood and his wife.

Scattered saga material

14. *Sumerian myth 'Inanna and the Gardener'*[s] : *plague of blood*

Translation of the text: S. N. Kramer, *ArOr* 17.1, 1949, 399ff.; id., *FTS*, 66ff. (= *GbS*, 63ff.).
Literature: ibid. and S. N. Kramer, *Sumerians*, 162f. and 196; M. Lambert, *RA* 55, 1961, 187f., no. 23; D. O. Edzard, *WM* I, 89; C. J. Gadd, *Iraq* 28, 1966, 117f.
The text of this myth is about 250 lines long, but is unfortunately destroyed at the end. It is part of the collection of Sumerian literature arranged by the early Babylonian scholars in Nippur and still awaits a scholarly edition; we owe our knowledge of it almost exclusively to S. N. Kramer. It belongs to the cycle of Inanna myths and tells of the work of the gardener Shukallituda,[t] who was the first to arrange a well-ordered plantation of trees to give shade. However, he committed an act of great wickedness. When Inanna,[u] wearied

[s] Title in Kramer, 'Inanna and Shukallituda'.   [t] Provisional reading of the name.
[u] Sumer's much-celebrated goddess of fertility and love, the Babylonian and Assyrian Ishtar.

after a long journey, entered his plot and rested in the shade of a tree, he had intercourse with her as she was helpless in a deep sleep, and then on his father's advice hid himself 'in the cities of the black-headed ones, his brothers', because he rightly feared the vengeance of the goddess. Inanna sought out the guilty one and punished men by three plagues which she brought upon the land (though without finding Shukallituda): first, all the water turned to blood; secondly, devastating storms came down; it is impossible to detect the form of the third visitation because of the damage to the text, which breaks off soon afterwards. For the first time so far we thus find in the literature of the ancient Near East the theme of the 'plague of blood' which we know from Ex. 7.14-25. We follow S. N. Kramer in reading the relevant verses:[v]

(But) what disaster the woman[w] then brought because of her womb!
Inanna – what she did because of her womb!
She filled all the springs of the land with blood,
she satiated all the hedges and the gardens of the land with blood.
The slaves collecting wood for burning – they drink nothing but blood,
the women slaves who come to draw water – they draw nothing but
    blood.
'I must find the one who lay with me, in all the lands', she said.
But she did not find the one who lay with her . . .

15. The Akkadian legend of Sargon: divine protection of the chosen child

Text and literature: L. W. King, *Chronicles Concerning Early Babylonian Kings* II, 1907, 87ff.; H. G. Guterbock, *ZA* 42, 1934, 62ff. (and earlier literature cited there); E. A. Speiser, *ANET*³, 119; H. Hirsch, *AfO* 20, 1963, 7; R. Labat, *RPOA* I, 307f.

This text of indeterminate age is preserved in three incomplete neo-Assyrian copies and a neo-Babylonian fragment. It is one of the many traditions about the figure of the first founder of a Semitic empire, Sargon of Akkad (about 2350-2294), and is the only one to provide a legend about his origin. What we have here may be a typical 'wandering theme',[x] which may also have been attached to other prominent ruler figures in the ancient Near East;[y] however, as yet we do not have other examples. The affinity with the story of the exposure of Moses and his subsequent discovery (Ex. 2.1-10) is unmistakable. After the section which is important for us here, the text enumerates Sargon's deeds; the ending is destroyed. Lines 1-14 run:

I am Sargon, the mighty king, the king of Akkad.

---

[v] *FTS*, p. 69, lines 1-8 (cf. p. 70, lines 3-10).
[w] Inanna.
[x] Cf. P. Jensen, 'Aussetzungsgeschichte', *RLA* I, 1928, 322ff.
[y] The story was useful to usurpers, since it could serve as a substitute for a genealogy and legitimate descent.

My mother was an *enitum* (i.e. an *entu*-priestess?),[z] I do not know my
   father;
the brother of my father loved the hills.
My city is Azupiranu, which lies on the bank of the Euphrates.
[5]The *enitum*, my mother, conceived me and bore me in secret.
She laid me in a basket of rushes, sealed my covering with asphalt[a]
(and) cast me on the river, which did not rise over me.[b]
The river bore me to Akki, the drawer of water.
Akki, the drawer of water, lifted me out as he dipped his ewer.
[10]Akki, the drawer of water, (took me) as son and reared me,
Akki, the drawer of water, made me his gardener.
When I was a gardener, Ishtar[c] gave me her love,
and for [fifty] four years I exercised kingship . . .[d]

II. HYMNS, PRAYERS AND LAMENTS

16. Sumerian hymn to Enlil

Translation and short commentary: the most recent edition is that of A.
Falkenstein, *SAHG*, 77ff. (no. 12) and 365; further references there.

   Because we have an early Babylonian copy as well as a neo-Assyrian one, it
is possible to date this text, in a way which is otherwise impracticable in cuneiform cultic literature, to the first third of the second millennium or even to a
date soon after the Sumerian era. This is an *ershemma* song in the poetic Emesal
dialect; poems of this kind were originally intended to be recited by priestesses.
The present song celebrates the fertility, power and glory – and also the
providence – of Enlil,[e] the great creator god of Nippur and its national deity
(later suppressed by Marduk or Ashur). The characteristics of hymnic diction
which it displays form points of contact with OT hymns, for example its use
of the doxological rhetorical question (cf. line 1 with Isa. 40.13; Ps. 92.5).

   [z] The interpretation of the word is not completely certain; if it is correct, it signifies
a high rank (e.g. 'high priestess'), often held by princesses. The *enitum* could marry,
but could not have children. E. A. Speiser, on the other hand, translates 'changeling'
(op. cit).
   [a] Literally 'door'.
   [b] 'Did not go over me.'
   [c] The warlike Ishtar Anunitum had a temple which was built for her in Akkad by
Sargon.
   [d] The narrative does not say explicitly that Ishtar set her favourite on the throne;
but it is to be assumed that it presupposes this.
   [e] Cf. D. O. Edzard, *WM* I, 59ff.

However, like the cultic poetry of Mesopotamia generally, it is not equal to the powerful compositions of the OT (cf. e.g. Pss. 103–105). The text follows Falkenstein, op. cit.:

Wise lord, the planner, who knows your will?
Endowed with strength, Lord of Ekur,[f]
born in the mountains, Lord of Esharra,[g]
storm of great might, father Enlil,[h]
you who were brought up by Dingirmach,[i] you go furiously to battle,
you scatter the hill-country like grain,[j] and mow (it) as the sickle mows
    barley!
You have taken your father's side[k] against the rebellious land,
you approach as the one who destroys the hills,
you break the hostile lands like a reed,
[10]make all your foes of one mind!
'I am the protective wall against all hostile lands and the one who
keeps them off.'[l]
You cast down the mighty, enter the door of heaven,
you grasp the bolt of heaven,
break open the heavenly lock,
[15]remove the closure of heaven,
you cast down the rebellious land in heaps!
You do not allow the rebellious, uncontrollable land to rise again.

6. Procession of the gods. Assyrian relief from
Malatya (about 700 BC).

    [f] 'Mountain house', the chief temple of Enlil in Nippur.
    [g] Another temple.
    [h] The scheme of introduction lying behind this poem cannot be demonstrated in the
OT hymns. Ps. 80.1 is still the best comparison.
    [i] 'Exalted god'.
    [j] As grain is scattered at a sacrifice.
    [k] An, the god of heaven.
    [l] Literally 'their lock'.

Lord, how long will you trouble the land which you made of one mind,
who can soften your angry heart?
20The sayings of your mouth are not despised,
who could rebel against them?
'I am the Lord, the lion of the holy An, the hero of Sumer,
I make the fishes of the sea glad, and see that the birds do not fall
    down,
the wise countryman, who ploughs the field, Enlil, I am he.'
25(Indeed) you are the lord who has grown great, the hero of your
    father!
No enemy can escape your right hand,
nor any wicked man flee from your left hand.

One verse is destroyed.

The hostile land over which your saying has gone forth, you will not
    allow to rise again,
30you leave no one in the rebellious land which you cursed.

One verse is destroyed.

Lord of Ekur, full of far-reaching power,
you are the first among the gods!
Chief of the Anunnaki,m
lord who guides the plough, Enlil, you are he,
(Indeed), chief of the Anunna gods,
you are the lord who guides the plough!

17. *Akkadian hymn to the sun god Shamash*

    Text: W. G. Lambert, *Babylonian Wisdom Literature*, 1960, 121ff.; further
literature, 124; textual information, 125; W. von Soden, *SAHG*, 240ff. (no.
4) and 381f.; R. Labat, *RPOA* I, 266ff.
    This 'great hymn to Shamash', which comes from the library of Ashurbanipal
but is in fact older, and is to be put towards the end of the second millennium
BC, is one of the most beautiful divine hymns from ancient Mesopotamia. It
contains about 200 lines (mostly combined in double verses) and celebrates
the sun god as the one who illuminates the earth, cares for men, is the longed-
for, victorious bringer of light, the guarantor of truth and justice, guardian of
the weak and the wretched, master of symbols and god of grace. Among the OT
psalms compare especially Pss. 19.4b-6; 95; 104; 107; 113; 136. The text has
not been preserved complete. The most striking extracts are given here:n

    m Anunnaki are originally the 'gods of the underworld', but the expression is also used
interchangeably with Igigi (originally 'gods of the world above') for the supreme deities.
    n Numbering of verses follows W. G. Lambert, op. cit.

[1-12]O illuminator . . . (in) the heavens,
who makes the darkness bright[o] . . . above and below,
Shamash, illuminator . . . (in) the heavens,
who makes the darkness bright . . . above and below!
[5]Your beams cover . . . like a net.
You lighten the darkness of the high hills!
At your appearing the rulers of the gods rejoice,
all the Igigi exult,[p]
your rays constantly grasp the secret things,[q]
[10]in your constant light their traces are visible.
Your blinding light constantly seeks out . . .
the four banks of the world, like Girru . . .[r]

[17-38]O illuminator of the darkness,[s] you open the 'nipples' of heaven,[t]
make the beard of light glow, the cornfield, the life of the land;
your rays cover the high mountains,
[20]your glowing light fills the surface of the lands,
you bow over the hills to survey the earth,
you suspend (?) from heaven the circle of the earth.
You protect all the people of the lands,
(and) all that Ea, king of the princes, has created is entrusted to you.
[25]You shepherd all that is endowed with the breath of life,
you are its shepherd above and below.[u]
Regularly and without ceasing you pass through the heavens,
you travel over the wide world day by day,
over the flood of the sea, the hills, over earth and heaven
[30]you go daily without ceasing like a . . .[v]
In the underworld you care for the princes(?) of the Kubu,[w] the
   Annunaki,
above, you direct the affairs of all men,
shepherd, of those below, guardian of the world above,
Shamash, you preserve the light of everything.
[35]Again and again you cross the sea in all its breadth,
whose deepest foundations not (even) the Igigi know.

[o] For this theme cf. Ps. 112.4, also Ps. 36.9 and Isa. 9.2.
[p] Cf. p. 101 n. m above.
[q] Cf. Ps. 19.6b.
[r] The god of fire.
[s] See n. o above.
[t] To give rain: emendation of R. Borger, *JCS* 18, 1964, 55.
[u] Cf. e.g. Ps. 95.7.
[v] Cf. Ps. 19.5f.
[w] Cf. B. Kienast, AS 16 (FS B. Landsberger), 1965, 146 n. 28.

Shamash, your blaze penetrates the abysses of the sea,
so that the monsters in the depths of the sea look on your light.
47-52When you rise, the gods of the land assemble,
an angry glare lies over the land.
What is planned by the lands of many tongues –
50you know and you recognize their way.
All mankind bows before you,
O Shamash, all the world longs for your light.

95-101If a man practises usury(?), you destroy his power,x
if a man acts maliciously, an end is made to him.
You (yourself) make the unjust judge discover prison,
you lay punishment on the one who accepts a bribe and commits
     injustice,
but the one who rejects a bribe and intercedes for the weak
100is well-pleasing to Shamash, and he will lengthen his life.y
The wise judge who gives righteous judgments,
completes(?) a palace and lives among the princes.

112The one who practises deception when he holds the corn measure,
who lends out (corn) according to the middle measure (and then)
     requires back a large measure,
the curse of the people will overtake him before his time.
115If he requires repayment before time, a burden will be laid on him,
his heir will not receive his possessions,
(and) his brothers will not (be able to) enter his house.
The honest merchant who lends corn according to the great measure,
     earns much respect,
he is well-pleasing to Shamash, and will prolong his life.
120He will found a great family, gain prosperity,
like the water of an ever-flowing spring his descendants will endure.

163-165You loose the bonds of those who bowed before you,
you ever accept the prayer of those who constantly bless you anew.
165(But) they praise your name with reverence
and worship your majesty for ever.

176Illuminator of the darkness, lightener of the gloom,
who dispels the dark and shines over the broad earth,
who makes the day to shine and sends down scorching heat on the
     earth at midday,

x Literally 'horns'.
y Cf. e.g. Ps. 146.7-9.

(and so) makes the broad earth glow like a flame,
[180](yet) shortens the days and lengthens the nights,
[brings] cold, frost, ice and snow.

At the end the text is damaged more and more.

18. Sumerian 'raising of the hand' prayer to the moon god Nanna-Suen (Sin)

Text: A. Sjöberg, *Der Mondgott Nanna-Suen in der sumerischen Überlieferung* I, 1960, 167ff.; A. Falkenstein, *SAHG*, 222ff. (no. 44) and 379; F. J. Stephens, *ANET*[3], 385ff.; R. Borger, *ZA* 61, 1971, 81f.

This text has been preserved in Ashurbanirpal's library, and like the hymn to Enlil (no. 16), is composed in the Emesal dialect, though the version in which it has come down to us is bilingual.[z] It is possibly from the 'post-early Babylonian'[a] period, but is nevertheless one of the earliest of its kind. The hymn, which was counted among the canonical[b] literature, is a 'public' prayer and celebrates in quite traditional formulae the creativeness, power, righteousness and exalted status of the moon god (the phrases used are by no means limited to the god celebrated here). The moon god was called Nanna or Suen (later Sin); his chief temple was the Ekishnugal in Ur.[c] Lines 29ff. in particular invite comparison with the OT hymn, Ps. 147, especially with vv. 6, 8f., 15-18. For the rejection of moon-worship in the OT, however, see Deut. 4.19; 17.3; II Kings 23.5 and Job 31.26ff.

[1f.]O lord, hero of the gods, who is exalted in heaven and on earth,[d]
father Nanna, lord Anshar,[e] hero of the gods . . .
[11-48]Fruit which is self-created,[f] of lofty form, beautiful to look on, of
  whose splendour man never grows tired,
womb that bears everything, sitting on a high throne above men,
glorious father, who holds the life of the whole country (protectively)
  in his hand.
Lord, like the distant heaven and the broad sea, your divinity is full of
  terror.

---

[z] Provided with an interlinear Akkadian translation.
[a] A common term; what is meant is the time from about 1400 BC onwards; cf. A. Falkenstein, *MDOG* 85, 1953, 9ff.
[b] The Babylonian literature was evidently incorporated in a canon during the period in question. Cf. H. Schmökel, *Kulturgeschichte des Alten Orient*, 1961, 230 (and 724 for further literature), and W. G. Lambert, *JCS* 16, 1962, 59ff.
[c] With its great ziggurat, which today has been partly restored.
[d] But cf. also Ps. 148.13.
[e] In himself the father of An, later identified in Assyria with the national god Ashur; here merely a title.
[f] A reference to the regular waxing of the moon.

[15]He has created the land, founded the sanctuaries (and) given them
  names,
the father, begetter of gods and men,[g] enthroned on high, who
  establishes sacrifices,
who calls kings, bestows sceptres (and) determines [destiny] for distant
  days,
who goes before all, the powerful one, whose secret will no god can
  descry,
who runs swiftly without tiring, who opens the way for his divine
  brothers,
[20]who goes from the base of heaven to its zenith, who opens the door
  of heaven (and) gives light to all men,
my father, all creatures [rejoice] when they see you, seek [your light]!
O lord, who decides destinies in heaven and on earth, whose saying no
  one can alter,
who holds water and fire in his hands, who guides living creatures –
  who among the gods is as you are?[h]
Who is exalted in heaven? You alone are exalted![i]
When you have spoken your word in heaven, the Igigi[j] pray to you,
when you have spoken your word on earth, the Anunnaki[k] kiss the
  ground.
When you have spoken your word above like a storm, it brings food
  and drink to the land in abundance,
when you have spoken your word on earth, the vegetation[l] flourishes
  luxuriantly.
Your word makes the sheepfold and the stall fat, makes living creatures
  numerous,
your word brings about justice and righteousness, and makes men
  speak the truth.
Your word is as remote as the heavens and as deep as the earth, so
  that no one can descry it.
Your word – who can know it, who can measure himself by it?
O lord, your rule has no counterpart in heaven nor your heroic power
  among your divine brothers on earth,

---

[g] In the theology of Ur (and certainly also of Harran, the second city with a moon
cult), Nanna Sin became the creator god, cf. also already v. 12.
[h] Cf. Ex. 15.11; Pss. 86.8; 97.9.
[i] Cf. Ps. 148.13.
[j] Here the gods of heaven.
[k] Here the gods of the earth or the underworld.
[l] Text: 'luxuriant plants'.

^{35}mighty one, exalted king, whose 'divine powers' no one dares to
    wrest from you –
none of the gods can be compared with your deity.
Wherever you [look] as a friend, there is grace,
wherever you raise your hand [to help], there is . . .
^{41}[Your] beloved spouse, the glorious woman,^{m} can say to you, 'Lord,
    be restrained!'
The young Utu,^{n} the lord, the great hero, can say to you, 'Lord, be
    restrained!'
^{47}The bolt of Ur, the exalted seal,^{o} can be moved,
the gods of heaven and earth can say to you, 'Lord, be restrained!'

19. *Sumerian temple hymn*

Text: A. S. Sjöberg et al., *The Collection of the Sumerian Temple Hymns*,
TCS 3, 1969, no. 35, 43ff., cf. 11 and 154.
    Mesopotamian hymns were addressed not only to the gods and – during the
period of their deification^p – to the kings, but also to the sanctuaries, which
were thought to be endowed with independent divine power and were worshipped with cultic hymns, sacrifices, petitions and thanksgiving. The hymn
quoted here comes from a collection of songs of this kind and is addressed to
the temple of the war god Zababa named Eduba, in the ancient Sumerian
city of Kish.^{q} It cannot be later than the early Babylonian period (twentieth to
seventeenth century BC), and is remotely reminiscent of Israel's hymns of
praise to Zion, cf. Pss. 48; 84; 87; 132, etc.

O house, richly built, through Kish its head is raised in splendour,
dwelling, firmly founded, no one can shake your great foundation.
Your encompassing wall (?) is a powerful wall, stretching wide and
    towering into the heavens,
your interior (is) a battle mace, a *meddu* weapon, beautifully adorned
    with . . .
^{5}Your right side makes the hills quake and your left side scatters the
    enemy (on the ground).
Your ruler (is) powerful and exalted, a great storm, which oppresses
    the earth in fear and terror.
Ekishiba, your lord, the warrior Zababa,
has built his temple,^{r} O house of Kish, on your . . ., has taken his
    place on your heights.

^{m} The goddess Ningal.
^{n} The sun god (Akkadian Shamash), who was regarded as the son of Nanna.
^{o} The temple of Nanna? ^{p} I.e. at least from about 2300 to about 1700 BC.
^{q} East of Babylon; the ziggurat of Zababa is situated on the narrow tell of El-Oheimir.
^{r} Literally again simply 'the house'.

20. Sumerian hymn to the king

Text: H. de Genouillac, *RA* 25, 1928, 144ff.; A. Falkenstein, *SAHG* 120ff. (no. 26) and 371; W. H. Römer, *Sumerische 'Königshymnen' der Isin-Zeit*, 1965, 209ff.; A. Sjöberg, *Or* NS 35, 1966, 302f.

This hymn of praise, which has been reconstructed from fourteen fragments, is addressed to Iddindagan, the third ruler of the West Semitic dynasty of Isin (1916-1896). It celebrates his call by the great gods of Sumer, glorifies his works, his wisdom and his righteousness, and calls down the blessing of the great gods on the ruler who, as son of Dagan, is himself of divine origin. These courtly poems, which were later excluded from the ongoing tradition, and perhaps had no direct relationship to the normal cult, are reminiscent of OT royal psalms, e.g. Pss. 2; 20; 21; 45; 72; 89; 101; 110, etc. Some extracts are enough to sketch out the type of this literary group.

[1-6]Iddindagan, An has determined a happy destiny for you in his exalted place,
to make your crown shine out brightly,
he has exalted you as shepherd over the land of Sumer,[s]
(and) has put your enemies under your feet.[t]
[5]Enlil has looked faithfully upon you,
(and) has spoken his immutable word, Iddindagan, to you.

[22-28]Make the good day dawn like Utu,
all eyes are directed towards you,
all foreign lands will be peaceful under your broad protection.
[25]You have made roads (and) paths straight,
filled the land of Sumer with joy,
put righteousness into every mouth,[u]
(and) made the worship of the gods shine forth.

[43-48](Truly) you are the (right) man for the Ekur,[v]
may your sacrifices never cease in the house of Enlil.
[45]May Ekur's bricks speak gloriously of you to Enlil (and) Ninlil.
May you be given great power, Iddindagan, at the good word of An (and) Enlil!
Your great name is worthy of praise in the land of Sumer,
your name shines to the bounds of heaven.

[55-63]Under your rule men will increase and extend,
hostile lands will rest in peace,
men will enjoy days of abundance.

[s] Substantially comparable with II Sam. 5.2 (I Chron. 11.2); Ps. 78.71f.
[t] With this phrase cf. Pss. 47.3 and 110.1.   [u] Compare especially Ps. 101.5ff.
[v] 'Mountain house', the chief temple of Enlil in Nippur.

As the gaze of the black-headed ones was directed to your father,[w]
(so,) Iddindagan, it will be directed to you.
[60]May Enlil, the lord who determines destinies,
lengthen your days![x]
May the one who knows all
look upon you in friendship and grace!

21. *Akkadian invocation to an anonymous god*

Text and literature: E. Ebeling, *OLZ* 19, 1916, 296ff.; W. von Soden,
SAHG 272f. (no. 19); W. G. Lambert, *JNES* 33, 1974, 267ff., esp. 281ff.,
lines 132-157.
This text is one of a group of penitential prayers which was evidently quoted
often. It has been handed down in Sumerian, in Akkadian and in a bilingual
text, and even has echoes in similar Hittite cultic poems.[y] The 'invocation'
included here is attested by eight fragments from Nineveh and Ashur. It is
presumably addressed to a personal guardian deity; it opens with a 'general
confession' and a first prayer for forgiveness, and then begins again with a
reference to the sinfulness of all mankind. It differs from most penitential
psalms by the fact that here the transgressions are not only cultic and ritual,
but also ethical. There are echoes of Pss. 6; 32; 38; 102; 143. (Numbering of
lines follows W. G. Lambert.)

[132]Who is there who has not sinned against his god,[z]
who has constantly obeyed the commandments?
Every man who lives is sinful.[a]
[135]I, your servant, have committed every kind of sin.
Indeed I served you, but in untruthfulness,
I spoke lies and thought little of my sins,
I spoke unseemly words – you know it all.[b]
I trespassed against the god who made me,
[140]acted abominably, constantly committing sins.
I looked at your broad possessions,
I lusted after your precious silver.
I raised my hand and defiled what was untouchable,
I went into the temple in a state of uncleanness.[c]

---

[w] Is the reference here to the earthly father of the king, his predecessor Shuilishu, or
his divine father, Dagan? On 'black-headed' see p. 110 n. j below.
[x] Cf. the similar intercession for the king, Ps. 61.6f.
[y] Cf. H. G. Güterbock, *JNES* 33, 1974, 323ff.
[z] Cf. Prov. 20.9; Job 4.17; 15.14; also Ps. 130.3.
[a] Cf. Gen. 8.21.
[b] Cf. Ps. 139.1-4.
[c] Cf. the liturgies of entry in Pss. 15 and 24.3-6.

[145]I constantly practised shameful dishonour against you,
I transgressed your commandments in every way that displeased you.
In the frenzy of my heart I blasphemed your divinity.
I constantly committed shameful acts, aware and unaware,
acted completely as I pleased, slipped back into wickedness.
[150]Enough, my god! Let your heart be still,
may the goddess, who was angry, be utterly soothed.
Desist from the anger which has risen so high in your heart![d]
May your . . . by which I swore be completely reconciled with me.[e]
Though my transgressions are many – free me of my guilt!
[155]Though my misdeeds are seven[f] – let your heart be still!
Though my sins be countless – show mercy and heal (me)!
(My god), I am exhausted, hold my hand . . .

Continuation fragmentary.

22. Akkadian invocation to Ishtar

Text and literature: L. W. King, *The Seven Tablets of Creation* I, 1902,
222ff.; E. Ebeling, *Die akkadische Gebetsserie 'Handerhebung'*, [2]1953, 130ff.;
W. von Soden, *SAHG*, 328ff. (no. 61) and 401; E. Reiner and H. Güterbock,
JCS 21, 1967, 255ff.; F. J. Stephens, *ANET*[3], 383ff.; R. Labat, *RPOA* I,
253ff.

This text has come down to us in a late Babylonian copy, but there is already
evidence of it from the Hittite capital Hattusa-Boghazköy. It comes from about
the middle of the second millennium BC. Despite the ritual instructions which
have been added, its content is hardly magical, and it is reminiscent of the
psalms of penitence and lament mentioned in no. 21. Its literary form is that
of the 'invocation',[g] the best known group of which is that of the so-called
'raising of the hand' prayers, which could largely have suppressed free private
prayer. These invocations were addressed to a great variety of deities, above
all to Shamash, Marduk and Ishtar; they were given a fixed literary form and a
rhythmic shape, and begin with what is very often an extended hymnic address,
followed by lamentation, petition and thanksgiving. This last is usually in the
form of a promise of future glorification for the deity who provides help (with
a vow of thanksgiving or praise). The petition is for a gracious acceptance of the
prayer, reconciliation of the angry god (who can also be a personal guardian
deity), blotting out of 'evil of every kind' and a breaking of the evil spell. Only
the name of the person who prays needs to be inserted, and then – after exor-
cisms, rites of purification and of course with the offering of the appointed

---

[d] The suppliant recognizes the degree of the divine wrath in the severity of the misfortune or the sickness which has befallen him.
[e] The deity is gracious in himself.
[f] Probably in the sense of 'countless'.
[g] Cf. W. G. Kunstmann, *Die babylonische Gebetsbeschwörung*, LSS NF 2, 1932.

sacrifices – it is presented by the competent priest in the holy of holies, before the statue of the deity. The text as a whole may be compared with the OT penitential psalms already mentioned in connection with no. 21 (Pss. 6; 32; 38; 102; 143). Its broad, hymn-like opening has parallels in Jer. 17.12–18 and above all in the unit made up of Pss. 9–10. There is much in the OT to correspond to the vow of thanksgiving or praise with which the 'invocation' ends, e.g. in Pss. 7.17; 13.6; 31.7f.; 35.9f., 27f. The most significant parts of the extensive Mesopotamian text are as follows.

[18-26]Anu, Enlil and Ea[h] have exalted you among the gods, made your dominion great,
made you high among the Igigi, made your position pre-eminent.
[20]As they think of your name, heaven and earth tremble,
the gods quake, the Anunnaki shudder.
Men praise your majestic name,[i]
for you are great and exalted,
all the black-headed ones,[j] the masses of mankind, praise your heroic might.[k]
You look upon the oppressed and the mistreated and daily bring justice (to them).[l]
[40-50]Where you look, the dead come alive again[m] and the sick arise,
the one who was treated unjustly flourishes again when he sees your face.[n]
I called to you, your wretched, exhausted, sorrowing servant,
look upon me,[o] O my mistress, hear my supplication,
look faithfully upon me, accept my prayer.
[45]Promise me forgiveness, and let your disposition be soothed towards me,
forgiveness for my tormented body, which is full of bewilderment and confusion,
forgiveness for my sick heart, which is full of tears and grief,
forgiveness for my afflicted house, which laments incessantly,
[50]forgiveness for my mind, which is sated with tears and woe.
[56-71]How long,[p] O my lady, are my enemies to look darkly upon me?

[h] The supreme Babylonian trinity.
[i] Cf. Pss. 7.17; 66.2; 68.4; 69.30.
[j] The inhabitants of Mesopotamia.
[k] Ishtar has a markedly warlike aspect – which is already true of the Sumerian Inanna.
[l] Cf. e.g. Ps. 146.7ff.
[m] Cf. e.g. Ps. 33.18f.
[n] Cf. e.g. Ps. 80.3, 7, 19.
[o] Cf. Pss. 102.3; 143.7.
[p] This question is also typical of OT laments: Pss. 6.3; 13.1ff.; 35.17.

are they to plan evil things against me with lies and deception,
are my persecutors and those who envy me to rejoice over me?
How long,ᴾ O my lady, are the cripples and the fools to pass by me (in
   contempt)?
⁶⁰(All too) long waiting (?) has shaped me, and so I have come to be
   hindered,
(for) whereas the weak grew strong, I became weak.
I am tossed to and fro like flood water, stirred up by an evil storm,
my heart flutters up and down like a bird of heaven.
I mourn like a dove night and day,
⁶⁵I am ablaze and cry bitterly,
my inward parts are utterly filled with 'Oh' and 'Alas'.
What have I done, my god and my goddess?
I am treated as though I had not feared my god and my goddess.
Sickness, headaches, corruption and annihilation came over me,
⁷⁰terror, disdain and raging anger came upon me,
anger, wrath (and) the fact that gods and men turned away from me.

⁸¹⁻⁹²Forgive my sin, my iniquity, my wickedness and my offence,
overlook my transgression (and) accept my prayer.
Loose my fetters, secure my deliverance,
guide my path aright, so that I can (again) go (my) way among men
   radiantly like a great man.
⁸⁵Give instruction so that at your word the angry (guardian) deity may
   be reconciled,
(and) the (guardian) goddess who was angry with me may turn to me
   (again).
May my brazier, which is (now) black and smoking, glow (again),
my torch, which has been extinguished, shine (again).
May my scattered family be reunited,
⁹⁰may my fold grow wide and my stable become greater (again).
Accept my (humble) footfall, hear my entreaties,
look in friendship upon me and graciously receive my petition.

⁹⁹⁻¹⁰⁵Let my prayers and my supplications come to you
¹⁰⁰(and) may all your grace be with me.
Those who see me in the street will glorify your name,
(and) I myself will praise your divinity and power loudly before the
   black-headed ones:
'Highly exalted is Ishtar, Ishtar is the (true) queen,
Highly exalted is the lady, the lady is the (true) queen!

ᴾ This question is also typical of OT laments: Pss. 6.3; 13.1ff.; 35.17.

[105]'There is none[q] like Irnini,[r] the heroic daughter of Sin.'

23. *Prayer of Gudea, ruler of Sumer, from his hymn on building a temple*

Text: F. Thureau-Dangin, *Les cylindres de Goudéa*, 1925; A. Falkenstein, *SAHG*, 137ff. (no. 32) and 372ff.

Literature: M. Lambert and R. Tournay, *RB* 55, 1948, 403ff., 520ff.; A. Falkenstein, *Die Inschriften Gudeas von Lagaš* I, 1966, 178ff.; S. N. Kramer, *Sumerians*, 137ff.; A. Baer, *RA* 65, 1971, 1ff.

In contrast to the OT, the religious literature of ancient Mesopotamia rarely presents free, personal prayer – this is most likely to be found, if at all, on the lips of rulers and kings, and particularly in their votive inscriptions and those on new buildings; in that case the prayer is addressed to the deity to whom a gift is offered or for whom the particular building has been erected or restored. In his famous hymn, seeming almost endless with its more than 1300 lines, and inscribed on two clay cylinders, Gudea of Lagash (about 2050) depicts the preliminaries to the building of the temple of Ningirsu, named Eninnu ('house of fifty'), in Girsu,[s] and then its construction, adornment and consecration. (Gudea was a pious ruler from the Ur III period, concerned to revive the earlier culture of Sumer.) Before the beginning of this great work, to which Ningirsu called him in a dream, Gudea visited by ship the sanctuaries of his land in order to offer sacrifices and prayers and to receive a detailed interpretation of his vision from a goddess skilled in dreams. Of course the prayers cited here were formulated by a temple poet, who was probably the author of the whole mammoth composition; however, they will have corresponded with Gudea's own faith and thus come close to a 'personal prayer'. An illustration from this, the earliest prayer preserved in Sumer of whose date we can be certain, cannot be omitted here (it is cited following Falkenstein).

Cylinder A
Col. II 23–44

In the temple of Bagara he[t] celebrated the *eshesh* festival.
The Ensi[u] went to the holiest of the holies of Gatumdu,[v] to her resting place,
[25]offered bread there, gave cool water,

[q] Cf. Pss. 40.5; 71.19; 86.8 etc.
[r] A name for Ishtar.
[s] The present-day Tello (about 120 miles north-west of Basra), at that time the metropolis of the Sumerian state of Lagash, which was dependent on Ur. The state took this name from its earlier capital, Lagash, which lay on the site of the present-day el-Hiba (about 12 miles east of Tello).
[t] Gudea.
[u] A deliberately archaic title.
[v] A local mother goddess.

went to noble Gatumdu
(and) spoke this prayer to her:
'My queen, daughter of majestic An,
queen of the needy, goddess with the exalted head,
³⁰who gives life in the land of Sumer,
knows what is due to her city,
queen, mother, who founded Lagash, you are she!
When you have directed your gaze on the people, abundance pours
   down on them,
the lusty youth upon whom you look will have a long life.
³⁵I have no mother – you are my mother,
I have no father – you are my father!
You received my seed,ʷ gave birth to me in the temple,ˣ
Gatumdu – sweet is your pure name!
In the night you lay there for me,
⁴⁰you are my great sickle which stands by my side,
you are the one who gives water to the grain in abundance,
who gave me life.
You are a broad bulwark, your shadowʸ
will I worship in reverence . . .ᶻ

24. Lamentation from a hymn of Ashurnasirpal I to Ishtar

Text: W. von Soden, *SAHG*, 264ff. (no. 14) and 386 (translation and first
edition since Brünnow, *ZA* 5, 1890, 66ff.).
   Literature: W. G. Lambert, *AnSt* 11, 1961, 157; W. von Soden, *Herrscher
im Alten Orient*, 1954, 76ff.; R. Labat, *RPOA* I, 250ff.
   This hymn to Ishtar has been preserved in fragments in a copy in the library
of Ashurbanipal. It goes back to the less well-known Middle Assyrian King
Ashurnasirpal I (about 1040 BC) who was evidently of 'unknown origin', i.e.
came from a subsidiary line of the dynasty and ruled during a time of distress
for his land. In a prayer which is incorporated in the hymn (and is unfortunately
in fragments), we hear for the first time from the mouth of a ruler of Assyria
not only a reference to his pious works but also mention of his own guilt and
repentance. These are reminiscent of the lamentation 'I will praise the Lord
of Wisdom',ᵃ which was perhaps known to the author.ᵇ The lines relating to
Ishtar, the 'merciful goddess', run as follows (after W. von Soden, *SAHG*,
op. cit.):

ʷ An allusion to the consummation of the sacred marriage? Cf. also line 39.
ˣ Exaggerated poetic diction: for Gudea, Gatumdu was both mother and bride at the
sacred marriage.
ʸ Cf. e.g. Ps. 91.1.
ᶻ Similar prayers appear in the text on cylinder A II, 10–19; IV 8 – V 9 etc.
ᵃ See no. 34 below.   ᵇ W. von Soden, op. cit., 387.

7. An Assyrian dignitary in prayer before the god Ashur.
Painted and glazed brick from Assyria (eighth century BC).

Recto 13f.May your ear be directed to my weary words
and your sense be softened by my grief-laden speech.
23I did not think of your dominion, did not pray constantly . . .
Verso 8 -12On my royal throne I dispense with (?) [. . .]
I do not go to the meal that I should eat,
life-sustaining beer [has become] repulsive to me,c
I do not hear the strings and the music which belong to . . .,
    adornment [. . .],
I dispense with the joy of the living [. . .]

    c Text: *daddaru*, i.e. a foul plant.

[16-19]I, Ashurnasirpal, the frightened, who fear you,
who seize the fringe of your divinity, who pray to you as mistress –
look upon me, lady, and then I will worship your decision (?)!
You who are angry, have mercy on me, so that your countenance may
   be soothed!

Further lamentations follow, ending with the promise that after he has been
saved Ashurnasirpal will praise the goddess.[d]

25. Prayer from a building inscription of Nebuchadnezzar II

Text: S. Langdon, *Die neubabylonischen Königsinschriften*, VAB 4, 1912,
100f.; no. 1, col. II, lines 16–32; W. von Soden, *SAHG*, 286 (no. 29) and 392.
   The text comes from Nebuchadnezzar II, king of the Chaldeans (605–562) –
the ruler who occupied Jerusalem for the first time in 597 and then destroyed
it in 587/86 and deported its inhabitants. It is addressed to Nabu of Borsippa,
the god of wisdom and writing, who was regarded as Marduk's son and for a
while almost exceeded the latter in power and the respect paid to him. The
passage given below forms the conclusion of an inscription relating to the
ziggurat of Nabu in Borsippa, which deals with the restoration of this building.[e]

Col. II 16–31

Nabu, rightful heir,[f] illustrious vizier,
victorious favourite of Marduk,
look upon my works graciously and with joy,
[19/20]give me everlasting life, fullness with a great old age,
an established throne, a long reign, victory over my enemies
(and) the conquest of the land of my foe.
Your tablets can be trusted; they lay down the limits of heaven and
   earth.
[25]Put on them that my days may be long, and inscribe on them an old
   age for me![g]
Before Marduk, the king of heaven and earth,
your corporeal father, may my works be well-pleasing.
Speak in my favour!
'Nebuchadnezzar
[30]is in truth a king who gives rich adornment!'
May these be the words of your mouth.

[d] Cf. also examples of OT vows of praise: Pss. 7.17; 13.6; 31.7f.; 35.9f., 27f.
[e] It still towers high to the south of Babylon as the ruin of Bir Nimrud.
[f] I.e. of Marduk.
[g] Cf. the OT prayer for the king in Ps. 61.6f., and also Ps. 21.4.

26. A Sumerian lamentation on the destruction of Ur

Text: H. de Genouillac, *Textes religieux Sumériens*, 1930, no. 40 and further fragments; S. N. Kramer, *Lamentation over the Destruction of Ur*, AS 12, 1940; id., *ANET*³, 455ff.; id. and Inez Bernhardt, *Sumerische literarische Texte aus Nippur* II, 1967, 16, on tablets 18-25; M. Witzel, *Or* NS 14, 1945, 185ff.; ibid., 15, 1946, 46ff.; A. Falkenstein, *SAHG*, 192ff. (no. 38) and 376f.; C. J. Gadd, *Ur Excavations Texts* 6/II, 1966, 1, on nos. 135-139; H. Limet, *RA* 63, 1969, 5ff.; H. Sauren, *JNES* 29, 1970, 42ff.; Y. Rosengarten, *Trois aspects de la pensée sumérienne*, 1971, 45ff.

Literature: T. Jacobsen, *AJSL* 58, 1941, 219ff.; id., in H. Frankfort et al., *Before Philosophy*, 1949, 207ff. (which includes a partial translation); M. Lambert, *RA* 55, 1961, 190f. (no. 38); S. N. Kramer, *Sumerians*, 142ff.; Y. Rosengarten, *RHR* 174, 1968, 117ff.

This text, which was composed partly in the so-called Emesal dialect and partly in the main dialect, has been retrieved only with considerable effort; it is over 430 verses long and in its present form comes from the early Babylonian period. Y. Rosengarten, op. cit., has attempted to interpret it as a kind of Sumerian tragedy to be performed with singers and a choir. The poem is probably connected with the destruction of Ur by the Elamites about 1955 BC. It is not without counterparts.[h] It is divided into eleven sections and first laments at some length over Sumer, which has been laid waste and abandoned by its gods. Then it turns to the fate of Ur and its temple to the moon, smitten by a disaster which even the gracious Ningal, the consort of the moon god Nanna-Sin, could not ward off, although the supreme gods twice interceded for it. Her lament over the lost sanctuary and the imploring plea of the singer who addresses the gods on behalf of his people are quoted verbatim. In contrast to the OT lamentations over the destruction of Jerusalem in 587/86 BC, especially in Lamentations 1f., we find no trace of the idea that these events are connected with human guilt and expiation: of course this late Sumerian poetry is 1500 years earlier than Lamentations. Nevertheless, a degree of parallelism cannot be disputed. As the text follows Sumerian style in repeating the same ideas several times with minor differences, and gives whole lists of cities, temples and their gods, only a few verses are quoted here as an example (lines are numbered following *ANET*).

[65f.]O city (of a great) name - now you are destroyed for me,[i]
city of high walls - your land has perished!

---

[h] An even more extensive and perhaps more gripping poem on the same theme, 'Lament on the Destruction of Sumer and Ur', also known as the 'Second Lament over Ur', has recently been published in an edition by S. N. Kramer in *ANET*³, 611ff. However, it is far removed from the actual historical situation. The Ibbisin lament, which was at first regarded as an independent work, also belongs here (Falkenstein, *WO* 1.5, 1950, 377ff. and *SAHG*, 189ff.); cf. Kramer, *Iraq* 25, 1963, 171ff.

[i] Ningal speaks.

[75f.]His[j] [righteous city] which has been destroyed – bitter is its lament,
his Ur which has been destroyed – bitter is its lament.
[128-133]Like a tent, a house in which grain [has been gathered],
like a house in which grain [has been gathered],[k] it is now given
  over to wind and rain
[130]O Ur, my exalted chamber –
my house in the ravaged city which has been destroyed,
which has been torn down like a shepherd's cot,
(and) my treasures which towered on high in the city, have been
  scattered (to all the winds).
[173-175]Enlil called the storm – the people groan.
He took the wind of abundance from the land – the people groan,
he denied the good wind to Sumer – the people groan.
[190-195]The day was robbed of the rising sun, of bright light (?),
the bright sun did not rise in the land, (but) shone (only) like a star in
  the evening,[l]
the night was deprived of joy . . . and by the (?) south wind (?),
its cup was filled with dust[m] – the people groan,
the winds swept over the black-headed ones – the people groan.
[195]The net fell upon Sumer[n] – the people groan.
[200-205]The storm which destroys the land did its work (?) in the city,
the all-destroying storm [meant annihilation].
The storm which makes fire rain down(?) brought (distress) upon the
  people,
the storm which Enlil sent in hate, the storm which wears away the
  land,
[205]covered Ur like a cloth, enveloped it like linen.

[227-229]In Ur both weak and strong died of hunger,
the old women and men who had not left their houses were overcome
  by fire,
the children on their mothers' laps were carried off like fish from the
  water.
[232-235]The council of the land was scattered – the people groan,
the mother left her daughter – the people groan,
the father turned away from his son – the people groan.
In the city the wife was abandoned, the child abandoned, possessions
  dwindled away.

[j] The moon god Nanna; the community or the singer is speaking.
[k] Similar comparisons, Isa. 1.8.
[l] Cf. e.g. Isa. 13.10; Amos 5.18.
[m] Cf. especially Ps. 11.6; also Isa. 51.17, 22; Lam. 4.21.
[n] There is a similar picture e.g. in Ezek. 12.13.

²⁵⁴⁻²⁵⁶Mother Ningal stands (as though she were) an enemy, outside the city,
the woman raises her lament over her shattered house,
the queen of Ur cries woe over her ruined sanctuary.
²⁸⁶⁻²⁸⁸'Woe is me – in my city, which has perished, I am no longer the queen!
My house is in ruins, my city destroyed.'

The poet calls to Ningal in the name of the city of Ur:

³⁶⁷⁻³⁷²In your channels, (once) built for great ships, [reeds] (now) grow,
on your streets, (once) made ready for chariots, the mountain thorn (now) grows.
O my mistress – your city weeps before you as before a mother,
Ur seeks you like a child lost in the streets,
your house stretches out its hand towards you – like a man who has lost everything,
the walls of your righteous house call like a man, 'Where are you?'
³⁸¹⁻³⁸³May An, the king of the gods,° speak for you, 'Now it is enough!'
May Enlil, the lord of all lands, decree (a good) fate for you.
May he restore your city for you, (and) may you (again) be its queen . . .

III. PREDICTIONS AND PROPHETIC SAYINGS

27. *'A ruler will come . . .'*

Text: A. K. Grayson and W. G. Lambert, *JCS* 18, 1964, 7ff. (p. 7 also gives earlier literature); R. D. Biggs, *ANET*³, 606ff.
Literature: R. D. Biggs, *Iraq* 29, 1967, 117ff.; W. W. Hallo, *IEJ* 16, 1966, 231ff.; W. G. Lambert, *Or* NS 39, 1970, 175ff.

Four texts of a prophetic kind, related in genre (A–D), which have become known in fragmentary copies from Ashur and Nineveh, describe the appearing of future kings (who are sometimes also called 'rulers'). Sometimes they even give the number of years these kings will reign, but they mention no names. The *Sitz im Leben*ᴾ of the works is hard to explain. There is also a dispute as to whether they are 'secular' or 'theological' writings, on the basis of the cyclical

---

° Cf. Ps. 95.3, and for the subject-matter also Pss. 96.4; 97.9, etc.
ᴾ For text C see also no. 28 (Shulgi prophecy); for text D no. 29, ('Prophetic speech of Marduk').

view of history, as W. W. Hallo[q] has ventured to suggest;[r] in any case, an interpretation of world history along the lines that history repeats itself after certain intervals and thus makes it possible to see the future, would offer one way of coming closer to the sense of the present documents. A certain parallelism can be established between them and Dan. 8.23-25; 11.2-45; to a lesser degree they also recall the Isaiah Apocalypse (Isa. 24-27) and kindred texts. Here are two examples from Text A:[s]

II 2[A prince will come] and reign eighteen years.
The land will live in safety and flourish and the people [will have] abundance.
The gods will make favourable decisions for the land, good winds will come.
5The . . . and the furrow will bring in an abundant yield,
Shakan and Nisaba[t] will constantly dwell in the land(?).
There will be rain and flood water, the people (?) of the land will make a feast.
(But) this ruler will be killed violently during a rebellion.
A ruler will come and reign for thirteen years.
10/11There will be an attack of the Elamites[u] on Akkad[v] and the booty (?) will be taken away from Akkad.
The temples of the great gods will be destroyed, and Akkad will suffer defeat.
There will be uproar, confusion and disorder in the land.
The nobles (?) will lose their respect, another unknown man will arise, will usurp the throne as king and deliver his[w] officials to the sword.
He will fill the brooks of Tupliash with half of the host of Akkad, the plains and the hills.[x]
The people will suffer a severe famine.

28. The Shulgi prophecy

Text: R. Borger, *BiOr* 28, 1971, 3ff., especially 14ff., 20ff.; A. K. Grayson and W. G. Lambert, *JCS* 18, 1964, 19ff.

An extensive prophecy was put on the lips of Shulgi, the second and most famous king of the third dynasty of Ur (about 2046-1998); already divinized in his lifetime, at a later date he was occasionally worshipped as a god. It

[q] See p. 71 above.
[r] W. G. Lambert, *Or* NS 31, 1962, 175 n. 7, differs categorically.
[s] Grayson and Lambert, op. cit., 12ff., 'First Side', Col. II, lines 2-18.
[t] The gods of animals and of grain.
[u] The eastern neighbours of Babylon, who were usually hostile.
[v] North Babylonia is meant here.
[w] I.e. the fallen king's?   [x] Corpses will lie everywhere.

begins with one of the usual speeches of the ruler in praise of himself, in which he describes himself as 'I, god Shulgi, the darling of Enlil and Ninlil'. The text continues with a series of sayings about the future (which are certainly to be regarded as *vaticinia ex eventu*) concerning the destinies of the cities of Nippur and Babylon[y] and their kings, and ends with a number of predictions which proclaim salvation and disaster in turn.[z] Here is an extract:[a]

Col. IV 2-22

. . . On the edge of the city[b] of Babylon
the builder of this palace will grieve.
This ruler will endure evil things,
[5]his heart will not be glad.
During his kingship
battle and slaughter
will not cease.
Under his rule brothers will consume one another,[c]
[10]the people will sell their children
for money.
All the lands will be thrown into confusion.
The husband will leave the wife
(and) the wife the husband.
[15]The mother will close her door before the daughter,[d]
the possessions of Babylon will go
to Subartu[e]
and to the land of Assyria.
The king of Babylon
[20]will hand over the possessions of his palace
to the ruler of Ashur,
his property to Ashur . . .[f]

29. *Prophetic speech of Marduk*

Text and translation: R. Borger, *BiOr* 28, 1971, 3ff., esp. 5ff., 16ff.; A. K. Grayson and W. G. Lambert, *JCS* 18, 1964, 21ff.

[y] In reality Babylon still played no kind of role at the time of Shulgi.
[z] With renewed echoes of the biblical book of Daniel, cf. Dan. 11.4, 6, 8f.; 12.1.
[a] According to Borger, op cit., 20f.
[b] Or 'at the conquest'?
[c] The same theme occurs in Isa. 9.19f.
[d] Cf. e.g. Micah 7.5f. or Isa. 3.5.   [e] An earlier name for Assyria.
[f] As far as we know this can only be an allusion to the destruction and sack of Babylon by the Assyrian king Tukultininurta I (*c.* 1233-1198) – which provides a *terminus post quem* for the dating of the text.

Literature: H. Güterbock, *ZA* 42, 1934, 72ff.

In the library of Ashurbanipal this text was included in a 'series' with the Shulgi prophecy (cf. no. 28). The original text of the fragments, which come from Ashur as well as Nineveh, is to be dated to the 'second dynasty of Isin', or more exactly to the reign of Nebuchadnezzar I (*c.* 1127-1105), when Marduk finally reached the summit of the Babylonian pantheon. This is the 'only divine autobiography to be found in cuneiform literature' (Borger). It is written as a speech of Marduk in praise of himself and addressed to the other gods. First it speaks of the three removals of Marduk's statue from Babylon which had taken place since then – though here they appear as the free decision of the god – and then continues with an extended prophecy of salvation which is doubtless addressed to Nebuchadnezzar I and in accordance with the wishes of the priests of Marduk is meant to seal the absolute pre-eminence of his god. Some of the individual details recall OT prophecies of salvation.[g] Its main content is an extensive 'list of wishes' made by these priests to the king, and the salvation proclaimed is made dependent on their being fulfilled. Their concern is with the restoration of the statue of Marduk which had been removed by the Elamites about 1160 BC on the fall of the Cassite dynasty, together with the impressive expansion and adornment of the temple of Marduk and the gods related to him. If the statue had not been restored at the time when this text was composed (the restoration did in fact take place), this section at least is a real prophecy of salvation. Here we shall quote the best-preserved passages from the closing section.[h]

Fragment from Ashur IV 4-8 and 21-24

. . . This ruler will be powerful and [will have no] rivals.
[5]He will take care of the city,[i] he will gather together those who are scattered.[j]
At the same time he will make the temple of Egalmach and the (other) sanctuaries splendid with precious stones.
[21-24]He will bring together and consolidate the scattered land.
The door of heaven will constantly be open (?)

Fragment from Nineveh III 6'-24'

The rivers will bring forth fish,
the field of the pasture (?) will be rich in produce,[k]
the winter grass will last until the summer,

[g] Cf. e.g. Isa. 1.26ff.; 4.5f.; 13.19; 14.22; 30.23; 31.8; 34.5b; 43.5; 60.4 or Amos 9.14f.; Micah 2.12; 4.6; Zech. 1.17 etc.
[h] According to R. Borger, op. cit., 16b, 17a.
[i] The reference is to Isin, the seat of the dynasty.
[j] Similarly also Ezek. 11.17; 20.34, 41.
[k] Cf. e.g. Lev. 26.4; Ezek. 34.27.

the summer grass will be enough for the winter,[1]
[10]the harvest of the country will flourish and its market value will be
favourable.
Evil will be turned into order,
gloom will be dispersed and evil will be dissipated.
Clouds will constantly be overhead.
One brother will have mercy on another brother,
[15]the son will worship his father like a god,
the mother [will] . . . her daughter,
the bride will be garlanded (?), she will honour her [husband].
Mercy will always be present among men.
Man's achievements [. . .] will stand firm.
[20]This ruler will reign over all the lands.
But I, all you gods,
have a covenant with him,[m]
he will destroy Elam,
he will destroy its cities . . .[n]

30. *Prophetic sayings from Mari*

Text and translation: *ARM* II 190; III 40, 78; X 4, 6-10, 50f., 53, 80f.;
XIII 23, 112-14; G. Dossin, *RA* 42, 1948, 142ff.; id. and A. Lods, *Studies in
Old Testament Prophecy*, FS T. H. Robinson, 1950, 103ff.; id., 'La divination
en Mésopotamie . . .', 1960, 77ff. The texts[o] have now been collected with a
commentary by F. Ellermeier, *Prophetie in Mari und Israel*, 1968, the more
recent ones from *ARM* X ('La correspondence féminine') and by W. L. Moran,
Bib 50, 1969, 15ff., cf. also *ANET*[3], 629ff.; W. von Soden, *UF* 1, 1969, 198;
P. R. Berger, ibid., 207ff.
Literature: already almost too extensive to describe, cf. the summary in
Ellermeier, op. cit., 21ff.; also 172f., 186 and 224ff., together with studies on
individual letters; in addition, the quotations in W. L. Moran, *Bib* 50, 1969,
15f. nn. 1-3 and passim; J. G. Heintz, *SVT* 17, 1969, 112ff.; id., *Bib* 52, 1971,
543ff.; W. Römer, *Frauenbriefe über Religion, Politik und Privatleben in Mari*,
1971; K. Koch, *UF* 4, 1972, 53ff.

[1] Cf. Lev. 26.5.
[m] The king.
[n] A clay tablet with similar content came to light during the 1969/1970 campaigns in
Uruk-Warka and elsewhere. To begin with it enumerates a series of kings of various
Babylonian cities who could not establish 'righteousness' in the land, and then goes on
to announce a ruler coming from Uruk who will bring justice, restore the glory of Uruk
and rule over the whole world, cf. H. Hunger, *UVB* 26/27, 1972, 87.
[o] Further texts belonging here are *ARM* X, 4, 9, 53, 94 and 117, cf. W. von Soden,
op. cit., and J. G. Heintz, *Bib* 52, 1971, 547f.

Among the thousands of letters in the archives of Mari[p] from the reign of Zimrilim[q] are a series of texts which for the first time bear witness to real Babylonian prophetic sayings. These are reports of prophetic proclamations in the temples of Mari and elsewhere - in neighbouring cities over the border. They were sent to King Zimrilim by administrative officials, diplomatic representatives or high-placed ladies of the court, above all Zimrilim's consort herself. The gods giving the inspiration are Dagan of Terqa, Tuttul and Mari(?), Anunitum, Belet-ekallim, Belet-biri and Itur-mer, all worshipped in the temples of the country or in the capital Mari, along with Adad of Aleppo and Shamash of Sippar.[r] The institution of cultic prophecy is unusual in the Babylonian sphere, but at this time it obviously commanded considerable respect and exercised political influence in Mari and its neighbourhood. What prophets of both sexes[s] and occasionally other cultic personnel or even lay people gave out as the word of their god on the basis of dreams, visions, auditions and sometimes in ecstasy was thought to be so important that a report was sent to the king about every case of any significance, and the content of the prophecy had to be 'attested' by a special ceremony.[t] The content covers a wide range: greater reverence to the deity who makes himself known, better adornment of his sanctuary, reminders of sacrifices which are due, political advice and warnings, and clear predictions of success for military undertakings of the king. Thus the prophecies of Mari are certainly parallel to the proclamations of official Israelite *nebiim* (which are not very well known to us),[u] though at the same time they also recall Isaiah's words of comfort to his people, to which he struggled through in the great distress of his country,[v] and the numerous secondary prophecies of salvation which have been inserted into the texts of the prophets and the announcements of consolation and salvation in Ezekiel and Deutero-Isaiah.

(*i*) Offering for a dead father (*ARM* III 40)[w]

[1]Say to my lord: Thus (says) Kibridagan,[x] your servant. [5]It is [well]

---

[p] Present-day Tell Hariri, excavated since 1933 by A. Parrot and his staff, lying on the Euphrates in north-east Syria near to the Iraq frontier.

[q] A contemporary and long-standing ally of Hammurabi, who was finally defeated by him and dethroned.

[r] Cf. Ellermeier, op. cit., 76ff.

[s] Babylonian *ap(i)lum* or *apiltum*, 'answerer' (male or female), *muḫḫum* or *muḫḫutum*, 'ecstatic' (male or female), and *qabbatum*, 'speaker'.

[t] Sending to the king a lock of hair and the fringe of the one making the pronouncement or of a witness giving a report.

[u] Cf. simply Isa. 28.7ff.; Jer. 5.31; 6.14; 14.13ff.; 23.9ff.; 27.9f.; 29.21ff.; Micah 3.5ff.; Zeph. 3.4; P. R. Berger (*UF* 1, 1969, 107) has also referred to Joel 2.28.

[v] Cf. Isa. 7.3ff.; 10.5ff.; 17.1ff.; 37.21ff.; II Kings 19.20ff.

[w] W. von Soden, *WO* 1, 5, 1950, 399; Ellermeier, op. cit., 32ff.; *ANET*[3], 624, e.

[x] Prefect of Terqa (present-day Ashara, forty-two miles north-west of Mari on the Euphrates).

with Dagan and Ikrubel,[y] (and) in Terqa and its district everything is in order. Furthermore, on the day on which I intended to send this letter to my lord, [10]the *muḫḫum* of Dagan came to me and said [to me]: 'The god has sent me![z] Write to the king in haste that the offerings for the dead must be made to the spirit of Jahdunlim.'[a] Thus the *muḫḫum* [20]said to me, and so I report it to my lord. May my lord do what seems good to him!

(*ii*) Warning and encouragement (*ARM* X 7)[b]

[1]Say to my lord: Thus (says) Shibtu,[c] your handmaid. All is in order in the palace. [5]Shelebum[d] fell into ecstasy in the temple of Anunitum[e] on the third day (of the month). Anunitum spoke thus:[f] 'Zimrilim, people will put you to the test by a rebellion.[g] Be careful! Take to yourself trusty (?) servants in whom you have confidence, [15](and) appoint them to watch over [you]. Do nothing alone! [20]I will give into your hands the men who [want to put you] to the test!' (With this message) I have sent[h] the lock of hair (and the fringe) [25]of the eun[uch][i] to [my lord].

(*iii*) Reprimand and promise of help (*ARM* X 8)[j]

[1]Say to my lord: Thus (says) Shibtu, your handmaid. [5]Akhatum, a daughter of Daganmalik, fell into ecstasy in the temple of Anunitum in

[y] The chief gods of Terqa; in addition, Dagan was the supreme god of the land of Mari.

[z] Cf. p. 125 n. s.

[a] The father of Zimrilim, whose cult of the dead was certainly instituted during the period of Assyrian lordship over Mari. Recollection of its resumption probably puts the text in the first period of Zimrilim's reign.

[b] Ellermeier, op. cit., 56ff.; Moran, op. cit., 29ff.; *ANET*[3], 630, l; Römer, op. cit., 19f.

[c] Consort of Zimrilim and daughter of King Jarimlim of Aleppo, who gave sanctuary to prince Zimrilim when he fled from Mari before the Assyrians. Shibtu writes from the palace of Mari (which also lent its name to the whole state) to her husband, who is away.

[d] A member of the cultic personnel, who also appears in *ARM* X 80 (see no. vi below).

[e] The form of manifestation of the warlike Ishtar, chief goddess of Mari. *ARM* X 8 gives a further, very attractive prophecy from the shrine of Anunitum (cf. the following text).

[f] Through the mouth of Shelebum.

[g] We do not hear elsewhere of such an event.

[h] To confirm the statement, for which the prophet is thus responsible; cf. p. 123 n. t.

[i] The translation is disputed, cf. Moran, op. cit., 30 n. 2; von Soden, op. cit., 198: 'sodomite'.

[j] Ellermeier, op. cit., 58ff.; Moran, op. cit., 31f.; *ANET*[3], 630, n; Römer, op. cit., 20f.

the centre of the city[k] and spoke as follows: 'Zimrilim, although you neglect me,[l] (for my part) I will continue to love you.[m] I will give your enemies into your hand.[n] (And) the men who rob me I will pounce on, I will put them in the belly[o] of Belet-ekallim!'[p] On the following day [20]the priest Akhum brought me this report, the lock of hair and the fringe, and so I am writing this to my lord. (With it) I have sealed the lock and the [25]fringe and have sent them to my lord.

(*iv*) Good news from Dagan about the Jaminites and a warning to pay more heed to the god (A 15)[q]

[1]Say to my lord, Thus (says) Iturashdu,[r] your servant: [5]On the day when I sent this my letter to my lord, Malikdagan, a man from Shakka, came to me and spoke to me as follows: 'In my dream I and the man with me were on the way [10]from the area of Sagaratum in the upper district to Mari. On the way (?) I went into Terqa, and when I entered there I went into the temple of Dagan and [15]bowed down before Dagan. When I lay at his feet, Dagan opened his mouth and spoke to me: 'Have the kings of the Jaminites and their people made peace with the people of Zimrilim, [20]who have come up here?' I replied, 'They have not made peace!' Just as I wanted to go out, he said to me (again): 'Why are there not constantly messengers [25]from Zimrilim before me, and why does he not constantly give me his news? Had this been so I would have long since given the kings of the Jaminites into the hand of Zimrilim! Now go, I have sent you!' To Zimrilim you shall speak thus; this is what you (have to say): Send your messengers to me [35]and share everything with me. Then I will have the kings of the Jaminites struggling in the catcher's basket and will present them before you!'[t] [40]This is what that man saw

[k] In Mari.
[l] The clergy of Anunitum in Mari obviously feel neglected by the king, like those of Dagan, cf. the following text.
[m] Hos. 3.1 is a limited parallel.
[n] I Kings 22.6, 12, 15; II Kings 3.15ff. are generally comparable.
[o] So according to von Soden, op. cit., ad loc.; the significance of the threat is obscure.
[p] 'Mistress of the palace', a manifestation of Inanna-Ishtar known since Ur III; she probably had a temple or a chapel in many cities with a royal residence, and in Mari has been shown to be the guardian deity of the dynasty.
[q] Ellermeier, op. cit., 24ff.; *ANET*[3], 623, a.
[r] Palace prefect in Mari and governor of Nahur.
[s] Cf. *ARM* III 40 (see no. i above), line 14, and XIII 114 (see no. viii below), line 11, and on this e.g. Jer. 26.12, 15; for the content see also Isa. 6.8f.; Jer. 1.7; Ezek. 2.3; Amos 7.15.
[t] The priests of Dagan, the chief god of Mari, evidently felt neglected because they received too few instructions from the king; they therefore complained in exactly the

in his dream and he reported it to me. I have written it down for my lord so that my lord may decide about this matter of the dream![u] [45]Furthermore, if it please my lord, may my lord give Dagan a full report, and may the messengers of my lord then be constantly on the way to Dagan. [50]The man who recounted this dream to me will offer the sacrifice of an animal to Dagan, which is why I am not sending him to you, and as this man[v] is reliable, he has not brought his[w] lock and his fringe with him.

(v) Warning against warlike adventures (*ARM* X 50)[x]

[1]Say to my lord: thus (says) Adduduri,[y] your handmaid. Since the fall[z] of your father's house I have never had this dream. [5]My earlier tokens pointed in the same direction . . .(?). In my dream I went into the temple of Belet-ekallim,[a] but Belet-ekallim was not there, and the statues standing before her were not there either.[b] I saw that and began to weep. I had this dream of mine in (the time of) the first night watch. Again I dreamed: Dada, the priest [15]of Ishtar . . .,[c] was on duty at the gate of Belet-ekallim and . . . kept calling out 'Come back, Dagan! [20] Come back,

---

same way as the priesthood of Anunitum (cf. the preceding text, no. iv line 9, and p. 125 n. l). They promise the king success in war or politics – here the subjection of the powerful and aggressive nomad tribe of the Jaminites – provided that representatives of Zimrilim are constantly stationed in the temple of Dagan, that the priests are kept regularly informed of political events and are given the function of advisers. The fact that a 'chance' visitor to the temple had this audition is meant to be especially impressive, but the matter-of-fact Zimrilim may hardly have been very impressed. It is hard to overlook the parallel here to the 'lying prophets' e.g. in Jer. 23.13, 16.

[u] Iturashdu also seems sceptical, but of course leaves the decision to the king.

[v] This must refer to the messenger whom Iturashdu sends to Zimrilim with the report of the 'word of god' in Dagan's temple in Terqa.

[w] The recipient of the dream.

[x] Ellermeier, op. cit., 64ff.; Moran, op. cit., 38ff.; *ANET*[3], 631, p; Römer, op. cit., 23, 26f.

[y] A lady of the court in Mari and therefore a lay person; referring to 'signs' which she has already received earlier – she reports two of her dreams of a prophetic nature and the supplementary saying of a *muḫḫutum* (ecstatic) of Anunitum, verifying her report by sending a lock of her hair and her own fringe. She is the sender of a number of reports of prophetic sayings that have come to Zimrilim's notice.

[z] Thus according to von Soden, op. cit., ad. loc., instead of 'restoration'; what is meant is the murder of the father and the brothers of Zimrilim and the sacking of Mari by Shamshiadad of Assur.

[a] See p. 125 n. p above.

[b] A threatening omen: in the vision the statue of Belet-ekallim and the statues of suppliants set before her are missing; i.e. the goddess, the guardian deity of the royal house, has left her place and is out of action. – Cf. Ezekiel's vision of the departure of the divine glory: Ezek. 8.1–11.25.

[c] I.e. the priest of another goddess of the type of Ishtar who so far has not been identified; the temple of Belet-ekallim is so to speak without a mistress.

Dagan!'[d] So the sound kept echoing. Furthermore: the *muḫḫutum* in the temple of Anunitum stood up and said: 'Zimrilim, do not go to war! Remain in Mari and I (myself) will undertake everything!'[e] My lord should not neglect to take heed. I myself am sealing up strands of hair and the fringe from the woman's garment and am sending it herewith to my lord.

(*vi*) Good news about Eshnunna (*ARM* X 80)[f]

[1]Say to 'my star':[g] Thus (says) Inibshina:[h] The eunuch (?)[i] Shelebum gave me an oracle [5]once before, and I have reported it to you. Now the *qabbatum*[j] of Dagan of Terqa came and spoke thus to me. Thus she spoke: 'The peace moves made by the "man of Eshnunna"[k] are sheer deception. The water runs under the dry reed![l] But I will catch him in [15]your net, which I am weaving.[m] I will put an end to his city[n] and I will destroy his possessions, which have not been attacked since ancient times! [20]This is what he[o] said to me!' Now be careful. Do not go into the centre of the city without a (favourable) omen! [25]I heard the following said: 'He[p] is

[d] Dagan, Mari's supreme lord, who once made Jahdunlim king, has departed in Adduduri's dream (cf. Ezek. 8-11); he is besought to return. The critical situation presupposed is probably the first phase of Zimrilim's final conflict with Babylon, which eventually led to the conquest of Mari by Hammurabi.

[e] Literally something like 'will give the answer'. Similarly (as Moran, op. cit., 40f., ad loc., points out), Ishtar of Arbela to Asshurbanipal, *ANET*[3], 451; cf. Isa. 7.3ff. in the OT.

[f] Ellermeier, op. cit., 68ff.; Moran, op. cit., 52ff., and *ANET*[3], 632, x; Römer, op. cit., 21ff.

[g] A tender family address, mostly used by Zimrilim's daughters; Inibshina is one of them (cf. Moran, op. cit., 33 ad loc.).

[h] Also the author of *ARM* X 81-83.

[i] Cf. p. 124 nn. d, i above.   [j] 'Speaker'.

[k] 'Man' is often used (in a derogatory way) for 'ruler' or 'king'. The king of Eshnunna (on the Dyala) was called Ibalpiel; he was a constant supporter of neighbouring Elam and in the time of Hammurabi played quite a significant role. For most of the time he was hostile to both Babylon and Mari. As long as the federation of these two states lasted, auxiliaries from Mari often fought alongside the Babylonians against Eshnunna. This text probably refers to such an enterprise; understandably it assigns Zimrilim the leading role (and rightly so, perhaps, during the earlier years).

[l] Literally 'straw'. There is evidently a proverb here, meaning something like 'do not trust outward appearances'.

[m] As, say, the god Ningirsu holds the enemies of Eannatum of Lagash - about eight hundred years earlier - in his net on the relief of the 'vulture stele', cf. A. Parrot, *Sumer*, 1960, 134, fig. 163b; A. Moortgat, *Die Kunst des Alten Mesopotamien*, 1967, plate 118. In the OT cf. e.g. Ezek. 12.13; 17.20.

[n] Eshnunna, present-day Tell Asmar.

[o] As the person who delivers the saying is a woman, 'he' can only refer to the god.

[p] Namely Zimrilim.

inwardly in constant unrest(?).' You have no reason to be disquieted![q]

(*vii*) Prophecy of victory (*ARM* XIII 23)[r]

[1]Say to my lord: Thus (says) Mukannishum,[s] your servant: I offered Dagan the sacrifice for the life of my lord. Then the *aplum* ('answerer') of Dagan of Tuttul stood up and spoke as follows: 'Babylon, what do you keep doing? I will [10]capture you in the net![t] Your god . . . a wild ox . . . The houses of the seven confederates[u] and all their possessions will I hand over to Zimrilim!' And the *aplum* of D[agan]. . . .

The remaining seven lines are destroyed.[v]

(*viii*) Good news about the threat from Hammurabi of Babylon (*ARM* XIII 114)[w]

[1]S[ay to my lord]: Thus (says) Kibri[dagan], your servant: [5]On the day when I prepared this my letter to my lord, the wife of a man[x] came to me before the darkness of the hill[y] and spoke to me thus about a report on Babylon: 'Dagan has sent me.[z] Write to your lord: He is not to be anxious . . . he is not to be anxious! [15]Hammurabi [the king of] Babylon . . .[a]

The other side is illegible.

[q] Translation not completely certain. The prophecy was in fact fulfilled; in the thirtieth year of his reign Hammurabi defeated Eshnunna. However, that did not do Zimrilim any good: a year later he, too, was defeated by the Babylonians and subjected to their rule – as a too wilful ally who had now become superfluous.

[r] Ellermeier, op. cit., 40ff.; *ANET*[3], 625, i.

[s] A palace official in Mari.

[t] Cf. also Ezek. 32.3; Hos. 7.12.

[u] Evidently a reference to Hammurabi, his partner in a coalition at that time; a letter from Mari, first published by G. Dossin in *Syr* 19, 1938, 117f., talks in a similar context even of 'ten to fifteen "kings" who go with the Babylonians'.

[v] Perhaps a further prophetic saying followed here.

[w] Ellermeier, op. cit., 46ff.; id., *Qohelet* I/2, [2]1970, 24ff.; *ANET*[3], 624, d.

[x] *awilum* here in the sense of 'free citizen'.

[y] Evidently a point of time, say, 'before the mountains become dark'. From Tell Hariri towards sunset one can see how the hills in the south-west become obscured (I am most grateful for this kind information to A. Parrot and M. Lambert, who supplied it by letter).

[z] See p. 125 n. s above. Cf. e.g. Jer. 26.12, 15 once again; Isa. 6.8f.; Jer. 1.7; Ezek. 2.3; Amos 7.15 are also relevant for the subject matter.

[a] Again a laywoman as prophetess with a new word of encouragement from Dagan (cf. the previous text) in connection with Zimrilim's quarrel with Hammurabi. The course of history shows that the prophecy of a good outcome was not fulfilled. Zimrilim was defeated and first of all allowed to remain in Mari as a vassal; after a rebellion, however, he was banished and we hear no more of his personal fate.

IV. CURSES IN TREATIES, CATALOGUES OF SINS

31. *Esarhaddon's vassal-treaty*

Text: D. J. Wiseman, *Iraq* 20, 1958, 1ff., esp. 29ff.; E. Reiner, *ANET³*, 534ff.
Literature: R. Borger, *ZA* 54, 1961, 173ff.; I. J. Gelb, *BiOr* 19, 1962, 159ff.; R. Frankena, *OTS* 14, 1965, 122ff.
After the middle of the second millennium BC and probably under Hittite influence, treaties begin to play a part in the life of ancient Near Eastern states. Official documents of this kind, like the donation documents (Kudurru) of the Cassite rulers and of the later Babylonian kings, and international treaties of the Hittites and Assyrians with their partners, were protected against possible infringement by a whole series of divine curses. More recent researches[b] have thought to discover parallels in OT texts (predominantly those in Deutero-nomy and the Deuteronomistic works) which deal with the covenants of Yahweh with his people, and also, say, with Abraham and David,[c] parallels in particular with the sections of the cuneiform documents mentioned above which contain curses.[d] Particular reference must be made to Deut. 28 and Lev. 26. However, the lamentations and threats of the prophets, especially in Isaiah and Jeremiah, also need to be considered.[e] The newest, best and most extensive instance of an ancient Near Eastern document of this kind[f] is the vassal-treaty of Esarhaddon of Assyria (680–669), almost 700 lines long, which was re-discovered in Nimrud, ancient Kalah, in 1955. It has proved possible to recon-struct it almost completely from its 350 fragments. This showed that more than 250 lines of it were taken up with curses. The most significant sections are listed here:

Lines 41–61

[41]A treaty which Esarhaddon, king of Assyria, has made with you before the great gods of heaven and earth, on behalf of the crown prince

[b] G. E. Mendenhall, *Law and Covenant in Israel and the Ancient Near East*, 1955; F. C. Fensham, *ZAW* 74, 1962, 1ff.; ibid., 75, 1963, 155f.; id., *ThZ* 23, 1967, 305ff.; D. J. McCarthy, *Treaty and Covenant*, AnBib 21, 1963; K. Baltzer, *The Covenant Formulary*, 1971; R. Frankena, *OTS* 14, 1965, 122ff.; M. Weinfeld, *Bib* 46, 1965, 417ff.; id., *JAOS* 90, 1970, 184ff.
[c] For Abraham see principally Gen. 15; for David, II Sam. 7.8ff.
[d] On this above all D. R. Hillers, *Treaty-Curses and the Old Testament Prophets*, BibOr 16, 1964 (the most striking instances are on pp. 43ff.); cf. further M. Weinfeld, *Bib* 46, 1965, 417f., and not least W. Schottroff, *Der altisraelitische Fluchspruch*, WMANT 30, 1969.
[e] Cf. e.g. Isa. 34.11–17.
[f] For the Assyrian treaties cf. also E. Weidner, *AfO* 8, 1932/33, 17ff.; R. Borger, *Die Inschriften Asarhaddons, Königs von Assyrien*, AfOB 9, 1956, 107ff.; E. Reiner, *ANET³*, 531ff.

designate Ashurbanipal, son of your lord Esarhaddon, king of Assyria, whom he has designated and named [45]as his successor. When Esarhaddon, king of Assyria, departs this life, you shall set the crown prince designate, Ashurbanipal, on the royal throne, and he shall exercise the kingship and rule of Assyria over you. (If) you do not protect [50]him in country and in city, do not fight and (even) die for him, do not always speak the whole truth to him, do not always advise him in utter loyalty, do not smooth the way for him in every respect, [55]if you displace him and put his older or younger brothers on the throne of Assyria in his stead, if you falsify a word of Esarhaddon, king of Assyria, if you are not subject to this crown prince designate Ashurbanipal, son of Esarhaddon, king of Assyria, your lord, [60]so that he cannot exercise kingship and rule over you . . .

Lines 385–396

If – as you stand here on the ground (on which) the oath (is given) – and give the oath (only) with words and lips and not with your whole heart, and do not pass on (the oath) to your sons who will live after this treaty,[g] [390]if you take the curse upon yourselves and do not purpose to keep the treaty of Esarhaddon, king of Assyria, in favour of the crown prince designate Ashurbanipal, then [395]your sons and grandsons will have to fear for ever your god Ashur and your lord, the crown prince designate Ashurbanipal.

Lines 414–430

Then may[h] Ashur, the king of the gods, who determines men's fate, [415]appoint for you an evil and unhappy fate and prevent you from becoming fathers, growing old, reaching old age.

May Ninlil,[i] his beloved consort, cause him to proclaim disaster for you, and may she make no intercession for you. May Anu, the king of the gods, rain down sickness, exhaustion, headaches, sleeplessness, care, ill-health! May Sin, the light of heaven and earth, [420]cover you with leprosy and so prevent your going in to god and king; (then) wander like a wild ass or a gazelle through the fields!

May Shamash, the light of heaven and earth, refuse you fair and righteous judgment, may he take away from you the light of your eyes; (then) wander in darkness!

[425]May Ninurta, leader of the gods,[j] strike you down with his grim

[g] I.e., later.
[h] As has been said, the curses cited in the following passage are particularly reminiscent of Deut. 28, and especially vv. 28–34; cf. Frankena, op. cit., 147f.
[i] With the heritage of Enlil, Ashur also took over his consort.
[j] In battle.

arrow, fill the field with your corpses and cast out your flesh as food for eagles and vultures.

May Venus,[k] the brightest among the stars, place your women in the arms of your enemy before your very eyes, may your sons [430]no (longer) call your house their own, may a foreign enemy divide your possessions among themselves.

Further curses follow.

Lines 528-532

May they (the gods) make your ground like iron, so that no one can plough[l] it. [530] As rain does not fall from an iron heaven, so may rain and dew not come upon your fields and pastures[m] . . .

32. Shurpu - the Akkadian series of adjurations

Text and commentary: E. Reiner, Šurpu, AfOB 11, 1958.

In the conditional sentences which precede the curses in Assyrian treaties, the actual conditions are presented as possible breaches of the treaty. Similarly, we find that moral law in the ancient Near East is presented predominantly in a negative form, as a catalogue of sins, which are collected together in the adjurations 'for everyone's use'. Thus these almost endless and often very detailed lists of possible transgressions, declaimed by the priest concerned with purification before or during the ritual on the assumption that one or the other would apply to the person seeking absolution, have only to be read correctly to present remarkable parallels to the ethical commandments and laws in the OT. Similarly, these are often garbed in a negative form, 'You shall not . . .' (there are references to examples in the notes). The classic cuneiform text of this very extensive and widespread genre[n] is the second tablet of Shurpu ('burning', i.e. a ritual of purification), a series of adjurations which take up nine tablets in all and have predominantly been preserved in copies from Nineveh and Ashur. It is hard to estimate the time of the composition of any work of this kind, but part of it at least may go back into the second millennium BC. Only sections of the adjuration are given here, but they contain most of the commandments in the Decalogue (Ex. 20.2-17; Deut. 5.6-21), albeit often with a number of qualifications; the adjurations sum up countless possible sins and misdeeds of all kinds under the basic formula which is repeated from time to time, 'May it be forgiven . . .'.[o]

---

[k] The planet of Ishtar.   [l] Literally 'cut'.
[m] Cf. Deut. 28.23; Lev. 26.19. The comparison is so contrived and extraordinary that the Assyrian original clearly shines through here. R. Borger, op. cit., 190f., on lines 528ff. is to be followed in his assumption that Deuteronomy knew the curse from a treaty between Assyria and Judah, perhaps that of Manasseh.
[n] B. Meissner, Babylonien und Assyrien II, 1925, 212ff., 229ff.
[o] Following E. Reiner, op. cit., 13f.

II 1-4[Adjuration. May it be forgiven,] you great gods,

[God and] goddess, lords of forgiveness!

[NN, son of] NN,[p] whose god is NN, whose goddess is NN,

[who . . .] sick, in danger (of death), in misery, in need.

6Who said 'no' for 'yes' and 'yes' for 'no',[q]

14f.who spoke falsely as a witness;[r]

who let the judge to make a wrong judgment.

20Who caused enmity between son and father,

22who caused enmity between daughter and mother.

29f.Who did not set free a prisoner, who did not release one who was in fetters,

who did not let the captive see the light (of day).

32Who does not know what is a transgression against the god or what is a sin against the goddess.

44f.He disinherited the son, the rightful heir, and did not accord him (his rights),

he cheated in drawing boundaries and laid down a false boundary.[s]

47-49He entered the house of his neighbour,

had dealings with his neighbour's wife,[t]

shed his neighbour's blood.[u]

55f.His mouth is honest (but) his heart is false,[v]

(when) his mouth says 'yes', his heart says 'no'.[w]

60-64He accuses, convicts and calumniates,

does wrong, plunders and incites to theft,

he has his hand in evil,

his mouth . . . is lying, his lips are false and violent,

he accedes to wrong and knows what is unseemly,

65he has his place among the evil,[x]

transgressed the bounds of right,

did unjust things,

had dealings with magic and witchcraft.[y]

---

p The name of the believer seeking absolution or healing was inserted here.

q Cf. lines 55f. and E. Kutsch, *EvTh* 20, 1960, 206ff.

r Cf. Ex. 20.16 (Deut. 5.20); Ex. 23.2.

s Cf. Deut. 19.14; 27.17 and also Prov. 22.28, etc.

t Cf. Ex. 20.14, 17 (Deut. 5.18, 21).

u Cf. Ex. 20.13 (Deut. 5.17); Ex. 21.12ff.

v Cf. Ps. 15.2b.

w See E. Kutsch, op. cit.; F. Thureau-Dangin, *RA* 21, 1924, 131-3, line 22; outside the Decalogue, Lev. 19.12; Num. 30.3; Deut. 23.23 and Ps. 50.16ff. (and in the New Testament Matt. 5.37).

x Cf. Ps. 26.4f.

y Cf. Ex. 22.18; Deut. 18.10f.

Because of the evil and forbidden things he has tasted,
[70]because of the countless sins which he has committed,
because of the assembly which he has set at variance,
because of the close community which he has scattered,
because of all his contempt for the god and goddess,
because he promised with heart and hand and then did not give.
[93-98]He was involved in shedding blood,
was there when blood flowed,
ate what was forbidden in his city,
betrayed the affairs of his city,
gave his city a bad reputation,
openly agreed with one under a curse.
[129]May it be forgiven, O Shamash, you judge,
[134]forgive it, you magician among the gods, gracious lord Marduk![z]

V. WISDOM

33. An Akkadian dialogue on the unrighteousness of the world[a]

Text: B. Landsberger, *ZA* 43, 1936, 32ff.; W. G. Lambert, *Babylonian Wisdom Literature*, 1960, 63ff.; W. von Soden, *MDOG* 96, 1965, 52ff.; R. H. Pfeiffer, *ANET²*, 438ff.; R. D. Biggs, *ANET³*, 601ff.

Literature: R. Labat, *RPOA* I, 320ff.; J. J. Stamm, *JEOL* 9, 1944, 101ff.; id., *Das Leiden des Unschuldigen in Babylon und Israel*, 1946, 19ff.; W. von Soden, op. cit., 41ff.

Sumerian and Babylonian wisdom literature,[b] like that of the OT, stands midway between theology and philosophy. Among its numerous tractates, fables, sayings, dialogues and other works, the only ones which are to be compared with the OT are the lamentations and poems concerned with theodicy, which prove to be parallels to Job, Ecclesiastes and the penitential psalms (especially Pss. 6; 31; 38; 102 and 142).[c] The first dialogue presented here is between a sufferer and his friend; it is artificially divided into twenty-seven sections each of eleven lines (each of four stresses; the lines tend to form

---

[z] An appeal to countless other gods for the absolution of the sinner follows.
[a] Also known under the title 'Acrostic Dialogue', 'Babylonian Theodicy' and 'Babylonian Koheleth'.
[b] For Sumero-Babylonian wisdom literature in general see the investigation by W. G. Lambert mentioned above, and J. J. van Dijk, *La sagesse suméro-accadienne*, 1953; also E. J. Gordon, *Sumerian Proverbs*, 1960; id., *BiOr* 17, 1960, 122ff.; S. N. Kramer, *Sumerians*, 217ff.
[c] There are also echoes of Proverbs and the Song of Songs.

double verses), and like Ps. 119 forms an acrostic.[d] It laments the suffering of the innocent in an unjust world. The text has its lacunae;[e] it comes predominantly from the neo-Assyrian and late Babylonian period. W. von Soden[f] thinks that he can date the work to around 800 BC; it is often difficult to understand, not least because of the constraints presented by the acrostic.

Lines 1, 4-11, 27-33

Sufferer[g]

[1]O wise man,[h] [. . .] let me speak to you.
[4][Then will I,] the sufferer, not cease to reverence you.
[5](For) where is a wise man like you,
where is a scholar who can compete with you,
where is a counsellor to whom I can unfold my grief?
I am devastated, am in the depth of distress.
When I was still a child, fate took my father from me,
[10]my mother who bore me departed to the 'land without return',
my father and my mother left me unprotected.
[27]My body is exhausted, weak from emaciation,
my good fortune is passed, my security (?) has gone.
My strength has vanished, my riches are consumed,
[30]sorrow and need have darkened my features,
the grain in my field (?) is not enough to satisfy me.
Spiced wine, which gives men strength, is too little for satiety.
Does a happy life (still) await me? I would like to know how!

Lines 56-66

Friend

O palm tree, tree of abundance,[i] my honoured brother,
endowed with all wisdom, golden(?) jewel,[j]
you are as steadfast as the earth – but the plan of the gods is
      concealed.[k]
Look at the proud wild ass on the [plain]:
[60]the arrow will hit the one who trampled on the fields.
Look at the lion you mentioned, the enemy of cattle:

[d] The Akkadian acrostic is made up of the twenty-seven initial syllables of the sections: *a-na-ku ša-ag-gi-il-ki-i-na-am ub-bi-ib ma-aš-ma-šu ka-ri-bu ša i-li u šar-ri-ma*, which means, 'I, Shaggil-kinam-ubbib, the incantation priest, am a worshipper of god and king' – certainly the way in which the author of the work introduces himself.
[e] Cf. Lambert, *Wisdom Literature*, 69.
[f] Op. cit., 52.
[g] The dialogue form is used in a similar way in Job.
[h] Forms of address at court which seem almost exaggerated.
[i] For this metaphor cf. e.g. Jer. 11.16; 17.8; Pss. 1.3; 52.8.
[j] See n. h above.
[k] Cf. e.g. Isa. 55.8f.; Eccles. 8.16f.; 11.5.

for the wickedness which the lion committed,[1] the trap awaits him.
The one endowed with riches, the newcomer, who heaps up profit,
will be burnt by the king in the fire before his appointed time.
[65]Do you want to go the way these have gone?
Seek rather the lasting grace (of your) god![m]

Lines 70-77, 133-41
Sufferer
 Those who do not seek (their) god, go the way of prosperity,
 (but) those who pray to (their) goddess, are impoverished and
  embittered.[n]
 When I was young I sought the will of (my) god,
 I sought my goddess with humility and prayer,
 and yet I had to do forced labour without reward,
 [75]instead of riches my god decreed poverty for me.
 The cripple is my superior, the fool has an advantage,
 the rogue has been promoted, but I have been brought low.
 [133]So I will abandon my house [. . .]
 I will desire no (more) property [. . .]
 [135]I will ignore the commands of (my) god and trample (his) ordinances
 underfoot.
 I will slaughter a calf and [. . .] food
 (then) I will set off (and) go to distant parts,
 open up a spring, give the wave free course,
 like a thief I will run a mile over the fields.
 [140]I will go from house to house to ward off my hunger,
 famished I will look around, wander about up and down the streets.

Lines 237-257
Friend
 The godless deceiver who gained wealth,
 the murderer pursues with his weapon.[o]
 If you do not seek the counsel of the god – how can you flourish?
 [240](But) the one who bears the yoke of his god, he has his livelihood,
  however small it may be.
 Seek the kindly breeze of the gods,
 then you will soon win back again what was lost in a year.[p]

[1] The image of the lion is also used in the OT in connection with the wicked man; cf.
especially Job 4.8-11, and for example Pss. 35.16f.; 58.6.
[m] Ps. 37 should also be compared with this section.
[n] Cf. Jer. 12.1 and above all Job 21.6ff.; Pss. 10.3ff.; 73.3ff.; Eccles. 8.9ff.
[o] Cf. e.g. Job 18.5-21.
[p] Cf. e.g. Job 8.5f.

Sufferer

I looked around among men in the world, but the signs were full of
contradictions.[q]
The god does not put anything in the way of the evil demon.[r]
²⁴⁵The father drags the boat along the canal,
while his firstborn son[s] lies (idly) in bed.
The oldest brother goes his proud way like a lion,
the second son may be happy to be a mule driver.
The heir goes along the road like an idler(?),
²⁵⁰the younger son must give bread to the poor.[t]
What can I still gain, I who have to humble myself before the
overseer (?)?
I have to bow even before the humble,
and the rich and haughty mock me (like) a child!

Friend

O wise and knowing man, rich in knowledge –
²⁵⁵your heart is evil and you blaspheme God.[u]
The heart of the god is unfathomable, like the middle of heaven,[v]
what he can do is hard to understand, and incomprehensible to men.
²⁶⁵Give heed, my friend, understand my views,
hear the careful expression of my speech.
They praise loudly the way of the famous man who knows how to
murder,
(but) oppress the lowly.
They assent to the evildoer to whom [righteousness] is an
abomination,
²⁷⁰but drive away the honest man who heeds God's word.

Lines 287–297
Sufferer

You are kind, my friend, behold (my) grief.
Help me, look on (my) distress, understand it.
I am a fearful slave who begs in humility.
²⁹⁰I have not seen help and support for one moment.

---

[q] Cf. Eccles. 3.16.
[r] Text: *sharrabu* demon, evidently an evil spirit.
[s] The privileges of the first-born in ancient Near Eastern culture seem to the sufferer
to be especially unjust.
[t] I.e., do menial work.
[u] Cf. e.g. Job 34.35–37.
[v] Cf. Job 11.7–9.

I modestly go through the squares of my city,
(my) voice was not loud and my speech was gentle.
I do not go about with head upraised, but look at the ground,
like a slave I do not praise (my God) in the assembly of my
   associates.
²⁹⁵May the god who has abandoned me help me,
may the goddess who (has betrayed me) show me mercy,
the shepherd, the sun of the people,ʷ be [gracious] to me like a god!

34. *'I will praise the Lord of Wisdom'*

Text: W. G. Lambert, *Babylonian Wisdom Literature*, 1960, 21ff.; W. von
Soden, *MDOG* 96, 1965, 49ff.; E. Leichty, *Or* NS 28, 1959, 361ff.; R. Labat,
RPOA I, 328ff.; R. H. Pfeiffer, *ANET²*, 434ff.; R. D. Biggs, *ANET³*, 596ff.
   Literature: W. von Soden, *ZDMG* 89, 1935, 155ff.; esp. 164ff.; T. Jacobsen,
in H. Frankfort et al., *Before Philosophy*, 1949, 227ff.; R. Borger, *JCS* 18,
1964, 49ff.
   This text,ˣ which is spread over four tablets,ʸ apparently consists of more than
400 lines with four stresses and is presented as the monologue of a well-read
and poetic Babylonian in a high position, who lived in the late Cassite period
and is probably describing his own misfortune. His name was probably
Shubshi-meshre-Shakan; as the pious servant of the highest of all gods, the
'lord of wisdom', Marduk, he sees him as both the author of his suffering, his
persecution and his sickness, and his saviour, whose saving intervention he
foresees in three dreams. As the introductory verse (the title) stresses, to
praise him is the concern of the poem: the problem of theodicy is dealt with in
a restrained fashion (tablet II, 12–38); the author probably regarded it as
insoluble. The work itself is probably to be dated in the twelfth century BC;
after an introduction which has been missing for a long time but has now re-
appeared, at least in part,ᶻ it presents four main themes with some subsidiary
material: the poet, like a true-blooded Pharisee, is conscious of no misdeeds,
but thinks that he has lived a pious life. He tells how the god withdrew his
hand from him, how he subsequently suffered, and how in dreams he then
experienced deliverance and how in fact this finally came about thanks to the
grace of Marduk.
   The evidence breaks off before a more detailed account of the change in his

   ʷ The king. – Cf. e.g. II Sam. 5.2 (I Chron. 11.2); Jer. 23.1f.; Ezek. 34.1-10; Ps.
78.71f.
   ˣ The text as arranged on the tablets is to be found in Lambert, op. cit., 31, 37, 47,
57.
   ʸ The fact that the fragmentary fourth tablet belongs to the text is now no longer
disputed.
   ᶻ The first twelve verses, cf. Leichty, op. cit.; they celebrate the power and fearfulness
of Marduk.

fortunes; we do, however, learn from an additional fragment at least that there
was a detailed description of the speedy recovery of the victim. His rehabilitation at court, in public opinion and in the family, and Marduk's renewed grace,
may have been the closing themes of the poem. Because of its connection with
the discourses of Job,[a] large sections of it are cited here.[b]

Tablet I, 43-56

My god has forsaken me and has disappeared,
my goddess has given me up and keeps her distance.[c]
[45]My guardian spirit, who walked at my side, has turned away,
the spirit who protected me has disappeared and is concerned with
    someone else.
My status has vanished and my appearance has become sombre,
my pride has run away and my protection made off.
Fearful omens are given to me,
[50]my house is forbidden me, and I wander around outside,
the organs of the animals which I inspect are swollen each day (?).
I must constantly go to the diviner and the interpreter of dreams.
My reputation is bad on the streets,
when I lie (on my bed) at night, my dream is full of terror.
[55]The heart of the king, the shoot of the gods,[d] the sun of his people,
is angry (with me) and is not easy to appease.

Tablet I 68-92

In their hearts they rage (the demons) against me, blaze like fire,
delight in acting against me with slander and lies.[e]
[70]They gagged my noble mouth like . . .
so that I, who was accustomed to speak, am like a dumb man.
My hearty shout is reduced to silence,
my head, which was (once) held high, is bowed down to the ground.
Fear has weakened my strong heart.
[75]Even a boy can turn back my (once) broad chest.
My arms, once strong, are both paralysed (?).
I, who (once) strode along as a noble, have learned to slip by unnoticed.
From being a dignitary I have become a slave.
Although (?) belonging (?) to a large family, I have become a recluse.
[80]When I go on the street, men point their finger (?) at me;

---

[a] Job 9f.; 12–14; 21; 29–31.
[b] The numbering of the verses follows Lambert.
[c] Note, too, the allusions to the language of OT lamentations, here e.g. Ps. 22.1.
[d] Literally, 'the flesh of the gods'; what is meant is perhaps 'the one who (cares for)
the well-being of the gods'.
[e] Cf. e.g. Ps. 35.11, 20f.

when I enter the palace, eyes follow me (?),
my city looks upon me as an enemy,
(indeed) my land is dark and evil,
the one who (was like a) brother to me has become a stranger,
[85]my companion has turned into a scoundrel and an adversary.[f]
In his rage my comrade denounces me,
my companions constantly sharpen (?) their weapons.
My good friend has put my life in danger,
my slave has cursed me for all to hear,
[90]my house . . . the mob calumniates me,
when an acquaintance sees me he goes past on the other side (?),
my family treat me as though I did not belong to them.

Tablet II 1-5

I waited for the next year, the appointed time passed,
(then) when I looked around, it (continued to be) very bad.
My misery became (still) greater, I did not find the right.
I called to (my) god, but he did not let me see his face,[g]
I prayed to my goddess, but she did not raise her head.

Tablet II 12f.

Like one who has not poured libations to (his) god
nor invoked (his) goddess at a meal,

Tablet II 17-27

Who was negligent and despised their (the gods') rites,
who taught his people neither reverence nor worship,
but ate his meal without calling on his god
[20]and despised his goddess by bringing her no meal offering,
like one who succumbed to vanity and forgot his lord,
frivolously swore a holy oath by his god, there I stand.
I was full of zeal in supplication and prayer,
[25]prayer was my will and sacrifice my rule,
the day for reverencing (my) god was a delight to my heart,
the date of the procession of (my) goddess gave me profit and gain,
the prayer for the king[h] was a joy to me.

Tablet II 36-42

But who knows the will of the heavenly ones,
who understands the plans of the gods in the underworld?

[f] Cf. e.g. Ps. 55.12ff., and for the context not least Job 19.13-20.
[g] Cf. e.g. Pss. 13.1; 88.14; 102.2; 143.7.
[h] Cf. Pss. 28.8f.; 61.6f.; 84.8f.; also I Sam. 2.10b.

Where have mortals (ever) understood what god does and what he does not do?[i]
The one who was yesterday still alive – today he is dead (?);
[40]darkness suddenly came over him, and then he soon rejoiced again.
One moment he was singing full of jubilation,
and now he is lamenting like a professional mourner . . .

Tablet II 112–118

My god did not come to my rescue, did not hold my hand,
my goddess did not look graciously on me, did not come to my side.
My grave was already waiting, and what was needed to bury me was ready.
[115]Lamentation rang out even before I was dead.
My whole country said, 'How he has been brought to an end!'
The one who envies me heard it and his countenance lit up,
the one who envies me was told it, and her heart was quickened.

35. 'Man and God' – the 'Sumerian Job'

Text: J. J. van Dijk, *La sagesse* (cf. p. 133 n. b), 122f.; S. N. Kramer, *HTR* 49, 1956, 9ff.; id., *FTS*, 147ff. (= *GbS*, 94ff.); id., *SVT* 3, 1960, 172ff.; id., *Sumerians*, 126ff.; id., *ANET*[3], 589ff.; J. J. van Dijk, in *HRG* I, 1971, 495ff.
Literature, partly as above, also E. J. Gordon, *BiOr* 17, 1960, 149; M. Lambert, *RA* 56, 1962, 82 no. 77; W. G. Lambert, *Babylonian Wisdom Literature*, 10.

This Sumerian counterpart to the preceding Akkadian poems about theodicy, which probably comes from the end of the third millennium, has only been known to us for a short time. S. N. Kramer has managed to reconstruct it from six fragments copied about 1800 BC and coming from Nippur. Far removed from all theological speculation, in 'Sumerian pragmatism', an anonymous man is introduced here who for no reason has been involved in misfortune. However, he does not protest, but asks for deliverance in humble lament and petition – for no man, he says, is free from guilt. In the end the pious sufferer is heard and saved, and finally praises his god. The nucleus of this simple piece of teaching is strongly reminiscent of the prose framework to the biblical book of Job (1.1–2.10; 42.7–9), though that is of course about 1500 years later. The text follows Kramer, *ANET*[3], and in part van Dijk, *HRG* I.

[1-5]Let a man constantly praise the supremacy of his god,
the young man[j] simply praise the words of his god;
(yet) may those who live in the land around (also) lament!

---

[i] Cf. Job 11.7ff.; Eccles. 8.16f.; 11.5.
[j] The Sumerian term means a young, strong (and highly regarded) man.

Let him comfort his friend and companion in the house of . . .
[5] let him soothe his[k] heart!

[26-38]I am a (young) man of understanding – (yet) though I have
    understanding, it is of no use to me,
My true word becomes lies.
The deceiver has brought the (destructive) south wind upon me, (and
    now) I must serve him.
If I have no understanding, I come to ruin before you,
[30]you have constantly brought new grief upon me;
when I go into the house, my senses are darkened,
when I go out on the street, a (respected) man, my heart is oppressed.
(Even) my trusty shepherd has become angry at me, a (respected) man,
    and looks at me askance,
he lifts his hand against me, though I am not his enemy.
[35]My companion does not say a good word to me,
my friends turn my true speech into lies,
the deceiver has noted down wicked things against me –
(but) do you, my god, take it not into reckoning.
[63-73]Ah, let my mother who bore me make no end to her lamentation
    before you,
let my sister strike up no joyful hymn, no happy song,
[65](rather) let them sadly lament my misfortune before you.
Let my wife name my sorrows in sadness,
let the lamenters bemoan my bitter lot.
My god – the day shines brightly over the land, (but) for me the day is
    dark,
the bright day, the good day . . .
[70]Tears, laments, distress and pain abide in me,
suffering overpowers me like one doomed to nothing but tears,
the evil spirit of destiny holds me in its hand and takes away my
    breath of life,
the malignant demon of sickness bathes in my body . . .

[100-103]How long[l] will you continue to leave me without guidance?
They, the great wise ones, proclaim a true and just word:
'A sinless child was never born of its mother,
there has never been an innocent boy from ancient times.'[m]

---

[k] I.e., the god's.
[l] A question which is also typical of the lamentations in the OT; cf. e.g. Pss. 6.3;
13.1f.
[m] Cf. Prov. 20.9; Job 15.14–16; 25.4–6; also Gen. 8.21 (J).

[118-129]The bitter tears and lamentations of the man found a hearing
with his god,
when the cries of woe and weeping with which he was overwhelmed
had soothed the heart of his god for him.
[120]The just utterance, the simple, pure word which he spoke was
accepted by his god,
the confession,[n] which the man earnestly made,
found grace before . . . his god, his god took his hand away in the face
of the oppressive words of disaster,
the demon of sickness who had encompassed him with widespread
wings rushed away,
the [suffering?] which had cast him down like . . ., he drove off.
[125]The demon of evil fate which had established itself, he commanded
to depart according to his verdict.
He changed the man's grief into joy,
gave him the . . . gracious . . . spirit as a protector and guardian,
(and) gave him a guardian spirit with a friendly countenance.
(But) the man did not cease to praise his god . . .

36. *Lament for Urnammu of Ur*

Text and commentary, G. Castellino, *ZA* 52, 1957, 1ff.; S. N. Kramer,
JCS 21, 1967, 104ff.; textual information on p. 112; M. Lambert, *RA* 55, 1961,
196, no. 74; C. Wilcke, *Actes de la XVIIe rencontre assyriologique*, Comité belge
de recherches en Mésopotamie, 1970, 81ff.

This Sumerian text was previously known to us only from a fragment, and
was at first thought to be epic or mythical. It has only recently been reconstructed
by S. N. Kramer and C. Wilcke from numerous fragments located in Philadelphia, Istanbul and Jena. It is a lament bewailing the apparently premature
and perhaps violent death of Urnammu, the founder of the Third Dynasty of
Ur and creator of the last Sumerian empire. The speaker is the king's widow,
and it may have been composed not long after the event, before 2000 BC. In
view of the mighty acts of Urnammu and his numerous works of piety, the
poem sees his death as an apparent injustice on the part of the gods An and
Enlil, who determine men's fate. This complaint is put on the lips of the
dead ruler himself, and he makes it from the underworld. The goddess Inanna
is particularly close to the king, since she is the sovereign lady of the city of
Uruk from which he comes, and vainly seeks to bring him help; towards the
end of the text she accuses these gods of breaking their word – probably
because of a very different pronouncement of An and Enlil to Urnammu which
had been given formerly at his enthronement. Thus this poem, too, is concerned

---

[n] Text: 'the words'.

with theodicy.° In contrast to the 'Sumerian Job', the concern here is not with any rehabilitation of the righteous sufferer. What is accorded to him is simply a posthumous reputation, thanks to the explanation given by Inanna.ᵖ The text runs to more than 230 verses. The beginning is uncertain and the end is damaged. At first it laments the misfortune which has come upon Sumer by Urnammu's premature end; it then goes on to speak - in phrases which are unfortunately obscure - of the death of the king and his funeral rites; it describes his entry into the underworld, his sacrifice for its gods and his inclusion in the hierarchy of the realm of the dead, which is brought about by his 'beloved brother Gilgamesh'. As Urnammu hears the 'lament of Sumer' from the world above, he utters his bitter reproaches against the gods who have determined his fate and have prepared so undeserved an end for him, the one who has been just and pious. The lamentation probably ended with Inanna's vain attempt to secure from Enlil the king's return to life. The sections which are most significant for our present purpose run as follows:

Introduction
6-11 (*JCS* 21, 116ff.)
Disaster came upon Sumer, the righteous shepherd�q was snatched away,
the righteous shepherd Urnammu was snatched away, (yes,) the righteous shepherd was snatched away.
An altered his holy word,ʳ his heart . . . was comfortless,
treacherous Enlil altered all the determinations of fate.
¹⁰Then Ninmahˢ began a lament in her . . .
Enkiᵗ closed the door before Eridu . . .

Urnammu's lament in the underworld
144-168 (*JCS* 21, 118ff.)
When seven, indeed ten days had passed,
¹⁴⁵the cries of woe from Sumer reached myᵘ king,
the cries of woe from Sumerᵛ reached Urnammu,
[the lamentation over] the walls of Ur which he had not been able to complete,

° Cf. Kramer, op. cit., 104; Wilcke, op. cit., 86.
ᵖ Wilcke, op. cit., 91f.
q For this designation for the king cf. (e.g.) again II Sam. 5.2; Ezek. 34.1-10; Ps. 78.71f.
ʳ Cf. Ps. 89.34f., 38ff.
ˏˢ Mother goddess.
ᵗ As usual, in opposition to An and Enlil.
ᵘ Urnammu's widow is speaking.
ᵛ What is meant is probably the cultic lament at the official mourning for the king in Ur.

over his new palace which he had built, but in which he had (as yet)
   had no joy –
[he,] the shepherd, who could no longer care for (?) his house –
¹⁵⁰[over] his spouse, whom he could no longer clasp to his breast,
[over] his son, whom he could no longer place on his knee . . .
[over] his little sisters, whom he could no longer . . .
[Then] . . . my king [wept],
the righteous shepherd burst out in heart-rending lamentations.
¹⁵⁵'What happened to me was appropriate:
I served the gods well, prepared for them . . .
gave to the Anunnaki what was well-pleasing to them,
overwhelmed with treasure their resting places, adorned with lapis
   lazuli.ʷ
Nevertheless, no godˣ supported me and soothed my heart.
¹⁶⁰. . . my favourable omen vanished into the depths of heaven,ʸ
I, who served the gods day and night – now the day ends sleeplessly
   for me.ᶻ
As though I were detained by a rainstorm (?) from heaven,
alas, now I cannot arrive at the turreted walls of Ur.
¹⁶⁵As though my wife were swallowed up (in it),
I spend my day in bitter tears and lamentations.
My strength has gone,
in one day the hand (?) of fate has . . . me, the warrior . . .'

Inanna's attempt at help and her lamentationᵃ
198–210 (Wilcke, op. cit., 86f.)

Inanna humbly [entered] the glistening Ekur,ᵇ
before Enlil's terrifying countenance with rolling eyes (?):
²⁰⁰'Great mistress of Eanna,ᶜ the one who has died no longer [returns]
   to us, even for your sake!
The righteous shepherd has abandoned Eanna, and [you will] not see
   him again!'

Line 202 is unclear

   ʷ There is archaeological and documentary evidence for Urnammu's extraordinary
measures to restore the cult and the temples after their decline during the Gutaean
period.
   ˣ Inanna's attitude is passed over here.
   ʸ Literally 'was as far as heaven'.
   ᶻ Metaphorical: without pay.
   ᵃ Note the translation variants in *JCS* 21, 1967, lines 198ff.
   ᵇ The chief temple of Enlil (the ruling god of Sumer) in Nippur.
   ᶜ Inanna, whose sanctuary in Uruk is called Eanna, is addressed: Enlil answers her
tacit question.

Inanna, the fearful light, the oldest daughter of Sin,[d]
shakes the heaven and makes the earth quake,[e]
[205]Inanna destroys the sheepfold and burns (?) the pen:
'I will hurl it at An, king of the gods,[f] as abuse,
Enlil has made me lift up my head with him[g] – who has changed this
      word?
The exalted word which King An has spoken – who has changed this
      word?
Are the rules which hold in the land, the commandments which are
      set up, to have no force?
[210]Will there no longer be abundance and . . . for the place of the
      gods[h] on which the sun rises?'[i]

---

[d] The moon god of Ur.
[e] In anger because of Enlil's refusal. Cf. e.g. Jer. 10.10; Ps. 68.8.
[f] Cf. Pss. 95.3; 96.4; 97.9.
[g] With Urnammu: the reference is probably to the rites of the sacred marriage.
[h] Meaning the Sumerian Olympus.
[i] The altering of Urnammu's destiny by An and Enlil would, Inanna charges, disrupt
the ordering of the world.

C

HITTITE TEXTS

INTRODUCTION

The remains of the Hittite capital of Hattusa near the modern Anatolian village of Boghazköy (about ninety miles east of Ankara as the crow flies) have already provided decisive material for our knowledge of the Old Testament. They were described for the first time in 1837 as a significant ruined city, and since H. Winckler's first visit in the year 1905 have been investigated almost constantly, at first somewhat inappropriately, but already with great initial success. More than ten thousand clay tablets inscribed with Babylonian cuneiform (only a very few of which have survived intact) have presented us with a great many texts[a] from which it is possible for us to construct a picture of the Hittite empire and its culture - though excavation, publication, reconstruction and editing are still far from complete.

Most of the Boghazköy texts are composed in Hittite, but there are also texts in foreign languages which serve as examples of cultural influence. We have evidence of Sumerian, which at that time was the classic language of educated men, of Akkadian, which was the international language of communication, of Hurrian, which was spoken above all in northern Mesopotamia, and Hattian, Palaic and Luwian, the languages of Asia Minor. The term 'Hittite' goes back to early research at the beginning of this century; the ancient name for it was Nesian; along with Palaic and Luwian, it represents the earliest written branch of the Indo-European group of languages.[b]

---

[a] E. Laroche, *Catalogue des textes hittites*, EeC 75, 1971, 192, reckons on a total number of 550–600 works or individual sections.

[b] Another element of this 'Anatolian' branch is the so-called 'hieroglyphic Hittite' of

The earliest document in Hittite may go back well into the eighteenth century BC (the copy we have is, of course, much later), and is still an isolated instance, but a series of significant inscriptions go back to the so-called Old Kingdom (the first half of the sixteenth to the beginning of the fifteenth century). After a period which is still largely obscure to us, the 'Middle Kingdom', there follows the era of the New Kingdom, from about the middle of the fourteenth to the end of the thirteenth century, from which the bulk of our texts derive.

Hittite literature is divided into a large number of genres – with an insignificant number of exceptions it comes from the state archives, and above all from the archives of the 'great temple' (the centre of the state cult in the capital) and also from the archives of the royal citadel. There is almost no trace at all so far in Boghazköy of private business texts and documents connected with private law, genres which are attested abundantly e.g. in Mesopotamia. What have emerged here are historical accounts, like chronicles, and historically significant genres, like the annals of rulers; domestic and foreign state correspondence; a collection of laws (primarily connected with the principle of compensation and not with that of retribution), edicts, state treaties, which are again significant for the history of the genre; investiture documents, instructions for state functionaries, regulations for court ceremonial, minutes of official hearings, inventories, lists of properties, general lists of places, officials and people which were needed for state administration; library catalogues, directions for the training of chariot horses (which were tactically important), lexical and literary teaching material for the education of scribes, stories resembling folk tales or romances, and written evidence of a religious and magical nature (in quantity and extent this represents by far the most significant part of the Hittite texts).[c] There is an abundance of descriptions of cultic practices and festivals of all kinds, partly with formulae and sayings in foreign languages,[d] lists of sacrifices, 'inventories of the cult' (lists with brief descriptions of representations of deities and their cults), myths, hymns, prayers, vows, questions put to oracles along with their answers, collections of omens and a large number of magical

---

inscriptions on rock and stone in Asia Minor and Syria, which is still difficult to master. This is better termed 'hieroglyphic' or 'pictorial' Luwian, like the Lycian and Lydian languages, which are first attested in the classical period.

[c] More than half of the numbers given in E. Laroche, op. cit. With a number of continuation tablets and duplicates they appear strikingly more often than the texts of other genres.

[d] The intention was to address the relevant deity effectively in his own language, if he belonged to another ethnic stratum.

rituals for all possible happenings and disasters in the life of the individual or the state.[e]

Texts from this sphere of religion and magic (and indeed those of other genres) begin from the recognition that history – which is not seen as moving towards a goal – and individual life are determined by a sequence of interactions between gods and men. The gods, the number of whom is legion (the texts speak of the 'thousand gods' in the land of the Hittites alone), are human beings writ large. (The exceptions are a few deities in the form of animals and some natural phenomena, abstract concepts, holy objects and places which are regarded as divine.) They are in possession of a 'divine power' which enables them to do all kinds of things impossible for men, whether existentially, physically or logically. Depending on their sphere of activity, they are divided into gods above the earth and gods below; some of the latter gods have a sinister or hostile attitude towards men, whereas otherwise the attitude of the gods is more positive or at least ambivalent.

Men, who are constantly and above all interested in a good life in this world, are at the service of the gods (at least until death, which changes them into sometimes dangerous spirits, *manes*, to whom sacrifices must therefore be offered, and transfers them to the underworld). However, as mankind has a tendency to evil, and indeed is in fact corrupt,[f] conflicts arise. For cultic and also moral transgressions provoke the wrath of the gods, which brings about sorrow, untimely death or, on a larger scale, catastrophes. The success of individuals or states is seen as a sign of the favour of the guardian deity or the pantheon of the state (usually well-deserved, but sometimes quite gratuitous). The gods of enemies are reconciled to this, or in the case of a conflict or a war (waged on both the human and the divine levels) must eventually bow to higher law and – if the conflict has been between states – be incorporated into the pantheon of the victor; at the least they must be guarantors of the treaty which is established when peace is made, along with the gods of the other nation.

The close interweaving of state and cult is expressed in the high-priestly functions of the king at many important divine festivals which were held throughout the land, and in his ultimate responsibility for national catastrophes (including natural disasters and epidemics). It was

[e] E. Laroche has counted about 170 surviving descriptions of cults, festivals and magic rituals; by a statistical comparison with the titles which appear in the library catalogues that have survived, he has estimated that there were once about 1200 works of this kind (op. cit.).

[f] For the sinfulness of men cf. no. 6 § 8 below. Other texts also mention this: the Arzawa state treaties assert that mankind is false or misled (J. Friedrich, MVÄG 31/2, 1926, 135, §21 etc.). Hattusilis III talks of the generally evil attitude of mankind in *KUB* I 1 + I 49 (A. Goetze, MVÄG 29/3, 1925, 11).

in accordance with this exposed position of the ruler that he was particularly concerned to protect himself against chance[g] ritual impurity or
ritual impurity conjured up by black magic, as against anything introduced from outside which would incur divine anger or misfortune. As
in the life of the common man, it is clear from this that not only ritual
neglect and other faults, but also unfriendly powers manipulated by man
('impurity', 'curse', 'evil tongue', etc.) could bring about disaster and
destruction. Thus the catalogue of counter-measures to be taken by

8. Extract from the great rock relief of the sanctuary of Yazilikaya
near Boghazköy, second half of the thirteenth century BC. The height
of the group of figures on the left is 2.52m. This is the meeting of
the chief gods in the middle of the procession: the Hurrian weather
god Teshub, standing on two subservient mountain gods, with his
bulls Seri and Hurri, before his consort Hebat and their son
Sarruma, who are standing on two wild cats. To the right - and out
of the picture - is a long procession of goddesses, while Teshub is
leading the procession of male deities (wearing horned crowns).
The more important gods (marked out by their inclusion near to
the middle of the picture or by their adornments and the number
of horns on their 'crowns') are denoted by hieroglyphic inscriptions
which confirm the Hurrian interpretation of the picture of the
pantheon. This and certain details of the pictorial representation
reflect the Hurrian influence which was exerted during the period
of the empire.

[g] E.g. through a hair which has carelessly been allowed to fall into water intended for
the palace. We can see how seriously such an incident was taken from the subsequent
execution of the careless water-carrier: *KUB* XIII 3 III 21-31 (J. Friedrich, *FS
B. Meissner*, MAOG 4, 1928, 50).

anyone afflicted by fate and in cases of catastrophe (and indeed in expectation of such blows) include magical means: the usual pious concern to earn the favour of the gods, the various methods of discovering their motives and their wills, prayer and vows, are supplemented by the attempt to influence and compel the deity by an incantation which combines petitions and magical rites and thus more or less openly introduces the constraint of magic – even when there is a concern to remove or ward off the effects or the fear of witchcraft. The ambivalence detectable in this attitude was hardly a problem, as is indicated by the myth that when the gods themselves are at a loss, they take refuge in magic.

The texts are therefore aware that the gods, who are otherwise so powerful, occasionally have need of such expedients. Even more, it is evident that these gods are virtually dependent on men, living on their sacrifices and sometimes on their accomplishments (which at times are dubious).

This is the point of contact for the religious ideas (liable to insignificant alteration through various ethnic influences) which form the background to the Hittite texts.

For reasons of space, the selection of texts which follows is a very limited one, but it may provide some useful comparative material to set against the Old Testament. From time to time an indication is given of the ethnic strata in which the particular evidence is rooted. It should be noted that the Hattian stratum should be regarded as the native, earliest material. It seems to have had a renaissance in the revival of the cult of Nerik around the middle of the thirteenth century. We must reckon with Hurrian influence after the encounter of the Old Kingdom with its Hurrian neighbours in the East. This influence is detectable to a greater extent after the beginning of the New Kingdom, and continues with increasing force down to its end. The mediating role of the Hurrians should be stressed here; they may have been instrumental in passing on both Sumero-Babylonian and Canaanite material to Anatolia. Numerous Luwian elements in the language of the New Kingdom bear witness to the strong influence exercised by the Luwians, who had settled in the south and south-east of Anatolia, on the thought and life of the Hittites, who were akin to them. We must be content here with noting that many Hittite ritual texts, for example, go back to Luwian authors.

It may be stressed that none of these texts can be later than the fall of Hattusa about or in the years soon after 1200 BC. However, in many cases it is clear that the work is to be dated earlier.

General bibliography:
A. Goetze, *Kleinasien, Kulturgeschichte des Altertums*, HAW III/1, [2]1957;

H. Otten, 'Das Hethiterreich', in H. Schmökel (ed.), *Kulturgeschichte des alten Orient*, 1961;
E. von Schuler, 'Kleinasien', in H. W. Haussig, *WM* I 1, 1965;
H. Otten, 'Die Religionen des Alten Kleinasien', in *Religionsgeschichte des alten Orients*, HO VIII/I/1, 1964;
G. Walser (ed.), *Neuere Hethiterforschung*, *Historia* Einzelschrift 7, 1964;
G. Steiner, 'Gott (nach hethitische Texten)', *RLA* III, 1971, 547–575;
O. R. Gurney, *The Hittites*, ²1954.

I. MYTHS

The following myths (and extracts from myths), which contrast with the Old Testament, come from a Hurrian and Hattian milieu; their different origin is also expressed in a difference in type. We have the myths of Hurrian origin in the form of epic poems. The gods whom they portray are clearly influenced by Babylon; this bears witness to their considerable age – they may go back to the end of the third millennium and the beginning of the second. Canaanite influence can also be seen; this is only to be expected in view of the close links between the Hurrians, the Amorites and the Canaanites. One of the chief concerns of Hurrian mythology seems to be to describe the development of the contemporary distribution of power among the gods with a wealth of imagination, a passion for detail and no ethical scruples.

The myths of Anatolian and Hattian origin are less entertaining: they set out to account for the origin and occasion of particular rites, to explain their significance and present use, and to show the relationship between gods and men. It is usual for a more or less extensive description of the rite in question to be added, and this also provides a formal demonstration of the auxiliary function of Hattian myth.

1. *From the Song of Ullikummi, tablet 3: the separation of heaven and earth*

Text: *KUB* XXXIII 106 III 23–55. Literature: H. G. Güterbock, *JCS* 6, 1952, 27ff.

References to the origin of the world are extremely rare in Hittite literature. The cycle of myths about the god Kumarbi, taken over from the Hurrians, has for long been the only material worth mentioning among this considerable scarcity of texts. Part of the cycle, the Song of Ullikummi, the son of the deposed king of the gods, makes a brief mention of the building of heaven and earth as a totality. It was evidently built by the 'age-old' gods, who were not even known by name, on the shoulders of the primaeval giant Upelluri. The separation of heaven and earth is also put somewhere in this obscure primal period (the theme can also be found in Sumerian and Egyptian mythology). The Song of Ullikummi mentions this event because the way in which it was achieved is a model for the way in which Teshub, the Hurrian weather god,[h] is able to defend and establish his rule over the gods in the face of the powerful rebel Ullikummi.

Genesis 1.4, 6, 7, 14, 18 are the most relevant comparative texts from the OT.

[23]When Ea had fi[nished speaking], he [began to go]. . . . And Upelluri [lifted up his] eyes [and he beheld (?)] Ea]. And Upelluri [began to say] to Ea, 'May you live, O Ea!' [And he arose(?). Then Ea began] to return a greeting to Upelluri: ['May you live,] Upelluri, in the dark earth, (you) upon whom [heaven and ear]th are built!' [30]Ea [again] began to [sa]y to Upelluri: 'Do you not know? Has no one, Upelluri, given you the news? Do you not know the speedy god,[i] whom Kumarbi created against the gods? And how Kumarbi, utterly intent on the death and destruction of the weather god, has created an [35]adversary for him? Do you not know the *kunkunuzzi* stone which grew down in the water? Like an . . . (embrasure? shield? mushroom?) it towers(?) on high and envelops/covers the houses of the gods and even Hebat![j] Do you really not know that speedy god, Upelluri, as the dark earth is distant (from what has happened)?' [40]Upelluri began to reply to Ea: 'When heaven and earth were built upon me, I was not aware (of it). Nor was I aware of the way in which they came and separated heaven and earth with an iron blade. And now something is hurting my right shoulder. But I do not know who that god is.' [45] When Ea heard these words, he looked at Upelluri's right shoulder. And behold, the *kunkunuzzi* stone was set on Upelluri's right shoulder like a . . .! Then Ea answered and began to say to the age-old gods: 'Hear my words, you age-old gods who know of [50]earlier things. Open up again the ancient storehouses of your mothers, fathers and forefathers. Bring the ancient ancestral seal so that the (houses) can be sealed up once again. And bring (out) the ancient saw with which heaven and earth were divided from one another, and sever Ullikummi, the *kunku-nuzzi* stone, whom Kumarbi raised to be the adversary of the gods, [55]at his feet.'

[h] 'Weather god' (or storm god) is a designation for the type of masculine fertility god whose activity was seen above all in tempest and storm, and in life-giving downpours. The Hittite pantheon knew countless local manifestations of the type.

[i] Ullikummi is given this name because of his wonderfully quick growth (or shooting up). In fifteen days he has grown up to heaven. The underlying idea is perhaps that of a volcano.

[j] Sun goddess, consort of Teshub, chief goddess of the Hurrian pantheon and as such 'queen of heaven'.

2. *The kingship in heaven*

Text: *KUB* XXXIII 120 + 119 = XXXVI 31. Duplicate XXXVI 1. Edited by H. G. Güterbock, *Kumarbi, Mythen vom churritischen Kronos*, 1946, 6ff.; H. Otten, *Mythen vom Gotte Kumarbi*, VIOF 3, 1950, 5ff. Date: not later than the first half of the fourteenth century BC.

In connection with the separation of heaven and earth and, according to the text to be discussed here, probably after that event, the beginning of a kingship was set 'in heaven'.[k] This was presumably meant to indicate a further step in cosmic organization. Two conceptions gave the Sumerians, Egyptians and Babylonians occasion to compose mythical accounts of historical facts, changes and pressures in the cult, in terms of relationships, descent and power-struggles among the gods: the notions that the gods have a human (indeed all too human) nature and that the strength of the gods, who produced sons and daughters, was subject to a certain process of aging. The myths about the Hurrian god Kumarbi occasionally go back to mythological features and names in Sumerian and Babylonian thought, but also display a creative freshness and strength of their own, which demonstrate that they are far removed from the often tedious phase of theological systematization. Informative and entertaining at the same time, they depict the course of universal rule, the history of the kingship in heaven. With great narrative skill they put the third king of heaven in a central position, as being the most interesting protagonist: Alalu and Anu each reigned over the gods for nine years until they were dethroned by their son, vizier and successor, and expelled. In addition, Kumarbi castrates his father Anu, but this action causes him special difficulties. He is miraculously made pregnant by Anu's 'manhood' and is compelled to give life to several other hostile gods including Teshub, the mighty weather god. Teshub succeeds in overthrowing Kumarbi. The Song of Ullikummi[l] describes how the crafty Kumarbi does not give up: by means of a rock thought of as being in female form, he fathers the stony Ullikummi, and succeeds in bringing him up on Upelluri's shoulder, without knowledge of the heavenly beings, in order to take his revenge. The passage quoted above described the threat presented to the perplexed group of gods round Teshub by the young stone giant; future developments are also indicated. Once severed from Upelluri's shoulder, Ulli-kummi loses his power and Teshub maintains and strengthens his rule. The story now follows the lines of the myth of the guardian deity: after some tem-

---

[k] It does not seem quite logical for the myth to localize rule in heaven in I 18, and then in I 22-24 to talk as though this were set on earth and heaven were a different region.
[l] There is a further myth which belongs here and which is very similar to the Song of Ullikummi in its conception. Unfortunately it has been preserved in a rather bad state: it deals with Kumarbi's son Hedammu, who has the form of a snake. He comes forth from the sea and undermines the rule of the king of heaven by wreaking devastation on earth. However, he is tricked by the seductive arts of the goddess Ishtar and is then presumably destroyed by the weather god and his helpers (cf. J. Siegelová, *Appu-Marchen und Hedammu-Mythus*, StBT 14, 1971).

porarily successful attacks by the guardian deity Lama (Hurrian Nubadig?), Teshub's supremacy is finally recognized by the gods (including Kumarbi).

Elements of the myth, in particular details of the sequence of generations, came to the West, probably passed on there by North Syrian and Aegean trade (cf. the later account e.g. in Hesiod's *Theogony*). OT parallels are provided by texts which assert Yahweh's kingship over the gods (thus Ps. 95.3, for content also Pss. 29 and 82; Pss. 96.4 and 97.7, 9, essentially also passages like I Kings 22.19ff.). Of course the OT, governed as it is by exclusive Yahweh worship, has no place for theomachies or theogonies. (Similarly, it is more concerned with Yahweh's kingship over Israel or individual Israelites; cf. e.g. Ex. 15.17f.; Deut. 33.5; I Sam. 8.7; 12.12; Pss. 44.4; 74.12 or 5.2; 84.3.)

Lines I 1-7 of this Hittite text are fragmentary. Prayers are made in them to pairs or groups of gods who are called upon elsewhere essentially to witness or guarantee oaths. Thus I 1-4 are addressed to the 'age-old' gods, who are thought of as long-departed divine ancestors, 'fathers and mothers', living in the underworld, with knowledge of all the past. I 5f. are addressed to Ishara, the god of oaths, and the two Sumerian gods Enlil and Ninlil (among others). The myth then begins:

Once upon a time Alalu was king. Alalu sat upon the throne and the mighty Anu, the first among the gods, stood before him [10](in service). He bowed down at (his) feet, whenever he handed him his cup to drink. Alalu was king in heaven for nine 'counted' years. In the ninth year Anu made war on Alalu. He defeated Alalu, who fled before him and went down to the dark earth. [15]He went down to the dark earth, and Anu (now) sat on his throne. Anu sat on his throne and the mighty Kumarbi waited on him with food. He bowed down at his feet, whenever he handed him his cup to drink.

Anu was king in heaven for nine 'counted' years. In the ninth year Anu made war on Kumarbi. Kumarbi, the offspring of Alalu, [20]made war on Anu. He could not withstand Kumarbi's gaze:[m] Anu extricated himself from Kumarbi's hand and he, Anu, flew up to heaven. Kumarbi pursued him. He seized Anu by the feet and dragged him down from heaven. [25]He bit (off) his genitals. His manhood slid(?) down into Kumarbi's body like iron. As Kumarbi gulped down Anu's manhood he rejoiced and laughed aloud. Anu turned to him and began to say, 'Do you rejoice because you have swallowed my manhood? [30]Do not rejoice for your body. I have laid a burden upon you in your body: first, I have made you pregnant with the mighty weather god. Secondly, I have made you pregnant with the untameable river Aranzah.[n] Thirdly, I have made you pregnant with the mighty god Tasmi(su). I have made you carry three

___

[m] Properly 'eyes'.
[n] The Hurrian name for the Tigris.

fearful gods as a burden in your body, and finally (in grief) you will come [35]to smite the rocks of Mount Tassa with your head!'
When Anu had finished speaking, he r[ose] up to heaven and hid himself. Kumarbi spat out of his mouth. The cunning king spat out of his mouth . . .

From this point on the text is in very bad condition; however, it indicates that the seed which was spat out impregnated (?) a mountain, but that to his rage Kumarbi still had to bear the three gods who had been foretold. In Nippur, the city of his Sumerian counterpart Enlil, the king of the gods, he counts the months of his pregnancy. When they have come to an end Anu seems to explain to the weather god, as yet unborn, the unusual modes of birth which are possible for him. The weather god, who promises to avenge Anu, who has begotten him, decides to emerge through an opening in the body which will not make him ritually unclean. But Kumarbi, tormented by fearful pain, has this exit magically secured with the help of men, and the weather god is born in a different way. Kumarbi's intention of devouring the weather god is frustrated. Instead of this the two fight. The conclusion of the tablet, which has not been preserved, may have told of Kumarbi's fall and of the enthronement of the weather god.

3. The weather god and the dragon Illuyankas

Text: *KBo* III 7 ('A'); *KUB* XVII 5 ('B'); *KUB* XVII 6 ('C'); *KUB* XII 66 ('D') and further fragments. Transcription in E. Laroche, *RHA* 77, 1965, 65ff. Translation: A. Goetze, *Kleinasien²*, op. cit., 139f. (the myth; for some of the ritual sections see V. Haas, *Der Kult von Nerik*, StP 4, 1970, 338). Date: this is a text of the Middle (?) Kingdom in later copies.
The text, which has not been preserved complete, gives two myths describing a fight with the dragon as aetiologies of the *purulli* festival.[o] This festival was Hattian in origin and was celebrated in the North Anatolian city of Nerik and its vicinity. The explanations accompanying the myths are concerned with some aspects of the great feast of Nerik, particularly with the thank-offering for rain on Mount Zali(ya)nu, which is deified in an anthropomorphic way, and with the evidently unusual status accorded to Zalinu and his consort in the course of a sacred procession in Nerik. The principal ideas behind the annual celebration of the lengthy *purulli* festival seem to have been the local fertility cult and the assembly of the gods in the temple of the weather god of Nerik to bring grace and reconciliation to the king and thus order and blessing to the land.[p]

[o] The interpretation of this Hattian designation is still not completely certain; it may be connected with the word *mur-* ('earth').
[p] For details cf. V. Haas, op. cit., 43ff. The description of the festival proper - one of the examples which has come down to us covers a series of thirty-two tablets - indicates a long festival.

The two myths of the fight with the dragon are to be interpreted cosmo-
logically. They have been handed on in a terse style by an 'anointed' priest
(possibly as earlier and later tradition). Their common elements are the initial
defeat of the weather god by the serpent Illuyankas ('dragon') and his final
victory, which is only made possible with human help. In the first instance it
is the goddess Inaras who through her complaisance towards the man Hupasiyas
enlists his help in a treacherous surprise attack on the dragon – the weather god
has only to strike the fatal blow. In the other instance, the weather god, deprived
of his heart and his eyes, fathers his saviour on a poor girl. On marrying into the

9. Late Hittite relief on a plinth from Malatya, eleventh to ninth century
BC, 47 cm. high (Ankara Museum). The weather god is fighting with the
dragon, on whom a storm shower (with hail?) is descending. The portrayal
is clearly reminiscent of the style of the period of the Hittite empire.

family of the dragon this saviour requires his father's heart and eyes as a wedding
present. He returns these to his father, so that once they are restored his father
is again able to take up the fight against the dragon and to prove victorious.

    In both the myths the human helper comes to grief at the hands of the weather
god. Hupasiyas pays for his hybris when he expresses a longing for his earthly
wife and children. The son of the poor woman falls in a heroic struggle at the
side of his father-in-law as a member of the clan: he has told his father not to
be concerned for him. This latter heroic version seems to follow the Hurrian-
Hittite myth of the dragon Hedammu[q] by transferring the battle to the sea
and makes an interpretation much more meaningful in terms of the victory of
the powers giving order to the world over the lower powers of chaos. Presumably this myth is not originally Hattian, but one which has been taken over from
south-east Anatolia or has been influenced from that direction. Finally, it
underlies the (Greek) story of Typhon in the library of Apollodorus and has
parallels in the Canaanite myth of Baal's fight with Lothan (OT Leviathan) or
Yam, which is even reflected in the OT in allusions and reinterpretations: cf.
above all Isa. 27.1; 51.9f.; Pss. 74.13f.; 89.9f.; Job 26.12f. The opposite
emphases are also worth noticing: see Pss. 104.26; 148.7, and not least Gen.

[q] See p. 153 n. 1 above.

1.21. Of course the idea that God is in need of human help – in a synergistic sense – to establish himself and his rule is alien to the OT.

First version

[A I 1]Thus says Kella, the 'anointed' of the weather god of Nerik, the heavenly weather god [. . .] the story of the *purulli* festival is no longer (?) told as follows: [5]'May the land grow and flourish and may the land be protected!' And when it grows and flourishes, they celebrate the *purulli* festival.

When the weather god and the dragon Illuyankas fought each other [10]in the city of Kiskilussa, Illuyankas defeated the weather god. The weather god appealed to all the gods, 'Come and help me.' The goddess Inaras prepared a feast. [15]All her preparations were generous: great pots of wine, great pots of *marnuant* beer, great pots of *walhi* beer. And she filled the pots to the brim. And [Inaras] went into the [city of Z]ikaratta [20]and found a man called Hupasiyàs. Then Inaras said to Hupasiyas, 'See, this is my plan, and you must help me!' Then Hupasiyas said to Inaras, [25]'If I may sleep with you, I will come and do what you wish.' So he slept with her. Then Inaras brought Hupasiyas with her [B I 4]and hid him. Inaras [5]adorned herself and summoned Illuyankas from his hole: 'Look, I want to hold a feast. So come to eat and drink.' Then up came Illuyankas and [his children]. [10]And they ate and drank and emptied every pot and got drunk. Then they could not get back into their hole. So Hupasiyas came up and bound Illuyankas with a rope. Then the weather god came and slew Illuyankas, and the gods were with him.

[C I 14]Then Inaras built herself a house on a rock in the district of Tarukka.[r] And she let Hupasiyas live in the house. And Inaras instructed him, 'When I go over the land do not look [20]out of the window. For if you look out, you will see your wife and children.' Now when the twentieth day came, he pushed open the window and saw his wife and his children. [25]And when Inaras came back from the country, he began to cry, 'Let me go home.'

[A II 9]And Ina[ras said, 'Did I not command you, 'Do not look(?)] out'?'

At this point the text becomes badly mutilated (A II 10ff.); it indicates that in an argument with Inaras, who is evidently assisted by the weather god, Hupasiyas is killed. Inaras seems to have handed over her house to the (Hittite) king, and this becomes the occasion for the celebration of the *purulli* festival. Lines A II 21ff. form a transition to the ritual event:

The herald from Nerik brings thick bread first of all to Mount Zalinu when he pours down rain in Nerik. [25]He has asked for rain from Mount Zalinu . . .

[r] A place (like Nerik) in the north of Anatolia.

The text becomes too fragmentary and then breaks off.

Second version

D III 3 . . . The dragon Il[luyankas] had defeated [the weather god] and robbed him [of his heart and his eyes]. And the weather god [thought how he might take vengeance on him (?).] A III 4 And he took as wife the daughter of a poor man [5]and she gave birth to a son.[s] When he was grown up, he took as bride a daughter of Illuyankas. The weather god instructed his son, [10]"When you enter the house of your bride, then ask of them (my) heart and (my) eyes."[t] So when he went in he asked for the heart and they gave it to him. [15]Later he asked for the eyes and they gave them to him also. Then he brought to the weather god, his father(, what he wanted). And the weather god took back his heart and his eyes.

[20]When his body had thus been restored to its former (complete) state he went off again to the sea to do battle, and when they came out to do battle with him he began to get the upper hand over the dragon Illuyankas. And the son of the weather god was with Illuyankas, and he cried out to heaven to his father, 'Smite me too! [30]Do not save me!' Thereupon the weather god slew the dragon Illuyankas and (with him) his (own) son. And this is the weather god [. . .

About fifteen lines are missing from the following explanations given by the 'anointed' Kella. The text begins again with D IV 1ff., which is concerned with the cultic practice of Nerik (as is the first version of the myth). Again the central position is occupied by the mountain god Zalinu.

D IV 1 . . .] the [forem]ost gods made themselves the last (?) for the 'anointed one' and the last (?) made themselves the foremost gods. [5]The store for the grain (offering) of the god Zalinu is great and that of Zashapuna the consort of Zalinu is greater than the weather god in Nerik. A IV 4 continues:The gods said to the 'anointed' Tahpurili: 'When we go to the weather god of Nerik, where shall we sit?' And the 'anointed' Tahpurili said, 'If you should sit on the stone thrones (?) and if they cast (?) the lot (?) for the "anointed one", then let the "anointed one" who holds Zalinu sit on the stone throne which is above the well.' Now all the gods come together (are summoned) and the lot(?) is cast (?). Then Zashapuna of Kastama is greater than all (the rest of) the gods. And because she is the consort of Zalinu, whereas Tazzuwasi is his concubine, these three are at Tanipia. And for that very reason, a field has been

[s] Cf. perhaps the mythical material which has been incorporated in Gen. 6.1–4.

[t] According to old Hittite law a man – especially one without means – could enter his wife's family and ask for a sum of money corresponding to the bride-price which would usually be exacted from him.

dedicated by the king in Tanipia: six measures of farmland, one measure
for a vineyard, house and threshing floor, and three houses for labourers;
there is a document relating to this and (in addition) the (property) of the
gods is holy to me. This I have told as it is (truthfully).

There follows the colophon, in part corresponding to the title of the book,
after the scribe's mark, which is put at the end of the tablet.

First tablet. Complete. The words of the 'anointed' Kella. The [scribe]
Pihaziti copied this in the presence of Walwi (?) the supervisor.

4. The myth of the disappearance of Telipinu

Text: First version: *KUB* XVII 10 ('A'); *KUB* XXXIII 2 ('B'); *KUB*
XXXIII 1 ('C'); *KUB* XXXIII 3 ('D'). Edited by H. Otten, *DieÜberlieferungen
des Telipinu-Mythus*, MVÄG 46/1, 1942; A. Goetze, *Kleinasien*[2], op. cit.,
143f. Date: the three versions of the present myth differ from one another in
minor details; the archetype may have been written down in the later Old
Kingdom, or at the latest, at the beginning of the Middle Kingdom. A number
of parallel versions deal with other vanished deities in place of Telipinu.

Telipinu, son of the weather god Taru and himself to be regarded as a 'weather
god', is a member of the Hattian pantheon. This text depicts his angry disappearance from active life and the general barrenness and drought which
results. Plants, animals, men and gods are brought to the brink of destruction.
After the gods, tormented by hunger, note the absence of Telipinu and seek
him in vain, an eagle is sent out to look for him. When it, too, returns unsuccessful, the mother goddess sends out a bee, which finally tracks down Telipinu to
his hiding place and arouses him by stinging him. This makes Telipinu even
more angry, and he gives vent to his wrath by means of a devastating flood.
Terrified, the gods seek safety in magic. The angry Telipinu is to be calmed by
an incantation. Kamrusepas, the goddess of health, first of all performs a ritual
invocation of the angry god by attracting him out into the open by means of
delicacies and soothing substances, at the same time calming him by what she
says. Once Telipinu has roared down in a storm, the main part of the incantation follows. Kamrusepas deals with Telipinu's body by burning parts of a
ram and waving them. All kinds of materials are either destroyed or shown to be
harmless or transitory, and in accordance with sympathetic magic, are identified with Telipinu's outbursts of anger, in order to bring him round. The
pantheon, which has arranged for the incantation to counter the threat to its
existence, assembles and promises itself renewed salvation and a long life.
Telipinu is declared to be free from all hostility.

Next comes a lacuna in the text in which there may have been an account
of the ineffectiveness of this approach – or perhaps it is said that Kamrusepas'
ritual was incomplete and needed to be supplemented. There then follows the
fragment of an incantation, performed by a human being. This is not just
confined to placating Telipinu; it is also concerned with freeing the whole of

nature from the wrath of Telipinu, who has been banished to the underworld. Telipinu, rid of his anger, resumes his usual beneficial activity. The world of nature, men and gods is restored to order, and the royal couple are endowed with long life and strength. A fleece is hoisted as a sign of the happy turn of events and of blessing.

The aim of the myth is to demonstrate the efficacy of the ritual against divine anger embedded in the action. The theme of the missing god, who, unlike the other gods in the vegetation myths to be found elsewhere in the ancient Near East, is not a dead god (cf. Dumuzi, Adonis, Osiris, etc.), may be of Hattian origin and is also applied to other Hittite gods. We can therefore find word-for-word parallels to the present myth, even to points of detail. There is evidence that the ritual was used time and again in periods of disaster. Two versions deal with the disappearance of the personal deities of queens of the Old and the Middle Kingdoms. There is evidence of severe catastrophes during the periods in question.

There is no parallel in OT ideas of God to the thought that the gods are dependent on help from men or even from animals, that they can be influenced by magic, that they are finite, that they are not omniscient, that they can be involved in earthly catastrophes, that they can be powerless in the face of their own unbridled passions.[u] There is, however, a parallel in the OT to the conviction that the angry departure of the deity can be seen in all kinds of catastrophes: cf. communal laments like Pss. 44.9ff.; 74; 79; narrative texts like II Sam. 21; 24; I Kings 17; 18; prophetic instances like Hos. 4.10; 9.14; Amos 1.2; Micah 6.14f.; cursing themes in Lev. 26; Deut. 28, and not least in the account in the framework of Judges: Judg. 2.14f.; 3.8, etc. Above all, however, the OT bears witness to the experience of the absence of God, in greater breadth and depth, in a way which is comparable and at the same time incomparable: see e.g. Isa. 1.15; 8.17; 29.14ff.; 45.19; 48.16a; 54.8; Jer. 12.7; 23.23f.; Hos. 5.6; and on the other hand Deut. 31.16-18; 32.20 or Pss. 44.24ff.; 89.38ff.; Lam. 5.20ff.

About twelve lines are missing from the beginning of the Hittite text; they may have dealt with the cause of Telipinu's deep resentment which gives rise to the following results (A 15ff.):

[5]Dust-clouds filled the window, smoke filled the house. The embers on the hearth were choked. The gods stifled on the altars, the sheep stifled in the fold. The oxen stifled in the stall. The ewe spurned her lamb and the cow spurned her calf.

[10]Telipinu went away. (With him) he took blessings on produce . . . fertility (?) and abundance in the field, in the meadow and in the wilderness.[v] And Telipinu went and put himself[w] in the wilderness (?). Weariness (?) overcame (?)[x] him. Then corn and grain ceased to grow. Oxen,

[u] In this connection cf. e.g. I Kings 18.27.

[v] It is unclear whether this is scrubland, marsh, steppe, or something else.

[w] More exactly, 'met with', 'slipped in'.   [x] Or, 'vegetation (?) overgrew (?) him'.

sheep and humans [15]ceased to conceive, and those who were pregnant were unable to give birth. The hills had no more moisture, the trees withered so that the buds could no longer shoot. The meadows were parched, the springs failed and a famine began in the land. Men and gods were in danger of dying of hunger.[y] The great sun god gave a feast and invited the thousand gods to it: they ate, [20]but they were not satisfied; they drank, but were unable to quench their thirst. Then the weather god thought of his son Telipinu: 'Telipinu my son is not here. He was angry and has taken away all good things with him.' The gods great and small began to search for Telipinu. The sun god sent out the swift eagle, (saying): 'Go, search the [25]high mountains, search the deep valleys, search the blue waves!' The eagle flew off, but he did not find him (Telipinu), and he reported to the sun god: 'I have not found him, Telipinu, the mighty god.' Then the weather god said to Hannahannas:[z] 'What are we to do? We shall [30]yet perish from hunger!' The 'exalted goddess' said to the weather god: 'Do something, weather god! Go and look for Telipinu yourself!'

The weather god searches vainly for Telipinu in his cult city, and after breaking down the door of the city, which was shut, gives up the search in despair.

Then Hannahannas sent out [35][the bee]: 'Go and look for Telipinu!' [The weather god sa]id [to the 'exalted goddess']: 'The gods great and small have looked [and not found] him; is this [bee] now to fly off and [find him? Its wi]ngs are tiny and it is tiny too. Will they (the gods) understand that?'

The gap which follows can be partially filled from fragments of the so-called second and third versions of the myth, *KUB* XXXIII 5 and 8–10:

The 'exalted goddess' said to the weather god: 'Leave that to me! It

---

[y] Gods can perish and die, at least in theory. Cf. also a passage from the myth of the disappearance of the weather god, *KUB* XXXIII 24 I 30–36: 'The father [of the weather god, who had disappeared] came to his (i.e. the weather god's) grandfather and reasoned with him: "Who has sinned [against(?)] m]e, that the seed has perished and everything is withered?" – His grandfather said, "No one (else) has sinned. You alone have sinned!" Thereupon the father of the weather god said, "I have not sinned." – And his grandfather said, "If I find it out, I will smite you! Now go, look for the weather god!"' It seems reasonable to assume that a dead god would have been restored to a similar status among the gods of the underworld. Here it is once again clear that only differences of degree were recognized between man and god.

[z] The Hittite mother goddess and goddess of birth, or the foremost of a group of goddesses of this type. She is also termed 'exalted goddess'. Her sphere of activity was especially affected by barrenness.

will [fly of]f and find him.' And she said to the bee: 'Go off, . . . and look for Telipinu. When you find him, sting him on his hands and feet and make him get up! Take wax, smear his eyes and his hands with it, cleanse him, and bring him back to me.' The bee [flew off]. It searched the high mountains, it searched the [deep valleys], it [searched the blue] waves. The store of honey in its [body] began to decay [and the wax (?) began to] decay, and then it (found) him (Telipinu) in a meadow near [Lihz]ina in the woods. It stung him on his hands and feet and made him get up[, it smeared his eyes and hands with wax and . . .]

[Then] Telipinu [said]: 'I was furious [and I went aw]ay. [Why have] you [woken] me from my sleep?[a] Why have you forced [me] to talk when I am angry?!' Telipinu was very angry.

The mutilated text indicates that in his wrath Telipinu caused a flood which destroyed cities and houses, killing men and animals. The gods, in terror and dismay, asked vainly what was to be done.

[Then] (one of the gods) said: '[Let us] summon the mortal (man). [He shall take (?) . . .] the . . . on (?) mount Ammyna and shall summon him (Telipinu)! He shall bring him here with an eagle's wing.[b] Yes, the mor[tal (man)] shall bring him here, he shall bring him with an eagle's wing!'

The next lines, which are very fragmentary (*KUB* XXXIII 8 + II 18-24, belonging to the second version), suggest that the gods involve the man. It is difficult to discover Telipinu's reaction, as the text breaks off. However, after material which would roughly fill in the gap in the first version, the second column of A introduces a ritual of propitiation or purification which is carried out, not by the man, but by Kamrusepas ('smoke spirit'?), the goddess of magic and healing arts. It is uncertain whether there is a discrepancy from the second version here, or whether the incantations of Kamrusepas and the man (the latter in A IV) are thought to go hand in hand – or perhaps to be in competition. In any case, the close connection of the ritual with the action of the myth should be observed. A II 1-32 is part of Telipinu's summons:

[9]See, there [is] 'water slopping about'.[c] [May it] please you, Telipinu, [to be gracious(?)!] [Turn to] the king in friendship! See, there is . . . [May it please you(?)] [13]to be content! . . . [16]. . . See, there [are] figs. [And] as [figs] are sweet, so may [your disposition,] Telipinu, become sweet! As the olive tree [has] oil in it [and as the vine] has [20]grape juice

[a] Cf. Pss. 44.23; 78.65.
[b] To be thought of as a magical ingredient and instrument in the hand of the one performing the incantation. It was also used for sprinkling.
[c] Sense obscure. Most likely to be a scribal error for 'turning water', a fluid used for ritual purification.

in it, so may you, Telipinu, have good intentions [for men(?)]. See, here
is anointing oil. May it anoint [your heart and mind(?)], Telipinu! As
malt and 'beer bread'[d] can be bound together within, so [may] your
disposition, [Telipinu,] be bound up with man's concerns. [As a grain
of wheat] is pure, so may Telipinu's disposition become pure. [As]
honey is sweet and butter mild, so may Telipinu's disposition become
sweet and mild. See, Telipinu, I have sprinkled your ways with fine oil.
Now, Telipinu, go along the ways sprinkled with fine oil! . . . As esparto
grass can be woven, so, Telipinu, may you be compliant.'

Then came Telipinu raging. With lightning and thunder[e] he alighted
on the dark earth. [35]Kamrusepas saw him and the eagle's wing bro[ught
him]. [III 1]Anger made him stop; wrat[h made him stop; rage] made him
stop; fury made him stop.

Kamrusepas said to the gods: 'Co[me], gods, the god Hapantallis is
p[asturing(?)] the sheep of the sun god. [5]So now seek out twelve rams. I
wish to perform magic on Telipinu [. . .][f] I have taken a shell (?) with 'a
thousand eyes' and . . . put the . . .[g] of Kamrusepas'(!) rams in it. I have
burnt (them?) for Telipinu here and there (as incense?), and thus driven
the evil out of Telipinu's body; I have taken away his anger, I have taken
away his wrath, I have taken away his rage, I have taken his fury. Telipinu
was angry, it choked his mind and his body (like damp) firewood.[h] In the
same way as they have [15]burnt this damp firewood, so too shall Telipinu's
anger, wrath, rage and fury be burnt up. As [malt] is dry so that it cannot
be t[aken] into the fields, and cannot be used as seed, and cannot be used
to make bread, but is put into a sealed granary, so too Telipinu's anger,
[wrath,] [20]rage and fury [will] become dry! Telipinu was angry: his mind
and body were like a raging fire. As this fire is put out, so too shall
(Telipinu's) anger, wrath and fury be put out. Telipinu, let go your anger,
let go your wrath, [25]let go your fury! As (water in the) gutter does not
flow [upwards], so shall Telipinu's [anger, wrath] and fury not re[turn!]

The gods [sat down (?) in their] ass[embly] under the *hatalkesna*
tree. And under the *hatalkesna* tree [I have brought about (?) salvation/
salvation is(?) brought about] over long [years]. [30]And all the gods were
there, (including) [Papaia, Isdustaia], the Gulses goddesses, the mother
goddesses,[i] the god Halki ('grain'), Mia[tanzipa] ('spirit of growth'),

[d] An ingredient in brewing.
[e] Cf. Ps. 18.7-14; II Sam. 22.8-15; Ps. 77.17ff.
[f] Probably an organ which was regarded as the seat of strong emotions.
[g] Possibly 'what has been cut off'.
[h] Or, 'his mind and his entrails were bundled up like firewood/brushwood'.
[i] The (groups of) goddesses enumerated so far were thought to be concerned with
determining fate or with the protection of the processes of birth. Like at least the two
following deities, they belong to the underworld.

Telipinu, the 'guardian deity', Hapantall[is . . .]. I have brought about salva[tion] for the gods over long years and I have purified him (Telipinu). [C][9][. . .] [I have taken] the evil from Telipinu['s body], I have taken away his [anger], I have taken away his wrath, [I have taken away his ra]ge, I have taken away his [fury], I have taken away the ["evil] tongue", [I have taken away the ev]il . . .'

The text of A IV 1ff. continues after a gap of about 15 lines. The propitiatory ritual of 'the man' (the completion of Kamrusepas' incantation or, if that had failed, the last way out of the cosmic crisis) has already begun:

['. . . You, O *hatalkesna* tree, wear white garments in the spring, but in the autumn your clothing is blood red. The ox goes beneath you[j] and] you rub off the hair on his forehead(?). The sheep [goe]s beneath you and you rub off its wool. (Now) rub off from Telipinu his anger, his wrath, his rage and his fury. If the weather god comes in fearful anger, [5]the 'man of the weather god'[k] brings him to a standstill. If the porridge pot threatens to boil over, the spoon brings the (porridge) to a standstill. In the same way, my words, the man's words, will bring Telipinu's anger, wrath and fury to a standstill. Telipinu's anger, rage, wrath and fury will depart. They will leave the house. They will leave [10]the central pillar (?). They will leave the window (also the hinge, the courtyard, the city gate, the gatehouse, the main road). They are not to go to the fertile field, to the garden, to the wood. They are to go the way of the sun god of the earth![l] The porter has opened the seven gateways,[m] he has withdrawn the seven beams. [15]Down below in the dark earth there are bronze vessels. Their covers are of lead and their rings (?) are of iron. What goes in never comes out, because it perishes in there. And they are to receive Telipinu's anger, rage, wrath and fury, and these are never to come out again!'

[20]Telipinu returned to his house and thought of his land. Then the dust-clouds left the window, the smoke left the house. The altars were subordinate to the gods/were reconciled with the gods. The hearth released the embers. The sheep rested in the fold. The oxen rested in the stall. The mother picked up her child. The ewe attended to her lamb. [25]The cow attended to her calf. And Telipinu took thought for the king and queen and endowed them with life, strength and many days.

[j] Supplemented along the lines of *KUB* XXXIII 54 + 47 II 15ff.

[k] A priest of a particular kind who functioned in a cult of a Hattian kind (Nerik), above all as one who invoked the deity (as here).

[l] The conception that the sun passes through the underworld during the course of the night has led to the religious development of a type of chthonic deity termed the night sun, who shares with the astral sun god his functions of ruling and judging.

[m] Those of the underworld. This is a feature of originally Sumerian mythology (cf. in the OT e.g. Ps. 9.13; 107.18; also Matt. 16.18).

Telipinu cared for the king. A staff was set up before Telipinu and a fleece was hung on the staff. And that means the fat of the sheep, that means corn, cattle [30] and wine. That means oxen and sheep. That means long years and the blessing of children. That means the good news of the lamb.[n] That means prosperity and good fortune.

The text becomes fragmentary and breaks off.

II. PRAYERS

Since there are only just over a dozen examples, it is doubtful whether Hittite prayer can be termed a genre of its own.[o] In so far as Hittite prayer is a genre, however, it may be said to be essentially argumentative petition. We have no traditions of thanksgivings, and independent hymns have been handed down only in the form of translations from the Akkadian or the Sumerian. The prayers are put on the lips of kings and queens named or unnamed, a royal prince and an anonymous person. The prayers are essentially concerned with divine support, health or its restoration, long life, the blessing of children, favourable weather, the fertility of fields and flocks, victory over enemies, the end of epidemics, the discovery of reasons for divine anger and even the forgiveness of guilt – in order to put an end to divine judgments. A subsidiary concern of those who make the prayers arises from their experience of the value of good relationships as it has been gained in the human sphere. To be safe, or at least not to have to fight a solitary way through a particular trouble, one can try for the mediation of the sun god, who is impartial and unconditionally respected in the pantheon, or for the intercession of divine satellites or supporters of the competent deity or the god in question. Consequently a text can consist of two or more prayers.

With or without an intercessor, the suppliant seeks through his argument to secure a favourable acceptance of his petitions: objectionable requests are to be ignored; he proclaims unconditional trust in divine help, stresses his dependence, recalls earlier signs of favour from the deity(ies), emphasizes his own achievements, his pious care in the ritual sphere, his reverence and service towards the gods, the temple and the cult. He promises consecrated gifts and dedications if his prayer is heard, along with praise of the deity through which his respect will be increased

[n] Probably a reference to favourable findings at the inspection of entrails.
[o] Not including the numerous petitions embedded in rituals or the more or less short (or abbreviated) prayers to be found there, e.g. no. 7 below.

among men and gods. In special cases the gods are reminded that they are essentially compelled to help: a pregnant woman can cite a proverb according to which the gods hear the prayer of a woman in labour; the king who asks for an end to a fearful epidemic points out that if the gods allow the plague to continue they are putting their own existence at risk, since there will soon be no one able to offer them sacrifices. Men under judgment plead for the recognition of mitigating circumstances and ask accordingly for the punishment to be stopped. It is argued that a man has transgressed unwittingly, or bears his father's guilt while being innocent himself; that he has voluntarily confessed to the guilt which he has inherited; or it is said that this has long been expiated, has already been atoned for many times over.

This is not the place for a comparison with OT petitions. Attention should, however be drawn to two perspectives which can be found in the OT as in Hittite prayers, indeed in the ones which are included here. First, arguments are made from the basic conviction that a transgression against the deity will be punished by a visitation; conversely, a blow which falls on a community or an individual indicates a wicked action which has been committed recently or even longer before. The following examples of this pattern of argument can be selected from a number of instances in the OT: II Sam. 21.1ff.; Jonah 1.2ff.; Ps. 38.1ff., and not least individual speeches by Job's friends, especially Job 4.7ff. If misfortune is to be warded off, its cause must first be discovered, and this is often by no means evident (cf. e.g. Jonah 1.7). This is where we find the second perspective: to clarify obscure situations and to discover the divine will, enquiries must be made of the deity. Significant differences emerge here. There are only partial agreements between the methods of enquiry among the Hittites and among the Israelites. The Hittites can make use of the following means: oracles in dreams and incubation in the temple, the intervention of inspired persons and oracle priests, including haruspices, the use of a kind of pendulum oracle and (according to the end of no. 3 above) what is presumably a form of drawing lots, which was particularly popular. In addition, the observation of birds, prophesying from cups and other practices of interpreting signs and making predictions are in vogue. The Old Testament is familiar with dreams and visions as means by which the divine will is made known (cf. I Sam. 28.6, 15), and also with the drawing of lots by priests (cf. Deut. 33.8; Josh. 7; I Sam. 14.41ff.; for the opposite point of view see I Sam. 9.9ff.; Jer. 23.16ff., 23ff.; Micah 3). On the other hand it rejects outright other forms of prediction and all forms of magic as illegitimate practices (cf. e.g. Lev. 19.26, 31; Deut. 18.9ff.; see of course also Gen. 44.5; Ezek. 21.21 and again I Sam. 28). The fact that the suppliants in the OT – in contrast to the Hittites – know that the existence of their God is not dependent on human sacrifices and other cultic practices (despite the argument in Ps. 30.9), should at least be noted as an important difference which indicates another kind of relationship to the deity.

5. *From the prayer of Kantuzilis*

Text: *KUB* XXX 10. Translation: A. Goetze, *ANET*[3], 400f. Date of composition: first half of the fourteenth century BC.

The beginning and end of the present text are missing. It is one of a group of prayers from the fourteenth century which begin with praise, followed by petition. Both elements, and especially that of the hymn, clearly draw on Babylonian hymns and prayers addressed to Shamash the sun god, without being mere translations. They are usually put on the lips of kings.

The hymnic section of this text is no longer extant. The text itself can be supplemented as being a parallel version of the anonymous prayer *KUB* XXXI 127 + (and duplicates). The hymn in this latter prayer is addressed to the Hattian sun god Istanu (edited by H. G. Güterbock, *JAOS* 78, 1958, 237ff.). The sun god also appears in our text; his function as a mediator can be clearly recognized. The second part is addressed to the personal deity of the suppliant and presents the real petition. A further address to the sun god appears on the verso of the tablet. The prayer arises from the distress of a person who is seriously ill. This version is put on the lips of a man called Kantuzilis, probably a royal prince from the time of Suppiluliumas I, the founder of the New Kingdom.

A parallel to the preliminary hymn (which is no longer extant) in the OT would be the praise of God which 'realizes salvation', found for example in Pss. 9.1ff. and 108.1ff. as an introduction to lamentation and petition. There are also formal parallels to assertions of innocence (lines 11ff.) and expressions of confidence in the OT psalter: e.g. Pss. 5.4ff.; 7.3ff.; 17.1ff.; 26.3ff. or in Pss. 27.1ff.; 31.1; 57.1; 71.1–6. Equally comparable is the way in which the distress is depicted and petitions are articulated (apart from those concerned with discovering transgressions still unknown). The Hittite comparative text runs as follows:

Recto [4]Sun god, when you go down into the earth, go and spe[ak] with my god[p] [and] pass on to him (my) words, the words of Kantuzilis. My god, ever since my mother gave birth to me, you have reared me. You alone, my god, are [my refuge(?)] and my stay.[q] You alone, [my god,] have put me among good men. You, my god, appointed me to stand in an influential place. [And you,] my god, have called me, Kantuzilis, to be your favourite servant [. . .][r] [10]From childhood onwards I have known

[p] A reference to a personal guardian deity, who in this case is one of the group of gods of the underworld.

[q] Literally 'binding'.

[r] Literally 'as servant of your body and soul'.

nothing but the gracious power of my god. [. . .]

And the more I grew, the more I bore witness to (?experienced?) my god's grace and wisdom in everything. I have never sworn falsely by my god. I have never broken an oath. I have never eaten what is holy to my god and therefore is not permissible for me to eat. I have never made my body unclean.

[15]I have never withheld an ox from your stall, nor (let) a sheep (depart) from your fold. When I found food, I never ate it without thinking, and when I found water, I never drank it without thinking.[s] Were I now to recover, would I not recover at your word, O god? Were I to come to (renewed) strength, would I not regain strength at your word, O god?

[20]Life is bound up with death and death is bound up with life. Man does not live for ever. The days of his life are numbered. Even if a man lived for ever – if bitter suffering befell him, would that not seem to him to be a punishment?

10. Rock relief from the sanctuary of Yazilikaya near Boghazköy, second half of the thirteenth century BC. The height of the figures is 1.64 and 1.07 m. King Tudhaliyas (IV) of Hatti is wearing cultic adornment, and is being embraced by the Hurrian god Sarruma (a gesture of protection!). The names are written in 'Hittite' hieroglyphs.

[s] I.e. without testing whether this were unclean or were a sacrifice or a drink-offering intended for the gods.

[Now] may my god freely[t] open his heart and his soul and t[ell] me my sins, [25]so that I may know them. May my god either speak to me in a dream – indeed, may my god open his heart to me [and] tell [me] my [sin]s, so that I may know them – or may a prophetess speak to me or may a seer of the sun god tell me (my sins) from (inspecting) a liver. Indeed, may my god freely[u] open his heart and his soul and tell me my sins, that I may know them.

[And] do you, my god, bestow upon me new [health] and [stren]gth!

The following sections on verso 1–13 are badly damaged. Lamentations over the loss of divine support and the incomprehensible, manifold suffering are coupled with heart-rending petitions for help and restoration.

[14]Through sickness my house has become a house of misery, and through misery my soul drops down to another place.[v] I have become like one who is sick at the turn of the year (?). Sickness and misery have now become too much for me. That I must continually tell you, my god.

At night sweet slumber does not embrace me on my bed. No improvement makes itself known to me. Now, [my god,] give me po(w)er [20]and strength![w] How you could once have foreordained [th]is sickness for me in your heart – I have never asked the seer that.

Now I cry for mercy in the presence of my god. So hear me, my god, [and] do not make me one who is unwelcome at the king's gate. Ackn[owl]-edge me before me[n]. Do not let my [cau]se be lost. Those to whom I d[id] good, [25]none of them refreshes me. You, my god, are [my father] and my mother. [. . .]

The text breaks off.

6. The so-called second plague prayer of Mursilis II

The text has been preserved in three copies, each of which is incomplete: in *KUB* XIV 8; *KUB* XIV 11; *KUB* XIV 10 + XXVI 86. The numbering by paragraphs which follows is based on the edition by A. Goetze (*Kleinasiatische Forschungen* I, 1929, 204–35, cf. *ANET*[3], 394ff.), except that §6, emended by means of the additional passage *KUB* XXVI 86, does not consist of two paragraphs, as Goetze assumes. So from §7 onwards the numbering is one figure lower. The date of composition is the third quarter of the fourteenth century BC.

A long-drawn-out and severe epidemic which is understood as a divine

[t] Literally 'with a whole heart'.
[u] See the previous note.
[v] The kingdom of the dead.
[w] Conjecture.

visitation causes King Mursilis II to address prayers at different times to individual gods or to all the gods, in order to make them bring an end to the plague. As a rule they centre on the acknowledgment of a transgression which has been shown or confirmed by an oracle to have a causal connection with pestilence. Expiatory actions are announced and along with the plea for them to be accepted there is a request to make known any other causes for the divine punishment, so that these too may be removed. Four 'plague' prayers[x] have come down to us in more or less good condition, the first of which sees the cause of the plague in a serious breach of an oath on the part of Mursilis' father Suppiluliumas I (along with supporters and 'the Hatti land'). Shortly or immediately before his accession, Suppiluliumas I had eliminated the ruler designate Tudhaliyas II, who indeed may already have become king. A further prayer sees at least a temporal connection between an Egyptian expedition of Suppiluliumas and the outbreak of the plague. The prayer quoted below seems to be the latest in sequence (the traditional description of it as the second plague prayer is derived from earlier scholarship); in addition to a breach of treaty caused by the Egyptian expedition it also deals with a cultic omission. In the tension between inherited guilt and the conviction of personal innocence Mursilis takes responsibility for the transgression in order to make atonement. The argument is strictly logical.

The understanding of causality which is able to associate historical events according to religious and legal principles (treaty under divine guarantee – breach of treaty – national catastrophe as a consequence of divine anger), was used by the Hittites to brilliant effect in their history writing. As has already been indicated, it can also be found in the OT: II Sam. 21.1–14 is a corresponding example: a three-year famine causes David to seek 'the face of Yahweh' (presumably to discover its cause). He is told that the cause is a violent breach of the treaty made with the Gibeonites at the time of Joshua (Josh. 9.3ff.), on the part of Saul. The offended Gibeonites fix an expiation – the execution of seven of Saul's male descendants. As a result the affected land is purified and reconciled to Yahweh.[y] Reference is made in the notes to detailed points of correspondence between the following text and the OT traditions.

§¹Weather god of Hatti,[z] my lord, [and you gods of Hatti,] my [lor]ds! [King] Murs[ilis], your servant, has sent me: 'Go to the [weather god] of Hatti, my lord, and to the gods, my lords, speak as follows:

"What is this that you have done? You have let a plague into the Hatti land, and the Hatti land has been sorely oppressed beyond measure by the plague.[a] For twenty years now men have kept on dying,[b] in the time

---

[x] For their order cf. H. G. Güterbock, *RHA* 66, 1960, 61f.

[y] For the latter cf. Num. 35.33f.; Gen. 9.5f.; for the parallelism as a whole see A. Malamat, *VT* 5, 1955, 1–12.

[z] The supreme national god (along with the sun goddess of Arinna).

[a] The question and the description of the distress can be found combined in a similar way in Pss. 74.1, 4ff.; 80.4ff., etc.

of my father and in the time of my brother, and now they are dying in my own days, since I became priest of the gods.^{c} Since the dying continues in the Hatti land, the plague has not been removed from the Hatti land. And I cannot suppress the disquiet in my heart; I can no longer suppress the anguish in my body."

In §2, which is badly damaged, Mursilis refers briefly to his exemplary worship of all the gods and his care of the temples,^{d} and then reports how useless have been his earlier pious efforts to free the land of the plague by prayer and sacrifice, or even to discover the reason for the onset of the plague, by means of oracles, dreams or prophetic sayings. This is all the more incomprehensible to him.

§3"Even the [few] people who[remain]ed to sacrifice thick bread [and wine]^e conti[nued to die. And again the mat]ter pressed heavily upon (my conscience), and [(once again) I enquired of an oracle the (cause of the) wrath] of the go[ds]. [Then I came] upon two old tablets. One tablet dealt with [the rite for the river Mala].^{f} The old kings [had] appointed an offering to the river Mala [for all tim]es. [Now,] (i.e.) since my father's days, d[ying has continu]ed in the Hatti land, and we have never performed the rite to the river Mala.^{g}

§4The second tablet concerns Kurustama. When the weather god of Hatti brought the people of the city of Kurustama to Egypt, and when the weather god of Hatti had made a treaty with the Hatti concerning them, they were then under oath to the weather god of Hatti. Now when the people of Hatti and the Egyptians were under oath to the weather god of Hatti, the people of Hatti transgressed the oath. The Hatti suddenly broke the oath. My father sent foot-soldiers and chariotry. They attacked the country of Amka,^{h} in Egyptian territory. And again he sent (troops) and again they attacked it. When the Egyptians became frightened, they asked my father outright to make one of his sons king.^{i}

---

^{b} Here and throughout there is the impersonal expression 'there was/is constant dying'.

^{c} An expression for the religious function of the Hittite king. For the subject cf. Ps. 110.4; Gen. 14.18; II Sam. 6.14, 18, and on the other hand II Chron. 26.16-18; Num. 3.10, 38.

^{d} The immaculate fulfilment of religious duties as a reason for asking god to intervene: Pss. 17.2-5; 26, etc.

^{e} The reference is to the inhabitants of the Hatti land in their religious function.

^{f} Hittite name for the Euphrates.

^{g} Cf. the account of Josiah's reform in II Kings 22; 23 and especially II Kings 22.13 and 23.21-23. Of course this is on quite a different level.

^{h} The depression between the Lebanon and Antilebanon.

^{i} This request was made by the widow of either Tutankhamun or his predecessor

But when my father gave them one of his sons and they took him there, they killed him.[j] Now my father was very angry and set out for Egypt and attacked Egypt and smote the foot-soldiers and chariotry of the country of Egypt. At that time the weather god of Hatti, my lord, allowed my father to win in the dispute, so that he was able to defeat the foot-soldiers and the chariotry of Egypt and to smite them.[k] But when they brought back the pris[oners] they had taken to the Hatti land, a plague broke out among the prisoners and they be[gan] to die.

§5When they brought the prisoners into the Hatti land, the prisoners brought the plague into the Hatti land and from that day there has been dying in the Hatti land. Now when I found the above-mentioned tablet dealing with Egypt, I made an enquiry to the god through an oracle:[l] 'Those arrangements which were made by the weather god of Hatti – that the Egyptians and the people of Hatti were put under oath by the weather god of Hatti and that the Damnassaras deities[m] were present in the temple of the weather god of Hatti, my lord, whereupon the people of Hatti suddenly broke this treaty – is thi(s the starting point for) the wrath of the weather god cf Hatti, my lord?'[n] And this was confirmed (by the oracle).

§6Because of the plague I also asked the oracle about the sacrifice for the [Mala] river. And there, too, it proved that I had to account for[o] that before the weather god of Hatti, my lord. Be[hold], now I have acknowledged [the trans]gression before [the weather god of Hatti]. It is so; we have done it. [But] it did [not] happen in my time; [it happened][p] in the time of my father ... . I know that well. [. . .] the matter, and the weather god [of Hatti, my lord, is] angr[y . . .] because of [this matter . . .]. In Hatti land the dying continues, s[ee (?), for this (very) rea]son I continue [in prayer t]o the weather god of Hatti, my lord. I prostrate myself on my knees before you and c[ry] for mercy. So hear me, weather god of Hatti, my lord, and the plague [will] be taken away from the Hatti land.

§7The causes of the plague which have been established, when I made

Amenophis IV (Akhenaten). Cf. H. G. Güterbock, *JCS* 10, 1956, 94ff. But cf. now D. B. Redford, *BASOR* 211, 1973, 36ff.

[j] The event may be attributed to a political revolution which is to be connected either with the accession of Pharaoh Ay or with that of Tutankhamun. Redford, op. cit., differs.

[k] The conception of divine judgment underlies this. Judges 11.27, for example, speaks in a similar way of a divine act of judgment in war.

[l] For this very point see again II Kings 22.13.

[m] A group of deities the position of which is still obscure to us.

[n] Compare especially Ezek. 17.11–21.

[o] Literally 'come before the weather god'.

[p] See p. 173 n. r below.

the matter the subject of an oracle, these I have removed, by making [atone]ment for each of them. In connection with the [breaking of the oa]th, which has been established as the cause of the plague, I have offered the sacrifice for [breaking the] oath before the weather god of Hatti[, my lord . . .] I have also sacrificed [before the (other) gods . . .] The [rite has been performed(?)] to you, the weather god of Hatti, and the rite [has been performed to them]. (As far as the omission) of the sacrifice for the Mala river (is concerned), which has been established [(as a contributory cause) o]f the pla[gue] – since I am now setting off for [the Ma]la river, forgive me, weather god of H[atti], my lord, and you gods, my lords, for the (neglect of the) sacrifice for the Mala river. I will now perform the rite for the [Mala] river and carry it out (properly). In the matter because of which I am performing it, namely because of the plague, be graciously inclined towards me, that the plague may be cured in the Hatti land!

§8Weather god of Hatti, my lord, and you gods, my lords. It is (sadly) the case that (men) are sinful.q My father too has sinned by transgressing against the word of the weather god of Hatti, my lord. But I have sinned in nothing. Now it is (true) that the father's sin falls on the son.r So the sin of my father has also fallen upon me. See, now I have confessed it to the weather god of Hatti, my lord, and to the gods, my lords: it is so, we have done it. Now because I have confessed my father's sin,s may the mind of the weather god, my lord, and the gods, my lords, again be pacified! Again be graciously inclined towards me, and drive the plague away from the Hatti land once again. And may the few who are left to offer thick bread and wine no longer continue to die.

§9See, I continue in prayer to the weather god, my lord, because of the plague. So hear me, weather god of Hatti, my lord, and save me! [I would like (?)] to re[mind you of this (?)]: the bird takes refuge in its nest (?), and the nest (?) saves it. Or, if anything becomes too difficult for a servant, he makes a request to his lord, and his lord hears him and [is kind towards] him and sets right what was too difficult for him.t Or, if a servant has transgressed, and confesses his transgression to his lord, his lord can do with him what he pleases. But because he has confessed his transgression to his lord, his lord's mind is pacified, [and the lord]

q Literally, 'they keep sinning'. In the OT cf. Gen. 6.5; 8.21; Job 4.17; 15.14; Prov. 20.9.
r For the 'corporate' liability of the sons for the transgressions of their fathers cf. II Sam. 21.5ff. and also Ex. 20.5; 34.7; Num. 14.18; Lam. 5.7; Ezek. 18.2. For the rejection of this liability see Ezek. 18; Jer. 31.29f.; Deut. 24.16.
s Cf. e.g. Ps. 32 and especially v.5.
t Cf. Ps. 123.2f.

will not punish that servant. Now I [have confess]ed my father's sin. It is so, I have done it. [I]f (there is to be) atonement, it is certain (that) because of the abundant [atonement that has already been made (?)] for th[at plag]ue . . .], for the [pri]soners which were brought back from Egypt and for the colonists which were [brought back] – for all the atonement that Hattusa has made with the plague, it has already [made] twenty-fold [restitution]. Yet the mind of the weather god of Hatti, my lord, and of my lord gods, has not been pacified. But if you want to lay upon me any additional expiation, tell me in a dream, and I will make it to you.

§10See, weather god of Hatti, I address my prayers [to you]: save me. [And i]f indeed it is for this reason that the dying continues, while I am putting (thin)gs in order once a[gain], may those who are still [left] to sacrifice thick bread and wine no longer continue to die. But if the dying continues for any other reason, may I either see (this) in a dream or may it be [establish]ed through an oracle or may an ecstatic announce it to me,u or may all the priests find out by incubation what I have asked of them. Weather god of Hatti, my lord, save me! And may the gods, my lords, show their divine power! Let someone see it in a dream. And may the reason why dying continues be established! We will hang the bronze clasp (?) from the *sarpa* wood.v So save me now, weather god of Hatti, my lord, and may the plague once again be t[aken] away from the Hatti land!"'

III. FROM ROYAL SUBSTITUTIONARY RITUALS

The magical practice of the 'prophylactic ritual' was used to ward off the appearance of disastrous omens and divine punishments which were forecast. This ritual provides for the replacement of the man threatened with judgment and disaster by a substitute who will take his place and will have to undergo what is feared – usually death. This argument has a cogency typical of magic.

The substitute is usually a living animal or a human effigy, and is identified with the person in danger, in a manner valid for magic, by the recitation of formulae of identification which can be accompanied by corresponding symbolic actions. It is then offered to the god who is angry or who plans disaster, and is usually destroyed during the course

---

u Cf. I Sam. 28.6.
v An obscure practice (a pendulum oracle?).

of the ritual. The deity is compelled to accept the substitute and allow the person whom it replaces to go unscathed.

The ritual of the substitute king is a special form of the substitute ritual. This requires the appointment of a living man to be substitute, which is otherwise very rare. He is used to replace the ruler threatened with a fatal disaster after having first been given royal status in a piece of ritual theatre which is meant in real earnest; sometimes he is even allowed to rule for a while. This practice was already known in Mesopotamia at the beginning of the second millennium BC, and there is certain evidence for it in the neo-Assyrian empire (seventh century BC). In one instance it was probably used in Babylon in the fourth century BC.

The two passages which follow belong to a series of Hittite rituals for a substitute king dating from the fourteenth to thirteenth centuries BC. It may be presupposed that they are related to Babylonian models. Whereas the first text comes from a ritual which took at least nine days and seems to have provided for the death of the 'substitute king' on the seventh day of the ritual, after he had reigned for several days previously, the second text presents a rather different notion: the substitute king, who as in the first text is a prisoner of war, is not ritually slain, but allowed back to his homeland, with the intention of removing the dreaded disaster completely from the Hatti land.

Both themes, the representative transference of guilt and disaster and the rite of elimination (unknown in Mesopotamia), which removes the evil from a particular human environment by loading it on to a carrier, can also be found in the OT. There, of course, the determining factors are atonement and the forgiveness of sins, and the possibilities of autonomous magic are never considered. Comparable passages are Lev. 16.20-28 (the ritual of the scapegoat); 14.7, 53; Lev. 4-5 in connection with the principle of Lev. 17.11. The themes are taken up in a new form in the servant song of Isa. 53: the 'servant' takes away the guilt of the 'many' by being despised, through sickness and death. Cf. esp. Isa. 53.4-7, 12; but see also Ex. 28.38; Num. 18.22f.

H. M. Kümmel has provided a comprehensive study of the Hittite substitute king ritual, putting it in a history-of-religions context, in *Ersatzrituale für den hethitischen König*, StBT 3, 1967.

7. *From the nine-day ritual of the substitute king*

Text: Of eleven known fragments, which are distributed among at least five documents, the following are used here: *KBo* XV 9 ('A'); *KBo* XV 2 ('B'); *KUB* XVII 14 + *KUB* XV 2 ('C'). First edition by H. M. Kümmel, StBT 3, 50ff.

The occasion for the ritual is an omen of the king's death, which is seen as the announcement of a visitation for 'something evil'. However, according to the text the king does not know of what kind this evil is. There is no mention anywhere of repentance; interest is entirely directed towards averting the punishment. To this end the ritual provides for a double substitute for the king. A prisoner of war is offered up to the gods of the world above who have a special responsibility for the living, and a wooden substitute effigy is offered to appease the wrath of the gods of the underworld (perhaps to be imagined as being like the metal effigies of dead kings who were given divine honours as prominent *manes*). After he has transferred his identity to the substitute, the king is driven out of his palace and, officially forgotten and ignored, retires to an unknown (?) place. Describing himself as a ghost among the ghosts, he laments his incomprehensible lot before the sun god, describing how he has been snatched away from the life foreordained for him by the gods, and asks to be restored to his own destiny, which was that of a long and happy reign under the eyes of the gods of heaven, only thereafter to be followed by death. The further course of the ritual, which unfortunately has come down to us only in fragments, points towards the fulfilment of this request and guarantees that it will be brought about. After ruling for a number of days the substitute king dies (of course, a violent death) and thus diverts the proclamation of doom which has intervened by fulfilling it. The king is ritually purified, and can go on to experience his own happy destiny.

B recto 5'-11', continued by C verso 5'-13', deals with a wooden effigy of the king, which is dressed up with clothes and given bedding, and is also provided with food.

C verso 14-23 supplemented from A I 12ff.

On the day when the prisoner sends out the king,[w] on that very day the king says to him: 'This man (the prisoner) is the living substitute for me (upon the earth). This effigy is the substitute for me (under the earth). If you gods above have marked me out for some evil fate, and have shortened my days, months and years, this living substitute is to take my pl[ace]. [20]Mark it well, you gods above! If (you) sun goddess of the earth[x] and you gods under (the earth) [have vis]ited me with some evil, [may] this effigy take my place, [and do (you), sun goddess of the earth] and you gods beneath (the earth) [mark] this well!

There follows A I 22-36, a section which is badly damaged. According to this the prisoner expels the king from the palace and takes possession of the throne. As he departs, the king seems to ask the gods what crime he has

---

[w] What is meant is the expulsion of the king by the substitute king, who has to demonstrate his authority in this way (and presumably at the same time has to confirm that he has taken over as representative). See A recto 24'.

[x] See p. 164 n. l above.

committed for them to rob him of the kingship.[y] The prayer is continued along
the lines of the purpose of the action with C recto 2′ ff.

'M[ay they(?)] take away all that evil[z] completely from the throne
[. . .], the land [. . .], the house, the army, [the chariotry and the labou]rers!
[5′]But may . [. . .] . me, my spirit, the cities of Hattusa, Katapa, [Nerik?],
Arinña, Zippalanda, women and children [. . .], oxen (?), land, house,
army, chariotry . . .

There follows in lines 7′ to 17′ a list of gods above and below the earth,
introduced by the heavenly sun god and the heavenly weather god, along with
other weather gods.

. . . with long years, with a (long) future, with life, [he]alth and strength
[20′], remember me [graci]ously. [Aft]er he has finished speaking these
words before the sun god, he goes [. . . out] of the palace . [. . .] [24′]. . . no
one calls him [by his na]me (?) again . [. . .

B verso 1′-7′ speaks of the withdrawn life of the real king (line 3′ 'no one
calls him "king" any more'). Lines 5′-7′ indicate a strict prohibition against
going out which is delivered to him.

[8′]Further, if anyone comes into the city, do not say to him 'In which
city the (real) king (is, etc.),' no (rather:) [10′]'In which city the new king
(is),' people are accustomed to say, 'ther[e is the king(?)]'. Furthermore,
the king prostrates himself day by day, early in the morning [. . .] before
the sun god of heaven and s[ays] before the sun god of heaven: 'Sun god
of heaven, my lord, what have I done that you have taken away the
t[hrone] [15′]from me and given it to another and [? . . . ha]ve summoned
me to join the spirits of the dead! S[ee,] now I am among the spirits of
the dead. I have shown myself (to you), the sun god of heaven, my lord.
So leave me once again to my divine fate,[a] to the gods of heaven, and
[free] me from the midst of the spirits of the dead!'
[20′]After that the rites of kingship[b] are performed on the new king.

[y] Supplemented following B verso 14′f.
[z] The text has the plural.
[a] The 'fate' of the king is only written without the sign for 'god' in one copy of the
text. The form of writing seems to point to a deification of the destiny brought about by
the gods (see especially C recto 5′-20′). The usual interpretation of the passage as proof
of an exaltation of the king after his death to a place among the heavenly gods begins
from a use of the word 'fate/destiny' for death which is well attested, but rather one-
sided; in my view, however, this does not do justice either to the full meaning of the
word, which is primarily concerned with this world, or to the meaning of the text,
which is completely oriented on earthly life. For the dead, a return to life means a change
from the lordship of the gods of the underworld to the lordship of the heavenly ones.
[b] I.e. the accession ceremonies; cf. the following text, recto 19′ff.

[Two men] from each (court) office, (namely) two [. . .] lords, two administrators, two cooks, two table people, [two . . .,] two bakers are [. . .] and give him food and drink. And his bed is prepared in the bedchamber. ²⁵'The men who are assigned to him keep watch over him by night, and when the cup-bearer gives him drink, they hold the *sertappila*ᶜ over the cup. And wherever the king is accustomed to sit, [he also si]ts beside ²⁹'him. On the seventh day he [dies (?)].

The next part of the text has many gaps in it. It speaks of the repetition of the king's prayer and above all of extended rites of purification, which suggest Babylonian origin. *KUB* XV 2, supplemented by further duplicate fragments, gives the following colophon on verso 5'-9':

First tablet, not completed. Invocation [. . .]: This is the ritual to be used if the king is assigned (?) to die, whether he sees it in a dream, whether it is shown to him in an oracle by animal or bird, or whether he enc[ount]ers any other fatal [om]en.

8. *From the ritual of the substitute king KUB XXIV 5 + IX 13*

The starting point of this ritual is a fatal omen sent by the moon god, who was primarily revered as an oracle giver in the Babylonian empire. The king offers various substitutes: a bull as a burnt offering for the moon god, offered in the presence of the cultic statues of deceased kings, simulating the solemn cremation of the threatened ruler. There is then mention of a substitute effigy. A request is made that the threatened doom, the 'evil omen', 'shortened years', 'short days (of life)' should accompany the substitute king, who has formally been appointed by anointing and robing in the royal regalia, to his foreign homeland. Further substitutes are offered to the sun god, to Lilwani, the queen of the underworld (who will in future be responsible for the candidate for death), and to the moon god, in the form of lambs.

The most recent edition of the text is in H. M. Kümmel, StBT 3, 7ff.

ᴿᵉᶜᵗᵒ ⁶'[Now when it is] night, he (the king) takes the images of the [former] Labarnasᵈ and goes to the *harpa*ᵉ of the moon god [. . .] and speaks as follows: 'Consider the reason [why] I have come [to] pr[ay]; hear me, moon god, my lord! [Moon god, my lord, you have sent] an omen, showing disaster for me. ¹⁰'Behold, I have [. . . a substitu]te in (my) place. Accept it, [and let me free!'] They now bring a living bull up on the *harpa* and [sacri]fice [him on] the *harpa*. The king goes up on the *harpa* [and] says: '[Consider] the reason why you, moon god, have

---

ᶜ An object which cannot be interpreted with any certainty.

ᵈ A title of the Hittite kings (roughly corresponding to Caesar).

ᵉ Perhaps a raised place for sacrifices.

sent an omen, [show]ing disaster for me, [. . . you de]sire to see the smoke of [. . . my] (cremation?)[f] with your own eyes. [15']See, I myself have come and have [offered this substi]tute. [So] behold [the smoke(?) fr]om it! They may die, but I must [no]t die!

There are gaps in lines 17'-18'. Among other things, there seems to have been mention of a substitute effigy.

[19']They now anoint the prisoner with the royal oil, [20']and he says (to the king): 'See, he is now king! [I have bestowed] the royal name[g] on this man, I have dressed him in the ro[yal apparel] and I have put the band on his forehead! Evil omen, short years, short days, mark [this] well! Go after this substitute.' And he goes out of the city. [He/they . . .] one shekel [of silver], one shekel of gold, one mina of copper, [25']one mina of tin, one mina of iron, one mina of lead. They assign [an] officer to the prisoner and he takes him back to his own land. The king[, however,] makes the prayer.[h] Afterwards the king immediately goes to wash.

As soon as it is light, the king makes the prayer. [Then] he performs the 'house ritual', the 'pure ritual'. When it is day, the king performs the '[pur]e' rites.

The king then sacrifices a lamb each to the sun god, Lilwani and the moon god, with the request that they shall accept the substitute in his place and acquit him, so that he may continue to see the sun. The text then breaks off.

IV. INSTRUCTIONS

Instructions, given by the king or even by the queen, represent an important genre of Hittite writing. The Hittites put them in the same category as treaties with other states – they too are guaranteed by an oath. With a request that they should be followed conscientiously and administered loyally, they are addressed to officials and particular professional groups which were predominantly active in the public interest: to administrative and military officials, to members of the army, to city governors, and also to palace officials and – as in the case of the following texts – to cultic functionaries in the broader sense.

[f] The Hittites practised cremation.
[g] 'Name of the kingship' probably means the official title.
[h] Literally 'the raising of the hand' (a gesture of prayer).

9. *Instructions for cultic officials and temple personnel*

Text: *KUB* XIII 4 ('A'), with duplicates *KUB* XIII 5 + XXXI 95 ('B'), *KUB* XIII 6 + 19 ('C') and *KUB* XXXI 94 ('H'). Date of origin: at the latest, the middle of the thirteenth century BC. Editions: E. Sturtevant, *JAOS* 54, 1934, 363ff.; id., *A Hittite Chrestomathy*, 1935, 129ff.; A. Goetze, in *ANET*[3], 207ff.

As a safeguard against abuse of office, fraud and negligence, the text (which is quoted here in an abbreviated form) covers the nature and the performance of various duties by associating special regulations concerning conduct with statements of principles about responsibility before the gods and the requirements of cultic purity. Particularly in connection with the theme of 'cleanliness' and 'uncleanliness', comparable material can be found in OT precepts and statements about the priesthood and the cult, though there the aspect of holiness[i] is supreme and makes far-reaching ethical demands. The regulations for priests e.g. in Lev. 10; 21f., or Ezek. 44.16ff. are comparable, as are the standards used for criticism in I Sam. 2.12–17, 22, 29f. and Mal. 1.6ff. As far as points of detail are concerned, there is also a similarity in the principle of conditional family liability (A I 28–38): cf. e.g. Ex. 20.5; 34.7; Num. 14.18; Josh. 7.24f.; I Sam. 2.29ff.; II Sam. 21.5ff.; Lam. 5.7 and Ezek. 18.2.[j] Finally, the description of scepticism in B II 27–31 ('Because he is a god, he will say nothing and do nothing to us') is reminiscent of the OT passages Zeph. 1.12; Pss. 10.1–4, 11; 14; 64.5; 73.3ff., 11; 94.7. There is a similar expression of the conviction of the divine visitation which is to be expected, but will be all the more searching, in Pss. 37.7, 9f., 13 and 73.17f.

The beginning of the first column is missing in the Hittite text.

[A I 14ff.]Furthermore, those who prepare the daily (sacrificial) bread are to be pure. [15]They are to be bathed and shaved, their [body?] hair and their na[ils] are to be cut. They are to wear clean clothes. They are not to prepare it [in an unclean state(?)]. (Only) those who are [agreeable] to the gods' soul and body are to prepare this (bread). The baking houses in which they prepare it are to be swept and [20]sprinkled. Furthermore, neither pigs nor dogs are to come to the door of the room where the bread is broken. Are the sensibilities of men and gods of a different kind? Not in that respect(?), by no means! (Their) sensibilities are the same.

[i] The concept of holiness itself is not unknown to the Hittites. It is used, for example, if something is to be described as belonging exclusively to a deity, primarily its divine nature, and then perhaps the territory of a hostile city which has been destroyed and dedicated to the god, and which is not to be built again (like Jericho). It is also used of temples, cultic utensils, priests, sacrifices, festivals (our texts gives the word in the context of the designation 'festivals of the holy priest' in A I 42).

[j] While collective liability is to be found in some cases, as in Israel (Deut. 24.16), individual liability is certainly more frequent and is the normal usage. It was common among the Hittites at least after the fifteenth century.

If a servant stands before his master, he is bathed and dressed in clean clothes and in this fashion gives him his food or drink. [25]And because his master eats and drinks, he is relaxed in (his) attitude and [fe]els one with him (the servant). Now if it is a matter of a god, will he (too) not be capable of feeling(?) disgust?[k] Is he likely to feel otherwise? If a servant makes his master angry in some way, they will either execute him or cut off his nose, his eyes, [30]his ears, or [they will seize] him and 'call him over',[l] together with his wife, his children, his brothers, his sisters, his married kinsfolk, his clan, even his male and female slaves – or they may do nothing at all. Now if [anyone] arouses the anger of a god, [35]does the god afflict that man alone? Does he not also afflict his wife, [his children,] his [descen]dants, his family, his slaves and slave girls, his cattle, his sheep and his crops, and in this way utterly destroy him? So be very careful indeed in the matter of a god, for your own good!

Furthermore, the festival of the month, the festival of the year, the festival of the stag, the autumn festival, [40]the spring festival, the festival of thunder . . .

The names of twelve further festivals are given; some of them are known but cannot be interpreted.

[45]. . . and whatever other festival (is celebrated) in Hattusa – if you do not celebrate them in order with all (the prescribed quantities of) oxen, sheep, bread, beer and wine, and if your temple officials enter into an arrangement with those who have to provide (all) that, you slight the gods.[m]

[50]Or if you take something that is part of the preparation (for a sacrifice) and do not set it before the gods, but withhold it from them and take it into your houses, and your wives, your children or your servants consume it, or if a relative by marriage or a friend, or one entitled to the protection due to a citizen,[n] comes to you and you [55]give it to him, and withhold it from the god, and do not set it before him, even if it is only a part and you only withhold a part, you will be made responsible for this diminution. You are not to diminish the sacrifice. Anyone who diminishes it shall die. There shall be no mitigation for him.

[60]You must offer all the bread, beer and wine in the temple. Let no

---

[k] Another suggestion for translation is 'finding fault'.

[l] An idiomatic expression, corresponding either to our 'help into eternity' or at least a legal term for summoning to a capital trial.

[m] Cf. I Sam. 2.12–17, 29ff. and the regulations in Lev. 2.10; 3.16b–17; 5.13, etc.

[n] A privileged foreigner who has been granted asylum and is allowed to take part in the cult and appear at court (see B II 11–13). It corresponds to the Hebrew *ger* (e.g. Num. 15.15f.).

one take for himself sacrificial bread (or) thin bread! Let no one pour beer (or) wine out of the cup! You shall allow it all to go to the god. And you shall say these words before the god: 'May the god, my lord, [punish] anyone who has taken any of this sacrificial bread ^{65}and wine, and may he hold his house responsible for it!'

BII 6-33 supplemented on the basis of CII and AII[Furthermore,] if you [wish to?] eat and drink on that day, [then?] eat and drink!° But if you cannot finish it, eat [until] the third day. [But . . .] your wives, your children, your servants ^{10}[. . . may] in no wise [cross] the threshhold of the gods. But if a befriended citizen wants to come to one (of you), [he may] enter the temple. For he may cross the threshhold of the gods and the king. [He is to be conducted(?)] up, and he is to eat and drink. But if he is a ^{15}[foreig]ner, if he is not a citizen of Hattusa, he may [not enter into the gods(?). And anyone] who (nevertheless) introduces him incurs the death penalty!

The following section prohibits the replacement of good sacrificial animals or their meat with less valuable animals or meat and completely forbids the removal of sacrificial animals and meat for sale or for private use or for any other purpose. There follows a rejoinder to the characteristically sceptical argument of the defrauder:

^{27}. . . 'Pecause he is a god, he will say nothing and do nothing to us.' Just think how a man reacts if someone snatches away food from before his eyes. The will of the gods is strong. It does not make haste to seize, but when it does seize, it does not let go again. So be very careful about the will of the gods!

A II ^{25}Furthermore, you are (only) caretakers of the silver and gold of the gods, their clothes and copper implements with which you deal (or: which you have). (You have) no (right to) the silver, the gold, the clothes and the bronze utensils of the gods, nor to anything else that is in the house of the gods: whatever it may be, it belongs only to the god (in question). So be very careful! No silver or gold at all should ^{30}belong to a temple official. He should not wear it on his body and he should not make any decoration for his wife or child out of it. And if anyone gives him silver, gold, clothes or bronze utensils as a gift from the palace, it should be designated: 'Possessor, so and so; the king has given it to him.' Its weight should also be written down. It should also be written down: 'On such and such a festival it was given to him,' and the names of the witnesses should be written down afterwards: 'So and so were present when it was given to him.' Furthermore, he should not bring it into his

_____

° The passage clearly relates to a cultic meal before the gods. Cultic meals were also normal religious celebrations among the Hittites. Cf. Deut. 16.11, 14; 26.11; I Sam. 1.3ff., where the family in the widest sense can attend the cultic meal.

house. Rather, he should sell it. ⁴⁰But if he does sell it, he should not sell it secretly. The lords of Hatti should be present and look on, and what he sells should be written down on a tablet and sealed. And when the king comes up to Hattusa, (he) should put it (the tablet) in the palace and they should seal it. But if he puts it up for sale on his own account, he is liable to the death penalty. The one who does not sell the royal gift which is designated by the king's name – and does not sell silver, gold, clothing, bronze utensils in the way outlined above – and the one who receives it and hides it and does not bring it to the king's gate,ᵖ both of them shall be liable to ⁵⁰the death penalty. Indeed, they both shall die. They are . . . to the gods. There shall in no way be any mitigation for them.

The following paragraphs are concerned with the punctilious observation of festivals (§9'), with the duties of the temple officials who are assigned to nocturnal duties and of the night watchmen (§10'), with other instructions for the temple watch (§11'), with disturbances to the cult (§12') and with putting out the fire in the temple at night (§13').

ᴬ ᴵᴵᴵ ⁵⁵Furthermore, all of you who are kitchen servants of the gods, cup-bearers, waiters at table, cooks, bakers, vintners, be very careful about the feelings of the gods! Devote much reverent care to the gods' bread and wine. The room where the bread is broken ⁶⁰must be swept and sprinkled. Dogs and pigs are not to cross its threshhold. You must bathe and put on clean clothes. Your (body?) hair and your nails must be cut, and the feelings of the gods must not be offended(?) by you. If a pig or a dog somehow touches wooden or earthen vessels ⁶⁵which you are using, and the kitchen master does not take this away, but offers the gods food in an unclean vessel, then the gods will give him dung to eat and urine to drink.q And if anyone goes and sleeps with a woman, he must go in (just) the same way as if he were seeing to the service of the gods, and were giving the god food ⁷⁰and drink. Furthermore, [. . .] when the sun (rises?) [he must bathe himself,] and in the morning, at the time when the gods eat, he must make haste to be present. And if he fails to do this, it will be a trespass for him. And if anyone sleeps with a woman, and his superior or overseer forces him afterwards (to take part in the cult) he shall say so. And if he is ashamedʳ to say it (to him), he must tell his colleague and must bathe. But if he knowingly keeps silence, and still has not bathed, and approaches the bread and ⁸⁰wine of the gods in a state of uncleanness, or if his colleague knows it or sees it and keeps

ᵖ The king's judgment place. At the same time the seat of the authorities of the highest court and the capital court.
q To be understood as punishment in the other world.
ʳ Literally 'if he does not dare to'.

[it] secret, and it later comes out, [they are both] liable to the death penalty. They must both die.

The following paragraphs (§§15′–19′) deal with the duties of the agricultural personnel of the temple, above all with the regulations for producing the sacrificial animals and fruit used for the cult, and with the prohibition against embezzlement.

D

UGARITIC TEXTS

INTRODUCTION

So far, no original texts of any significant length have been discovered from the immediate Canaanite background to the Old Testament. Our knowledge of the culture and religion of South Canaan at the time before the foundation of Israel rests exclusively on the information given in the Old Testament and on the mute testimony of archaeological excavations. This information has been supplemented in some respects by the reports of ancient authors and the church fathers on Phoenician religion, which was closely related to the cults in neighbouring south Canaan, later to become Palestine. In addition, in the nineteenth century a series of inscriptions of Phoenician original texts was discovered, though they do not all go back to the early period of Israel. We also have some information from Egyptian sources.

This unsatisfactory situation was fundamentally changed by the extensive discovery of texts on the North Syrian tell of Ras esh-Shamra, ancient Ugarit. The texts unearthed from the archives and libraries of this ancient trading city on the North Phoenician coast since 1929 are written predominantly in the Akkadian language and script and relate to all areas of life. A second equally extensive group of texts is of particular importance for the Old Testament and its world. These are clay tablets inscribed with a peculiar alphabetical cuneiform, for which so far there is evidence only in quite isolated discoveries outside Ugarit. The language of these texts is a North Canaanite dialect, which has now come to be termed 'Ugaritic'. In many respects it is closely related to Hebrew. The same alphabetical cuneiform was also used in Ugarit to write down Hurrian texts.

In content the North Canaanite tablets from Ras Shamra are partly archive material and partly mythical or epic texts. The second group of texts is of extraordinary significance for the history of religion; its most extensive and most important documents were discovered during the first archaeological campaigns. It gives us an original and comprehensive view of the religious ideas and cults prevalent in ancient North Canaan. It is important that the mythical texts can be supplemented with material related to the administration of the cult, especially with lists of gods and sacrifices, and with all kinds of archaeological finds in the ruins of temples, effigies of gods and apparatus used in the cult. Thanks to these rich and varied sources, our knowledge of the nature of the cult in ancient Ugarit has become more exact and more extensive than that of the cult of any other city in ancient Syria and Phoenicia before the time of the Romans.

Archaeological stratigraphy, combined with the historical features in the texts themselves, makes possible quite an exact dating of the alphabetical cuneiform texts from Ras Shamra. In essentials, they originate in the thirteenth century BC, i.e. the last period of the history of ancient Ugarit. In about 1200, Ugarit was destroyed in connection with the so-called 'invasion of the Sea Peoples'. Of course, this only indicates the period when the texts were written down. The basic material in the myths is certainly very old indeed. At any rate, they reproduce religious conceptions which were alive in Canaan in the thirteenth century BC. Thus the texts are evidence for a period of the utmost significance for Israelite history and religion – perhaps even of fundamental significance. From what we know, the phase of the consolidation of Israelite tribes in southern Canaan begins at the end of the thirteenth century. The Old Testament indicates that conflict with the cults practised in the agricultural land of Canaan and with the general pattern of agricultural civilization played a considerable part in this development. Because the Old Testament tradition is so hostile to Canaan, we can discover little from it about the religion which the Israelite groups found in ancient Canaan, and what there is is presented in the context of polemics. The Ras Shamra texts, however, give an objective picture of Canaanite religion for this very period. The gods, cults and mythical conceptions which the Israelites began to encounter as they settled in Canaan may roughly have corresponded to what we can infer in this respect from the Ugaritic texts.

We learn more not only about the Canaanite deities mentioned in the Old Testament, their significance and the forms in which they were worshipped, but also about the influence of Canaanite cults on the religion of Israel. As the material has been studied more and more closely, it has become increasingly clear that Yahwistic religion assimilated far more Canaanite elements than had generally been supposed. Thus we already find in ancient Ugarit the various forms of sacrifice which occur in the

INTRODUCTION   187

Old Testament and the terminology for them. Influences of this kind are
not restricted to cultic usages; they can also be seen in conceptions of
the gods. This is especially the case with the transference of the functions
of the Canaanite god of weather and fertility, Baal/Hadad, to Yahweh.
Such observations should not really surprise us. They simply confirm
the justification for prophetic polemic against the Canaanite influence on
Yahwistic religion. Old Testament cultic poetry, above all, makes it clear
how far these influences could go in detail. Here we come up against a
wealth of phrases and poetic imagery which are already characteristic of
Ugaritic myths – sometimes there are even exact verbal parallels. On the
basis of such a comparison, Psalm 29, which is very early, can be identified
as an ancient Canaanite cultic hymn which has been superficially adapted
in terms of Yahweh. The pattern of *parallelismus membrorum*, i.e. couplets
which are the same in form and content, is a characteristic element of
poetic expression in Ugaritic myths and epics even before it appears in
the Old Testament.

   Thus the Ugaritic texts not only inform us about the religion of ancient
Canaan before the arrival of Israel, but also present us with a wealth of
material to explain the Old Testament traditions and to help us to understand them better. However, we should not overlook the fact that the
Ugaritic texts only come from the wider Canaanite background to the
Old Testament. The mere fact of the distance between Ugarit, in
Northern Syria, and Israel, in Palestine, is important. In addition, there
were no diplomatic or territorial links between the two areas. In its hey-
day Ugarit controlled only the coastal strip as far as Beirut. Thus there
are no political reasons why specifically Ugaritic gods should have been
worshipped in Canaan, in the south. Nor can it be said that religion in the
West Semitic and Canaanite area of Asia Minor was the same everywhere,
although there were far-ranging similarities in cult and in myth. While
the most important gods and types of gods were to be found all over the
coastal region of Western Asia, within the pantheon of individual city
states each will have had a differing position. Accordingly there must also
have been some differences in the myths which told of these gods and their
relationship to each other.

   It is clear, then, that as well as showing many features which we also
find elsewhere, the myths in Ugarit have an unmistakable local colouring.
The significant position of the goddess Ashirat, the 'mistress of the sea',
and her following, can be explained from the topographical position of
the coastal city. The massif of the 'hill of the north' (present-day Jebel
el-Aqra), which lay to the north of Ugarit and dominated the landscape,
was revered as the home of the chief god Baal and played a corresponding
role in mythology. As stories about the gods, the myths also reflect cultic

conditions in the city. Thus to all appearances Baal was late in achieving his dominant position in the pantheon and in the cultic life of Ugarit, as the city god of Ugarit (*b'l ugrt*). This emerges, *inter alia*, from the fact that he needs the support of the goddess Anat before he can attempt to build a palace (= temple). The supreme god El hesitates before acceding to his plan and has to be persuaded by very vigorous threats from the goddess Anat. In general, rivalry between El and Baal is unmistakable. Significantly, Baal is not regarded, like the other Ugaritic gods, as the son of the father-god El and the mother-goddess Ashirat. As successor to the earlier vegetation god Dagan, he is called 'son of Dagan'. Thus genealogically he is alien in the Ugaritic pantheon.

Among other local specialities in the world of the gods and in the myths of Ugarit are the signs of influences from neighbouring cultures and religions. As a significant trading city and port with far-reaching connections and a mixed population, Ugarit was especially exposed to influences of this kind. Thus in Ugaritic myth the chief influences are Hurrian and Aegean. One of the favourite divine figures, the artistic Kusharu-Hasisu, is expressly said to have his home in Crete. The depiction of divine feasts and the strongly anthropomorphic treatment of the gods which are often to be found in the mythical texts are reminiscent of the world of the Homeric deities.

These few allusions make it clear that one cannot transfer the religious statements in the Ugaritic texts to conditions in southern Canaan in the thirteenth century BC without considerable qualification. In fact there are also considerable differences with respect to the gods and their functions. Thus in Ugarit the sun deity plays only a modest role in cult and myth and is feminine. She is called Shapash or Shapshu, whereas in Palestine the masculine sun god Shamash is worshipped. The goddess Ashirat of Ugarit is a goddess of the sea. On the other hand Asherah, who is mentioned in the Old Testament, is a tree goddess. In general, it is impossible to imagine too much variety in the divine world of ancient Canaan. Two elements above all may have played their part in this development: first the general tendency to differentiate in cult religions between the local manifestations of the divine figures who were chiefly worshipped, and secondly the division of Syria-Palestine into a large number of small states or city states, which understandably had each its own cult and its own pantheon. Nevertheless, the relationship between the cults and myths of this area is so close that we may certainly suppose that myths were also told in southern Canaan which will have been very similar to those of Ugarit in their themes, the chief features of their content and their poetic language.

One word should also be said about the tradition of the mythical texts from Ugarit, which are in fact the main source for our knowledge of Ugaritic religion. The texts have a predominantly literary character. In the form in which they have come down to us they were clearly not intended for liturgical use - apart from the myth of the birth of the gods Shahar and Shalem. But that does not mean that in the last resort they did not have their home in the cult. This is less probable, however, in the special group of semi-mythical or epic texts (the Daniil and Krt texts) which tell predominantly of earthly events. Perhaps these epics are poetic accounts of particular periods of the early history of the dynasty of Ugarit elaborated with mythical elements. The main theme of the two great epic texts is in any case the preservation of the dynasty despite all kinds of threats to its continuance.

Select bibliography

Introduction

W. Baumgartner, 'Ras Schamra und das Alte Testament', *ThR* 12, 1940, 163-88; 13, 1941, 1-20, 85-102, 157-83; id., 'Ugaritische Probleme und ihre Tragweite für das Alte Testament', *ThZ* 3, 1947, 81-100; G. Fohrer, 'Die wiederentdeckte kanaanäische Religion', *TLZ* 78, 1953, cols. 193-200; E. Jacob, *Ras-Shamra Ugarit et l'Ancien Testament*, 1900; C. F. Pfeifer, *Ras Shamra and the Bible*, 1962; A. S. Kapelrud, *The Ras Shamra Discoveries and the Old Testament*, 1965.

Language

A. Aistleitner, *Untersuchungen zur Grammatik des Ugaritischen*, BSAW, PH 100. 6, 1954; G. D. Young, *Concordance of Ugaritic*, AnOr 36, 1956; C. H. Gordon, *Ugaritic Textbook*, AnOr 38, 1965; A. Aistleitner, *Wörterbuch der ugaritischen Sprache*, BSAW, PH 106. 3, [3]1967.

Editions of the texts

A. Herdner, *Corpus des tablettes en cunéiformes alphabétiques*, vols. I-III, 1963; C. H. Gordon, *Ugaritic Textbook*, AnOr 38, 1965. Texts discovered since the appearance of the collections have been published in *Ugaritica* 5-6, 1968/69.

Translations

C. H. Gordon, *Ugaritic Literature*, 1949; H. L. Ginsberg, 'Ugaritic Myths and Epics', in I. Mendelsohn, *Religions of the Ancient Near East*, 1955, 221-79; id., in *ANET*[2], 1955, 129-55; G. R. Driver, *Canaanite Myths and Legends*, OTS 3, 1956; A. Jirku, *Kanaanäische Mythen und Epen aus Ras Schamra-Ugarit*, 1962; J. Aistleitner, *Die mythologischen und kultischen Texte aus Ras-Schamra*, [2]1964.

Mythology and Cult

J. Obermann, *Ugaritic Mythology*, 1948; M. H. Pope and W. Röllig, in H. W. Haussig, *WM*, 1965, 219-312; J. Gray, *The Legacy of Canaan*, SVT 5, ²1965; A. Jirku, *Der Mythus der Kanaanäer*, 1966. - For individual gods, O. Eissfeldt, *El im ugaritischen Pantheon*, BSAW, PH 98. 4, 1951; A. S. Kapelrud, *Baal in the Ras Shamra Texts*, 1952; M. H. Pope, *El in the Ugaritic Texts*, SVT 2, 1955.

For the cultural background

A. van Selms, *Marriage and Family Life in Ugaritic Literature*, 1954; A. F. Rainey, *The Social Structure of Ugarit*, 1967; id., *The Scribe at Ugarit*, 1968.

Special relationships to the Old Testament

J. H. Patton, *Canaanite Parallels in the Book of Psalms*, 1944; W. H. Schmidt, *Königtum Gottes in Ugarit und Israel*, BZAW 80, ²1966; O. Kaiser, *Die mythische Bedeutung des Meeres in Ägypten, Ugarit und Israel*, BZAW 78, 1962; M. Dahood, *Ugaritic-Hebrew Philology*, BibOr 17, 1965; W. F. Albright, *Yahweh and the Gods of Canaan*, 1968; L. R. Fischer (ed.), *Ras Shamra Parallels*, vol. I, AnOr 49, 1972.

Abbreviations of text numberings:

CTA = A. Herdner, *Corpus des tablettes en cunéiformes alphabetiques* . . .
I AB etc. = designations by C. Virolleaud in the first publications
Gordon = C. H. Gordon, *Ugaritic Textbook*.

I. MYTHS

By far the greatest number of mythical texts from Ugarit deal predominantly with the god Baal and his consort Anat. This corresponds with the dominant position of Baal in the cult of the city. However, another factor may be the circumstance that with few exceptions the mythical tablets and fragments were discovered in the library of the temple of Baal. The Baal texts have the character of a more or less closely connected cycle of myths which narrates the 'history' of the god.[a] As our series of

[a] It is clear from the many close connections in content, and from the uniformity of style and writing, that the six large tablets (*CTA* 1-6) belong together. Furthermore, the signatures in *CTA* 4. VIII and *CTA* 6. VI show that the text has been produced by the same 'scribe Ilimilku'. This Ilimilku also appears in similar signatures (colophons) to the Daniil and Krt texts. Presumably he is identical with the man of the same name to whom a certain Belubur announces, in a letter composed in Akkadian (*Syr* 16, 1935, 188ff.), that he is sending some tablets which are to be presented to the queen. It seems likely that these tablets contained mythological or epic texts. If this is correct, then Ilimilku may have been a learned man of ancient Ugarit with an international reputation.

Baal texts is not complete, and some of the tablets that have survived are only fragmentary, the sequence of the parts of the cycle can only be reconstructed with reservations.[b] The Baal-Hadad text (*CTA* 12, Gordon 75) seems to belong to quite another group of myths altogether. Here El emerges as the real adversary of Baal. There are also special features in both the language and the tradition.

The Baal myths have a more or less clear connection with the process of nature. Recognizing this context, F. F. Hvidberg was the first to put forward the view that both the central theme and the cultic point of reference of all the Ugaritic myths was to be sought in the autumn vegetation festival, the New Year Festival.[c] Hvidberg's approach was developed above all by I. Engnell, who attempted to demonstrate the probability that both the mythical and the epic Ras Shamra texts had their origin in a cultic pattern which was widespread throughout the ancient Near East. They assigned the king the chief role as the representative of the vegetation god in the cultic and dramatic presentation of the myths at the New Year Festival.[d] However, this view has not been able to command general assent. The very variety of the themes of the Baal myths goes against their being related to a single feast in the year, quite apart from the difficulties presented by an interpretation of the texts as a cultic-dramatic ritual. The attempt to understand the group of Baal myths as a reflection of the natural course of the year, in which each of the gods embodies a particular season, also fails to do justice to the content of the text.[e] The latest variant of this hypothesis recognizes in the Baal texts references to features of climate, agriculture and the cult which accompany the course of the Ugaritic calendar year, which begins in the autumn.[f] According to this, only the first two columns of *CTA* 3 can be connected with the theme of the New Year Festival.[g] However, all

---

At any rate, he is to be regarded as more than the copyist of the texts, which had already taken on a stereotyped form. Cf. O. Eissfeldt, *Sanchunjaton von Berut und Ilumilku von Ugarit*, BRGA 5, 1952, 77ff.; M. Dietrich/O. Loretz, *UF* 4, 1972, 31f.

[b] J. C. de Moor, *The Seasonal Pattern in the Ugaritic Myth of Ba'lu According to the Version of Ilimilku*, AOAT 16, 1971, has most recently suggested the sequence *CTA* 3, 1, 2, 4-6. J. Aistleitner, for example, differs, rejecting any more exact identification because of various overlaps in content. The following partial translation follows the order proposed by J. C. de Moor.

[c] *Graad og Latter i det Gamle Testamente*, 1938; English edition, edited by A. S. Kapelrud: *Weeping and Laughter in the Old Testament*, 1962.

[d] *Studies in Divine Kingship in the Ancient Near East*, 1943.

[e] This interpretation was developed by T. H. Gaster, *Thespis*, 1950, [2]1961.

[f] Cf. J. C. de Moor, op. cit.

[g] However, even this cannot be established with any certainty. Cf. below the introductory remarks on col. II, 'Anat's war'.

the Baal myths may have been recited solemnly in their present form at this festival, in order to help to guarantee the unbroken and prosperous succession of the seasons in the sequence laid down in the divine history contained in the myth. G. R. Driver rejects any connection with the seasons at all.[h] In his view, the texts are concerned with the introduction of the young god Baal as a fertility god into the Ugaritic pantheon and with the establishment of his supremacy over all the other gods under the patronage of the supreme god El. There are also weighty arguments in favour of this interpretation. However, in any case it is impossible to make a decision exclusively in favour of one or the other interpretation. This situation probably derives from the conception of the myth itself, which shows the 'history' of Baal, i.e. his rise in the Ugaritic pantheon, in his function during the cultic year of Ugarit.

1. A banquet for Baal

Text: *CTA* 3, col. I = V AB-A = ʿnt I.
The text gives us no indication of the occasion for the festivity. It seems to be the supreme god El himself who arranges the banquet. It is improbable that the cycle of Baal myths began with this banqueting scene. However, among the tablets so far found there is none that we can put before it with any certainty.
The scene is very reminiscent of descriptions of feasts of the gods and sacrifices in Homer (especially *Iliad* I, 458-74, 595-604; II, 421-31). The OT is familiar with the image of the great feast which God will prepare for the peoples (Isa. 25.6ff.). There is also the conception of the cup of wrath which God gives to the kings of the nations far and near (Jer. 25.15ff.). There are no mythical pictures of a feast of the gods in monotheistic Yahwistic religion. OT criticism of sacrifice rejects the view that sacrifice is a meal for God (Ps. 50.8ff.). However, sacrifice is occasionally described as food for God (Lev. 3.1, 16; Num. 28.24). The picture of wine, 'which delights the hearts of gods and men' (Judg. 9.3), is reminiscent of ancient Canaanite ideas.

2. . . . He[i] serves Baal, the mighty,
honours the prince, the lord of the earth.
He raised himself up, set it before him and ⁵gave him food.
He divided a breast before him,
the forepart of the fatling with a sharp knife.
He approached, offered the wine, and gave him drink.

¹⁰He puts the cup in his hand,
the goblet in his two hands –
a great tankard of mighty size,

[h] *Canaanite Myths and Legends*, OTS 3, 1956.
[i] El seems to be meant.

a holy cup, a woman may not look upon it,
a cup, [15]a goddess[j] may not look upon it.
It holds a thousand jars of wine,
ten thousand may be mixed in it.

They began to play and to sing,
a musician with cymbals in his hand.
[20]A young man sang with a fine voice,
about Baal, who dwells on the peaks of the mountain of the north:[k]
'Baal looks at his daughter,
he looks at Pidraya, the daughter of cloud,
and at Talaya, [25]the daughter of rain . . .'[l]

2. *Anat's war*

Text: *CTA* 3 II = V AB-B = ʿ*nt* II.
There is a gap of about twenty-five lines between the first and the second
columns of the text. This unknown part of the myth must have related the
reason for the blood-bath which Anat now instigates. No connection with events
in the seasons can be discerned. Nevertheless, scholars have thought to see in
the passage the mythical basis of a fertility rite aimed at overcoming periods
of drought by the shedding of blood.[m] Nor is there any point of contact for
connecting this passage with the myth of the battle with chaos.[n] Since Anat,
Baal's sister, constantly intervenes on her brother's behalf in the texts of the
Baal cycle, as goddess of war, we may have a similar occasion here, a threat to
Baal's rights.
The text is important because of its vivid description of the bloody terror
which is disseminated by the goddess of war. Anat is not mentioned in the OT.

[j] The name of Ashirat appears in the text, but here it is simply used as a designation
for a goddess.
[k] The mountain of Baal Zaphon is still a place of worship even now (cf. O. Eissfeldt,
Baal Zaphon, Zeus Kasios und der Durchzug der Israeliten durchs Meer, BRGA 1, 1932,
30ff.). Presumably there was a temple somewhere near its summit, or perhaps merely a
place in the open for sacrifices (perhaps with a 'divine throne' hewn out of rock, cf.
K.-H. Bernhardt, *Gott und Bild*, 1956, 146). Such locations are often to be found on
hills associated with gods. One very well preserved example from the Hellenistic-Roman
period is the cultic place above Sefire in northern Lebanon. It consists of a large temple
with ancillary buildings at the foot of the mountain, a small intermediate sanctuary half
way up and the place of sacrifice at the top. – From his throne on the mountain Baal
looks out on the rain clouds which surround the massif of the mountain below its
summit. This impressive natural phenomenon is familiar to pilgrims to Mount Zaphon
today, as it was in ancient times.
[l] Talaya and Pidraya are names with meanings (*ṭl* = dew, *pdr* = thunder mace(?), cf.
J. Aistleitner, *Wörterbuch*, 254).
[m] Cf. J. Gray, *The Legacy of Canaan*, SVT 5, [2]1965, 45.
[n] The only thing to be considered would be a translation of the battle with chaos
into the historical dimension.

She does, however, appear in ancient place names (Beth Anath, Anathoth). She was worshipped alongside Yahweh by the Jews of Elephantine. Some OT descriptions of Yahweh's appearance as the god of war and judgment are reminiscent of Anat's rage (e.g. Deut. 32.40ff.; Isa. 34.5ff.).

11. Anat as goddess of war.

3
. . . .

After Anat had shut the doors of the palace,
she encountered the young men [5]at the foot of the mountain (?).
And then Anat fought in the plain,
she mows down the cities,
she shatters the inhabitants of the coasts,
she annihilates the men of the sunrise.

Beneath her, heads lie like balls;
[10]Hands (fly) over her like locusts,
the hands of the shield-bearers like hacked-off stubble.[o]

Soon the heads towered up to her back,
the hands stretched up to her lap.

She bathes her knees in the blood of soldiers,
her rings in the life-blood of [15]the shield-bearers.
With the staff she drives away the old,
she aims at the thigh with her bow.

Then Anat returns to her house,
the goddess comes to her palace.
And she has not become sated by the battle in the plain,
[20]by mowing down the inhabitants of the cities.

She hurls stools against the shield-bearers,
throws tables against the warriors,
footstools against the heroes.

She lays many low and looks upon the scene (with pleasure);
Anat mows and enjoys herself.
[25]Her inwards swell in jubilation;
her heart is filled with joy.
Anat's inwards rejoice,
when she bathes her knees in the blood of soldiers,
her rings in the life-blood of the shield-bearers.
She slaughters in the house until she is sated,
[30]she mows between the tables.

The blood of the soldiers was washed away in the house;
the oil of peace (?) was poured out.
The virgin Anat washed her hands in a shell,
the Yabamat Limim her fingers.[p]
She washes the blood of soldiers from her hands,
[35]the life-blood of shield-bearers from her fingers.
She ranges [stool] on stool,
table on table,
footstool on footstool.
She draws water and washes herself –
dew of the heaven, fat of the earth,

[o] The image probably derives from the treatment of grain with a threshing-sled on the threshing floor.
[p] A name for Anat. The meaning is uncertain.

a shower of rain [40]from the rider on the clouds,[q]
the dew of heaven which the clouds pour down,
which is given by the stars.

[42]She puts on perfume. . . .

3. Baal's plan to build a temple

Text: CTA 3. III–IV = V AB–C/D = 'nt III–IV. Columns III (the last
of the recto of the tablet) and IV (the first of the verso) follow one another
without a gap.

The connection with the two preceding scenes is easy to recognize. First of
all Baal is introduced in his function as a fertility god and is honoured by El
through a banquet. But nothing has yet been decided about the erection of a
dwelling-place for Baal on Mount Zaphon and its counterpart in the city of
Ugarit. Baal cherishes the understandable wish to be on a level with the other
gods in this respect. But he himself is not active 'in the highest circles'; he
makes use of the help of his energetic and experienced sister Anat, the goddess
of war. With this the myth arrives at its real theme. In this larger context the
second scene seems simply to have the purpose of depicting Anat in her
activity as goddess of war and to demonstrate that she is a suitable help for
Baal in his plan. About fifteen lines are missing at the beginning of the third
scene (cols. III–IV); they probably gave an account of the preparation for
Anat's invitation. Baal's daughters evidently also had some kind of share in
this preparation. Anyway, one of them is mentioned in the first of the lines
which has been preserved. Then there follows the precise order to Baal's two
messengers.

[5]So, young men, go in!
Bow yourselves down before Anat,
and fall down, abasing yourselves, in her honour!
And say to the virgin Anat,
present this message to the Yabamat Limim:
[10]'Message of the mighty Baal,
a word from the one who is exalted among the heroes!
Come to me from the land of battle!
Bring love into the earth,
pour peace into the heart of the earth,
much love into the depths of the fields![r]

[q] Cf. the OT conception of Yahweh as the rider on the clouds: Isa. 19.1; Ps. 68.4;
also Deut. 33.26; II Sam. 22.11; Pss. 18.10; 68.33.
[r] There is an allusion here to Anat's double function as goddess of war and goddess
of love.

Plate III   Akkadian cuneiform tablet: Creation Epic, Tablet IV

15
. . . s
Your feet are to hasten to me,
your legs are to run to me.
Behold, I have a saying and I will utter it for you,
a word, and I will report it to you.
It is a word [20]of the tree and an invocation of the stone.[t]

The heaven will whisper to the earth,
the ocean to the stars:
I wish to build a palace the like of which the heavens do not know,
something that men do not know
and the [25]hordes of the earth do not understand.

Come quickly, for I truly will establish it (?)
In the midst of my mountain, (I) the god of Zaphon,[u]
in the holy precinct, on the hill which I possess,[v]
in a pleasant place, on the hill which displays my power.'

And behold, when Anat looked on the two gods,
[30]her legs trembled,
they collapsed at the hips,
sweat covered her face,
the skin of her loins quivered,
the flesh (?) of her back.

And she raised her voice and cried:
'Why have Gapan and Ugar come?[w]
Has some enemy shown himself against Baal,
is there [35]hostility against the one who rides on the clouds?

Have I not smashed El's darling, Yam?[x]

    [s] The translation of this line is uncertain. It perhaps names three attributes of Anat
to support her summons, e.g. '(By) your . . ., your staff (?), your weapon (?).'
    [t] Perhaps this means that Baal's decision, which has become a word of command, is
addressed specifically to tree and stone as being the most important materials for the
planned palace.
    [u] In the OT cf. Isa. 14.13; Ps. 48.2; possibly Ps. 89.12.
    [v] Cf. here also Ex. 15.17f.
    [w] Gpn (vine) and 'ugr (meadow) are names with meanings, appropriate for the func-
tion of messengers of the god of fertility. It is also possible to see them as representatives
of Byblos (Egyptian kpn) and Ugarit, the extreme south of the sphere of Ugaritic
influence and the capital itself. Cf. J. A. Montgomery, JAOS 53, 1933, 110.
    [x] The god Yam (sea) is one of the chief adversaries of the fertility god Baal. There is
a reflection here of a natural experience of those living on the coast of Syria. During
the winter storms the waves of the sea often flooded those areas of cultivated land which
were only a little above sea level. Loss of land, above all by the hollowing out of rocky

Have I not made an end to Nahar, the great god?[y]
Have I not crushed Tannin? Yes, I crushed him![z]
I shattered the wounded snake,
[39]the powerful (?) one with the seven heads . . .'[a]

There follows an enumeration of the other opponents of Baal defeated by
Anat, whose titles cannot be determined in any detail. It is clear that they
belong to the group of the gods of the earth, and especially Mut, the god of the
underworld, whose name is probably also mentioned. His following includes
'fire, the hound of the gods', and 'flame, the daughter of El'.

[43] . . . .

'I will fight and will take possession of the weapon (?) of anyone
who seeks to drive Baal [45]from the heights of Zaphon,[b]
who seeks to seize his ears like a bird,
who seeks to dispossess him from the throne of his kingdom,
from the high place, the seat of his rule!

Has any enemy shown himself against Baal,
is there hostility against the one who rides on the clouds?'
The young men answered and replied to her:

---

bluffs, could be seen continually and bore witness to the rage of the god Yam. It is striking that Anat boasts of her victory over the enemies of Baal. Here she works indepen-
dently and not merely as a helper of Baal in the fight with the powers of chaos (cf. no. 7
below). This accords with the basic tendency of this part of the cycle, which assigns the
greatest share of the activity to Anat.

[y] Nahar means the same deity as Yam (see no. 7 below). However, we should probably
see him as another manifestation. It is true that *nhr* can be translated 'swell' or 'wave',
but the usual meaning of 'river' seems more appropriate. Natural phenomena, which
recur annually, can also be seen behind this designation of the ruler of the waters of
chaos. Violent rainstorms or sudden melting of snow can often turn the watercourses
coming down from the hills into rushing torrents, which can do considerable damage.
Thus Yam/Nahar is responsible for all water which threatens agriculture and human
existence generally. Cf. O. Kaiser, *Die mythische Bedeutung des Meeres*, 44ff. – Yam is
also known to the OT tradition as the power of chaos (Isa. 51.10; Job 26.12f.).

[z] The helpers of Yam/Nahar are mentioned here and in the following verses. Tannin
(usually translated 'dragon') also appears occasionally in the OT as a chaos monster
hostile to creation, which Yahweh conquered in primaeval times (Isa. 51.9; Ps. 74.13).
Otherwise it designates great sea monsters (Gen. 1.21; Ps. 148.7) or snakes (Ex. 7.9f.,
etc), or is used metaphorically (Isa. 27.1; Ezek. 29.3; 32.2).

[a] The 'wounded snake' is mentioned metaphorically in Isa. 27.1 as a chaos monster
or sea monster. There, as in Ugaritic (*ltn, CTA* 5. I, 1 = I* AB l. 1 = Gordon 67, I, 1),
it bears the name Leviathan.

[b] The OT also talks very frequently of 'mountains of God' (cf. e.g. Ex. 3.1; 24.13;
I Kings 19.8; Pss. 68.8, 17; 87.1f.), particularly in connection with the royal throne of
God (cf. e.g. Ex. 15.17f.; Pss. 9.11; 74.2, 12).

'No enemy has shown himself ^{50}against Baal,
there is no hostility against the one who rides on the clouds!
A message from the mighty Baal,
a word from the one who is exalted ^{52}among the heroes:
"Come to me from the land of slaughter . . ." '

We already know the message which has been given by Baal to his envoys;
this is now presented again almost word for word, apart from a few omissions.
Such repetitions are characteristic of Ugaritic myths and epics. They are an
ingredient of the style of oral presentation through a singer or story-teller.
The answer given by Anat also begins with the verses 'I will come from the
land of slaughter . . .', and after an invitation to Baal (only fragments of which
have been preserved) it begins again a second time with them. In this way the
content of Baal's message of peace is made particularly impressive. After the
messengers have been sent back, Anat herself sets out:

^{81}Then in truth she went to Baal,
on the heights of Zaphon,
over a thousand pastures and ten thousand fields.
Baal sees the coming of his sister,
the approach of the daughter (?) of his father.
He sent women to meet her,
^{85}he set an ox before her,
a fatted calf before her countenance.
They drew water and she washed herself,
dew of the heaven, fat of the earth,
dew of the heaven which the clouds pour down,
which is given by the stars.
^{89}She put on perfume . . .

4. Anat's audience with El

Text: *CTA* 3. V = V AB, E = ʿnt V.
The beginning of the fourth scene has been destroyed. It is possible to
supplement some of it by the use of parallels. We must assume that in the meantime Baal has communicated the details of his concerns to Anat, once she has
recovered from the exertions of her journey. The explanations given by Baal
culminate in the lament that he has no dwelling-place like other gods, even
including his daughters. Anat responds here also in a most vigorous way:

^{7}Then [the virgin] Anat retorted:
'The Bull^{c} El, [my father],^{d} will agree,

---

^{c} A name for El which characterizes his strength and also his function as god of creation and fertility. – According to Ex. 32.4; I Kings 12.28f., statues of bulls sometimes

he will agree with me and . . .
¹⁰. . . (or) I will smite him to the ground like a lamb,
I will bloody his grey hair,
make his grey beard [run with blood],
if he does not give Baal a house like the (other) gods,
[a temple] like the sons of Ashirat!'ᵉ
[She stamped her] foot,
and the earth [quaked].ᶠ

And behold, she [turned her fa]ce ¹⁵[towards El],
[and she went to El at the place] where the floods begin,
to the midst of [the source] of the two [seas].ᵍ
She ascended the mountain of El,ʰ
. . . and arrived [at the ab]ode of the king, the father of the exalted ones
    (?).
. . .
The Bull [El], her father, [heard] her coming,
²⁰in the seven rooms, in the eight chambers.ⁱ
. . .

El speaks to welcome Anat and observes: 'The light of the gods, Shapshu,
is scorching,/the heavens are in distress because of Mut, the son of the gods.'
Evidently El takes some delight in making this allusion to the rule of Mut, the
god of the underworld, over the earth. At any rate, Anat begins her reply (so
far as we have it) with the words, 'Do not delight . . .' The sorry state of the
earth during the period of drought is certainly connected with the fact that Baal
still has no abode. This passage is a clear indication of the amalgamation of the
aetiological legend of the cult with the rhythm of the seasons, which realizes
the 'history' of the god. – Anat then threatens to beat in El's brains, using the

---

had a role even in Yahweh worship. But see also Hos. 8.5; 13.2.
  ᵈ The designation of El as father of Anat complicates her relationship to Baal as his
sister, since Baal is not one of El's sons.
  ᵉ 'Sons of Ashirat' means the totality of the gods in El's pantheon, as Ashirat is the
mother of the gods in her capacity as El's consort.
  ᶠ Cf. Hab. 3.6.
  ᵍ The two seas are the primal waters, one of which extends above the firmament of
heaven and the other of which extends under the earth. This conception of the cosmos
is also presupposed by the Priestly account of creation in Gen. 1.7 (cf. also the OT parallels to the wording of the two verses in Job 38.11, 16f.; Ps. 18.15). The starting point
for the primal waters is the 'primal mountain' on which El has his dwelling. For the
location of El's abode cf. p. 202 n. k below.
  ʰ See p. 198 n. b above.
  ⁱ This is a way of describing an indeterminate but large number of rooms. Cf. the
corresponding usage in the OT: Micah 5.5; Eccles. 11.2.

same words which she had already spoken in her first reaction to Baal's lament:
'I will bloody your gray hair . . .'

[34]El replied in the seven rooms, yes, in the eight chambers:
'I have (long since) known, my daughter, that you are like a man;
for no one among the goddesses is so presumptuous(?). –
What is your desire, virgin Anat?'
Then the virgin Anat replied:
'Your decree, O El, is wise.
May your wisdom [40]endure for ever!
A happy life is your decree. –
May our king[j] be the mighty Baal, our judge!
No one shall be over him.
It shall be our duty to hand to him the goblet,
We shall both give him the cup.'
Then Bull El, her father, truly cried out aloud,
El, [45]the king, who created her;
Ashirat and her sons cried out,
the goddess and the horde of her kin:

'Alas, Baal does not have a house like the gods,
an abode like the sons of Ashirat,
a dwelling-place (like) El,
an abode (like) [his sons],
a dwelling place (like) the lady Ashirat [50]of the sea,
a dwelling place (like) [Pidra]ya, the daughter of cloud,
[a home] (like) Talaya, [the daughter] of rain,
[an abode [52]like Arsiya, the daughter of Yaabdar] . . .'

Thus Anat achieves through flattery and praise of El's wisdom what she
could not achieve through crude threats. It is striking that Anat does not present
Baal's plan, but raises the further demand that Baal shall be made king of the
gods, a demand which contains within itself the seeds of conflict. However,
El and the assembly of the gods do not react to this. Rather, they raise the very
complaint made by Baal at the beginning of the scene with Anat. To all
appearances the consequence of this agreement is the resolve to build a dwelling-
place for Baal.

5. *The message to Kusharu-hasisu, the master-builder*

Text: *CTA* 3. VI = V AB, F = *ʿnt* VI.
Only about ten lines are missing from the beginning of the text. Accordingly,
El puts his resolve to help Baal build a house into action. Within this short

---

[j] According to Ps. 95.3; 96.4; 97.9; 136.2, Yahweh is king over the gods.

space, at any rate, we should not expect the narrative to be taken further by means of new actions. El now sends the relevant message to Kusharu-hasisu (i.e. something like 'skilful and cunning'), the master-builder of the gods. As he lives in Caphtor (Crete), two messengers of the goddess Ashirat, goddess of the sea, who are skilled in seafaring, are sent to him:

7
. . .

'Go through Gabal, go through Qaal,
go through Ihat-Nop Shamim![k]
Make haste, [10]you two fishers of Ashirat,
go, Qadesh-Amurru.[l]
See, truly you are to turn your face to the midst of Chikupta,
Caphtor belongs to the god, all of it, [15]the throne of his residence,
Chikupta is the land of his possession.
Over a thousand meadows and ten thousand fields.
Bow yourselves before Kusharu and fall down,
prostrate [20]yourselves in honour of him!
And say to Kusharu-hasisu,

[k] Of the three places, Gabal can be identified clearly. This is Byblos (Akkadian *gubla*, Phoenician *gbl*, Hebrew *g[e]bal*, cf. Ezek. 27.9). From this fixed topographical point El's abode can also be determined with some degree of confidence. It should be sought in the shrine of the spring of Afqa on the upper course of the Nahr Ibrahim. The Arabic name Afqa corresponds to the Ugaritic *apq* ('source') in the phrase *apq thmtm* ('source of the two seas'), which is used here and in other places to describe El's abode. Geographically, these two seas could be identified with the Mediterranean and the lake Yammuneh which lies east of the ridge of the Lebanon; from ancient times a number of popular traditions were current about a secret subterranean connection between this and the Afqa spring (cf. for details M. H. Pope, *El in the Ugaritic Texts*, 75ff.). The processional route which leads from Byblos to Afqa and from there over the mountain ridge (which at this point is flatter), also seems to be old. This geographical localization does not go against the conception of the cosmic seat of the god El, which is inaccessible to men. Both the cosmic seat and its earthly counterpart always go together. Thus in the religious thinking of Israel Yahweh, too, has his throne above the heavens. At the same time, however, he resides in the distant mountain of Horeb, the mountain of God (I Kings 19), and nearer, on his holy hill in Jerusalem. Similarly, in the mythical story of the building of a temple for Baal the erection of a cosmic abode is connected with the building of an earthly temple. Similarly, too, *thm* can denote both mythical primal water and earthly tracts of water.

[l] This is a twofold deity who has been fused more or less consistently into a single figure. Behind the deity stand greater deities, but they played no more significant role in the cult and the myth of Ugarit. In the case of Amurru we should think of the national god of the Amurru; Ashratum (= Ashirat?) appears as his consort in Akkadian texts of the second millennium BC. The female deity Qadesh also often appears as an independent figure in the Ugaritic texts. Thus the hero of the Krt text is termed son of El and Qadesh (II K. I–II. 11, 22). Possibly this Qadesh is identical with Ashirat.

bear before Hayin,[m] the skilful one,
a message from the mig[hty Baal],
[25]a word of the exalted one among the heroes!"[n]

6. The dispute over the permission for the building

Further events can only be guessed at. Text *CTA* 1 (= VI AB = *'nt*, pl. IX), which in all probability forms the continuation, has been preserved in a very bad state. The possibility cannot be ruled out that a further tablet *CTA* 1, unknown to us, preceded it. At any rate it becomes clear that the building of Baal's palace is not yet taking place. A further message to Kusharu-hasisu seems necessary, and El entrusts the goddess Anat with this.[o] The divine master-builder now, it seems, accepts the commission and obeys El's command to begin building. However, there is a further delay before work can begin: now Ashirat, mistress of the sea, intervenes on behalf of her son Yam, who like Baal is without an abode.[p] *CTA* 1 ends with a scene which probably described the challenge to a duel in which Baal was to take part.

The following group of texts in the Baal cycle (*CTA* 2 = III AB) is in much better condition. We can infer from the tablet which is probably to be put first (*CTA* 2. III = III AB-C = Gordon 129) that Ashtar, the god of the underworld (who is also without an abode), appears as an opponent of the building of a palace for Yam. But this Ashtar has no hope, especially as he is unmarried. El declares: 'Governor Nahar, you are king!'

7. The fight between Baal and Yam

Text: *CTA* 2. I-II, IV = III AB-B A = Gordon 137; 68.

Now that Yam has achieved his aim, he can proceed to the elimination of his rival Baal. Some grim threats made by Baal at the fragmentary beginning of the second tablet of the group *CTA* 2 justify this plan. Yam sends out two messengers, having first carefully trained them in their commission.

[B 19]The young men departed,
they did not return.

---

[m] Hayin is another name for the twofold deity Kusharu-hasisu. But he also appears occasionally as a special figure, cf. no. 8 below.

[n] Remarkably, a message of Baal is mentioned here, whereas one would have expected a message from El. A possible explanation is that El simply hands on Baal's concern without making any contribution of his own. This would accord with the detachment which El generally displays towards Baal.

[o] Characteristically, El's communication of his decision to Anat also begins with the 'word of peace', 'Come to me from the land of battle . . .' Thus this saying is usual in conversation with Anat. It is evidently meant to placate Anat's constant tendency towards warlike rage, so that she is prepared at least to listen to the messengers.

[p] At this point the connection with the cycle of the seasons is again clear. During the winter months Yam, the god of the sea, is Baal's rival for rule over the earth.

[See,] they turned [their faces] [20]to the midst of Mount Il,[q]
to the assembly.
The gods were [at table],
the holy ones[r] were sitting down to dine.
Baal was beside El.
Now then the gods saw them,
when they saw the messengers of Yam,
the envoys of the governor Nahar,
the gods dropped their heads to their knees
and on the throne of their princeliness.
But Baal rebuked them:
'Why, O gods, do you hang
[25]your heads on your knees
and on the throne of your princeliness?
I see that the gods are oppressed in the face of the power of the
    messengers of Yam,   .
the envoys of the governor Nahar!
O gods, raise your heads from your knees,
from the throne of your princeliness!
I will answer the messengers of Yam,
the envoys of the governor Nahar!'
The gods raised their heads from their knees,
from the throne of [their] princeliness.

[30]Then the messengers of Yam approached,
the envoys of the governor Nahar.
They did not bow down at the feet of El,
they did not abase themselves before the assembly.
Standing [. . .]
[And they presented] their message.
One fire, two fires, burn;
[their eyes] are a whetted sword.
They say to the Bull, his father El:[s]
'Message of Yam, your master,
your lord, the governor Nahar.
Surrender, O El, the one whom you protect,
the one who is protected [35]by a [horde (of men)]!
Give up Baal and his servants,

    [q] The text has *ll* instead of *il* (scribal error?).
    [r] *bn qds* can also be translated 'sons of Qadesh'. For the identification of Ashirat and
Qadesh see p. 202 n. l above.
    [s] I.e. Yam's father.

the son of Dagan, so that I may take possession of his battle-axe!"ᵗ
[And] the Bull [replied], his father, El:
'Your slave, O Yam, your slave Baal will be ³⁷(for ever),
the son of Dagan will truly be your prisoner . . .'

Further assurances by El follow. Tablet *CTA* 2. IV first reports Baal's
reaction; but at that point the final battle is already beginning. There is thus a
considerable gap in the course of the action, probably amounting to one tablet.
The skilful and devious Kusharu-hasisu proves to be a very useful helper for
Baal:

⁷Then up rose Kusharu-hasisu:
'Truly, I have said to you, prince Baal,
I have advised you, rider on the clouds.
See, O Baal, your enemy,
you should smite your enemy;
see, you should annihilate your adversary.
¹⁰You should take possession of your eternal kingship,
your everlasting rule!'ᵘ

Kusharu brought a double-axe
and gave it a name:
'Your name shall be Yagrush.ᵛ
Yagrush, drive out Yam,
drive Yam from his throne,
Nahar from his seat of rule.
You shall swoop down from Baal's hand,
like an eagle from his fingers.
Smite the shoulders of Prince Yam,
between the handsʷ ¹⁵of the governor Nahar.

The battle-axe swoops down from Baal's hand,
like an eagle from his fingers.
It smites the shoulders of Prince Yam,
between the hands of the governor Nahar.

Yam is strong, he does not collapse,
his legs are not bowed,

ᵗ The Ugaritic word translated in this way can also mean 'fine gold'. However, the
question is not one of gold, but of making Baal powerless. The battle-axe is the symbol
of Baal's power in his capacity as weather god.
ᵛ ᵘ Cf. Ex. 15.18 in the OT 'Song of the Sea', in connection with Ex. 15.8, 10, 11. Cf.
also Ps. 29 (esp. v. 10); Ps. 93 (vv. 2, 5), and for the context in general Hab. 3.8, 15;
Ps. 77.16ff.; 89.9f.; 104.7 and p. 198 nn. y, z, a above.
ᵛ A name meaning 'He is driven out'.
ʷ Meaning the front of the upper part of the body.

his frame is [18]not broken . . .

Kusharu-hasisu quickly provides another, stronger double-axe. It strikes Yam on the skull. This decides the battle in Baal's favour. Surprisingly, the goddess Ashtarat, famed for her beauty, now appears.[x] She had been held prisoner by Yam. She congratulates Baal on his victory and asks him to 'dissolve' Yam, i.e. to make him become the element that he embodies as god of the sea. 'Yam is truly dead, Baal should be king!'

8. *Ashirat and Baal*

Text: *CTA* 4.I-III = II AB. I-III = Gordon 51. I-III.

Nothing now seems to stand in the way of Baal's building plans. Once again the lament is heard, 'Baal does not have a house like the other gods . . .' Then Kusharu gets to work and provides the valuable substances for decorating the interior of Baal's palace. Here we see how useful it proves for him to embody three divine figures. They divide in the smithy. Hayin can blow the bellows and Hasisu hold the tongs. With forethought Kusharu exercises his skill first in making the furniture; for El's permission to build has yet to be given. Above all, Ashirat's opposition must be taken into consideration. She is in a state of anger and grief because of Yam's death, the loss of her dominion. The wise Kusharu advises Baal and Anat to go together to seek Ashirat, mother of the gods, and this they do. She immediately begins to lament over Yam – as far as we can see from the fragmentary text.

[II 12]As she raises her eyes,
Ashirat sees Baal coming.
And she also sees the approach of the virgin [15]Anat,
the coming of Yabamat [Limim].
Her legs tremble,
they collapse at the hips,
sweat covers her face,
the skin of her loins quivers,
[20]the flesh (?) of her back.[y]

She raised her voice and cried:
'Why has the mighty Baal come?
Why has the virgin Anat come?
The two who have murdered (?) him, [25]my son . . .'

Baal and Anat attempt to quieten Ashirat and give her presents of silver and gold, gifts which Ashirat then delights in. After a complaint by Baal about an

---

[x] Ashtarat is to be found through the West Semitic area as a special goddess of fertility. In the OT there is a fight against the cult of 'Astarte', who is often mentioned as a Phoenician goddess (I Kings 11.5, 33; II Kings 23.13).

[y] Ashirat's agitation is described in the same words as are used of Anat in scene 3.

insult which he has received in the assembly of the sons of the gods (only part
of it is preserved and therefore it is incomprehensible), the visitors state their
purpose:

III 23When the mighty Baal had arrived,
the virgin Anat had arrived,
25they stated their case to Lady Ashirat of the sea,
made their plea to the creator of the gods.
And Lady Ashirat of the sea replied:
'Why do you state your case to Lady Ashirat of the sea,
why do you make your plea 30to the creator of the gods?
Have you stated your case to Bull El, the gracious one,
have you made your plea 32to the creator of the creatures?'

The two goddesses now resolve to do this together. Before they set out the
three deities first further strengthen themselves with a hearty meal.

9. A temple for Baal!

Text: CTA 4. IV-V = II AB. IV-V = Gordon 51. IV-V.
Even before daybreak, Ashirat, Anat and Baal set out on their journey. The
mother of the gods rides on an animal, as being the highest in rank. The twofold deity Qadesh-Amurru shows her many-sidedness in this scene in preparing
for the journey and carrying it through.

IV 9He saddled an ass,
harnessed the jackass.
10He attached a bridle of silver,
a snaffle of gold.
He arranged the bridle on her she-ass.z
Qadesh-Amurru harnessed (it);
he set Ashirat on the back of the ass,
15on the splendid back of the jackass.
Qadesh began to drive the animal on;
Amurru was like a star in front,a
the virgin Anat behind.
19But Baal went (?) to the heights of Zaphon.b

z Obviously only one animal is meant, and that is always the same one.
a It can be seen how Qadesh-Amurru can carry on two different activities at the same
time. One drives the donkey, while the other runs in front and lights the way.
b The translation does not follow the text exactly (read yb'a instead of tb'a?). However,
the context clearly requires that Baal shall be on Zaphon during the negotiations between
the two goddesses and El. An appearance before El, relations with whom are always
tense, would hardly further the purpose of the journey.

In this way the two goddesses reach El's palace at the source of the two seas. El is clearly delighted to see his wife. He laughs and stamps his feet on the platform of his throne. Evidently a 'cold buffet' is always at hand in his throne room:

IV,35'Eat! Drink!
Eat bread from the table,
drink wine from the jars,
the blood of the trees from a golden cup.
See, El's affection will arouse you,
the love of the Bull will charm you!'

40Lady Ashirat of the sea replied:
'Your decree, O El, is wise!
May your wisdom last for ever!
A happy life is 43your decree.
Let our king be the mighty Baal' 44. . .

The poet puts the same words in Ashirat's mouth as have already been used in the fourth scene with Anat. Here, too, the chorus of assembled gods joins in Baal's 'lament': 'Baal does not have a house . . .' As soon as the chorus has fallen silent, El announces his decision. This happens in a very diplomatic way, as he has already given permission for the building:

IV 58Then spoke the kindly El, the gracious one:
'Am I a slave, a servant of Ashirat?
60Am I then a slave who seizes a shovel?
Or am I a handmaid of Ashirat to make bricks,
so that a house can be built for Baal
V 63like that of the gods,
and a sanctuary like that of the sons of Ashirat!'

Lady Ashirat of the sea then replied:
65'O El, you are great, and indeed wise,
your grey beard instructs you . . .
. . .
And now Baal will appoint the time of his rain.c
. . . d

---

c Damaged, translation uncertain. – The conviction that Baal gives rain and appoints the time of his rain is contested in the OT: cf. especially the Elijah tradition, I Kings 17-19, esp. 17.1; 18.1, 21-46, and also Hos. 2.2-13. The rain is understood as Yahweh's gift; cf. e.g. Deut. 11.11-17; 28.12, 24; Judg. 5.4; I Sam. 12.16-18; I Kings 8.35f.; Jer. 10.13; Amos 4.7f.; Hab. 3.10; Zech. 10.1; Pss. 68.8f.; 77.17.
d Translation uncertain: perhaps 'The time when the ships are caught in a storm' (cf. E. Lipiński, UF 3, 1971, 86).

[70]And he will make his voice ring out in the clouds,
by flashing his lightning to the earth.[e]
He is to build the house of cedar,[f]
yes, he is to erect the house of bricks.[g]
So, let it be told to the mighty Baal:

[75]'Summon labourers into your palace,
builders (?) into the midst of your temple!
The mountains will bring you much silver,
the hills desirable gold.
Camels will bring you precious stones,
[80]and build a palace of silver and gold,
a palace of pure lapis lazuli.'
The virgin Anat rejoices.
She stamps her feet,
so that the earth quakes.
Then she turns her face [85]to Baal
on the heights of Zaphon,
over a thousand meadows, ten thousand fields.
The virgin Anat laughs,
she raises her voice and calls;
she congratulates Baal:
'I have to bring you good tidings!
A house will be [90]built for you
like that of your brothers . . .'

Once again she repeats the words of Ashirat, to pass them on to Baal.

10. *The temple window*

Text: *CTA* 4. V. 106-27 and VI-VIII = II AB V. 106-27 and VI-VII =
Gordon 51. V. 106-27 and VI-VII.
The action now moves to Mount Zaphon, where Kusharu-hasisu has meanwhile arrived. When the craftsman has eaten a fatling, Baal tells him the details
of his building plans. Above all, everything must be done quickly, so that he
can soon enter upon his rule. There is a difference of opinion between the
builder and the architect over the question of introducing a window.

---

[e] According to OT conceptions, Yahweh too speaks through thunder (Pss. 18.13;
29.3ff.; Job 37.2ff. etc.). He sends out his lightning like arrows (Ps. 18.14; Hab. 3.9f.,
etc.).
[f] Yahweh's temple in Jerusalem is also described as a house of cedar, II Sam. 7.7;
I Chron. 17.6.
[g] The use of bricks for representations and cultic buildings was unusual in Ugarit of
the late bronze age.

V 121'Hear, O mighty Baal,
mark well, rider on the clouds!ʰ
I would like to have a casement in the pa[lace],
a window in the temple.'
125But mighty Baal replied:
'You shall not make a casement in the pa[lace],
127[a window] in the temple.'ⁱ

Kusharu-hasisu again repeats his proposal, and again it is rejected. However, Baal adds a reason which can be understood, although the tablet is badly damaged. He is afraid that his daughters Pidraya, the daughter of cloud, and Talaya, the daughter of rain, may get in through the opening. And above all, Yam might have the possibility of spying on him. Put in earthly terms, Baal is afraid that cloud and rain will get into his fine palace, and also the waves of the hostile sea. Meanwhile, the building of the temple proceeds apace:

VI 20'They [brought(?)] from Lebanon and its forest,
from Sirion, the most precious of its cedars.ʲ
They set fire to the palace,
flame to the temple.

See, for one day and a second,
fire 25devoured the palace,
and flame the temple,
a third, fourth day.
. . .
See, 32on the seventh [day] the fire went out in the palace,
the flame in the temple:
silver turned to blocks,

ʰ As an epithet of Yahweh, Isa. 19.1; Ps. 68.4; cf. also Deut. 33.26; II Sam. 22.11; Pss. 18.10; 68.33.
ⁱThis argument recalls I Kings 8.12, where it is said that Yahweh wants 'to dwell in darkness'. However, what is meant is dwelling in clouds of darkness. Nevertheless, a lack of windows is one of the characteristics of ancient Canaanite temple buildings; in this they contrast with similar Hittite buildings. Cf. p. 211 n. l below.
ʲ Sirion is probably a term for the Antilebanon, but this is not a place where cedars grow. Presumably the passage is meant to indicate that the best cedars were brought from the most famous forests (cf. I Kings 5.6ff.; II Chron. 2.2ff.; Ezra 3.7). Perhaps, too, the cedar woods on the massif of Mount Zaphon were exhausted at the time of the composition of the myth, so that economic realities compelled the importation of trees from the southern hills. Jebel Aqra still has the remains of cedars, as does the northern Jebel el-Ansariye near Slenfe, about eighteen miles south-east of Ugarit.

gold ^{35}turned to bricks . . .^{k}

When the temple is ready, it is consecrated by a great banquet, to which all the gods, the 'seventy sons of Ashirat', are invited. Bulls, calves, rams, lambs and goats are provided, and also eight different kinds of nectar (cf. Judg. 9.13). Baal then visits his empire, the cities in his possession. When he returns, he has to note that further work is still needed on the splendid temple building.

$^{VII\,14}$Then the mighty ^{15}Baal began to speak:
'I command you, Kusharu, build this (very) day,
Kusharu, build immediately.
A window will be opened in the palace,
a ca[sement] in the midst of the temple,
a rift will be opened in the clouds!'
^{20}. . . [. . .] Kusharu-hasisu laughed.
Kusharu-hasisu raised [his voice] and cried:
'Truly I said to you, mighty Baal,
you will agree, O Baal, ^{25}with my words!'

He opened a window in the palace,
a casement in the temple.
Baal opened a rift in the [clouds].
^{29}Ba[al] made his holy voice [resound] . . .^{1}

11. *Who is king?*

Text: *CTA* 4. VII. 35ff. = II AB. VII. 35ff. = Gordon 51. VII. 35ff.

Baal has now reached the summit of his power:

^{k} The idea of a powerful smelting furnace may underlie this remarkable method of building. This would also explain the use of bricks as building material, i.e. as a forme for the metal, which could be smelted between the brick walls.
^{1} The parallel between the temple window and the rift in the clouds through which Baal, as weather god, sends thunder and lightning, provides the key for understanding what is happening in the building of the temple. According to mythical ideas Baal's shrine is in the clouds round the top of Zaphon, indeed this shrine is formed by the mighty clouds themselves, from which the god's lightning is sent down. When the sun shines on the towering clouds after the rain, the walls of this marvellous divine palace glisten with silver, gold and precious stones. - Obviously the myth also has in mind the earthly counterpart of this heavenly dwelling, the solid 'cedar house' of Baal.

35Baal's enemy has taken to the woods,
Hadad's opponent to the caves in the
hill.[m]
And mighty Baal began to speak:
'O enemy of Hadad, why are you afraid?
Why do you fear the weapon Damarun?'[n]
Baal's eyes are directed to his hand,
when it raises (?) the cedar in his right
hand (for a blow).[o]
Thus (?) Baal sits enthroned in his
palace,
'A king or a commoner,
who seeks to make the earth his
dominion(?),
45him will I sent to Mut, the son of
El . . .'

12. Baal, with a cedar in his left
hand. Stele from Ras Shamra.

Baal finally goes so far as to claim, 'I alone am the one who will rule over the gods!' Immediately after this boastful word (lines 49f.), to which Pss. 95.3; 96.4; 97.9; 136.2 in particular correspond in the OT, the limitations of his power appear: the first signs of the approaching dry season. The battle with Mut, the lord of death and the underworld, who rules over the earth during the dry period of the year, is in view.[p]

[m] Baal's enemies have had to retreat into inhospitable regions. The West Semitic god of fertility, Hadad, is often identified with Baal.

[n] Translation uncertain. Baal's outcry is obviously meant ironically.

[o] The sense of the phrase is to indicate that Baal finds the target with his weapon. It is also possible to translate, 'Baal's eyes are before his hand', i.e. he first looks carefully for his target before letting fly. For the idea of the cedar in Baal's hand see the relief depicting the god which comes from Ugarit (*Syr* 14, 1933, plate XVI, see fig. 12 above). On this stele Baal is carrying a battle-axe in one hand and a tree in the other. See also the magical formula in an Egyptian incantation: 'May Baal smite you down with the cedar which is in his hand' (*ANET*[2], 249).

[p] Mut ('death') occasionally appears as a personalized figure even in the OT, cf. Isa. 28.15; Job 18.13.

12. *Baal's message to Mut*

Text: primarily *CTA* 4. VIII = II AB. VIII = Gordon 51. VIII; then *CTA* 5. I-II = I* AB. 1-II = Gordon 67. I-II.
Baal sends his messengers Gapan and Ugar[q] to Mut in the underworld (which is also often mentioned in the OT). There is a vivid description of the dangers of this journey.

[7]'And go down into the "underworld"'[r] of the earth.
You will be numbered among those
who have descended into the earth.[s]
[10]Then, indeed, turn your face to his city Hmry![t]
Decay (?) is the throne on which he sits;
loathsomeness (?) is the land of his possession.
But be watchful, [15]you servants of the gods,
do not draw near to Mut, the son of El,
so that he does not swallow you up in his mouth like a sheep,
snatch you in his jaws [20]like a lamb.[u]
The light of the gods, Shapshu,[v] is scorching,
the heavens are thirsty through the power of El's darling, Mut.
Over a [25]thousand meadows, ten thousand fields,
cast yourselves down at [27]the feet of Mut. . . .

Only the beginning of Baal's message to Mut has been preserved. Baal proudly reports the completion of his palace. This is an indication that after his victory over Yam he now summons Mut to subjection. The concrete occasion for this demand is the display of Mut's power, which damages Baal's work of furthering fertility and vegetation. The text with Mut's answer is badly damaged. All that can be grasped from Mut's speech, which is hard to understand, is that he for his part summons Baal to admit defeat and to come down to him in the realm of the dead. Mut is ready to accept him:

[2][One lip to ear]th, one lip to heaven
[and the tongue] to the stars,
that [Baa]l can enter into him,

> [q] See p. 197 n. w above.
> [r] The text has *bt ḫptt* ('house of the outcast', or something of the kind). The same expression is used in II Kings 15.5 for the place occupied by the leprous king Azariah. (It is questionable whether the Hebrew text of Ps. 88.5a may be used in connection with this designation. Cf. N. J. Tromp, *Primitive Conceptions of Death and the Nether World in the Old Testament*, BibOr 21, 1969, 157ff.)
> [s] I.e., they are counted among the dead. Ps. 88.4 is phrased in a similar way.
> [t] A name with a meaning, perhaps 'maw'.
> [u] For the idea of the greedy maw of the underworld (Sheol) cf. Isa. 5.14; Hab. 2.5; Prov. 1.12; 30.16.
> [v] See the introduction, p. 188 above.

descend into his maw,
[5]like ripe olives which the earth bears,[w]
and the fruits of trees.

Then mighty Baal was afraid,
the rider on the clouds was terrified:
'Begone, say to Mut, the son of El,
bear before El's favourite, the prince:
[10]Message from the mighty Baal,
a word of the exalted one among the heroes.
Greetings, Mut, O son of El!
I am your slave, your subordinate!'[x]

The two divine messengers again undertake their journey into the underworld and deliver Baal's message. 'Then Mut, the son of El, rejoiced' (line 20).

13. Baal's entry into the underworld

Text: *CTA* 5. V = I* AB. V = Gordon 67. V.
Once Baal has decided to submit to Mut, presumably all sorts of preparations
are made before his resolve is carried out. No more detail can be gathered from
the text between the end of col. II and the beginning of col. IV, which is
almost completely destroyed. The remains of col. IV show that questions are
already being asked in the assembly of the gods about Baal's whereabouts. We
next find an undamaged section of the text in the middle of col. V. Here someone (Mut, or a messenger sent by him?) is instructing Baal on the way in which
he has to enter the underworld:

[6]'And you, take your clouds,
your wind, your pitcher(?),[y] your rain!
Let your seven boys be with you,
your eight boars!'[z]
[10]Let Pidraya be with you, the daughter of cloud,
let Talaya be with you, the daughter of rain,
truly turn your face to Mount Knkny,
take the mountain in both hands,

[w] I.e., fruits which grow on the earth (berries etc.).
[x] The terror caused by Mut's answer is itself enough to make Baal prepared to submit. This surprisingly fatalistic attitude of Baal, who as king of the gods is so active and
so conscious of his rule, makes the power of the god of the dead seem especially uncanny.
[y] If this translation is right, then we should think in terms of the vessels from which
Baal pours rain on the earth. See no. 18 below.
[z] Nothing is known about the function of these servants of Baal in animal form.
Baal's entry into the underworld, with all the personnel and appurtenances of the rain
god, reflects especially the observation that drought in the land was caused by absorption
of water into the earth.

the hill between both palms[a]
and descend into the underworld.
You will be counted among those who have descended into the earth,[b]
and you will come to know the nothingnesses, [17]as though you were
   dead.
Mighty Baal obeyed.

Immediately before Baal descends to the underworld, he is seized with love
for a cow, which bears him a 'son'.[c] This last action of the fertility god has a
twofold significance. First, it shows that Baal's activity will also survive the
period of his stay in the underworld. And secondly, it is associated with the
seasons. The period immediately before the end of the rains and the withering
of the vegetation is the time for mating cattle among Syrian herdsmen.[d]

14. Lament over Baal

Text: *CTA* 5. VI = I*, AB. VI = Gordon 67. VI and *CTA* 6. I = I AB.
I* = Gordon 62.
   Two ceremonial lamentations are depicted. First El, as the supreme god,
observes the usual customs after two messengers – presumably Gapan and
Ugar – have reported Baal's death.

[11]Thereupon kindly El, the gracious one,
descends from his throne.
He sits on the footstool,
and from the footstool he sits on the earth.
He scatters ashes [15]of mourning upon his head,
dust in which he has rolled himself, on his skull.
He covers his garments with a robe of mourning;
he gashes his skin with a stone;
he cuts off his sleeping locks (?) with a knife;
he makes deep furrows in his cheeks and his chin.
[20]He harrows the length of his arm,
his chest like a garden,
he ploughs his back like a valley.[e]
He lifts up his voice and cries, 'Baal is dead:

[a] This is the usual formality for a descent to the underworld, which has already been
fulfilled by Baal's messengers. What is probably meant is that the mountain conceals
the hole leading to the underworld. It has to be raised before the descent can be made.
[b] Cf. the phrase in Ps. 88.4a.
[c] See p. 221 n. w below.
[d] Cf. J. Gray, *The Legacy of Canaan*, 60.
[e] The same mourning customs are often mentioned in the OT. Cf. especially II Sam.
1.2; Isa. 15.2; Jer. 16.6; 41.5; 47.5; 48.37; Ezek. 24.17; Amos 8.10; Job 2.8. Contrast
Deut. 14.1; Lev. 19.27f.; 21.5, which prohibit cutting the skin and shaving off hair.

What will become of the people of the son of Dagan?
What will become of the many?
²⁵I (too) will follow Baal and descend into the earth.'

Anat, too, performs these mourning ceremonies, which are described with the same words. But whereas the traditional forms are enough for El, she searches for Baal and goes up and down the land and into the interior of the earth. Finally she finds Baal's body. Only then does she begin her lament.[f]

⁸Shapshu the light of the gods went down to her.
Until she had had her fill of weeping,
¹⁰she drank the tears like wine.
She called loudly to Shapshu the light of the gods:
'Lift the mighty Baal on to me!'
Shapshu the light of the gods heard her.
She lifted up mighty Baal,
she laid him down on the shoulders ¹⁵of Anat.
She brings him to the summit of Zaphon,
she bewails him and buries him,
lays him in the caves of ¹⁸the gods of the earth.[g]

Anat offers a great sacrifice of seventy wild oxen, seventy oxen, seventy sheep, seventy deer,[h] seventy mountain goats and seventy asses[i] to the dead Baal.

15. *Ashtar's abortive enthronement*

Text: *CTA* 6. I. 30ff. = I AB. I = Gordon 49. I.
News of the death of the mighty Baal delights the goddess Ashirat and her sons. Her plea for the building of Baal's temple was evidently forced on her by the pressure of circumstances. She rushes to El in order to have one of her sons appointed as Baal's successor. As soon as she mentions it, El agrees with this plan and asks Ashirat to name a candidate.

[f] Lamentation for the dead is usually above all a matter for women ('wailing women', Jer. 9.17ff.). The weeping and lamentation of women for the dead god plays a prominent role in the cult of the dying and rising vegetation deities (Baal, Hadad, Tammuz, Adonis). The cult of such fertility gods also found its way into the practice of women in Israel (Ezek. 8.14; Zech. 12.11).

[g] Probably meaning ghosts of the dead. In the OT cf. I Sam. 28.8; Isa. 8.19; 29.4 and in addition Lev. 19.31; Deut. 18.11.

[h] According to OT regulations for sacrifice, deer are not included among sacrificial animals (Deut. 12.15; 14.5).

[i] Offerings to the dead of asses, horses and mules are attested by archaeological evidence from the Hittite capital Hattusa. Cf. K. Bittel et al., *Die hethitischen Grabfunde von Osmankayasi*, WVDOG 71, 1958. – In the OT see the special value placed on the ass in Ex. 34.19f.

[53]Then answered Lady Ashirat of the sea:
'Should we not make Ashtar, the terrible, king?[j]
[55]May Ashtar, the terrible, be king!'

Then Ashtar, the terrible, went up to the summit of Zaphon.
He sat on the throne of the mighty Baal.
[60](But) his feet did not reach the footstool,
his head did not reach its end.[k]

And Ashtar, the terrible, spoke:
'I cannot be king on the summit of Zaphon!'
Then Ashtar, the terrible, went down,
he went down from the throne of the mighty Baal.
[65]And he ruled on earth as its god.[l]

16. Anat's conflict with Mut

Text: *CTA* 6. II = I AB. II = Gordon 49. II.
Anat does not give up her search for Baal; for the burial of his body only
means that the seasonal period has come to an end. The god himself is immortal;
but Anat must find him in order to free him from the power of the god of the
dead and assist him towards a new period of activity.

[6]As the heart of a cow longs for its calf,
as the heart of a ewe longs for its lamb,
so the heart of Anat (longs for) Baal.
She seizes Mut [10]by the fold of his garment,
grasps him by the hem of his robe.
She raises her voice and calls:
'O Mut, give me my brother!'

---

[j] Cf. scene 6 above, where Ashtar also emerges as a competitor in the search for permission to build a temple.

[k] I.e. the end of the back-rest of the throne.

[l] It is hard to define Ashtar's function within the rhythm of the seasons. The assumption of T. H. Gaster, *Thespis*, [2]1961, 126f., that he is to be seen as the god of artificial irrigation is still the most illuminating suggestion. In this capacity he cannot completely replace Baal, the god of rain; but for the time being he is king on earth. His epithet 'the terrible' may be connected with his association with the gods of the underworld, who on a number of occasions are also regarded as fertility deities, because not only rain but the earth itself is the basis for vegetation. (It cannot be demonstrated that the Ugaritic Ashtar has an astral character. For the 'international history' of the Ashtar figure cf. F. Stolz, *Strukturen und Figuren im Kult von Jerusalem*, BZAW 118, 1970, 191ff., 201ff.). The two following lines, only part of which has been preserved, speak of 'drawing water in jars'. Although there is no more rain, the springs are not yet exhausted and the supplies of water above the earth are not yet dried up. Perhaps Ashtar is the god who is responsible for this kind of water. Cf. G. R. Driver, op. cit., 12f., 71ff.

And Mut, El's son, replied:
'What do you desire, O Anat?
[15]Indeed, I wander and encompass
every mountain to the heart of the earth,
every hill to the interior of the fields.
(My) throat (?) lacks the sons of men
(my) throat the masses on earth.

I came to the pleasant land [20]of the plague god (?),
to the lovely field of the lion Mamit (?),
I met the mighty Baal.
I quickly put him in my maw like a lamb,
like a small goat in my jaws I crushed him,
he was swallowed up.
Shapshu, the light of the gods, is scorching,
[25]the heavens have become thirsty through the power of Mut, the son
    of El.'

One day, two days pass,
days become [27]months.
The maiden Anat approaches him.

. . .

[30]She seizes [31]Mut, the son of El,
with the knife she cuts him,
with the shovel she winnows him,
with fire she burns him,
with millstones she grinds him,
on the field [35]she throws him.
The birds eat his remains,
the feathered ones make an end [37]to what is left over.[m]

17. *Baal's victory over Mut*

Text: *CTA* 6. III–VI = I AB. III–VI = Gordon 49 III–VI.
Baal's revival is near. The supreme god El first experiences it in a dream:

[III 10]In a dream of kindly El, the gracious one,
in a vision of the creator of creatures,

---

[m] Anat treats Mut like grain on the threshing floor. This is a common picture for the
annihilation of an enemy (also in the OT, cf. Isa. 21.10; Hos. 10.11; Amos 1.3; Micah
4.13, etc.). In the context of the Baal myth there is doubtless an allusion to the seasonal
cycle. Mut has a completely positive function in connection with the seasonal changes
in vegetation. Under his rule the scorching rays from Shapshu are able to ripen the grain
that Baal helped to grow.

the heavens rain oil,
the wadis bring forth honey.[n]
The kindly El, the gracious one, rejoices.
[15]He puts his feet firmly on his footstool;
he opens his mouth (?) wide and laughs;
he raises his voice and shouts:

'I will sit and take my rest,[o]
and my soul shall be at ease in my breast,
[20]for the mighty Baal is alive,
[21]the prince, the lord of the earth exists!'

However, there is still no trace of the return of Baal. El sends Anat to Shap-shu, who as sun goddess has the best view of the earth: 'Where is the mighty Baal, where is the prince, the lord of the earth?' Shapshu is ready to look for Baal. But first she arranges the pouring out of wine from Anat's goblet as a special sacrificial offering for the revival of Baal. The scene then changes quickly – only a few lines are missing – to the final battle between Baal and Mut. The fact that the two gods are again 'alive' in this scene corresponds to their own immortality. Their 'death' is merely the period of their powerlessness. This fits in generally with the idea of death and life in the ancient Near East. Death is not simply the end of existence, but the end of a particular form of existence. For men the transition into the shadowy realm of the dead may be final, but this is not the case for the gods, especially if they represent processes in nature which involves regular disappearance and return.

Unfortunately the last two columns of *CTA* 6 are in a very fragmentary state, so that the context can only be reconstructed very tentatively. First of all Baal seems to fight against Mut and to overthrow him from the throne of his dominion. That would really be the end of the annual cycle, and it would be possible to begin again with the feast for Baal in scene 1. But now the action ceases to be associated with the course of a seasonal year.

V [7]Months become months,
and years [. . .], but in the seventh year,[p]
when the son of El, Mut,
[10]against the mighty Baal,
lifted up his voice and cried:
'Because of you, O Baal, (?) I have undergone humiliation,
because of you I have been cleft with the knife (!),
because of you I have been burnt with fire . . .'

[n] Cf. here the two words used in the OT in praise of cultivated land: Ex. 3.8, 17; 13.5; 33.3 etc.

[o] Can Gen. 2.2f.; Ex. 20.11; 31.17 be considered as counterparts to this rest of the 'creator of creatures' (line 11)?

[p] The seventh year also has a special role in the OT; cf. e.g. Ex. 23. 10f.; Lev. 25.3ff.; Deut. 15.1ff.; 31.10f.

Here Mut is alluding to his destruction by Anat in the previous scene, even if the wording is not quite the same. After a considerable gap, at least part of the description of the duel between Baal and Mut has been preserved:

VI 17 Mut is strong, Baal is strong!
They come together like wild oxen.
Mut is strong, Baal is strong,
they bite one another like snakes.
20 Mut is strong, Baal is strong,
they lash out like stallions (?).
Mut falls down, Baal falls down on top of him!

Shapshu calls to Mut,
'Listen, Mut, son of El!
How can you fight 25 with the mighty Baal?
Will not Bull El, your father, hear of this?
Truly, he will snatch away the support of your seat,
truly, he will overthrow the throne of your kingdom,
truly, he will break the sceptre of your power.'
30 Mut, the son of El, is afraid,
the darling of El, the hero, is terrified . . .

The text evidently ends with the further fall of Mut. It remains obscure why this additional battle between Baal and Mut takes place in the seventh year or in each seventh year. Still, it seems reasonable to suppose that we have here the influence of a seven-year agricultural cycle, in which the seventh year was a fallow year. Overcoming the consequences of this year of rest may be the reason for the second vigorous conflict between Baal and Mut at the end of the seventh year.[q]

18. Baal as weather god

A whole series of fragments of text of varying lengths testify to further scenes in the Baal myth. They cannot be incorporated in the great cycle, though the language and content are very close to it.[r] This is also true of the following text, which was published in 1968: Ugaritica 5, 557 = Gordon 603. Translation and commentary, E. Lipiński, UF 3, 1971, 81-92.

This is probably not a fragment from a wider context, but a complete cultic hymn in honour of the weather god; to interpret it as an enthronement ritual is at the least very risky.[s] Ps. 18.13f. and 29.1-10 in particular are comparative material in the OT.

[q] Cf. J. Gray, op. cit., 73f., with reference to Ex. 23.10f. and Lev. 25.3-7.
[r] Cf. pp. 190f. above.
[s] For this conception cf. L. R. Fischer and F. B. Knutson, JNES 28, 1969, 155-69.

. . .
Recto 1Baal has taken his seat,
the mountain is like a throne.
Hadad has [rested on the mountain],
like a storm(?) in the midst of his mountain,
the god of Zaphon in [a pleasant place(?)],
on the mountain where he shows his power.
He sends forth seven lightnings,
eight bundles of terror,
the 'tree' of lightning [descends(?)].ᵗ

5[On] his head (is) the noble (?) Talaya,
between [his] eyes [the daughters of rain],
the youngest (?) covers his feet.ᵘ
[His] horns [shi]ne above him,
his head is in . . ., in the heavens.

9[He makes his voice] ring out(?), the Bull,
his mouth is like two clouds.
. . .ᵛ
[He tips(?)] the vessel [of heaven],
Verso 4he pours the fat of salvation in the shell.
The virgin Anat 5[washes] her hands,
the [Yabamat] Limim [her] fingers.
She takes her lyre in [her] hand,
[she puts] the adornment (?) on her breast.
She sings of her love for mighty 8Baal,
whom she adores.ʷ

ᵗ Cf. p. 212 n. o above.
ᵘ Here the three daughters represent three different levels of cloud.
ᵛ The last two lines of the recto are damaged, as are the first two lines of the verso.
ʷ This introduces the theme of the love between Baal and Anat, a theme which lies very much in the background in the great cycle, but occupies a central position in other texts. Cf. CTA 10 (= IV AB = Gordon 76), where Baal (in the form of a bull) makes love to Anat (in the form of a cow), after which the goddess brings a calf into the world. A similar theme also plays an important role in CTA 12 (= Baal and Houd = Gordon 75). Here it seems that El makes use of Baal's sexual activity to put an end to him. The most vivid expression of this is the myth of the birth of the gods Shahar and Shalem (CTA 23 = Gordon 53), in contrast to the divine wedding song 'Yarich and Nikal' (CTA 24 = Nikkal and the Kathirat = Gordon 73).

II. PRAYER

19. *Prayer-song to El and the assembly of the gods*

The text *CTA* 30 = Gordon 107 is illuminating in connection with the position of El in the Ugaritic pantheon. In a situation of specific distress, appeal is made to all the other members of the family of the gods as well as El, in order to ensure their support. Then, however, the petition is addressed to El alone, as being the most powerful among the gods. The sacrifice mentioned at the end of the text is also offered to him. The petition has various points of contact with OT texts; for details see the footnotes.

[1]O El! O sons of El![x]
O assembly of the sons of El!
O meeting of the sons of El![y]
O Tkmn and Shnm![z]
[5]O El and Ashirat!

Be gracious, O El![a]
Be a support, O El!
Be salvation, O El!
O El, hasten, come swiftly![b]
[10]To the help of Zaphon,
to the help of Ugarit.[c]
With the lance, O El,
with the upraised (?), O El.
With the battle-axe, O El,
[15]with the shattering, O El.
Because of the burnt offering, O El,
because of the appointed sacrifice (?), O El,
because of the morning sacrifice, O El.[d]

[x] Cf. e.g. Pss. 29.1; 82.1, 6; 89.6.
[y] Cf. especially Pss. 82.1; 89.7 and Job 1-2.
[z] Probably names for or cosmographic descriptions of the places where the gods assemble.
[a] Cf. e.g. Ps. 51.1.
[b] Cf. e.g. Ps. 70.1, 5.
[c] Ugarit is here identified with its holy mountain, the abode of Baal.
[d] For sacrifice in situations of crisis, cf. in the OT e.g. I Sam. 7.9; Jer. 14.12 or Ps. 5.3, but contrast Ps. 4.5; 51.16f.

III. EPICS

20. *Keret*[e]

Text: *CTA* 14 = I K = Gordon *krt* and *CTA* 16. VI = II K. VI = Gordon 127. J. Gray, *The Krt Text in the Literature of Ras Shamra*, [2]1964; H. Sauren and G. Kestemont, *UF* 3, 1971, 181–221, provide new critical editions with transcription, translation and commentary.

The Krt text deals with the existence of a dynasty, in all probability the dynasty of Ugarit.[f] However, the epic goes far back into legendary times. The pattern of the action is very simple. Like the biblical Job, Keret loses all his family, wife and children, through illnesses, accidents or even war. He marries again and his wife produces a large number of sons and daughters. Then Keret falls sick. Restored to health again with the help of El, he suffers the rebellion of his oldest son, who himself wants to become king. At this point the text of the epic which has survived - largely only in fragments - breaks off.

The Krt text affords us a glimpse of the sacral character of a minor kingdom in ancient Canaan and at the same time of the social position of its ruler. For this very reason the epic is significant for our understanding of the early history of the Israelite state and the OT view of kingship. The connection between Keret and the world of the gods is close. He himself is of divine origin and is in close contact with the gods. The communication of divine instructions through dreams has a very significant function. All essential events are first communicated (down to minor details) as instructions in dreams, the wording corresponding exactly to the description of their earthly realization which follows in each case. The dreams are not only advice or instruction about the future; rather, the royal dreamer is himself active and presents his concerns to the deity. A parallel in the OT is the narrative of the dream of King Solomon in I Kings 3.4-15.

After Keret has lamented the loss of his family, sleep overcomes him (*CTA* 14 = I K = Gordon *krt*):

[35]Then El came down [36]in his dream,[g]
the father of the exalted ones in his vision.
And he approached and asked Keret:
'What is it with Keret that he weeps,
[40]that the beloved servant of El sheds tears?
Does he desire the kingship of the [Bu]ll, his father,
desire [43]to be like the father of men?'

---

[e] As with the majority of Ugaritic proper names, the vocalization is arbitrary: the names have come down to us only in Ugaritic cuneiform.

[f] Ugarit is not mentioned in the Krt text; but all the indications are that the action takes place in Ugarit.

[g] Cf. also the dream of the patriarch Jacob in Gen. 28.10-22.

Keret presents his wish for numerous descendants. Thén El's instructions follow (col. II):

^{62}"You must wash and adorn yourself (?),^{h}
wash your hands (as far as) the elbow,
[your] fin[gers] as far as the shoulder!
^{65}Enter [into the shadow of . . .],
take a lam[b in your hand],
a [sacri]ficial lamb [in] your right hand,
a young goat from [the herd]!
All [the food] for guests!
^{70}Take a . . ., a bird for sacrifice,
po[ur] wine [into the] silver [cup],
mead into the [gol]den cup.
Go up to the platform of the [tow]er,
yes, to the platform of the [tow]er!
Put yourself astride (?) ^{75}the pinnacle of the wall!
Raise your hand to heaven,
sacrifice to the Bull, to your father El,
serve Baal by your sacrifice,
the son of Dagan ^{79}by your food!
Then Keret may ^{80}come down from the roof . . ."^{i}

Instructions to prepare a great military expedition follow, in order to win a bride for Keret. Remarkably enough, at the end of the Krt text the rebellious usurper does not act on the instructions of a god. His plans are his own: 'And his heart told him . . .' The gist of his complaint to his father is that during his illness his father has not been able to discharge his royal duties to society, and is therefore incapable of continuing to act as ruler (*CTA* 16. VI = II K. VI = Gordon 127).

^{45}"You do not give the widow her rights,
you do not judge the cause of the one whose life is threatened,
you do not overthrow those who oppress the poor!
The orphans are not fed by you,
nor are the widows fed behind ^{50}your back;^{j}

^{h} Literally 'rouge yourself'. This can mean either the use of henna as a cosmetic or simply 'refresh oneself'.

^{i} This remarkable sacrifice is thought of as taking place, not on the platform of a tower-like building (*mgdl* = tower), but on the roof (*gg*) of the temple. Syrian temples – including the temple of Baal at Ugarit – tend to have a massive stairway leading to the roof (cf. the interesting use of *migdal* in Judg. 9.46ff.). The sacrifice is offered on the roof so as to be nearer to the deity, who cannot easily overlook an offering which is made here.

^{j} This group corresponds to the ideas of the social obligations of a ruler which are

for grief is the sister (of your) bed,
(and) sickness is the wife of (your) bed.
Come down from your royal throne! [53]I will be king! ...'

21. Daniil

Text: *CTA* 17. I = II D. I = Gordon 2 Aqht. I. There is a critical edition
with a transcription, translation and commentary by P. Fronzaroli, *Leggenda
di Aqhat*, 1955.
The epic of Daniil belongs to the same group of themes as the Keret text.
However, here the boundary between the world of the gods and the world of
men is drawn less clearly. Granted, dealings with the deity also have a role in
the Daniil text, in the form of dreams and visions, but both gods and men make
a personal appearance on the scene.
In a similar way to the Keret epic, the action begins with the promise of a
son to Daniil. Comparisons may be made with OT texts containing a similar
promise: the testimony to the promise of descendants in the patriarchal
traditions, and also in royal oracles (cf. e.g. Gen. 12.1ff.; 18.1off.; 22.25ff. or
II Sam. 7, especially 11ff.). The duties of the promised son of the king relate
to the personal care of the ruler, but are above all of a cultic and ritual nature,[k]
and are connected not least with the continuity of worship of an ancestral god.
This suggests the criterion given to the kings of the Davidic dynasty (cf. I Kings
15.3, 11; II Kings 16.2; 18.3; 22.2; II Chron. 28.1; 29.2; 34,2f.). There is also
the question whether mention of the ancestral god (line 27) could be connected
with the worship of ancestral gods associated with the patriarchs even in pre-
Palestinian times (cf. e.g. Gen. 26.24; 28.13; 31.53; 49.25; Ex. 3.6, 15). The
enumeration of the duties of the successor to the throne (in a dodecalogue
corresponding in form to the OT decalogues, Lev. 18.7ff.; Deut. 27.15ff.) is
evidence of an area about which we otherwise know nothing:

[26]'And let there be his son in the house,
a descendant in the midst of his palace,
who sets up a stele to his ancestral god,
a memorial stone (?) in the sanctuary to his kindred,
who makes his incense arise from the Earth,
who makes his burnt offering (?) ascend (?) from the dust,
who wards off the threats [30]of those who despise(?) him,
who casts down those who rebel against him.

---

customary in the ancient Near East. Cf. II Sam. 14.7f.; I Kings 2.2ff.; Ps. 72.1ff., 12ff.
and Ps. 101, together with the prophetic sayings in Isa. 1.23; Jer. 22.2f.; Ezek. 22.6f.
Some instances are not connected with kings or princes but with all Israelites: Ex.
22.22ff.; 23.3, 6; Deut. 10.17; Isa. 1.17; Jer. 7.5f.; Zech. 7.10; Prov. 22.22f. and many
other passages.
[k] K. Koch, *ZA* 58, 1967, 211-21, thinks exclusively of cultic and ritual obligations.

Who holds his hand in his drunkenness,
who supports him when he is overcome with wine.
Who eats his portion in the house of Baal,
his share in the house of El.
Who rolls out his roof on the day ³⁴of mire,[1]
who washes his clothes on the day of defilement.'

The craftsman Kusharu-hasisu presents the son of Daniil, whose name is Aqhat, with a valuable hunting bow. The war goddess Anat is envious of it. As he will not hand it over to the goddess, even in return for eternal life like that of the gods, she has him killed by one of her warriors, whom she turns into an eagle.

The effects of Aqhat's death on the vegetation are particularly striking. Everything becomes dried up; for seven, indeed for eight years, there is no rain. Here we see a connection (which is not unknown in the OT) between the prosperity of the ruling dynasty and the prosperity of the fruits of the field (cf. Ps. 72.16f., and in contrast II Sam. 21.1, 9, 10).

The outcome of the epic is unknown. The text breaks off with a description of the preparations made by Pgt, the sister of Aqhat, to seek out the murderer of her brother and to kill him.

---

[1] This presupposes a flat roof with a layer of clay to seal it.

E

NORTH SEMITIC TEXTS
from the first millennium BC

INTRODUCTION

Almost all North Semitic texts from the first millennium BC contribute in one way or another to our better understanding of the Old Testament; they come from the same cultural region, Syria-Palestine, from about the same period of time, and this fact is expressed in their linguistic affinity. Thus any selection from the multiplicity of North Semitic texts is to some degree subjective. It is not, however, subjective to adopt the perspective of presenting only those texts which are relevant for the history of religions. Nor is it subjective to leave out texts which are already available in K. Galling's *Textbuch zur Geschichte Israels* and elsewhere, even if they are of interest for the history of religion. Consequently this book does not contain the inscription from the sarcophagus of Ahiram of Byblos (tenth century),[a] the petition of the Jews of Elephantine to Bagoas (407 BC),[b] the 'memorandum concerning the rebuilding of the temple in Elephantine' (407/6 BC),[c] the tablet from the forecourt of Herod's temple in Jerusalem,[d] or the inscription from a Jerusalem synagogue (first century AD).[e] The inclusion of the Mesha inscription, which is also to be found in *TGI*, is the exception that proves the rule: it is of extraordinary significance, particularly in the religious sphere.

The material collected in the following pages comes from the territory of present-day Israel, from Transjordania, Syria, the Lebanon, Egypt, south-east Turkey and the Phoenician and Punic colonies in the Medi-

[a] *TGI*, 49; *ANET*[3], 661.
[b] *TGI*, 84ff.; *ANET*[3], 491f.
[c] *TGI*, 88; *ANET*[3], 492.
[d] *TGI*, 89f.; *TDNT* I, 266f.; A. Deissmann, *Light from the Ancient East*, [3]1927, 439ff.
[e] *TGI*, 92; Deissmann, op. cit., 80.

terranean. The languages in which it is written include Phoenician (or Punic), Aramaic, Hebrew and a related language of Transjordania. The main genres represented are inscriptions on buildings and tombs, and votive inscriptions; there are also letters and cylindrical seals. Attention is paid to the texts of state treaties as well as incantations. So far, mythological texts, hymns and prayers have yet to be found in the area with which we are concerned. However, we do have quotations dealing with mythology from the *Phoenician History* of Philo of Byblos.

Sometimes it is uncertain how proper names were pronounced. Names of people and geographical names are given in a vocalized form, even when there is either inadequate or contradictory evidence for their vocalization. In such cases the form of pronunciation has always been chosen which seems most probable, or which is generally accepted.

I. VOTIVE INSCRIPTIONS

1. *The Melqart stele of Bar-hadad*

13. Melqart, the 'Baal of Tyre', who was also worshipped in Aram and Israel in the ninth century BC. The figure is wearing a cap of the kind worn by gods, and an apron. In his left hand is a battle-axe and in his right the Egyptian symbol of life.

The text comes from a basalt stele (1.15 m. high and 43 mm. wide) found at Breij (about four miles north of Aleppo in Syria). It consists of five lines inscribed below a relief portrait of the god Melqart (see fig. 13, and *ANEP*²,

Plate IV A clay tablet from Ras Shamra:
Epic of Aqhat the Son of Danill

fig. 499). The stele is now in the museum at Aleppo. First publication: M. Dunand, *BMB* 3, 1939, 65ff., pl. XIII.

This is an Old Aramaic votive inscription for Melqart, the chief god of Tyre, also called 'Baal of Tyre' (cf. *CIS* I, no. 122 = *KAI*, no. 47). His worshipper, Bar-hadad, was a brother of the king of the Aramaean state of Damascus, whose rulers exercised control over weaker Aramaean states. This hegemony even extended as far as North Syria (see no. 2 below); that is where the stele was found. The Bar-hadad mentioned on it was a son of Idri-shamash, who was probably the father of King Hazael or the grandfather of King Bar-hadad II (the biblical Ben-hadad). Thus the inscription dates from the last decades of the ninth century BC and is the earliest evidence so far for the worship of the god Melqart, whose name is really an epithet and means 'king of the city'. Melqart appears with Baal of Tyre among the gods attesting the treaty of Esarhaddon in the seventh century BC (R. Borger, AfOB 9, 1956, 104, col. IV, 14). Later there is evidence of his cult throughout the Mediterranean - often under the name of Heracles, with whom he was identified as early as the sixth century BC among the Greeks (and later also among the Romans). He is mentioned by this name in II Macc. 4.18-20 and in Josephus (*Antt.* VIII. 5. 13, §146; *C.Ap.* I. 18, §119).

The Melqart stele is evidence for the cult of this god, who is really native to Tyre, in Aramaean territory. I Kings 16.31f. (cf. I Kings 18.16-40; II Kings 10.18-27) bears witness to the establishment of a similar cult in the northern kingdom of Israel; the Baal of Jezebel, the daughter of the king of Tyre, can only have been Baal of Tyre.

There are instances in the OT of vows and fulfilments of vows comparable to those in the inscription; cf. e.g. Pss. 22.25; 116 14-19; Isa. 38.20; Jonah 2.9. Perhaps the practice of setting up a memorial followed similar lines among the Israelites; cf. I Sam. 15.12, which must be a reference to a victory monument.

Literature: *KAI* no. 201; *WM* I, 297f.; *ANET*[3], 655; F. M. Cross, *BASOR* 205, 1972, 36ff. (which also has a new photograph); E. Lipiński, *Studies in Aramaic Inscriptions and Onomastics* I, 1975, 15ff.

[1]The stele which was set up by Bar-ha[2]dad, the son of Idri-shamash, who (was) father of the [3]king of Aram, for his lord, for Melqart, [4]because he[f] had made a vow and he[g] had hearkened to [5]his [4]voice.

2. The Zakkur inscription

The text is on a basalt stele which has been preserved only in fragments, little more than 2 m. high and 27-30 cm. wide; it was found in Afis (about twenty-five miles south-west of Aleppo). It has an inscription in Old Aramaic amounting to seventeen lines on the lower part of the front (A), twenty-eight lines on the left side (B) and two lines on the right (C). The front also has a relief

[f] Bar-hadad.
[g] Melqart.

portrait of a figure in human form, in profile, probably that of the god Ilu-wer. Only the fringe of the garment and the feet are really preserved. The fragments are now in the Louvre in Paris. First publication of the text: H. Pognon, *Inscriptions sémitiques de la Syrie, de la Mésopotamie et de la région de Mossoul*, 1907-1908, 156ff., plates IX-X, XXXV and XXXVI.

The stele and the inscription are dated about 785 BC for palaeographic reasons and because of the content. The inscription is a votive inscription of King Zakkur for Ilu-wer ('god Wer') who was worshipped on the central Euphrates from the third millennium BC on. About 800 BC, perhaps with the help of the Assyrians, Zakkur became king of the double kingdom of Hamath and Luash in northern Syria with Hazrak as his capital. He was probably a usurper, but following the pattern of the ideology of kingship in the ancient Near East he claimed that Baal-shamayim ('the lord of heaven'), the heavenly weather god who was worshipped throughout Syria and Palestine, had bestowed the kingship on him in Hazrak. This divine election was taken to be confirmed by the liberation of the capital, to which Bar-hadad II, king of Damascus, had laid siege with his North Syrian vassals. Presumably the liberation of the city had been achieved by the intervention of the Assyrian king Adad-nirari III (810-783). This probably took place in 796 BC, since in this year there was an Assyrian expedition 'as far as Mansuate' in Northern Syria (*RLA* II, 429, line 21). On the other hand, it seems that Hazael was still ruling over Damascus during the earlier expeditions of Adad-nirari III.

From a religious point of view, the Zakkur inscription is particularly interesting for the history of prophecy (and especially of the genre of the prophetic oracle of salvation) and for the investigation of the terminology connected with enthronements in the North-west Semitic sphere. It should be mentioned in passing that the siege of the capital Hazrak (Zech. 9.1: 'Hadrach') discussed in the inscription is reminiscent of the parallel event of the siege of Samaria by the same Bar-hadad II (cf. I Kings 20.1ff.; II Kings 6.24ff.).

Literature: M. Noth, *ZDPV* 52, 1929, 124 = *Aufsätze zur biblischen Landes- und Altertumskunde* II, 1971, 135ff.; *DOTT*, 242ff.; *KAI*, no. 202; G. Buccel-latti, *Studies presented to A. L. Oppenheim*, 1964, 54ff.; *ANET*[3], 655ff.; J. F. Ross, *HTR* 63, 1970, 1ff.; H.-J. Zobel, *VT* 21, 1971, 91ff.; E. Lipiński, *AION* 31, 1971, 393ff.; id., *Studies in Aramaic Inscriptions and Onomastica* I, 1975, 19ff.; J. C. Greenfield, 'The Zakir Inscription and the Danklied', *Proceedings of the Fifth World Congress of Jewish Studies* I, 1972, 174ff.

[A1] The [st]ele which was set up by Zakkur, the king of [Ha] math[h] and Luash[i] for Ilu-wer,[j] [his god.[k] [2] I] am Zakkur, king of Hamath and Luash.

---

[h] Hamath, present-day Hama, is a large city in central Syria, on the Orontes, which is often mentioned in the Bible.

[i] Written *l'š* in Old Aramaic.

[j] Ilu-wer is akin to the god Itur-mer of Mari and Terqa. Wer and Mer are phonetic variants of the same name. If the name is Semitic, W/Mer seems originally to have been a corn-deity: Mer < *mayr*; cf. Arabic *mara* (*myr*): 'bring in grain'.

I was a humble man, but [3]the lord of heaven [rescued me][l] and stood by me, and the lord of heav[en] made me king [in [4]Ha]zrak.[m] Bar-hadad, the son of Hazael, king of Aram, made an alliance of s[even[5]t]een kings against me: Bar-hadad and his army, Bar-gush[n] and his army, the [ki[6]ng] of Kue[o] and his army, the king of Umq[p] and his army, the king of Gurgu[m[q] [7]and] his army, the king of Sam'al[r] and his a[rmy], the king of Milid[s] [and his a]rm[y, the kin[8]g of . . . .][l]; [they we]re [9]sev[enteen] and their armies. And all these kings constructed a siege wall against Hazra[k] [10]and erected a wall higher than the wall of Hazrak, and made a moat deeper than [its] moat. [11]But I lifted up my hands to the lord of h[eave]n, and the lord of heav[en] answered me. [And] [12]the lord of heaven [spoke] to me [through] seers and through messengers. [And] [13]the lord of heaven said [to me]: 'Fear not,[u] for I have [made you] king, [and I [14]shall sta]nd by you and I shall save you from all [these kings who] [15]have set up a siege wall against you!' [The lord of heaven] spoke thus to [me, and he put all these kings to flight (?)] [16]who had set up [a

---

[k] It is improbable that we should supply either 'his lord' (in apposition to Ilu-wer) or 'in Hazrak' here: in all instances in Old Aramaic, 'lord' comes before the proper name, and in votive inscriptions it is unusual to have a place name at this point. But 'god' can well stand after the name of the deity.

[l] The addition is based on the detection of chiasmus in the sequence of verbs. Cf. lines 13f. with lines 2f.

[m] Comparison of the Old Aramaic writing *ḥzrk* with the rather later writing *ḥdrk* (Zech. 9.1) and the vocalized Assyrian rendering *ḥatarika* shows that the name was really Hadarik. – For the formula 'make king in the capital' or 'become king', cf. the notices of enthronements in the OT, e.g. II Sam. 15.10; I Kings 22.52; II Kings 13.1; 14.23; 15.8; Isa. 24.23; Micah 4.7.

[n] Bar-gush ('son of Gush') is the dynastic name of the ruler of a North Syrian state, the centre of which was the city of Arpad, often mentioned in the OT (Tell Refad, about eighteen miles north-east of Aleppo; cf. e.g. II Kings 18.34; 19.13; Isa. 10.9; Jer. 49.23). Gush was probably the name of the founder of the dynasty.

[o] A state and district in south-eastern Asia Minor (Cilicia), mentioned in I Kings 10.28.

[p] A small state in northern Syria, Assyrian Unqi, in the plain of el-Amq, north-east of Antioch (present-day Antakye).

[q] A small state in the northern Amanus mountains on the border between Cilicia, Cappadocia and northern Syria.

[r] Sam'al, present-day Zinjirli, on the eastern edge of the Amanus mountains, was the capital of the small state of Ya'di, which is regularly called Sam'al in neo-Assyrian inscriptions, after the royal residence.

[s] Milid (Aramaic *mlz*, Assyrian Milid), a small state on the upper Euphrates; corresponds to the territory of the later city of Melitene, present-day Malatya.

[t] There is room for two complete descriptions of rulers in the gap. Lesser kings were not mentioned by name.

[u] In the OT cf. e.g. Isa. 41.13ff.; 43.1ff.; 44.2ff.; 54.4ff.; Jer. 30.10f.

siege wall against . . . [17]. . .] and this wall whi[ch they . . .].
[B1][. . .] Hazrak [. . . [2]. . .] with chariots [and] with horsemen [3][. . .] its king in its midst.[v]
[4]I [enlarge]d Hazrak and adde[5][d to it] the whole district of [6][. . .] a, and I made it que[en] of [7]its [daughter citi]es.[w] [7][I built] [8]these fortifications throughout the district. [9]I [bu]ilt temples for the gods [10]throughout m[y land]. And I built [. . . [11]. . .] Apish[x] and [. . . [12]. . .] house [. . . [13]. . .]. I have set up this stele before Ilu-[14]wer and have written [15]on it the works of my hands [. . . [16]. . . W]hoever removes the wor[ks [17]of the hands of] Zakkur, king of Hama[th and Lu][18]ash, from this stele and whoeve[r [19]shall] remove this stele [20]from [befo]re Ilu-wer and shall take it away fro[m] [21]its [pla]ce or shall lay [hands o]n it, [22][to . . ., [23]. . . may] the l[ord] of heaven and Ilu-[24][wer and . . .] and Shamash and Sehr[y] [25][and . . .] and the gods of heav[en [26]and the god]s of the earth and the Baal of [27][. . . make a] st[ench arise from his cor]pse[z] and his [28][. . . and may they tear up] his ro[ot][a] and [his . . . .
[C1] . . . [. . . may] the name of Zakkur and the name of [. . . stand for ever].

3. Votive inscription of a Melqart worshipper from Cyprus

Text: Phoenician inscription on a semi-circular pedestal which was discovered in Lapethos (Lambousa) in 1893. The purpose of the two holes on the upper surface is probably to serve as part of the fastening for the votive effigy which is mentioned in the inscription. First published: P. Berger, *RA* 3, 1894-95, 69ff., plate IV.

The votive inscription dates from the eleventh year of a Ptolemy, probably Ptolemy II Philadelphus. That would put it in the year 273/272 BC.

The OT also expresses concern for the continuation of 'name' and 'seed' in a similar way to this inscription: cf. e.g. Gen. 12.2f.; Deut. 25.5f.; Josh. 7.9; Ruth 4.5, 10; I Sam. 24.22; II Sam. 14.7; 18.18; Isa. 66.22. Individual expressions, particularly those of a cultic nature, also have points of contact with OT terminology (see the footnotes).

Literature: *Répertoire d'Épigraphie Sémitique* III. 1, 1916, 1211; A. M. Honeyman, *JEA* 26, 1940, 57ff.; plate XI; *KAI*, no. 43; H. L. Ginsberg, 'Roots

---

[v] Probably the king of the Assyrian army, Adad-nirari III. The account of the siege and liberation of the capital Hazrak ends here.
[w] For the daughter-cities cf. Num. 21.25, 32; 32.42, etc. On Phoenician coins the capital is called 'mother' of the cities which belong to its territory.
[x] Probably the present-day Afis, where the stele was found.
[y] The sun god and the moon god.
[z] Expansion uncertain. But cf. Isa. 34.3; Joel 2.20; Amos 4.10.
[a] If the expansion is correct, this is presumably the root of the family of the evildoers. Cf. the formulation of Isa. 11.1.

below and Fruit above'.... *Hebrew and Semitic Studies presented to G. R. Driver*, 1963, 72ff.; A. van Branden, *OrAnt* 3, 1964, 245ff.; J. Swetman, 'Some observations on the Background of *ṣdjq* in Jeremias 23, 5a', *Bib* 46, 1965, 29ff.

[1]Votive image for good fortune! [2]This statue is a votive image. I am Yaton-baal, governor, son of Ger-ashtart, governor, son of Abd-[ashtart, governor, son of Abd-o]siris, [3]son of Ger-ashtart, son of Shillem, fruit of Carmel.[b] I have set this up in the sanctuary of Melqart as a mon[ument] to my name [among the living to bring me good fort]une [4]in the new moon of the 'sacrifice for the (god) Sasm'[c] of the eleventh year of Ptolemy the lord of kings, son of Ptolemy the lord of kings, [5]which is the thirty-third year for the people of Lapethos. The priest of the lord of kings[d] was Abd-ashtart, son of Ger-ashtart, [6]the steward, fruit of Carmel.[e] And in the month Mepa[f] of the fourth year of [7]Ptolemy the lord of kings, in the lifetime of my father, I set up the votive image of the face of my father in bronze in the sanctuary of Melqart. And in the month [8]Peullot[g] of the fifth year of Ptolemy the lord of kings, the son of Ptolemy the lord of kings, during the lifetime [9]of my father, I offered and dedicated in the borders of the pasturage of Narnaka[h] many beasts to my lord Melqart. [10][And] I came back, I came with [fa]t beasts to the place of refuge of the people,[i] to the altars of my lord Melqart, [11]for the sake of my life and for the sake of the life of my seed, day by day, and for the legitimate seed[j]

---

[b] The expression rendered 'fruit of Carmel' here and in line 6 should be taken in connection with the metaphorical use of 'root', 'stump' for the family (line 16). The same expression can be found in II Kings 19.30; Isa. 14.29; 37.31; Hos. 9.16; Amos 2.9 (cf. also Isa. 11.10; 53.2; Ezek. 17.9; Ps. 21.10). The more detailed designation 'fruit of Carmel' is a stereotyped expression which must be understood in the light of the metaphorical use of 'Carmel' (Isa. 19.23; 35.2; Jer. 46.18; Songs of Songs 7.5 etc.). The ridge, extending for about twelve miles and reaching a height of more than 552 metres between the Mediterranean and the plain of Jezreel, was proverbial for its overwhelming beauty, its dense woods and its holiness. The expression 'fruit of Carmel' is a piece of hyperbole verging on the colossal and the heroic, which stresses the majesty of the ancestor of the family.

[c] The name of a month. Its position in the calendar is still obscure. For Sasm see also no. 14 below and especially p. 248 n. m.

[d] I.e. the deified Ptolemy I Soter (305–283).

[e] This Abd-ashtart was probably a brother of Yaton-baal. Cf. n. b above.

[f] The name of a month; its position in the calendar is similarly still obscure.

[g] The name of a month, which was perhaps the month of the 'results' of agricultural work.

[h] Present-day Larnaca, near Lapethos, on the north-west side of the island.

[i] We read *[m]šbt b`t b(!)hyt šmn `l tqmt `m*. The word *tqmt*, 'place of refuge', also occurs in Lev. 26.37 (*hapax legomenon* in the OT).

[j] The same expression as in Jer. 23.5 and 33.15. Here it denotes the legitimate king of the Ptolemaic dynasty. Cf. also Zech. 3.8; 6.12.

[and] for [his] fat[her]s and for his people, [12][at the new mo]ons and at the full moons, month by month for ever as before, according to the bronze tablet [13][which] I [wro]te and which is fixed on the wall there as my gift of friendship.[k] And I have been making burnt offerings[l] of [14][beasts until] this day(?), and also a model temple in si[l]ver,[m] 102 kars[n] heavy, and I have consecrated this to [my] lord [15][Melqa]rt. May authority[o] and good fortune be secure for me and my seed. And may Melqart remember me [16][and establish] the good fortune of my stock.[p]

4. Punic votive inscriptions

Texts: we have knowledge of several thousand votive inscriptions on stelae from the Punic empire of Carthage. Those that have been included here relate to the Molok sacrifice. The first two inscriptions were found in 1945 and 1950 in Carthage on the so-called Tophet Salambo, a field of stelae and urns with the remains of sacrifices, mostly of children. They were published by J. G. Février in *CIS* I, 5684 and 5685, plates XCVIII and XCIX, and are among the earliest Punic inscriptions so far known to us (about 600 BC). The third inscription comes from the same site and was published by R. Dussaud in 1922 (*BAr* 1922, 246, no. 2 = *CIS* I, 3785 = *KAI*, no. 79). The other inscriptions from stelae translated here were discovered in 1950 at El-Hofra, in Constantine, and published by A. Berthier and R. Charlier (*Le sanctuaire punique d'El-Hofra à Constantine*, 1955): nos. 28, 35, 47, 55; plates IIA, IVA, VA, VIIA (= *KAI* nos. 106-109). They belong to the third to second century BC.

The word *mlk* is a term from Punic sacrificial terminology and etymologically has the meaning 'bringing' (a verbal noun from the causative of *hlk*, 'go'). Four later inscriptions from Ngaus (formerly Nicivibus) in Algeria (made about AD 200), in which the term *mlk* appears in an otherwise Latin context (*in molchomor*), leave no doubt as to what was meant by the Molok sacrifice: it was a nocturnal sacrifice, offered voluntarily to a chthonic deity. The stele with its inscription is meant to keep the god in mind of the sacrifice for ever. The expression *molchomor*, which occurs in Punic inscriptions in the form *mlk 'mr*, is usually translated 'lamb-offering'. However, the expression *-omor* points to the participle of the verb *'mr*, in English 'to speak' or 'to promise'. The parallel formulations *mlk .b'l* and *mlk 'dm bśrm btm* are to be translated similarly, 'votive offering of the giver' or 'votive offering of the man giving

---

[k] The word translated 'gift' similarly denotes in the OT a present made to the deity.

[l] For the expression 'make a burnt-offering' cf. e.g. Num. 29.2; Judg. 13.16; I Kings 8.64; Ezek. 45.23. For the association of the terms for gift and 'burnt offering' cf. e.g. Ps. 20.3.

[m] We read: *mp'lt 'nk 'lt*[14] *[hyt 'd] hym z'p bt bk[s]p*.

[n] An unknown weight. If *kr* were an abbreviation for the Persian and Aramaean *karsha*, it would be more than eighteen pounds.

[o] For *pqt*, 'official authority', cf. Akkadian *piqittu*.

[p] Literally 'the root', see p. 233 n. b above.

completely generously'.[q] All in all there can hardly be any doubt about the purpose of these expressions: they were meant to describe the votive offering as the exclusive gift of the person who had promised it and made it, and who wanted to honour and satisfy the god voluntarily and at his own expense. The inscriptions, at any rate, offer no support for the view that the Molok sacrifice was often a child-sacrifice: this can only be concluded from archaeological discoveries and OT accounts.

On the basis of a variety of OT texts (Lev. 18.21; 20.2–5; II Kings 23.10; Isa. 30.33; Jer. 32.35) it was long thought that worship of a god Moloch had also to be inferred in Israel, and that child-sacrifice was a characteristic of this worship (cf. Gen. 22; Judg. 11.30–40; II Kings 3.27; 16.3; 21.6; II Chron. 28.3; 33.6; Jer. 7.31ff.; 19.4ff.; Ezek. 16.20f.). However, the word *mlk* must be understood in the same terms as the contemporary Punic *mlk*, and its use in Carthage will have corresponded to that in the mother country of Phoenicia. Similarly, the god Baal-hammon, 'god of the fire pit(?)' or 'of the fire altar (?)', to whom the Molok sacrifice was offered in Africa, had his origin in Phoenicia. It seems that in Israel a Molok sacrifice to Baal was also known; Jer. 19.5 and 32.35 support this assumption (but cf. Jer. 7.31). It seems to be presupposed in Jer. 7.32 and 19.6, 11 that this sacrifice was intended for a deity of the world of the dead (cf. Jer. 32.35; II Kings 23.10; II Chron. 28.3; 33.6).

Literature: O. Eissfeldt, *Molk als Opferbegriff im Punischen und Hebräischen und das Ende des Gottes Moloch*, 1935; A. Alt, *ZAW* 52, 1934, 303ff. = *Kleine Schriften* I, [2]1959, 341ff.; id., *WO* 1, 1947–52, 282f.; W. Kornfeld, *WZKM* 51, 1952, 287ff.; R. Charlier, *Karthago* 6, 1953, 3ff.; J.-G. Février, *JA* 243, 1955, 49ff., and 248, 1960, 167ff.; also 250, 1962, 1ff.; *REJ* 124, 1964, 7ff.; J. Hoftijzer, *VT* 8, 1958, 288ff.; R. de Vaux, *Ancient Israel*, 1961, 444ff.; *KAI* nos. 61ff.; A. M. Bisi, *Le stele puniche*, 1967; *ANET*[3], 658.

(i) A stele of the votive offering of the giver,[r] set up by Bodisi, son of Melqart-gad, to the lord Baal-hammon.

(ii) A stele of the votive offering of the giver, which Magon, son of Hanno, gave to Baal-hammon.

(iii) To the mistress, the Tinnit-in-the-face-of-Baal,[s] and to the lord Baal-hammon.

Which was vowed by Kenemi, servant of Eshmun-amos, son of Baal-yaton, his benefactor.[t] May she bless him. And Tinnit-in-the-face-of-Baal will take the breath away from anyone who moves this stone away

---

[q] In Punic inscriptions *b'l* is the giver of the sacrifice. *'dm* has a collective meaning. The much-discussed *bśrm* is apparently the plural of the verbal adjective of *bśr*, 'take delight in'. *btm*, completely, is paralleled by *de sua pecunia* in bilingual inscriptions and accordingly means 'without support from others'.

[r] Here *mlkt b'l*: *mlkt* is probably plural. (Many masculine nouns have a plural ending in *-ot*.)

[s] Consort of Baal-hammon; perhaps of Libyan origin.

[t] Perhaps 'his liberator'.

14. The Mesha inscription.

or who acts without my consent or the consent of someone (acting) in my name.

(iv) To the lord Baal-hammon. A votive offering of the man giving completely generously,[u] which Apishshichar vowed, for he[v] heard his voice and blessed him.

(v) To the lord Baal-hammon. A vow which Adoni-baal made, son of Abd-eshmun. A votive offering of the man made in complete generosity.[w] He[x] heard his voice and blessed him.

(vi) To the lord Baal-hammon. A vow made by Shapot, son of Apollonius, who is completely generous. May you hear his voice and bless him!

(vii) To the lord Baal-hammon. A votive offering of the one who promises it. A vow made by Akborat, daughter of [. . .][y]

II. INSCRIPTIONS ON BUILDINGS

5. *The Mesha inscription*

Text: on a stele of black basalt, about 1.10 m. high, narrowing upwards from 68 to 60 cm. wide, still preserved intact. It was discovered in 1868 near Diban (formerly Dibon) in Transjordania. A cast was made of it in 1869, shortly before it was broken in pieces. The reconstructed stele and the copy are now in the Louvre in Paris (see fig. 14). 34 lines of the inscription were published in the first detailed edition by C. Clermont-Ganneau, *La stèle de Dhiban ou stèle de Mesa, roi de Moab*, 1870.

The inscription is in Moabite, a language closely related to the Hebrew of the OT. It derives from the Moabite king Mesha, who is also known from the OT (cf. II Kings 3.4ff.). When he had succeeded in making Moab once again independent from the northern kingdom of Israel, and in addition had annexed part of the territory of Gad, about 830 BC he set up the stele with its inscription in Qarhoh, the acropolis of Dibon, to commemorate the erection of a temple in thanksgiving to Chemosh, the chief god of Moab.[z]

[u] See p. 235 n. q above.

[v] I.e. Baal-hammon.

[w] Here *mlk 'dm bšrm bn'tm*, where *bn'* is a strengthened preposition *bn* with the Punic *mater lectionis* for *e* or *i*.

[x] I.e., Baal-hammon.

[y] Although the votive offering has been made by a woman here, all grammatical forms are masculine. That shows that the votive inscriptions follow, almost slavishly, a fixed pattern.

[z] Fragments of a second Mesha inscription have been discovered in Kerak. Cf. W. L. Reed and F. V. Winnett, *BASOR* 172, 1963, 1ff.; D. N. Freedman, *BASOR* 175, 1964, 50f.

The inscription is significant for the history of Israel in the ninth century BC; it is also relevant for the history of religion. That is not so much the case because it mentions Yahweh, the God of the OT (line 18) – unfortunately in a fragmentary context. Its chief importance in this respect is that it indicates a religious interpretation of history similar to that to be found in the OT: God's anger is manifested in oppression by enemies (line 5, cf. Judg. 2.14; 3.8; 10.7f.; Ps. 106. 40–42, etc.). The abatement of the divine anger is attested by a turn for the better (lines 6ff., cf. Judg. 2.16; 3.9ff.; 10.10ff.; Ps. 106.43, etc.). Military actions are carried out at God's command (line 32, cf. Judg. 20.23, 28; I Sam. 14.37, and above all I Sam. 23.2, 4). Not least, like the OT the Moabite text is familiar with the 'ban', i.e. the dedication of booty to God (lines 16f., 11f.; Deut. 7.2; 20.17; Josh. 7; 8.2 etc.). There is also evidence of a total ban in the OT (cf. e.g. Josh. 6.18–24; I Sam. 15; also Deut. 13.12–17). Furthermore, it is worth noting that like some OT texts, the inscription is aware of cultic high places (line 3; cf. e.g. I Sam. 9.13, 14, 19, 25; II Kings 16.4; 17.9f.; Ezek. 20.28f.). I Kings 11.7 mentions a special parallel.

Literature: R. Smend and A. Socin, *Die Inschrift des Königs Mesa von Moab*, 1886; M. Lidzbarski, *Handbuch der nordsemitischen Epigraphik* II, 1898, plate I, and *Ephemeris für semitische Epigraphik* I, 1902, 1ff.; R. Dussaud, *Les monuments palestiniens et judaiques*, 1912, 4ff.; *AOT*[2], 440ff.; S. Sergert, 'Die Sprache der moabitischen Königsinschrift', *ArOr* 29, 1961, 197ff.; *KAI*, no. 181; F. I. Andersen, *Or* 35, 1966, 81ff.; *ANET*[3], 320f.; J. C. L. Gibson, *Textbook of Syrian Semitic Inscriptions I, Hebrew and Moabite Inscriptions*, 1971, 71ff.; E. Lipiński, *Or* 40, 1971, 325ff.

[1]I am Mesha, son of Chemosh [yatt], king of Moab, the D[2]ibonite. My father ruled over Moab for thirty years, and I became king [3]after my father. And I made this high place for Chemosh in Qarhoh. [I] built it as a sign of [vic][4]tory,[a] for he saved me from all the kings and let me see my desire on all my enemies.[b] Omr[5]i was king of Israel,[c] and he oppressed Moab for a long time, for Chemosh was angry with his land. [6]And his son succeeded him[d] and he too said: 'I will oppress Moab.' In my days Che[mosh] spoke thus, [7]and I looked down on him and on his house.[e] And it was Israel which perished for ever, although Omri had taken possession of the whole la[8]nd of Madeba. And he dwelt in it during his days and half the days of his son, forty years,[f] but [9]Chemosh dwe[lt] in

[a] Read *bn[t]h [.n]*[4] *š*.
[b] Probably an allusion to the attack by the coalition of Israel, Judah and Edom (II Kings 3.4–27). For 'making one look in triumph on the enemy' cf. Pss. 59.10; 118.7.
[c] Cf. I Kings 16.16ff.
[d] Cf. I Kings 16.28ff.; 22.52ff.; II Kings 1.1; 3.1ff.
[e] An allusion to the fall of the dynasty of Omri in 841 BC.
[f] The period of a human life is seventy years (cf. Ps. 90.10; Isa. 23.15). Thus 'half the days' of a man (cf. Jer. 17.11; Ps. 102.24) are thirty-five years; the last years of the reign of Omri (about five years) and 'half the days' of his offspring (about thirty-five years)

it in my days. And I built Baal-meon and made the reservoir in it, and I built [10]Kiryathan. And the people of Gad had long dwelt in the land of Ataroth, and the king of I[11]srael had [10]built Ataroth for himself. [11]And I fought against the city and conquered it. And I killed all the people [outside] [12]the city as an atonement for Chemosh and for Moab. And I brought from there Uriel, their David, and I drag[13]ged him before Chemosh in Karyoth.[g] And I settled there the people of Sharon and the people of [14]Macharot. And Chemosh said to me, 'Go, take Nebo against Israel!' And I [15]went by night and fought against them from dawn until midday. And I to[16]ok it and slew [them] all: seven thousand w[arri]ors and [ol]d men – together with women and [old wom][17]en and maidens – for I had consecrated it for Ashtar-chemosh.[h] And I took from there the [r][18]am of Yahweh and dragged it before Chemosh.[i] And the king of Israel had built [19]Jahaz and he remained in it while fighting against me. But Chemosh drove him out before me,[j] [when] [20]I took from Moab two hundred men, all its brave men. And I led them against Jahaz and conquered it, [21]to annex it to Dibon.

I built Qarhoh: the walls of the parkland and the walls [22]of the acropolis. And I built its gates and I built its towers. And [23]I built the royal palace and I made both the condui[ts for the spr]ing insid[e] [24]the city. And there was no cistern inside the city, in Qarhoh, and I said to all the people, 'Make [25]yourselves each one a cistern in his house!' And I made an alliance for Qarhoh by binding [26]Israel.

I built Aroer and I made the road by the Arnon. [27]I built Beth-bamoth, for it was a ruin. I built Bezer, for [it was] a pile of ruins. [28][And the peop]le of Dibon were ready for war, for all Dibon was a company. And I appointed [29][the governors] of the hundreds to rule[k] in the cities which I had annexed to the country. And I built [30][Beth-made]ba and Beth-diblathan – also Beth-baal-maon, to which I brought [my] shep[her]ds [31][in order to protect] the cattle of the land.[l] And as for Hauronan, the house of Wa[. . .] lived in it. [32][. . . And] Chemosh said to me: 'Go down,

---

total forty years, i.e. from about 881–841 BC. For the duration of foreign rule see Judg. 13.1.

[g] In order to kill him. Cf. I Sam. 15.8, 33.

[h] Probably a combination of two gods. Worship of this particular god involved human sacrifice.

[i] 'Ram' of Yahweh: my conjecture. In my view it probably belonged to the royal sanctuary of Bethel. (For the ram as a sacrificial animal in the worship of Yahweh see e.g. Isa. 1.11 or Micah 6.6–7a.) Mesha would have sacrificed this ram to Chemosh.

[j] For an exact parallel see e.g. Deut. 4.38; Josh. 23.9; Judg. 6.9; Ps. 78.55. Cf. above all Judg. 11.23f.

[k] *Mlkty*, intensive root, as in the Old Aramaic of Zinjirli ('of Jaudi').

[l] A possible expansion is *'t.nq [d[31]y. lšmr.'t] ṣ'n.h'rṣ.*

fight against Hauronan!' And I went down [and I [33]fought against it and captured it. And] Chemosh [lived] in it in my days, and the moth [re]-moved injustice from there.[m] [. . . [34]. . .] years of pouring rain. And I [. . .]

6. The Karatepe inscriptions

Text: this is the longest Phoenician inscription found so far. It is in three versions, and is taken from a bilingual text in which hieroglyphic and Luwian versions are set side by side. It was discovered in 1946/47 in the ruins in Kara-tepe (east of Adana in Turkey). The version of the text which in what follows (as in *KAI*) will be called C covers four columns; it is carved on a great statue of Baal, with a smaller part on the bull-shaped pedestal on which the statue was set up. It has been published in H. T. Bossert and U. B. Alkim, *Karatepe* II, 1947, plates XXIX–XXXI, XL–XLIV, emended by H. T. Bossert, *BTTK* 17, 1953, 143ff.; figs. 7–11. The second version (B) is for the most part on the body of a gate lion. It is published in H. T. Bossert, op. cit., figs. 12–13. The best version of the text, called A in what follows, consists of three columns which are inscribed on orthostats and pedestals and (with a closing section) again on the body of a gate lion. Publication: H.Çambel, *Oriens* 1, 1948, 162, plate I; H. T. Bossert et al., *Die Ausgrabungen auf dem Karatepe*, 1950, plate XIV, 70; id., *BTTK* 17, 1953, figs. 1–6. The last-mentioned text, A, is used as the main text. (All earlier publications are merely preliminary reports.)[n]

The versions of the inscription give an autobiographical account by the vizier Azitawada. They were composed for the dedication of the citadel and the city discovered in Karatepe. Azitawada was evidently the chief minister of King Awarik of Kue and Adana in Cilicia, who is known under the name Urik(ki) as a tributary of Tiglath-pileser III of Assyria in the year 738 BC. According to his inscription Azitawada did good service to the kingdom of Adana and enthroned the descendants of Awarik. So the inscription must be dated after the death of Awarik, probably around 730 BC.

It has points of contact with the OT in many details, not only in its diction ('from the rising of the sun to its setting': Isa. 45.6; Mal. 1.11; Pss. 50.1; 113.3; 'a man of renown': Gen. 6.4; Num. 16.2, etc.) but also in its reference to gods (El + epithet: Gen. 14.19, 22; 'sons of God': Gen. 6.2, 4; Pss. 29.1; 89.6; Job 1.6; 2.1; 38.7; Rashap/Resheph: Hab. 3.5; Job 5.7) or to cultic apparatus and terms ('molten images': Num. 33.52; Deut. 9.12; Isa. 30.22 etc.). Features like blessing and curse also appear (cf. e.g. Deut. 28; especially Ps. 61.6). Not least, the Phoenician text recalls features of the Joseph story (Gen. 37–50), as when it stresses Azitawada's system of storehouses (Gen. 41.34ff., 47ff.) or his wisdom (Gen. 41.39), or when it describes him with a word which is

[m] Cf. Isa. 50.9; 51.8; Hos. 5.12.
[n] The hieroglyphic and Luwian parts of the bilingual inscription may be found in P. Meriggi, *Manuale di eteo geroglifico* II/1, 1967, no. 24, following Bossert's publications and photographs.

evidently used in a comparable way in Gen. 41.43. Finally, when it praises the removal of 'evildoers' or 'violent men', or the provision of peace and security, the inscription comes close to OT royal hymns, which make this very matter a duty for the rulers of Israel (cf. esp. Pss. 101.8 and 72.7).

Literature: *KAI* no. 26; *ANET*[3], 653f.; also A. Alt, *WO* 1, 1947–52, 272ff., and 2, 1954–59, 172ff.; M. Weippert, *XVII. Deutscher Orientalistentag, Vorträge I*, 1969, 191ff.; E. Lipiński, *RSF* 2, 1974, 45ff.

Text A, B, C

[11]I am Azitawada, vizier° of Baal, servant of [2]Baal, whom Awarik, king of the Adanites,ᵖ has made powerful. Baal made me a father and a mother to the Adanites. I have restored [4]the Adanites. I have expanded the land of the plain of Adana from the rising of the su[5]n to its setting. And in my days the Adanites had all good things and [6]full storehouses and prosperity. And I filled the temples of Paʿr.ᑫ I [7]added horse to horse and shield to shield and army to [8]army according to the will of Baal and of the gods. I shattered the violent [9]and removed every evildoer who was in the country. And I restored [10]the house of my lords to good shape and was benevolent to the family of my lord. [11]And I made them sit on the throne of their father and I made peace with [12]every king. Indeed every king reckoned me among the fathersʳ because of my righteousness and [13]because of my wisdom and because of the goodness of my heart. And I built strong fortresses [14]in all the outposts on the frontiers in the places where wicked men were, [15]gang leaders, none of whom had been a subject [16]of the house of Mopsos. I, Azitawada, placed them under my feet. [17]And I built fortresses at those places so that the Adanites might live in them [18]in peace of mind. And I subjected strong lands in the west, [19]which the kings who were before me had not been able to subdue. But I, [20]Azitawada, subdued them. I brought them down. I made them dwell [21]at the frontier in the east. And I have [II 1]established Adanites there, and in my days they were on all the [2]frontiers of the plain of Adana, from the rising of the sun [3]to its setting. And in places where [4]formerly there had been fear, where a man was afraid to walk [5]on a

° 'Vizier', *hbrk*; the same form occurs in Gen. 41.43 in the form *ʾbrk*. Cf. Akkadian *abarakku*, 'steward'. In the hieroglyphic-Luwian parallel the reading 'man of my sun', i.e. man of the king, should be adopted. Thus the epithet points to a high royal official. In this parallel there is no word to correspond to the first 'of Baal', so that the text reads, 'I am Azitawada, the man of my sun, the servant of the weather god'.

ᵖ The hieroglyphic-Luwian text has 'king of Adana'. The *dnnym*, 'Adanites', are thus the inhabitants of Adana. As the ruling dynasty of Adana was called 'house of Mopsos', the *dnnym* and Adana can hardly be dissociated from the 'Danaeans' of the Greeks.

ᑫ Paʿr was the residence of the kings of Kue and Adana. For *ʿequrrot*, 'temples', see Akkadian *ekurru* (Sumerian loan word) and Aramaic *ʾgwr*.

ʳ I.e. among 'the wise', 'the counsellors'. Cf. Gen. 45.8; Isa. 22.21.

road, in my days a woman could happily twirl spindles[s] according to the will of Baal and the gods. [7]And in all my days the storehouses were full, there was prosperity, the living was good [8]and there was peace of mind for the Adanites and for all the pla[9]in of Adana. And I built this city. I have given it [10]the name Azitawadya, for Baal and Rashap of the [11]he-goats[t] sent me to build it. And I built it according to [12]the will of Baal and according to the will of the Rashap of the he-goats with [13]full storehouses and with prosperity and with good living and with peace of [14]mind, so that it might be a protection for the plains of Adana and for the ho[15]use of Mopsos. For in my days the land of the plain of A[16]dana had full storehouses and prosperity, and no one among the Adanites was discontented[u] [17]in my days. And I built this city. [18]I gave it the name Azitawadya. I established Baal krntryš[v] in it and offered sacrifices for all the [III][1]molten images;[w] as a daily sacrifice[x] an ox and at the [time of plo]ughing [2]a sheep and at the time of harvest a sheep. And may Baal kr[n]³trys bless Azitawada with life and salvation [4]and mighty strength beyond any king, so that Baal krntryš [5]and all the gods of the city may give him, Azitawada, length of days and number [6]of years and good authority and mighty strength beyond any king. [7]And may this city possess full storehouses and wine,[y] and may [8]this people which dwells in it possess oxen and poss[9]ess cattle and possess[z] full storehouses and wine. And may they give birth to many (children) [10]and by virtue of the many may they be powerful, and may the many serve Azi[11]tawada and the house of Mopsos according to the will of Baal and of the gods.

Text A:

[12]Now if a king among the kings, or a prince among the princes, or a

---

[s] Hieroglyphic-Luwian: 'even women walked with the spindle'. For the causative root *ydl*, cf. Aramaic-Syriac *dul*, 'move', Akkadian *dalu*, 'go round', Arabic *dala*, 'go to and fro'. There is evidence of the causative root in the Talmud with the meaning 'roll up', 'spin'.

[t] This is a better translation than 'Rashap of the birds', as a divine 'stag' corresponds to this god in the hieroglyphic-Luwian texts. Rashap was a North Semitic god of the underworld and of fatal illness.

[u] Here we follow texts B and C. For *mtmll* cf. Arabic *malla* in the fifth form, 'be disturbed'.

[v] The inscription on the statue, C III 16, has: 'this god, Baal krntrys'. C places A II 19b-III 2a between A III 6 and 7. Baal krntryš escapes closer definition. The epithet *krntryš*, which is certainly not Semitic, causes problems.

[w] 'Molten images', *massekot*, as in the OT (see the preliminary remarks).

[x] In I Sam. 1.21; 2.19 and 20.6 the same expression is usually translated 'annual sacrifice'. Cf. M. Haran, *VT* 19, 1969, 11f. and 372f.

[y] The same expression as in Prov. 3.10.

[z] Text B breaks off here.

m^{13}an who is a man of renown, wipes out the name of Azitawada ^{14}from this gate and puts his own name (on it), if he even has good intentions ^{15}towards this city, but tears down this gate made by ^{16}Azitawada, or makes into a new gate and puts his name on it, ^{17}or if he tears it down with good intentions (or) if he tears it down out of hatred and malice, ^{18}may the lord of heaven and El, the possessor of the earth, ^{19}and the eternal sun god[a] and the whole group of the sons of the gods[b] wipe out that kingdom and that king and $^{IV\,1}$that man who is a man of renown. Only ^{2}may the name of Azitawada endure for ever like the names ^{3}of the sun and the moon.[c]

Text C: Inscription on the statue

$^{IV\,13}$Now i[f] a king among the kings, or a prince among the princes, ^{14}i[f] a man who is a man of renown com^{15}man[ds] that the name of Azitawada shall be wiped out on this statue of the go[d], ^{16}and puts his own name (on it), even if he does it with good intentions towards this city, ^{17}and says, 'I will make ^{18}another statue', and puts his name on it, and ^{19}the statue of god which Azitawada has made for Baal *krntryš*, which is at the king's entrance in ^{21} . . . [. . . $^{V\,1-5}$ . . . Only may the name of] ^{6}Azitawada endure for ever like the name ^{7}of the sun and of the moon.[d]

7. *The inscription from Pyrgi*

Text: A gold plate, 9.2 × 18.7/19.3 cm., found in 1964 (along with two gold plates with Etruscan inscriptions) in Pyrgi (S. Severa), about 24 miles north-west of Rome. It contains nine lines of a Phoenician text. First publication: G. Garbini, *ArCl* 16, 1964, 64ff., plate XXXVII.

This is a votive inscription from a building set up by the Etruscan ruler of Caere (Cerveteri) in honour of the goddess Astarte, whom the Etruscan text identifies with Juno. The date is disputed, but it cannot be later than the fourth century BC.

The day of the burial of the goddess (in the month of Kirar, probably at the beginning of the year) was the second day of the festival of the dying and rising of the god Melqart. On the third day he came alive again through the mediation of the 'reviver of the deity, the patron who supports Astarte', the bearer of a cultic office (see *KAI* nos. 44.2; 70.3; 90.3; 93.4 etc.), which appertained to the king or the highest minister of the state. One of the obligations of this 'reviver of the deity' was probably a sacred marriage with a priestess of Astarte. Hosea

[a] But cf. also Gen. 21.33.

[b] The parallel expression in the hieroglyphic-Luwian text is 'the Tarhuis (weather god) of heaven, the sun god of heaven, Aa (Ea, the Babylonian god of the sweet-water ocean, thought to be under the earth) and all the gods'. Accordingly Aa is probably to be identified with 'El, the possessor of the earth'.

[c] Ps. 72.17 is very similar.

[d] Again cf. Ps. 72.17.

6.2 seems to allude to such a festival of Melqart, as perhaps does Ezek. 28.1-19, since Melqart was the 'king of the city' of Tyre.

Literature: G. Garbini, *AION* 28, 1968, 229ff.; W. Fischer and H. Rix, *GGA* 220, 1968, 64ff.; *KAI²*, no. 277; W. Röllig, *WO* 5, 1969-70, 108ff.; E. Lipiński, in *Actes de la XVIIᵉ Rencontre Assyriologique Internationale*, 1970, 30ff.; E. Lipiński, *RSF* 2, 1974, 59ff.

¹To the lady, to Astarte. This (is) the holy place ²which was made and given by ³Tiberie Welianash, who rules over ⁴Caere, in the month of the 'sacrifice ⁵for the sun god', as a gift in the temple. And he built ⁶the niche, for Astarte desired (it) of him,ᵉ ⁷in the third year of his reign, in the mon⁸th Kirar, on the day of the burial ⁹of the deity. And may the showpiecesᶠ in the votive offering for the deity ¹⁰in her temple be as brilliant as those ¹¹stars.

8. Inscription of a Chemosh worshipper

Text: an Aramaic inscription from the land of Moab found in the centre of the city of Kerak. The four lines of which it consists are inscribed on an altar stone. The text was first published in an edition by J. T. Milik, *SBFLA* 9, 1958-59, 331ff.

The inscription dates from the Hellenistic epoch; on palaeographic grounds it is put in the first half of the third century BC. It is evidence that the worship of the old Moabite god Chemosh continued down to this late period and gives *Sr'* as the name of his consort. This is probably quite simply the Arabic noun for 'good fortune'. In any case, the other proper names mentioned in the inscription and the word for 'shelter' (in line 1) are Arabic. We cannot exclude the possibility that the name of the consort of Chemosh is a translation of the Greek divine name Tyche.

The inscription is significant, if only because it mentions the name of the Moabite god Chemosh, who appears at various places in the OT (cf. e.g. Num. 21.29; Judg. 11.24; I Kings 11.7, 33; II Kings 23.13). It is particularly fascinating because of the prophecy directed against Moab and Chemosh in Jer. 48, but it shows that the cult of Chemosh continued in the land of Moab despite the threatened deportation of the god and his priesthood (cf. Jer. 48.7); it would, of course, have been carried on by the Arabs who took the place of the Moabites (cf. Jer. 48.13, 46).

Literature: J. A. Fitzmyer, *JBL* 78, 1959, 60ff.

ᵉ Or 'for Astarte will be married through his mediation', in which case there is an allusion to the *hieros gamos*, the sacred marriage.

ᶠ Literally 'brilliant (objects)' (line 9) and 'brilliant' (line 10); for *šnt* cf. Arabic *sana*, 'shine', and D. W. Thomas, *ZAW* 52, 1934, 236ff., and 55, 1937, 174ff.; E. Lipiński, *Syr* 42, 1965, 47f., and 44, 1967, 285. Nails with gilded heads were found with the gold plate. Perhaps they were *clavi annales*.

[1]Shelter[g] of Sarra, the queen. [2]The servant of Chemosh, Hilal, the son of Amma, made [3]this altar and its space[h] [4]for the same house in the fifteenth year.

III. SEPULCHRAL INSCRIPTIONS

9. *Sepulchral inscription of King Tabnit of Sidon*

Text: a Phoenician inscription of eight lines at the foot end of an Egyptian anthropoid sarcophagus (i.e. one in human form), found in 1887 in a necropolis in Sidon. Now in the museum in Istanbul. First publication: E. Renan, *Comptes Rendus de l'Académie des Inscriptions et Belles-Lettres*, 1887, 182f.

To judge from the Egyptian inscription on the cover and inside the sarcophagus this originally belonged to the Egyptian general Penptah; afterwards, at the end of the sixth century BC, it was used again for the burial of the king of Sidon.

The text is notable above all because of the priestly and royal titles given to the ruler of Sidon. (Incidentally, Ittobaal, king of Tyre in the ninth century BC, was priest of Astarte: Josephus, *C.Ap.* I. 18, §123; Abbarus, king of Tyre in the sixth century, was high priest, Josephus, op. cit., I. 21, §157.) The contemporary text Zech. 6.11-13 is comparative material from the OT, as are Gen. 14. 18 and Ps. 110. Not least, it is also worth mentioning that the inscription uses the expression *t'bt* for 'taboo'; this is to be found in the OT in the form *to'eba*; cf. e.g. Lev. 18.27, 29; Jer. 6.15.

The text has also been translated in *KAI*, no. 13, and *ANET*[3], 662. Cf. recently also E. Lipiński, *RSF* 2, 1974, 55f.

[1]I, Tabnit, priest of Astarte, king of the Sidonians, son [2]of Eshmunazor, priest of Astarte, king of the Sidonians, lie in this sarcophagus. [3]Whoever you may be who comes across this sarcophagus, do not [4]open it and do not disturb me. For they have collected no silver for me, nor have they collected any [5]gold nor any other kind of valuable. Only I am lying in this sarcophagus. You must not op[6]en it and you must not disturb me, for that would be taboo to Astarte. And if nevertheless you [7]do open it and do destroy me, may (you) not have any seed among the living under the sun [8]nor a resting place among the spirits of the dead![i]

10. *Early Jewish sepulchral inscription*

Text: A two-line Aramaic inscription on the cover of an ossuary (a container

---

[g] The exact meaning of the word *wagr* in this context is uncertain.
[h] The Aramaic word is *niška*, which also appears in Neh. 3.30; 12.44; 13.7.
[i] The underlying word here also occurs in the OT: cf. e.g. Isa. 14.9; 26.14; Ps. 88.10.

for bones) from the tomb in Jebel Ḥallet et-Turi, south-east of Jerusalem. First publication: J. T. Milik, *SBFLA* 7, 1956–57, 232ff.

Date of composition: end of the first century BC.

This inscription is intended to deter grave robbers and recalls the expression used in the OT at Num. 9.13 and 31.50, '*qorban* Yahweh', i.e. offering for Yahweh, or better, 'consecrated property of Yahweh'. Here, of course, the divine name Yahweh has already been replaced by the Aramaic word for 'God'. Cf. Lev. 23.14. (In later times *qorban* was used alone. Cf. Mark 7.11; Matt. 15.5.)

[1]To any man who may appropriate this ossuary,[j] [2]it is the property of God consecrated[k] to him by the person who lies therein.

IV. SEALS

11. *Seal of an Edomite king*

Text: impression of a royal seal stamped on clay, 1.9 × 1.6 cm., with an inscription and the picture of a sphinx on the move. It was found in 1965 in the high-lying Edomite settlement of Umm el-Biyara in the immediate neighbourhood of the later Nabatean city Reqem-petra. First publication: C. M. Bennett, *RB* 73, 1966, 372ff. (cf. 399ff., plate XXIIb).

The king mentioned on it is very probably identical with the Qaush-gabri who is mentioned in Assyrian inscriptions at the time of Esarhaddon (680–669 BC), and further in the first year of Ashurbanipal (668 BC), alongside Manasseh, king of Judah (cf. R. Borger, AfOB 9, 1956, 60, line 56; M. Streck, *Assurbanipal*, VAB 7, 1916, 139, 24f.).

Qaus was the chief god of the Edomites; he was later worshipped in North Arabia. The name Qaus-gabr, 'Qaus is a hero' or 'Qaus is bold', largely corresponds to the throne name El-gibbor in Isa. 9.6b.

[1]Belonging to Qaus-ga [br], [2]the king of E[dom].

12. *Seal of a prophet of Melqart*

This early Phoenician seal was in the possession of the English consul in Beirut, whose name was Moore, when it was published through Count R. de Vogüé, *Mélanges d'archéologie orientale*, 1868, 81.

---

[j] The underlying word here denotes the sarcophagus in the Eshmunazor inscription (cf. *KAI*, no. 14. 3, 5, 7, 11, 21).

[k] *qorban*, 'consecrated material', is here almost synonymous with 'ban', an expression which can denote both the consecrated gift and the material subject to the ban (see the introduction to no. 5 above; cf. e.g. Lev. 27.21, 28; Num. 18.14 or Josh. 7.12).

In the inscription on the seal the office of the owner is mentioned after his name and his piety is stressed, as also happens in other inscriptions of this kind. For Melqart see no. 1 above.

'Man of God' is a designation which is regularly applied to prophets in the OT. Prophets of Baal of Tyre, i.e. Melqart, are mentioned in I Kings 18.19ff.; 19.1 and II Kings 10.19.

Literature: M. A. Levy, *Siegel und Gemmen*, 1869, 31, Phoenician inscription no. 18, and plate II, 17; E. Lipiński, *RSF* 2, 1974, 54f.

Belonging to Baal-yaton, the man of God, who depends on Melqart.[1]

13. *Seal of a priest of the moon god*

This early Syrian pictorial seal was also published through Comte R. de Vogüé, op. cit., no. 14. The inscription consists simply of the name of the owner and that of his father.

15. This seal depicts a priest by an incense altar; above the altar is a sickle moon as a symbol of the moon god.

The proper name of the owner, '*b'd*, corresponds exactly to the third throne name in Isa. 9.6b and probably means 'my father is judge'. 'My father' here is doubtless a theophoric element.

Literature: M. A. Levy, *Siegel und Gemmen*, 1869, 28, Phoenician inscription no. 13, and plate II, 12; E. Lipiński, *Sem* 20, 1970, 52.

Belonging to 'Abi-'ed, the son of Zakir.

V. INCANTATIONS

14. *First amulet from Arslan Tash*

A small limestone plaque measuring 8.2 × 6.7 cm., with an incantation, composed in a mixed dialect of Aramaic and Phoenician, acquired in Arslan Tash, ancient Hadattu (between Carchemish and Harran), in 1933. In the eighth century Arslan Tash was the seat of an Assyrian governor. The face of the plaque depicts a winged sphinx ('flyer') with a pointed helmet, and under it a lioness couchant with a scorpion's tail, which is swallowing a man (cf.

---

[1] The underlying word should apparently be understood in the light of the Arabic *raṣufa*, 'be dependent on'.

*ANEP*², no. 662). The obverse depicts a god – perhaps Sasm^m – walking, dressed in a short Assyrian tunic and a long coat and swinging a double axe. The piece is worked in the style of provincial Assyrian art of the seventh century.

First publication: Comte du Mesnil du Buisson, *Mélanges syriens* I, 1939, 421ff.

The plaque functioned as an amulet intended to protect the house against nocturnal demons. It dates from the seventh century BC. The incantations are directed against the two female demons who are depicted on the amulet. 'Two strangling goddesses' are also mentioned in Ugarit (*CTA* no. 34, line 18; *Ugaritica* 5, 594f., A, line 13).

The discovery is interesting in connection with the OT, since amulets and incantations also play a part – of a kind – there. For the former see Zech. 14.20; Song of Songs 4.9 and the views expressed on them in Gen. 35.4; Ex. 32.3; Judg. 8.21, 26; Isa. 3.18, 20. For incantations see Isa. 19.3; 47.9, 12; Jer. 8.17; Dan. 1.20; 2.2, and the explicit prohibition in Deut. 18.11 (and II Kings 23.24). The example of a Syro-Phoenician incantation reproduced here has points of contact with all this, and individual expressions are also parallel to the language of the OT.

Literature: *KAI* no. 27 (with earlier literature); *ANET*³, 658; F. M. Cross and R. J. Saley, *BASOR* 197, 1970, 42ff.; A. Caquot, *The Gaster Festschrift* (*JNES* 5), 1973, 45ff. (new deciphering); W. Röllig, *NESE* 2, 1974, 17ff.

¹Incantation for the right moment.^n The treaty of ²Sasm, the son of Pidri. ³Speak the following, ⁴and say to the strangling deities: ⁵'The house I enter ⁶you shall not enter, ⁷and the courtyard I tread ⁸you shall not tread. He (Sasm) ⁹has made a treaty with us° ¹⁰for ever.^p He has made out a bond ¹¹for us, (he) and all the sons of god,^q ¹²and the supreme one of the circle of all the holy ones,^r (a bond) ¹³with the treaty of heaven and earth, ¹⁴the eternal witnesses,^s with the treaty of Baal, ¹⁵[the lord of the who]le earth,^t with [his (Sasm's)] treat[y].

On the margins at the side and above:

¹[Incant]ation of Hauron,^u who has bound her (the strangler's) mouth,

^m For this god cf. A. Caquot and O. Masson, *Syr* 45, 1968, 317ff.

^n The reading *l't'* is certain.

° I.e., 'in our favour' (*ln*). What is meant is the whole family living in the house. For the expression *krt 'lt* cf. Deut. 29.1. The treaty assures the family the support of the gods and deters the night demons.

^p Cf. the corresponding formula in Gen. 9.12, 16 and elsewhere.

^q The same expression as in Pss. 29.1; 89.6.

^r Cf. Ps. 89.5, 7.

^s For an appeal to heaven and earth to guarantee a treaty see Deut. 4.26; 30.19; 31.28; 32.1; Isa. 1.2; Ps. 50.4 (Jer. 2.12; Micah 6.2) and the inscription from Sefire (no. 24 below), I A 11. Cf. M. Delcor, *VT* 16, 1966, 8ff.

^t The same expression as in Josh. 3.11, 13; Micah 4.13; Zech. 4.14; 6.5; Ps. 97.5.

^u The Canaanite god Hauron, to whom an appeal is also made in an incantation from

[2]and her seven co-wives and the ei[3]ght wives[v] of holy Baal.

On the winged sphinx:

[1]To the female one who flies: 'Along the dark chamber [2]the night beings have passed step by step.'

On the lioness with the tail of scorpions:

'They have come out of the h[ou]se.'

On and near the figure of the man:

[1]'He has arrived at [2]my door, [3]and he has [4]illuminated the [5]doorposts, the sun has risen! [6]They[w] groaned, [7]they went away and [8]flew off for ever.'

15. *Second amulet from Arslan Tash*

Text: a limestone plaque measuring 5.3 × 3.3 cm., with two incantations in Phoenician. Like the first amulet, it was bought in Arslan Tash in 1933. One side of the plaque shows a figure like a man with large eyes and scorpion feet. It is swallowing a man and so probably depicts the being with the evil eye.

First publication: A. Caquot and R. du Mesnil du Buisson, *Syr* 48, 1971, 391ff.

This is again an amulet, the incantation on which is intended to protect the house against the evil eye. The other side gives the text of an incantation for rain. The user is to sprinkle his fields and at the same time recite a formula of sympathetic magic. Probably both incantations are taken from a scroll containing a collection of Phoenician incantations. The amulet comes from the seventh century BC; the incantations themselves are probably earlier.

This discovery, too, is of significance for OT texts which presuppose amulets and incantation (for amulets cf. Gen. 35.4; Ex. 32.3; Judg. 8.21, 26; Isa. 3.18, 20; Zech. 14.20; Song of Songs 4.9, and for incantation Deut. 18.11; II Kings 23.24; Isa. 19.3; 47.9, 12; Jer. 8.17; Dan. 1.20 and 2.2). It also gives a vivid impression of fear of the evil eye, of which there are also traces in the OT (cf. the Hebrew text of Deut. 28.54, 56; Prov. 6.13; 10.10; 16.30). I Sam. 7.6, 10b might possibly be considered a parallel to a rite of sympathetic magic to produce rain. In any case, it is interesting to compare this with the conviction in the OT that Yahweh only blesses with a gift of rain when his commandments

---

Ugarit (*Ugaritica* 5, 564ff.), probably had a sanctuary in the two Beth-horons in Ephraim (Josh. 16.3, 5; 18.13). Cf. *WM* I, 288f.

[v] For the early Canaanite parallelism 7//8, cf. Micah 5.5; Eccles. 11.2.

[w] The female night demons. – The perfect is used in the magical sayings addressed to the sphinx, the lioness and the walking god, just as it is in wishes and execrations in Arabic. This use of the perfect has a religious significance, in that the expulsion of evil spirits by the use of the magical formula is represented as settled and as good as finished.

are fulfilled (so Lev. 26.4; Deut. 11.11ff.; 28.1f., 12). The expectation in the Phoenician incantation that rain will come from the 'Cyprian' and therefore, as in I Kings 18.41–46, from the sea, corresponds with geographical and climatic conditions.

Literature: T. H. Gaster, *BASOR* 209, 1973, 18ff.; W. Röllig, *NESE* 2, 1974, 28ff.; M. Liverani, *RSF* 2, 1974, 35ff.; E. Lipiński, *RSF* 2, 1974, 50ff.

A[1]Incantation for the sprinkler.[x]
'Baal [2]has harnessed his chariot,[y]
and an overpowering fountain [3]is with him.
The Cyprian has sent [4]his fire on the fields,
[4]and the wave of water [5]on the field.
Where is the Cyp[6]rian? He is hardened!'

B[1]«With bolts I have fastened [2]your eye. [3]He has taken flight, the one who casts the evil eye [4]on the womb, on the head of the one who comprehends all [5]wisdom, on the head of the dreamer, for [6]I have completely smitten the eye, his eye!'
[7]My incantation(s) is (are) as in the scroll.

VI. CULTIC INSCRIPTION

16. *The incense altar from Lachish*

A stone altar, rectangular in cross-section, 15 cm. high and 10 cm. wide, found outside the holy precinct of Lachish. There are three lines on the front. First publication: A. Dupont-Sommer in O. Tufnell, *Lachish III. The Iron Age*, 1953, I, 358f.; II, plates 49 and 68. Now in the Rockefeller Museum in Jerusalem.

To judge from the place where the small incense altar was found, it could have been used for private offerings. However, four similar incense altars were found in 1968 in pre-exilic strata of the holy precinct itself. The inscribed incense altar may therefore also have been part of the cultic furniture of the sanctuary of Lachish. Most scholars date it around 450 BC; but from the point of view of its epigraphy it can also belong to the exilic period.

The burning of incense seems to have been part of public and private worship for a long time – not least with an apotropaic function. In the OT Lev. 16.12f. bears witness to the burning of incense as part of the celebration of the great Day of Atonement; it seems to have had the purpose of providing concealment (v. 13b). The incense altar is attested in Ex. 30.1, 27 (and perhaps also in

[x] The same word is used in Num. 19.21 of the one who sprinkles the 'water against uncleanness'.
[y] Cf. e.g. Pss. 68.17; 104.3.

I Kings 7.48). The incense offering played a similar part (Lev. 2.1, 15; 24.7; Deut. 33.10; I Sam. 2.28; Jer. 6.20, cf. also Ps. 141.2). It was reintroduced to temple worship by Nehemiah after the exile (Neh. 13.9).
   Literature: R. Degen, *NESE* 1, 1972, 39ff.; A. Lemaire, *RB* 81, 1974, 63ff. and plate I; E. Lipiński, *Studies in Aramaic Inscriptions and Onomastics* I, 1975, 143ff.

[1]The incense altar of J[oa][2]s(?) son of Me[hir] (?) [3]to Yah the Lord of heaven.[z]

VII. GRAFFITI

17. *Hebrew graffiti from a chamber tomb*

   Hebrew graffiti, discovered in 1961 in a chamber tomb at Ḥirbet Beit Ley (about 5 miles east of Lachish). First publication: J. Naveh, *IEJ* 13, 1963, 74ff., plates 9-13.
   This type of tomb belongs to Iron Age II C (800-587 BC); the few utensils found in the tomb suggest the fifth century BC as a *terminus ad quem*. On orthographic and palaeographic grounds the three longer inscriptions are best dated to about 500 BC.
   This is evidence of private Jewish belief from the time of the prophets Haggai and Zechariah or from the period immediately afterwards. Inscription B evidently identifies the place Moriah (cf. Gen. 22.2) with the temple mount, as does II Chron. 3.1.
   Literature: J. C. L. Gibson, *Textbook of Syrian Semitic Inscriptions* I, *Hebrew and Moabite Inscriptions*, 1971, 57f.

A. [1]Yahweh is the God of the whole earth. The [2]mountains of Judah belong to him,[a] the God of Jerusalem.

B. For you yourself have blessed Moriah, the dwelling place of Yah, O Yahweh!

C. Deliver, O [Ya]hweh!

[z] Translator's note: This is the version of A. Dupont-Sommer, op. cit. The German text here reads: [2]Der einschläft, der setze [1]Rauchwerk wieder [auf], [2]an[3]genehm des Feu[ers] wegen.
   [a] In this context cf. e.g. Ps. 2.6; 24.3; 48.1f., 11; 121.1. – The reference here is, of course, to the hills of Judah (cf. Josh. 11.21; 20.7; 21.11).

252 NORTH SEMITIC TEXTS [E

VIII. ADMINISTRATIVE TEXTS

18. *The Ophel ostracon*

Text: a potsherd with eight lines, about 10 cm. × 8 cm., discovered in the west of Jerusalem in 1924. The left part of the ostracon and lines 4-7 are no longer legible. First publication: S. A. Cooke, *PEF* 56, 1924, 180ff., plate VI.

The character of the writing, which is similar to that on the Lachish and Arad ostraca, suggests that this ostracon fragment comes from the beginning of the sixth century BC. The content is part of a list of citizens and, it seems, their places of work.

The text twice mentions the 'valley of stelae' (literally 'of hands') which is also known from the Babylonian Talmud, Gittin 57.[b] To all appearances this valley, probably to the south-west of Jerusalem (between the wadi Sikke and the wadi Rababe) was a necropolis; it is referred to in Jer. 31.40.

Literature: J. T. Milik, *RB* 66, 1959, 550ff., plate XIII (with new deciphering) and *KAI*, no. 190.

[1]Hizqiyahu,[c] son of Qor'eh, in the field of the wool-carders; Jeho [...]; [2]Ahiyahu, son of the carder, in the valley of stelae; ... [3]Zephanyahu, son of Qari, in the valley of stelae; [... [4-7] ...]; [8]Hodiyahu, the [...].

19. *Document from Elephantine*

Text: A broad papyrus from the discovery made in 1906/07 on the island of Elephantine, in the Nile in Upper Egypt, opposite Aswan. First publication: E. Sachau, *Aramäische Papyrus und Ostraka aus einer jüdischen Militärkolonie zu Elephantine*, 1911, plates 17-19.

The text comes either from the year 419 (the fifth year of Darius II) or from the year 400 BC (the fifth year of king Amyrtaeus). It contains the names of the 123 colonists who paid the temple tax.

The tax list indicates that worship was offered at Elephantine to Yahweh (Yahu), Ashim-bethel and Anath-bethel. (For Ashim-bethel cf. II Kings 17.30.)

Literature: A. Ungnad, *Aramäische Papyrus aus Elephantine*, 1911, no. 19; A. Cowley, *Aramaic Papyri of the Fifth Century B.C.*, 1923, no. 22; E. G. Kraeling, *The Brooklyn Museum Aramaic Papyri*, 1953, 62f., 87ff.; *ANET*[3], 491; B. Porten, *Archives from Elephantine*, 1968, 160ff., 319ff.

[1]On the third of Phamenoth,[d] year 5. This are (sic) the names of the Jewish garrison, who gave silver to the God Yahu, [two shekels] of silver each. [2-119, 126-135] 123 names are listed. [120-121]The silver which was

---

[b] The reading of the text in lines 2f. presupposed here is certain.

[c] Old Testament evidence in II Kings 20.10 etc.

[d] An ancient Egyptian name for a month.

collected on this day of the month Phamenoth in the hand of Jedoniah, the son of Gemariah: [122]31 karash 8 shekels of silver. [123]And: for Yahu 12 karash 6 shekels; [124]for Ashim-bethel 7 karash; [125]for Anath-bethel 12 karash of silver.

IX. CORRESPONDENCE

20. *An Arad ostracon*

One of the inscribed Jewish ostraca which were found in 1964 in level VI of Tell Arad below a thick stratum of burnt material and debris. The potsherd is about 6.5 cm. × 4.4 cm., and contains nine lines of Hebrew text on the face and one line on the obverse. The writing is like that of the Lachish ostraca. The text contains two signs for units of measure or commodities which can no longer be interpreted. First publication: Y. Aharoni, *Yediot* 30, 1966, 32ff. = *IEJ* 16, 1966, 1ff., plate I.

Internal evidence and palaeography would put the ostracon before 587 BC, probably shortly before the first expedition of Nebuchadnezzar II against Judah in 598/597 BC. The recipient of the letter is a certain Eliashib who, it appears, was a royal administrator of Arad.

The conclusion of the letter refers to the temple at Jerusalem; at that time the Jewish temple at Arad had already disappeared; it was evidently pulled down under Josiah (640-609 BC). The sender of the letter, a subordinate of Eliashib, was therefore in all probability in the capital when he sent this letter to Arad.

Literature: *ANEP²*, no. 807.

[1]To my lord Elia[2]shib. May Yahweh [3]desire your welfare! Now, [4]Give Shemaryahu [5]X and Qerosi [6]Y. And concerning the mat[7]ter which [8]you commanded me, all is in order: [10]he is dwelling [9]in the temple of Yahweh.

21. *A letter from Tahpanhes*

A six-line Phoenician text on a complete papyrus (7 × 21 cm. in format), found in the shaft of a mastaba (tomb site) in Saqqara. First publication: N. Aimé-Giron: *ASAE* 40, 1940, 433ff., plates XL-XLII.

This is a letter. It comes from about the sixth century BC. It was probably sent, by messengers, from a place Tahpanhes (east of the Nile delta, cf. Jer. 43.7ff.) to Memphis. It is written by a Phoenician woman to 'her sister', i.e. her equal.

The text mentions the deity Baal-Zaphon, also well-known from Ugarit, who was worshipped on Mount Casius (lying to the east of the eastern branch

of the Nile at Pelusium, cf. Ex. 14.2, 9; Num. 33.7) and the gods of the neighbouring city of Tahpanhes, to which refugees from Judah, including the prophet Jeremiah, came in 587 (cf. Jer. 43.7-9; 44.11ff.; 46.14; cf. 2.16; Ezek.
30.18).
Literature: A. Dupont-Sommer, *PEQ* 81, 1949, 52ff., and *KAI*, no. 50.

[1]To Arishot, daughter of Eshmun-ya[ton]. [2]Say to my sister Arishot:
Your sister Bisha[e] said: Are things well with you? They are also well
with me! I wish you blessings from Ba[3]al-Zaphon and from all the gods
of Tahpanhes. May they further your welfare. I wish I had the silver
that you sent me! . . .

The rest deals with business matters.

22. The passover letter from Elephantine

Text: a papyrus fragment from Elephantine with writing in Aramaic on
both sides, found in 1906/07 (recto lines 1-7; verso lines 8-11). Like the Aramaic
letters from Hermopolis in central Egypt, this papyrus letter was probably
folded only once lengthwise. The right half of lines 4-10 has been lost; however, it seems that only a little is missing at the end of the lines. First publication:
E. Sachau, *Aramäische Papyrus und Ostraka aus einer jüdischen Militärkolonie
zu Elephantine*, 1911, plate 6.
This letter is one of the most important documents from Elephantine,
where a Jewish military colony with a temple to Yahweh was in existence
during the period of Persian rule over Egypt. The letter was written in the
fifth year of the reign of Darius II, i.e. in the year 419 BC, by the royal envoy
Hananiah to the Jewish ethnarch Yedoniah, who seems to have brought to
the satrap Arsham the royal command by which the passover was to be regulated
among the Jews of Egypt.
The festival mentioned in this 'passover letter' accords completely with the
ordinances for the festival given in the Priestly Writing (cf. Ex. 12.1-20,
especially 15-20, and Lev. 7.20f.; 23.5-8, 15f.; Num. 28.16-18, 25, and II
Chron. 30.15-18, 21; 35.2, 17; Ezra 6.19-22). The OT parallel passages can
even be used to help to fill in the gaps. The plural address is directed towards
the Jewish ethnarch and his colleagues.
Literature: A. Ungnad, *Aramäische Papyrus aus Elephantine*, 1911, no. 6;
A. Cowley, *Aramaic Papyri of the Fifth Century B.C.*, 1923, no. 21; A. Vincent,
La religion des Judéo-araméens d'Éléphantine, 1937, 234ff.; P. Grelot, *VT* 4,
1954, 349ff.; ibid., 5, 1955, 250ff.; ibid. 6, 1956, 174ff.; ibid. 17, 1967, 114ff.,
201ff., 481ff.; B. Porten, *Archives from Elephantine*, 1968, 128ff., 279ff., 311ff.;
P. Grelot, *Documents araméens d'Égypte*, 1972, 95ff.

[1][To] my [brother [2]Ye]doniah and his colleagues the [J]ewish gar-
[rison], your brother Hanan[iah]. The welfare of my brothers may the

[e] The exact pronunciation is unknown.

gods [ensure]. [3]Now, this year, the fifth year of King Darius, word was sent from the king to Arsham [. . . [4] . . .] . . . Now, count fou[rteen [5]days from the first day of Nisan, and observe the pass]over. And from the fifteenth day to the twenty-first day of [Nisan [6]observe the feast of unleavened bread. Now,] you are to be ritually clean and you are to take heed that you do not work [[7]on the fifteenth day and on the twenty-first day of Nisan]. You are not to drink [intoxicating drink] and [you are not to eat] anything which has leaven in it. [[8]You are to eat unleavened bread from the fourteenth day of Nisan at] sundown until the twenty-first day of Nisa[n at sun[9]down. You are not to bring anything leavened] into your houses for seven whole days, but you are to keep (it) away during [those] days. [10][. . . [11]To] my brothers Yedoniah and his colleagues, the Jewish garrison, your brother Hananiah.

23. A letter from Memphis to Aswan

Text: a complete papyrus with fifteen lines in Aramaic, found in 1945 in Tuna el-Jebel (western Hermopolis) along with seven other Aramaic letters. First published by E. Bresciani and M. Kamul, *Le lettere aramaiche di Hermopoli* (Atti della Accademia Nazionale dei Lincei, Memorie. Classe di Scienze morali, storiche e filologische, Ser. VIII, vol. XII, fasc. 5), 1966, no. IV.

These letters were sent from Memphis to Aswan and Luxor. Their content is personal requests and wishes, and they come from the late sixth or early fifth century BC, from an Aramaean, non-Jewish milieu. Letter IV was sent by a Nabusheh/Nabushezib, who was staying on business in Memphis, the capital of Persian Egypt, to his wife Nanaykham in Aswan. Maccibanit is his son-in-law, who has married their daughter Tashi; there are greetings to parents and brothers in lines 13f.

These papyri shed light on the religious conditions in which the Jews lived during the Persian period in Egypt. Among other things, papyrus IV mentions the 'queen of heaven', who was already worshipped in Jerusalem in the seventh century, and afterwards by the Jews in the Nile Delta, in Memphis and in Upper Egypt: Jer. 7.18; 44.17-19, 25; cf. 44.1.

Literature: J. T. Milik, *Bib* 48, 1967, 546ff.; B. Porten, *JNES* 28, 1969, 116ff.; P. Grelot, op. cit., 160ff.; B. Porten and J. C. Greenfield, *Jews of Elephantine and Arameans of Syrene*, 1975, 158f.

[1]Greetings to the temple of Bethel and also to the temple of the queen of heaven.[f] To my sister Nanaykham [2]from your brother Nabu-

[f] As the letter was sent to Aswan (according to line 15), the temple must have been in that city. There is evidence of the god Bethel (literally = house of god) about 676 BC in the treaty of Esarhaddon with King Baal of Tyre. This seems originally to have been a deified meteorite, which was perhaps worshipped in Sidon. The Jewish colonists in Elephantine and Aswan were similarly dependants of the god Bethel, because they lived in the neighbourhood of his sanctuary. The queen of heaven is possibly the goddess

sheh.[g] I wish you the blessings of Ptah,[h] that he may show me your face in health. [3]Greetings to Bethel-nathan. Greetings to Naki and Ashah and Tashi and Anati and Ati and Ra.

[4]Now, the dress-coat which you sent me has arrived, but it felt just like rough cloth and [5]I did not like it. When I see how it can be replaced, I will give it [6]to Ati as a coat. I am wearing the very dress-coat which you brought to me at Aswan. [7]Now, you must send us castor oil, and I will send some olive oil in exchange. Do not [8]worry about us, myself and Maccibanit. We are thinking about you. Take care [9]of Bethel-nathan because of the river. Now, if I find someone reliable, [10]I will send something to you. Greetings to Shabbatai the son of Shug! Greetings to Pasi! [11]Greetings to Ader, the son of Pasi! Greetings to Shail, the son of Patihorti and to Asha, [12]the son of Patikhnum! Greetings to all the neighbours! I have written this letter to send greetings to you. [13]Greetings to my father Psami from your servant Nabusheh! Greetings to my mother [14]Mamah and greetings to my brother Betay and his wife. Greetings to Wakhfra!

Address:[15]To Nanaykham of Nabushezib, the son of Patikhum, Aswan.

X. TREATY INSCRIPTIONS

24. State treaties between Katk and Arpad

Fragments of three basalt stelae discovered in 1930 at Sefire (fourteen miles south-east of Aleppo). Stelae I and II took the form of a truncated pyramid, each about 1.30 m. high; in each case the inscription was on three sides (A, B and C). Stele III was a block 0.82 m. high and 1.25 m. wide. First publication: S. Ronzevalle, MUSJ 15.4, 1930-31, 237ff. (stele I); A. Dupont-Sommer and J. Starcky, *Les inscriptions araméennes de Sfiré (Stèles I et II)*, *Mémoires présentés par divers savants à l'Académie des Inscriptions et Belles Lettres* 15, 1958, 197ff., plates I-XXIX; A. Dupont-Sommer and J. Starcky, *BMB* 13, 1956, 23ff., plates I-VI (stele III).

These are Old Aramaic state treaties between king Bar-gaya of Katak (Aramaic Ktk, Assyrian Kask/Kashk, in south-east Asia Minor) and Mati-el of Arpad (about eighteen miles north of Aleppo) from the middle of the eighth

---

Anath-bethel, who is mentioned in Esarhaddon's treaty with Baal of Tyre immediately after the god Bethel and was worshipped by the Jews of Elephantine and Aswan alongside an Anat-yahu. The queen of heaven would accordingly have been Anath.

[g] 'Sister' and 'brother' are used here for 'wife' and 'husband'.

[h] The chief god of Memphis.

century BC (before 740, the date of the conquest of Arpad by Tiglath-pileser III). Stele III was perhaps written before stelae I and II, as the king of Arpad still seems to have had considerable political independence and power. We cannot rule out the possibility that stele III belongs to the time before 754, when Mati-el was compelled to make a treaty with Ashurnirari V of Assyria. Stelae I and II would belong in the period after 754.

If these are not treaties to regulate Mati-el's vassal relationship with Bar-gaya, they are at least documentation of an alliance between unequal partners: the weaker king of Arpad had to concede greater rights to the stronger king of Katk, but had to take over increased obligations himself. Behind this was certainly pressure in the direction of an alliance against Assyria, especially for political and military security against the immediate threat to the kingdom of Arpad from the neo-Assyrian empire.

So far, the inscriptions of Sefire are the only state treaties in a North-west Semitic language. They are therefore important for the discussion of the problems surrounding the covenant and the covenant formulary in the OT. In particular, the way in which they threaten sanctions if the treaty is broken invites comparison with the OT: cf. Stele I A 21ff. and Stele II A 1ff. with Lev. 26.26; Deut. 28.38–40; Hos. 4.10; 9.12, 16; Amos 5.11; Micah 6.14f.; Zeph. 1.13; Hag. 1.6 and other passages. There are also interesting points of comparison in other individual features, as is indicated in the notes.

Literature: M. Noth, 'Der historische Hintergrund der Inschriften von *sefire*', *ZDPV* 77, 1961, 118ff. = *Aufsätze zur biblischen Landes und Alter-tumskunde* II, 1971, 161ff.; *KAI*, nos. 222–4; J. A. Fitzmyer, *The Aramaic Inscriptions of Sefire*, 1967, and *ANET*[3], 659ff. For the reconstruction of the gaps in the text see E. Lipiński, *Studies in Aramaic Inscriptions and Onomastica* I, 1975, 24ff.

Stele I

A [1]The treaty of Bar-gaya, king of Katk, with Mati-el, the son of Attar-sumki, the king of [Arpad, and the trea] [2]ty of the sons of Bar-gaya with the sons of Mati-el, and the treaty of the sons of the sons of Bar-ga[ya and] his [descendants] [3]with the descendants of Mati-el, the son of Attar-sumki, the king of Arpad, and the treaty of Katk with the [treaty of] [4]Arpad, and the treaty of the citizens of Katk with the treaty of the citizens of Arpad, and the treaty of one confed[erate with the other] [5]and with all Aram[i] and with Misr[j] and with his sons who will come up in [his] place, and [with the kings of the] [6]whole of upper and lower Aram and with anyone entering or l[eav]ing the royal house. They have set

[i] The expression refers to the community of minor Aramaean states, 'upper Aram (in the interior) and lower Aram (situated towards the Mediterranean)' (line 6).

[j] Very probably the shortened form of a neo-Hittite personal name, similar to the name Misramuwa, belonging to a ruler of Carchemish in the thirteenth century BC. It seems reasonable to assume that the person mentioned was king of this kingdom of Carchemish.

this treaty [7][on th]is [stele];[k] and this is the treaty which Bar-ga[ya] has made [before . . .][8] and Mullesh[l] and before Marduk and Sarpanitu[m] and before Nabu and Ta[shmetu[n] and before Erra and Nus][9]ku[o] and before Nergal and Las[p] and before Shamash and Nuru[q] and before S[in and Nikkal of . . .][r] and be][10]fore Nikkar and Kadia[s] and before all the gods of the steppe and of the cultivated lan[d and before Hadad of A][11]leppo and before the sevenfold deity and before El and Elyon[t] and before the heave[n and the earth[u] and before the depths of] [12]the sea and the fountains and before day and night. All [these] gods are witnesses. [O all you go[13]ds,] open your eyes to see that [Mati-el, the king of Arpad, keeps] the treaty of Bar-gaya.

[14]And if Mati-el, the son of Attar-sumki, the ki[ng of Arpad,] is false [to Bar-ga[15]ya, the king of Katk, and i]f the descendants of Mati-el [are false to the descendants of Bar-gaya, the kin[16]g of Katk, and if the sons of] Gush[v] as [. . . . [17]ff. there is a large gap here . . . [20] . . .] from [the . . . [21]and seven rams will cover] a ewe, and she will not become pregnant;[w] and seven wet[-nurses] will anoin[t their breasts (?) and] [22]suckle a child,[x] and it will not be filled; and seven mares will suckle a colt and it will not be fil[led; and seven] [23]cows will suckle a calf and it will not be filled; and seven sheep will suckle a lamb, and [it will not be filled]; and seven of his hens will go around during the famine, and they will not be

[k] The expression 'on this stele' is to be found in C 17: the expansion has been made accordingly. The subjects of 'have set' are Bar-gaya and Mati-el.
[l] The proper name of an unknown deity. She formed a pair with the god who is mentioned at the end of line 7, and is therefore presumably a female deity.
[m] The chief god of Babylon and his consort.
[n] The Babylonian god of Borsippa and his consort.
[o] The Babylonian plague god Erra and the fire god Nusku make up a pair in the parallel enumeration of divine guarantors in Ashurnirari's treaty with Mati-el.
[p] The Babylonian god of the underworld and his consort.
[q] The Babylonian sun god and his consort Aya, who is called Nuru ('light') here.
[r] The Babylonian moon god and his consort Ninkal/Ningal > Nikkal ('great lady') who is known from earlier North Syrian state treaties as 'Nikkal, the lady of Gurat', or 'Nikkal, the lady of Nuban' (cf. PRU 4, 1956, 52, 65, 157). The word Nikkal was probably followed by the phrase 'of Gurat' or 'of Nuban'.
[s] The proper names of two deities who have not yet been identified; they probably belonged to the pantheon of the king of Katk in Asia Minor.
[t] 'El and Elyon' should be compared with the OT El Elyon ('the supreme god'). Cf. Gen. 14.18ff.; Num. 24.16; Ps. 57.2; 73.11; 77.9f.; 78.35; 107.11. The names of deities who are concerned with an epithet by 'and' often occur in Ugaritic.
[u] Cf. Deut. 31.28; 32.1; Isa. 1.2; Ps. 50.4 and p. 248 n. s above.
[v] Ancestor of the ruling dynasty of Arpad.
[w] There are threats of sanctions after the gap. Cf. the OT parallels mentioned above.
[x] For the theme cf. again Hos. 9.14; Lam. 4.3f.; Gen. 49.25.

killed! And if Mati[-el is false to] [25]his son[y] and to his descendants, his kingdom will become like a kingdom of sand, a kingdom of dreams, ruled over by Assyria; [in that case may Ha] [26]dad [pour out] all evil upon earth and in heaven and every ill;[z] and he will pour out [ha][27]il [stones] over Arpad![a] And the locusts will devour for seven years. And the worm will devour for seven years. And the lament[b] [will ari]se [28]from the face of its land [for seven years], but no plants will appear, and nothing green will be seen so that its grass [will not be seen]! [29]And the sound of the zither will not be heard in Arpad, but among its people there will be the moans of the sick and the [tumult] of [cry]ing [30] and lamentation. And may the gods send every devouring pest against Arpad, and its people [will be devoured by the mout]h [31]of the snake and the mouth of the scorpion and the mouth of the bear of woe[c] and the mouth of the panther and the moth and the flea and the w[asp. A des][32]troyer of houses will tear it down! Its pastures [will be dev]astated and become a wilderness, and Arpad will become a ruined hill, [the lair of the stag and] [33]the gazelle and the fox and the hare and the wild cat and the owl and [the screech-owl] and the magpie![d] And no mention will be made of [that] ci[ty and of] [34]Medura and Meriba and Mazeh and Mabbula and Sharun and Tuwim and Bethel and Bayyanan and [. . . and A][35]rneh and Hazaz and Adam![e] As this wax is burnt in fire, so will Arpad and the [surroun]ding [cities] be burnt![f] [36]And Hadad will sow salt and cress in them![g] And you may not say, 'This thief and [this his shame], [37]this is Mati-el and his shame!'[h] As this wax is burnt in the fire, so Ma[ti-el will be burnt in

[y] I.e. the son of Bar-gaya.   [z] Cf. e.g. Deut. 28.23f.
[a] Cf. Isa. 30.30; Ezek. 13.11, 13; 38.22.
[b] The underlying word *tmy* is a substantive for the interjection *may* ('Alas'), an allusion to penitential ceremonies in times of need.
[c] We divide the words here as *db hh* ('bear of woe'). The Aramaic and Hebrew (Ezek. 30.2) word *hah* means 'alas'. See the similar expressions 'lurking bear' (Lam. 3.10), charging bear (Prov. 28.15), 'deprived she-bear' (II Sam. 17.8; Hos. 13.8; Prov. 17.12). Cf. this excerpt (A 30f.) and Stele II A 9 with Lev. 26.22 and Ezek. 14.15.
[d] Cf. e.g. Zeph. 21.3f. or Isa. 13.21f.; 34.10ff.
[e] The vocalization of the majority of these place names is hypothetical. Sharun, Tuwim and Hazaz are known from contemporary Assyrian documents. All these places seem to have belonged to the region close to Arpad.
[f] An allusion to magical actions which were performed at the time of concluding the treaties. Wax figures were evidently thrown into the fire. Cf. *mutatis mutandis* Ps. 68.2 (also Pss. 22.14; 97.5; Micah 1.4).
[g] For scattering salt see Judg. 9.45; Jer. 17.6; Zeph. 2.9 (also Deut. 29.23; Job 39.6). Cf. F. C. Fensham, *BA* 25, 1962, 48ff.
[h] 'This thief', who is identified with Mati-el, is the thief who is probably mentioned in line 42. At the time of the covenant ceremony he plays the role of a representative of the king; the 'shame' which accrues to him in the context of the action is similarly to come upon Mati-el if he breaks the treaty. Cf. p. 260 n. m below.

the fi]³⁸re, and as the bow and these arrows are broken, so will Inurta[i] and Hadad break [the bow of Mati-el] ³⁹and the bow of his nobles! And as the man of wax is blinded, so will Mati-e[l] be blinded![j] [And ⁴⁰as] this calf is cut up, so will Mati-el be cut up and so will his nobles be cut up![k] [And as ⁴¹th]is is [laid bare],[l] so will the wives of Mati-el and the wives of his descendants and the wives of his no[bles be laid bare. And as ⁴²this thief is taken and fettered] and robbed of his sight, so will [Mati-el] be taken and [fettered] and [he will ⁴³be robbed of his sight[m] . . .]

    ᴮ[The treaty of Bar-gaya, king of Katk, with Mati-el, the son of Atta¹r-sumki, the king of Ar]pad, and the treaty of the sons of Bar-gaya with the sons of Mati-el and the treaty of the [so²ns of the sons of Bar-]gaya with the descendants of Mati-el and with the descendants of any king who ³[will arise in Arpad] in his place, and with the sons of Gush and with the house of Silul[n] and with [all] Ar⁴[am and the tre]aty of Katk with the treaty⁵[of Arpad and the treaty of the citizens of Katk with the trea⁵[ty of the citizens of A]rpad and with its people and the treaty of the gods of Katk with the treaty of the g⁶[ods of Arpad] – this is the treaty of the gods which the gods have made.

    Happy the king ⁷[whose throne (rests) on the ste]adfastness of a great king and like thi[s] tr[eat]y (stands) [on the firma]ment of heaven! And [all the gods] ⁸will preserve [this] treaty and none of the words of thi[s] inscription will be silent! ⁹[And they will be heard from] Arqu to Yad[i and Buz], from Lebanon to Jab¹⁰[rud and . . . from Damas]cus to Aro and Ma[nsu]wa[t, from Beqa to Katk.° ¹¹[All the gods will protect the h]ouse of Gush and his people with their places of worship![p ¹²[Arpad will

    [i] Inurta or Ninurta was the Assyrian war god. He himself and the storm god Hadad used bows and arrows. An appeal is made to them here to break the bows and arrows of Mari-el if he breaks the treaty.
    [j] For the blinding of a king who breaks a treaty cf. II Kings 25.7; Jer. 39.7; 52.11 (also Ezek. 12.12f.).
    [k] For cutting up a calf at the time of concluding a treaty cf. Gen. 15.9–18; Jer. 34.18. For the significance of this ritual action cf. J. Henninger, *Bib* 34, 1953, 344f.
    [l] Flaying the hide of the dead calf serves as an image of unclothing the wives of Mati-el. For unclothing women as a shameful punishment cf. Jer. 13.26; Ezek. 16.37; Hos. 2.3; Nah. 3.5.
    [m] The thief was evidently struck at the moment when the treaty was concluded; cf. p. 259 n. h above.
    [n] The personal name Silulu is known from Assyrian documents. The house of Silul in Arpad was evidently a prominent family, along with the family of Gush, from which kings were descended.
    ° Lines 9–10 seem to contain an enumeration of geographical names in Syria in a certain order. This is probably a demarcation of the territory within which the treaty was valid.
    [p] The expression 'place of worship' here is a rendering of the Aramaic 'šrh/t. In a

preserve] thi[s] treaty, [if] his [h]ouse leaves him chi[ldl]ess or co[mes to not]hing in oppression and quarrelling.[q] [13][. . .] for Mati-el, the son of [14][Attar-sumki . . . [15-21]. . .] for your house. And if Mati-el does not obey [and if his sons do not obey and if his people does not obey [22]or if] all the kings who will enter upon rule in Arpad [do not obey] the w[ords of this inscription which will be [23]heard beneath the who]le heaven, then you will be false to all the gods of the treaty wh[ich is in this inscription. But if you do [24]obey and obser]ve this treaty and say, '[I] am a party to this treaty,' [then I will not [25]be able to stretch out my hand] against you and my son will not be able to stretch out his hand against [your] son and my descendants will not be able to stretch out their hand against [your] descen[dants. And if] [26]one of the kings or one of my enemies [says anything] against me, and you say to s[ome] king, 'What do you [want]?'[r] [and he stre[27]tches out his hand against] my son and kills him and stretches out his hand and takes any of my land or my possessions, then you are f[28][alse to the trea]ty which is in this inscription. And if one of the kings comes and encircles me, then come with [all your [29]battle force and] all your bow[men] and all your warrior[s], so that you may fall on the one who encircles me and fight against him. [Other[30]wise I will come] and surely heap up corpse upon corpse in Ar[p]ad. [No] single king [will] be a [safe] place of refuge for the fugitives and th[ey will [31]be] kil[led] without exception.

And if you do not come with your battle force on the day on which the gods [have appointed] suffering [for me], and [32]if al[l of you do not co]me with your battle force to help my ho[u]se to victory, [and if your descend]-ant[s do not] come to help [my] descendants to victory, [33][then you will be false to] the gods of the treaty which is in this inscription. And if the confed[erates] become weary with me, I can [34]ha[ve water brought up from my spring], but anyone who encircles [th]at spring will not be ab[le] to cut off access nor to stretch out his hand to the water of the spr[ing]. [35][And as for] the [king] who may come up and rob you of your heart, he and [his] batt[le force and anyone] who would rob [you of your heart] – [I will] have [36][their heads, to] root out the might of the aggressor [and] his [wicke]dness fr[om among the peo]ples. So have we sworn in the city,

---

similar way, the OT often has Asherah for 'place of worship'. – According to E. Lipiński (*OLP* 3, 1973, 112ff.), the reference may be to a sacred grove (Judg. 6.25-30; Ex. 34.13; Deut. 7.5; 12.3; 16.21; II Kings 18.4; 23.14f.; II Chron. 14.2; 31.1; Micah 5.14) or even a 'chapel' (I Kings 14.15, 23; 15.13; 16.33; II Kings 13.6; 14.23; 17.10, 16; 21.3, 7; 23.6f.; II Chron. 15.16; 19.3; 24.18; 33.3f., 7, 19).

[q] This is the ruling family of Arpad.

[r] This question expresses the readiness of the king of Arpad to recognize another overlord.

and if (it) is does not (happen), then we are fal[37][se in all this]. – And if
the [locus]ts have ea[ten] al[l] my br[ead or the d]rought has taken away
all my bread you are to send [me provisions to e]at. [38]And if you do not
supply my bread and do not bring me bread and do not lavish it, then
you will be false to this treaty. [39][And if you] can[not] contribute the
bread that is needed, because terror comes upon you and your throat
desires it and a[ll the grain] goes out [40]of your [cit]y and your house, you
will slaughter cattle as pro[visions] for my throat [and for ev]ery throat
in my house and for those under [my protect]ion, [41]and your son [will
delight in] his [hea]rt and the kings of A[rpad] will not cut [off any]thing
of the time [42]of l[ife. And if my son does not care] for those under his
protection, or (if) he has sunk down and disappeared, wherever you find
relief for your throat, Ame[n! [43]. . .] as he has done with you, so you
will cut the latecomer in two. And if [. . . [44]. . .] he strengthens the armour[s]
of my house against . . . [. . . [45]. . . against] my son or against one of my
eunuchs. And if one of them flees and come[s . . .]

[C1]Thus have we spoken [and thus] have we [writ]ten. What [2]I, [Mati]-
el, have written is an admo[3]nition for my son [and for the son] of my son
[4]who shall arise in my [place]. May [they] act [in accordance with] this
treaty of friendship [5][under] the sun [6][in favour of my] ro[yal h]ouse,
[so] that nothing [7]ba[d happens to the] house of Ma[8][ti-el and of his son
and the son] of his son fo[r [9]ever . . . [10-14]. . . Any] e[vil [15]may] the gods
keep far from his da[16]ys and from his house. And if [17]anyone does not
observe the words of the inscription which are on this stele, [18]but says,
'I will blot out your words!', [19]or, 'I will overthrow the treaty of friendship and return [20][to] wickedness!' – on the day that he [21]ac[ts] in this
way, may the gods overthrow [th]at ma[n] [22]and his house and everything
that is [in] [23]it, and may they make his humblest servant [24][sup]reme!
And his trib[e] will not have [25]a name!

Stele II

[A1][. . . and seven mares [1]will suckle a colt, and it will not be filled;
and seven cows will suckle a calf, and it will not] be filled; and seven
[2][sheep will suckle a lamb and it will not be filled; and seven goats will
suc]kle a kid, and it will not be [3]fil[led; and seven hens will go around
during the time of famine, and they will not be killed. And if he is fal]se
to Bar-gaya and to [4][his son and to his descendants, his kingdom will
become like a kingdom of sand, and his name will be for]gotten and [his]
tom[b] will be . . . [5][. . . And for se]ven years a copse of thorns [will] force

---

[s] Possible meaning, derived from *qelab* > *qelap* 'peel (off)'.
[t] For the text and its expansion see also stele I A 21 ff.

out the co[6][rn and for sev]en years his [. . . [7]. . .] among all the nobles of
[. . . [8]. . .] and his land. And a cr[9][y . . . And] the mouth of the lion and
the mouth of the [. . .] and the mouth of the panthe[r . . . devour . . .
[10-14] . . .]

B [1][. . . are] [2]the treaty and the friendship whi[ch] the gods have brought
about in [Katk and Arpad. And if Mati-el does not obey] and if his sons
do not obey, [3]if his nobles do not obey and if his people does not obey
and if [all the kings of Arpad] do not ob[ey, the gods of ter][4]ror will arise,
who are to bear witness to it.[u] But if you obey, the repose [of your] bi[er
will . . . and] [5]if you say in your throat and think in [your] heart, ['I am
a party to the treaty and I will serve Bar-gaya] [6]and his sons and his
descendants,' then I will not be able to stretch out my ha[nd against you,
nor my son against your son nor my descendants against your descen-
dants], [7]either to smite them or to destroy their name. And [if my son
says in his throat, 'I will arise in my father's] [8]place,'[v] and my son becomes
demented or grows old and wants [to have my head, to kill me, and you
say in your throat, 'Let him] [9]kill[w] whom he wants to kill', then you will
be false to all the go[ds of the treaty which is in this inscription. And the
gods [10]will] cast you out, and the house of Gush and the house of Silul.
And [. . . [11]. . .] of my [murder]er and the corpse of your son on the corpse
[. . . [12]. . .] by me. And on the day of wrath against all [. . . [13]. . .] . . . he
comes in fe[ar] of my son and the sons of [my] sons [. . .] [14]from the hand
of my enemies [. . .] . . ., you will be false [to this treaty . . .] [15]of the
great [. . .]; thorns [. . .] on your [. . .] and on [your] streets, [16]and no one
will oppress him. If he oppresses in the ci[ty . . .] [17]. . . [. . .]. If you desire
and do not [. . . you have become [18]fal]se to all the [gods of the tre]aty
which is in [this] inscription [. . . [19]And] he is not to . . . [. . .] . . . for a
par[ty] to the treaty [. . . [20]And] if [. . .], who is more powerful than you
[. . . [21]. . .]

C [1][And if anyone] gives [2]the command to remove [th]ese inscriptions
from the houses [3]of the gods,[x] where they have been eng[rav]ed, and
[4][s]ays: 'I wish to destroy the inscrip[t]ions and I will utterl[5]y annihilate
Katk and its king' - [6]even if he is afraid to remove the inscri[pt]ions
[7]from the temples (himself) and he says to [8]someone who does not understand, 'I hire you', and [9]commands him, 'Remove these [inscrip]tions
from the [10]houses of the [go]ds!' - he shall die oppressed by tor[ment
- he] [11]and his son! [12]. . ., all [13]the go[ds of the trea]ty which is in [thi]s

.[u] Cf. also stele I B 22, 39.
[v] Cf. stele I A 5; B 3; C 4 and stele II B 5.
[w] Cf. stele III 11.
[x] The 'houses of the gods' in this inscription are the sanctuaries in which the stelae
containing the treaties were housed. Cf. Josh. 24.25-27; Judg. 9.6.

inscription [will not carry off]^y ^{14}Mati-el and his son and the son of his son ^{15}and his descendants and all the kings of Arpad and all his nob^{16}les and their people from their houses and from ^{17}the days of their (life)!

Stele III

'[. . . And whoever comes to you] ^{1}or to your son or to your descendants or to one of the kings of Arpad and spe[a]ks [ag]ainst me or against my son or against the son of my son or against my descendants, any^{2}one who blows breath through his nostrils^z and says wicked words about me, [you must not] take the words from (his) hand. You must deliver them into my hands, and your ^{3}son must hand (them) over to my son and your descendants must hand (them) over to my descendants, and the descendant [of each of the kin]gs of Arpad must hand (them) over to me. Whatever is good in my eyes, I will do to them. ^{4}Otherwise you will be false to all the gods of the treaty which is in [this] inscription. And if a fugitive runs away from me, one of my high officials or one of my brothers or one of ^{5}my eunuchs or anyone from the people which is subject to me, and they go to Aleppo, you must not provide bread for [th]em and must not say to them, 'Stay peacefully in your place', and must not make ^{6}them be disdainful about me. You must quieten them and return them to me. And if they do not want to s[ta]y in your country, (then) quieten them until I myself come and placate them! But if you do cause them to be disdainful about me ^{7}and give them bread and say to them, 'Stay where you are, and do not go back to his place', then you will be false to this treaty. And all the kings around ^{8}me, or anyone who is well disposed to me and to w[h]om I send my messengers on a peaceful mission or for any other of my concerns or who sends me his messengers: May the ^{9}way be open for me! You shall not exercise control over me in this respect or raise any objection aga[inst] me! Otherwise you will be false to this treaty. And if it happens that any of my brothers or any of the ^{10}house of my father of any of my sons or any of my commanders or any of my [hig]h officials or any of my subjects or any of my enemies seeks ^{11}to have my head to kill me and to kill my son and my descendants – if they kill m[e], (then) you shall come yourself and avenge my blood on the hand of my enemy, and your son shall come; ^{12}he shall avenge the bloo[d of my son] on his enemies; and the son of your son shall come; he shall avenge the bloo[d of the son] of my son; and your descendants shall come; they shall avenge the blood of my descendants, and if it is a city,

---

^{y} It is probable that a formula of blessing like that in stele I C 15/16 should be supplied in the gap.

^{z} I.e., 'who is angry', 'who seeks a quarrel'. For this terminology see also Isa. 64.1; Prov. 1.23. Cf. F. Vattioni, *AION* 13, 1963, 279ff.

[13]you shall smite it utterly with the sword. And if it is one of my brothers or one of my vassals or [one] of my high officials or anyone from the people which is subject to me, you shall kill him and his descendants and his [14]relatives and his friends with the sword. Otherwise you are false to all the gods of the [tre]aty which is in this inscription. And if it comes into your heart and you bring (it) upon your [15]lips to kill me, and if it comes into the heart of the son of your son and he brings (it) to his lips to kill the son of my son, of it it comes into the heart of your descendants [16]and they bring (it) to their lips to kill my descendants, and if it comes into the [he]art of the kings of Arpad (and) if a son of man[a] dies in any way, you are false to all [17]the gods of the treaty which is in this inscription. And if one of his brothers disputes the right of [my] son who has set himself upon my throne or seeks to depose him, you shall not loose your [18]tongue between them and say to him, 'Kill your brother' or 'Take him prisoner and do [not] set him free'. [On the other hand,] if you make peace between them, he will not kill him and will not imprison him. [19]But if you do not make peace between them, (then) you will be false to this treaty. And concerning the [kin]gs around me, if a fugitive of mine flees to one of them and if a [20]fugitive of theirs flees and comes to me – if he gives back mine, I will give back [his]; [and] you yourself may not prevent me. Otherwise you will be false to this treaty. [21]And you shall not loose your tongue in my house and between my sons and between [my] br[others and between] my [de]scendants and between my people and say to them, 'Kill your [22]ruler', and 'Be his successor'. For I would renounce in his favour and in that case someone would take vengeance for [my blood]. [And if you] use deceit towards me or towards my son or towards [my] descendants, [23](then) you will be false towards all the gods of the treaty which is in thi[s] inscription. [And Talay]im[b] and its villages and its citizens and its territory belong to my father and [24][to his house for] ever. And when the gods had smitten the house [of my father, it belong]ed to someone else. But now the gods have restored the position[c] of the hous[25][e of my father], [and the house] of my father [has conquered], and Talayim has been restored for ever to [Bar-ga]ya and to his son and to the son of his son and to his descendants for ever. And [26][if one of the kings disputes the right of my son and the right of the son

---

[a] So far the earliest evidence of the expression *bar 'enosh*, 'son of man', i.e. here 'prince of the blood'. The Akkadian word 'man' can also mean 'king'.

[b] A city, perhaps in the region of the Habor triangle or the upper Balikh.

[c] The expression 'restore the position', 'bring about a change (of fortune)' is also used frequently in the OT: cf. e.g. Jer. 32.44; 33.7, 11; 49.6: Ezek. 39.25; Pss. 14.7; 53.6; 126.1.

of my son and the right of my descendants to Talayim and its village and its citizens,[d] - whoever raises [27] . . . t[he kin]gs of Arpad [shall . . .; but if you . . .] him, you are false in respect of this treaty. And if [28][. . .] and they bribe any king, he will [29][. . . all that i]s beautiful and all that [is goo]d [. . .

XI. MYTHOGRAPHY

25. Fragments from Philo of Byblos

So far no North Semitic texts of a mythological kind from the first millennium BC have come to light. However, the *Praeparatio Evangelica* of Eusebius of Caesarea (I. 9. 20-10. 55) does include fragments from the so-called *Phoenician History* of Philo of Byblos (born AD 64) who in turn made use of an earlier work, written in Phoenician, by a certain Sanchuniaton. These fragments deal with theogony and cosmogony. - There is a critical edition of the text by K. Mras, Eusebius, *Werke* VIII, *Praeparatio evangelica* (GCS 43) I, 1954, 39-54.

Philo worked over the basic material from Sanchuniaton in the spirit of his time, but his work without doubt contains ancient elements of a mythological, cultic and religious character; this is demonstrated above all from a comparison with the literature of Ugarit.

The fragments from Philo/Sanchuniaton are significant in that they provide parallels to the tradition about creation in the OT, to a number of mythical and theological concepts, and to the Molok sacrifice.

Literature: C. Clemen, *Die phönikische Religion nach Philo von Byblos*, MVÄG 42/3, 1939; O. Eissfeldt, *Ras-Schamra und Sanchunjaton*, BRGA 4, 1939; id., *Taautos und Sanchunjaton*, 1952; id., *Sanchunjaton von Berut und Ilumilku von Ugarit*, BRGA 5, 1952; id., in *Kleine Schriften* III, 1966, 398ff.; P. Nautin, *RB* 56, 1949, 259ff., 573ff.

(i) *The Molok sacrifice*[e]

(a) Porphyry, *De abstinentia* II.56 = Eusebius, *Praeparatio evangelica* IV. 16. 6.

At times of great disaster because of wars, plagues or droughts . . . the Phoenicians sacrificed one of their dearest ones by consecrating him to Kronos; and the *Phoenician History* which Sanchuniaton wrote in the language of the Phoenicians and Philo of Byblos translated into Greek

---

[d] Cf. line 17 and stele I B 28. This does not refer to the kings of Arpad, but the rulers of the 'other' house (cf. line 24).

[e] Cf. also no. 4 above.

in eight books is full of people who have made such sacrifices.[f]

(b) Eusebius, *Praeparatio evangelica* I. 10. 44.

Among the ancients it was the custom that at times of great danger and misfortune, instead of losing all, the rulers of a city or a people offered the dearest of their children as a sacrifice and a ransom to the vengeful demons;[g] those who were offered up were sacrificed with mystic rites. Thus Kronos, whom the Phoenicians call El, as ruler over the country and later, towards the end of his life, divinized as the star of Kronos, had an only son by a nymph of the country, Anobret by name. Him they called Jedud ('beloved'), a name which is still used for only sons among the Phoenicians even today. Now when very great dangers came upon the land as the result of a war, he sacrificed his son, after adorning him with royal regalia and preparing an altar.

(ii) *The beginning of the world*[h]

Eusebius, *Praeparatio evangelica* I. 10. 1.

As the beginning of all things he (Sanchuniaton) assumes that there was dark and windy air or a breath of dark air and a black, gloomy chaos. This was infinite and for a long time had no end. But – he says – when the wind made love to his own beginnings and a commingling took place, this combination became Pothos ('desire'). It was the beginning of the creation of all things. But he himself (the wind) did not recognize his creation, and from his commingling (i.e. the wind's) there arose Mot ('death').

(iii) *The assigning of rule over the world*[i]

Eusebius, *Praeparatio evangelica* I. 10. 32, 35, 38.

And when Kronos travelled over the inhabited earth he gave his daughter Athena rule over Attica . . . Then Kronos gave the city of Byblos to the goddess Baaltis, who is also called Dione, and Berytus he gave to Poseidon and the Kabirs . . . And when Kronos had come to the land of the south wind he gave the whole of Egypt to the god Tauthos so that it might be his royal residence.

---

[f] In the OT see II Kings 3.26f. and especially Micah 6.7.
[g] Cf. II Kings 3.26f.
[h] Cf. Gen. 1.1f. or Gen. 3.
[i] Cf. Deut. 32.8 (4Q and LXX).

(iv) *El-elyon*[j]

Eusebius, *Praeparatio evangelica* I. 10. 14.

In their time (i.e., that of the Kabirs) their appeared a certain Elyun, who was called the Hypsistos,[k] and a woman by the name of Beruth, who also lived around Byblos.

[j] Cf. e.g. Gen. 14.18ff.
[k] I.e., the highest.

INDEX OF NAMES AND SUBJECTS

Abandonment by God, 137
Abomination, 57f., 136; *see also* Taboo
Absence of God, 45, 126f., 159-65
Abu Simbel, 25
Accusation against gods, *see* Theodicy
Acrostic, 134
Adad, 93, 95f., 123
Adad-nirari III, 230, 232
Adam, 88
Adana, 240-2
Adjuration, 131-3
Adonis, 160, 216
Adultery, 132
Akhenaten, 13f., 16-19, 40, 172
Alalu, 153f.
Aleppo, 123f., 228f., 231, 264
Altar, 233, 237, 247, 250f.
Amenemope, 1, 48, 49ff.
Amenophis I, 39f.
Amenophis III, 30
Amon-Re, 41
Amulet, 247-50
Amun, 7, 13, 15, 20, 24-6, 29-34, 36, 40-44
An, 69, 74, 76, 78ff., 100f., 104, 107, 113, 118, 142f., 145; *see also* Anu
Anat, 188, 190f., 193-201, 203, 206f., 209, 216-21, 226
Anath-Bethel, 252f., 256
Anat-yahu, 256
Ani, 48f.
Anobret, 267
Anointed one, 157f.
Anointing, 178
Anshar, 104
Anthropomorphism, 148, 152-5, 161f., 180-3, 188
Anu, 69, 78, 83, 94f., 110, 130, 153-5
Anunitum, 123-7; *see* Ishtar

Anunnaki, 84, 95, 101f., 105, 110, 144
Apish, 232
Apocalypses, 71, 119
Apsu, 69, 76, 81f., 92, 94f.
Aqhat, 226
Arable land, 53f., 66
Aranzah (= Tigris), 154
Aratta, 86
Arbela, 127
Ark, 8, 90ff.
Arpad, 231, 256ff.
Arsiya, 201
Arslan Tash, 247, 249
Aruru, 69, 77
Asherah, 188, 261
Ashim-bethel, 252f.
Ashirat, 187f., 193, 201-4, 206-9, 211, 217, 222
Ashratum, 202
Ashtar, 203, 217
Ashtarat, 206
Ashtar-chemosh, 239
Ashur (god), 81, 99, 114, 130
 (city), 108, 118, 120f., 126, 131
Ashurbanipal, 127, 130, 246
 library of, 88, 90, 93, 104, 113, 121
Ashurnasirpal, 113, 115
Ashurnirari, 258
Ass, 207, 216
Astarte, 206, 243-5
Astrology, 71
Aswan, 252, 255f.
Aten, 15, 16-19, 55
Athena, 267
Atonement, 170-5, 239
 day of, 250
Atrahasis, 77, 81, 89, 91-4
Attica, 267
Atum, 11-13, 15, 26, 41

Audition, 71, 123, 126
Avenger of blood, 264f.
Ay, 172
Aya, 258
Azitawada, 240-3

Baal, 82, 156, 187f., 190-3, 196-221, 224,
    226, 232, 241f., 248-50
    -hammon, 235, 237
    krntryš, 242f.
    of Tyre, 228f., 247
    -shamayim, 230
Baaltis, 267
Baal-Zaphon, 253f.
Babi, 67
Babylon, 81, 119-21, 128, 175
Ban, 238f.; see also consecrated,
    forbidden, thing
Bar-gaya, 257ff.
Bar-gush, 231
Bar-hadad, 228, 231
Barrenness, 159f., 259, 262
Battle-axe, 205f., 212, 222, 228, 248
Beauty, 26
Bee, 21, 159, 161f.
Beer, 10, 62, 114, 157, 181
Belet-biri, 123
Belet-ekallim, 123, 125f.
Ben-hadad (= Bar-hadad II), 229f.
Berossus, 81, 88f.
Berytus, 267
Bethel, 255
Blasphemy, 65f.
Blessedness, 52, 85
Blindness, 36f.
Blood, 10, 65, 82-4, 132f., 193-5, 200,
    264f.
    plague of, 98
Borsippa, 115
Boundaries, 53f., 79, 132
Bread, 54, 61, 66, 262, 264
    date bread, 95
    sacrificial, 23, 65f., 112, 157, 171,
        173f., 180, 182f.
Bribery, 59, 85, 103, 182f.
Bull, 33, 149, 178, 221, 240
Bull-El, 199-201, 204, 207, 220, 223f.
Burial of deity, 243f.
Byblos, 197, 202, 227f., 266-8

Caere, 243f.
Carchemish, 257
Carmel, 233
Carthage, 235
Cedar, 21, 209-12
Chaos, 3f., 11, 156, 193, 198, 216f., 267
Chemosh(yatt), 237-40, 244f.
Circumcision, 28
Cloud, 84, 93, 193, 196, 198f., 209, 211,
    214, 221
    rider on the, 196-9, 205, 210, 214
Confession of sin, 32-4, 36, 108, 173f.
    of innocence, 63-7
    of faith, 32ff., 41
Confusion of tongues, 70; reversed, 86f.
Consecrated thing, 246
Corn, 16, 95, 100, 103, 218, 230, 262
    corn deity, 230
Covenant, 99, 122, 129, 153, 257; see
    also Treaty
Covetousness, 57
Cow, 5, 10f., 215, 221
Creation, 3ff., 13ff., 24f., 46, 69, 74ff., 84,
    89, 104, 152, 198, 200, 266f.
    through the word, 4, 7, 13f., 24, 26, 77
    narrative, 3ff., 89, 200
    of gods, 9, 13, 81f.
    see also God as creator
Crete, 188, 202
Crocodile, 24, 26, 51, 53, 60
Cults, inventories of, 147, 186
    officials of, 179-84
Curse, 72, 79, 101, 103, 129-33, 149, 232,
    235-7, 240, 243, 245, 258-60, 262f.
    cursing formulae, 72
Cyprus, 232

Dagan, 107f., 123-8, 188, 205, 216, 224
Damascus, 229f., 260
Damnassaras deities, 172
Daniil, 189f., 225f.
Darius, 255
Darkness, 6, 11, 16, 18, 36f., 102f., 128,
    267
Dead, book of, 4, 6f., 11, 64
    cult of, 2, 6, 11, 16, 30, 41, 65-7, 123f.,
        148
    god of, 212ff., 235; see Mut
    judgment of, 63-7

kingdom of, 7, 11, 134, 143, 169, 213, 245
mourning for, 140-4, 206, 215f.
offerings to, 66f., 123f., 216
spirits of, 123f., 148, 176f., 212, 245
Death, 12, 16, 39, 52, 61ff., 85, 148, 168, 212ff.
messenger of, 63
of gods, 161, 219
Debt, remission of, 58
Decalogue, 24, 131-3, 225
Deir el-Medina, 32, 36, 47
Demons, 120, 136, 138, 141f., 247-50
Destiny, 24f., 38f., 76, 105, 107, 141, 176f.
Destruction and building up, 55, 61
of mankind, 8, 10, 81, 89ff., 96
Deuteronomy, 72, 131
Dew, 131, 193, 196, 199
Dibon, 237, 239
Dione, 267
Divination, 71, 138
Djedef-Hor, 46
Dodecalogue, 225
Dogs, 85f.
Dove, 86, 97
Doxology, 36
Dragon, 81f., 156-8, 198
Dreams, 71, 91, 112, 123, 126, 137f., 166, 169, 171, 174, 178, 218, 223, 225
Drink-offering, 97, 139, 219
Drought, 91, 200, 214, 261
Dumuzi, 80, 88, 160

Ea, see Enki(-Ea)
Eagle, 159, 161-3, 226
Eanna, 80, 144
Earthquake, 106, 145, 200, 209
Ecstasy, 123f., 126
Eden, garden of, 8
Egg, primal, 3
El, 188, 192, 196-208, 213-6, 218-24, 226, 243
El Elyon (Elyun), 258, 267f.
Elamites, 116, 119, 121f., 127
Election, 27-30, 38f., 43, 99, 107, 230f.
Elephantine, 10, 194, 227, 252, 254-6
Elimination, rite of, 175ff.
End of the world, 11f.

Enki(-Ea), 69, 76-80, 83-7, 91f., 94f., 102, 110, 143, 152, 243
Enkidu, 74, 77, 93
Enlil, 69, 74-83, 87, 91f., 94f., 97, 99-101, 104, 107f., 110, 117f., 120, 130, 142-5, 154f.
Enmerkar, 86
Ennugi, 94
Enoch, 88
Enthronement, 142, 216f., 220, 230f.
Eragal, 95
Ereshkigal, 74
Eridu, 69, 76, 79, 87f., 143
Erra, 258
Esangila, 82
Esarhaddon, 72, 129f., 229, 246, 255
Eternity, 22, 26
Euphrates, 79, 94, 99, 123
Eusebius, 266-8
Evil eye, 249f.
Exposure of infants, 98
Eyes of God, 4, 6, 9, 13f., 22, 24, 28, 154
stolen from weather god, 158

Fate, 24, 45, 52, 54, 77, 82, 115, 118, 130, 134, 142f., 150, 163, 169, 176ff.; see also Destiny
Fear, 6, 9, 20f., 25f., 54-6, 106, 111, 115, 130, 138, 145; see also Gods feeling fear
Fertility, 5, 18, 26, 79f., 100, 105, 107, 119, 121f., 154f., 157-9, 162f., 165, 187, 196f., 213, 217, 226, 242
gods, 187, 192, 197, 199, 206, 212, 215-7
rite, 193
Festival, 155, 181
New Year, 6, 81, 191
Fire, 7, 102, 105, 163, 183, 235, 250
god of, 102
Flock (of God), 13, 15, 26f., 40, 46, 65
Flood, 8, 70, 89-97, 159
Forbidden thing, 133
Foreigner, rights of, 181f.
Forgiveness, 108, 110f., 131-3, 165, 175
Fraud, 180
Funeral rites, 143

Galumdu, 112f.
Gapan, 197, 213, 215

Geb, 8
Generosity, 49, 58
Gilgamesh, 74, 86, 89, 91-4, 143
Girru, 102
God, as creator, 5ff., 13ff., 35f., 84, 99,
    104f., 199, 207, 218
  as healer, 23, 110
  hidden, 25, 45
  as king, 9, 13, 80, 87, 102, 104f., 115,
    200f., 203, 206
  as king of gods, 8, 44, 84, 118, 145,
    153ff., 201, 206, 214
  as possessor, 23, 26, 37, 59, 63
  as protector, 22ff., 26, 30, 38f., 42,
    101f., 113, 167f.; see also Guardian
    deities
  righteous, 37
  care for men, 13-27, 41, 45f., 99, 101
  face (= favour) of, 110, 113, 140, 142,
    144, 170
  feeling anger, 32, 34, 84, 101, 109, 111,
    115, 145, 148, 159f., 162-4, 165,
    174, 181, 238
    disgust, 180-3
    envy, 226
    fear, 96, 110, 162, 214, 220
    hate, 117
  grace of, 33-5, 37f., 59, 101, 106, 109,
    111, 135, 137f., 142, 168, 173, 240
  hand of, 32, 35f., 41, 44f., 57, 59, 61,
    105f., 142
  love of, 13f., 23, 27f., 30, 40-42, 47,
    62, 99
  perfection of, 14, 16, 19, 65
  punishing sin, 35-7, 47, 98, 103, 148,
    165, 170, 173f., 176, 182
  resting, 5, 219
  sleeping, 162
  supremacy of, 23, 104, 192, 219, 248
  uniqueness of, 14f., 18f., 25, 36, 41,
    105f., 112, 212
Gods, generation of, 105, 152-5, 189, 221
  complain of having to work, 76, 91
  aging of, 152-4
  enemies of, 11, 13, 66, 100; see also
    Rebellion against, War waged by
  lists of, 69, 186
  of the dead, 235
  banquet of, 188, 192f., 196, 204,
    207-9, 211, 219

wedding song for, 239
  man as image of, 46, 77
Gold, 8, 21, 75, 182f., 206f., 209, 211,
    243-5
Golden age, 87
Good and evil, 6-10, 35
Gossip, 48
Grain, see Corn
Guardian deities, 108f., 111, 138, 148,
    153f., 164, 167
Gudea, 112
Guilt, 67, 165, 170, 175
Gulses goddesses, 163

Hadad, 187, 191, 212, 216, 221, 258-60
Hair, 124-7, 180, 183
Halki, 163
Haluppu-tree, 74
Hammurabi, 71, 123, 127f.
Hannahannas, 161
Hanish, 95
Hapantallis, 163f.
Harakhti, 15, 22, 26, 28
Harran, 105
Harsaphes, 43
Hatalkesna tree, 163f.
Hathor, 9, 39
Hatshepsut, 30
Hattusa-Boghazköy, 109, 146f., 177,
    181-3
Hauron, 248f.
Hayin, 203, 206
Hazael, 229, 231
Hazrak, 230-2
Healing, 23, 109; see also God as healer
Health, 23, 27, 36, 55
  goddess of, 159
Heart, 5, 7, 9, 12, 14, 23-5, 30, 35f.,
    39-42, 46, 48, 50, 52, 54-60, 63f.,
    84, 93, 109f., 120, 132, 136, 138,
    141, 158, 169, 195, 217, 224, 261f.
Heaven, court of, 7, 9
  door of, 100, 105, 121
  lord of, see Baal-shamayim
  and earth, separation of, 74f., 151f.
Hebat, 149, 152
Hedammu, 153, 156
Heliopolis, 4, 10, 27, 66
Heracleopolis, 43, 66
Heracles, 229

Hermopolis, 43, 62, 254
Hesiod, 154
High place, cultic, 238
History, 71, 119, 147, 170, 189, 238
  primal, 69, 88ff.
Holiness, of God, 33, 204, 265
  of property of gods, 159, 168, 233
  in OT, 180
Homosexuality, 66
Honey, 219
Horeb, 202
Horses, 241
Horus, 6, 22, 67
Hospitality, 181
Hot (= angry), 27, 51f., 55-7
Hupasiyas, 157
Hypsistos, 268

'I am the Lord', 101
Iah, 37
Iddindagan, 107f.
Igigi, 101f., 105, 110
Ikrubal, 124
Ilimilku, 190
Illness, see sickness
Illuyankas, 155-8
Ilu-wer, 230-2
Image, 45, 52, 147, 174, 176, 178, 233,
  240, 242
  of God, man as, 27, 46, 76f.
  as substitute, 174, 176, 178; see also
    statue, stele
Immortality, 85, 93f., 97, 219
Impurity, uncleanness, 108, 149, 155,
  168, 180ff.
Inanna(-Ishtar), 69, 74, 78f., 80, 97f.,
  110, 125, 142-5
Inaras, 156f.
Incantation, 77, 150, 159-65, 228, 247-50
Incense, 21, 97, 163, 247, 250f.
Incubation, 166, 174
Injustice, 54, 65, 132f., 145, 224
Intercession, 43f., 108, 116, 130, 165
  for the king, 139
Intoxication, 8-10, 76
Inundation of Nile, 6-8, 14, 19, 54, 66
Invocation, 107, 109ff., 159, 178, 197
Ipuwer, 2f.
Irrigation, 78, 80, 217
Ishara, 154

Ished tree, 67
Ishkur, 79
Ishtar, 69, 74, 78, 80, 96, 97, 109-13,
  115, 124-7, 153
  -Anunitum, 99
Isdustaia, 163
Isian, 88, 107, 121
Isis, 5
Istanu, 167
Itur-mer, 123, 230

Jebel el-Aqra, 187
Jedud, 267
Jerusalem, 202, 227, 246, 253, 255
Jezebel, 229
Job, 3, 72, 223
Josephus, 229, 245
Josiah, 72, 171
Joy, of gods, 102, 195
Judgment of God, 14, 45, 51, 63f., 165,
  224
  of the dead, 63ff.
  place of, 58, 60
Juno, 243
Justice, 45f., 51, 101, 103, 105, 110, 130

Ka (spirit), 18, 35
Kadia, 258
Kamrusepas, 159, 162f.
Karatepe, 240
Karnak, 14, 29f., 33, 41
Keret, 189, 223-5
Khepri, 13
Khnum, 56
King, as son of God, 16, 19, 27, 29, 107,
  113, 138, 223
  elect of God, 28, 98f., 231
  divinized, 39
  knows God, 19, 27
  as sun of his people, 137f., 241
  as bringer of salvation, 29
  promised, 118f., 121f.
  duties of, 224f., 241
  cultic functions of, 148, 243
  hymn to, 107f., 241
  lament for, 143-5
  prophecies of, 120, 122
  successor to, 130, 225
  substitute for, 175-9

Kingdom, kingship, origin of, 89
    primaeval, 87-9
    of God, 20, 22, 153, 198, 205, 220, 223
Kingu, 82, 84
Knowledge, creation by, 4
    of sin, 169
Kronos, 266f.
Kumarbi, 151-5
Kur, 82
Kusharu-Hasisu, 188, 201-3, 205f.,
    209-11, 226

Lachish, 250-3
Lagash, 112f., 127
Lahamu, 82
Lama, 154
Lament, lamentation, 41, 70, 86, 93,
    110f., 113-8, 133-45, 160, 206, 215f.
Lamu, 82
Language, 18, 70, 87
Lapethos, 232f.
Lapis lazuli, 8, 21, 75, 144, 209
Las, 258
Last/first, 47, 158
Law, 69, 131, 147
Laziness, 47
Leaven, 255
Lebanon, 210
Leviathan, 156, 198
Libation, see Drink-offering
Life, 19, 31, 45, 50, 53, 58, 60, 63
    eternal, 115
    long, 11, 103, 108, 113, 115, 159f.,
        164f., 177, 242
    after death, 11f., 16, 62
    symbol of, 31, 228
Light, 6, 11, 46, 75, 101-3, 105, 117
Lightning, 79, 163, 209, 211, 221
Lilwani, 178f.
Lion, 40, 86, 134, 218, 262
Lioness, 247, 249
Liturgy of entry, 108
Lot, drawing of, 158, 166
Lothan, 156; see also Leviathan
Love, 5, 125, 196, 267
    of man for God, 14, 21, 30
    of Baal for Anat, 215, 221
    see also God, love of
Lugalbanda, 86
Luxor, 255

Lying, 57ff., 132, 141

Maat, 13, 36, 40, 52, 59, 64f., 67
Mace, 106
Madeba, 238
Magic, 6, 24, 46, 64f., 69, 81, 109, 132,
    147, 150, 155, 159f., 162f., 166,
    174f., 247ff.
    sympathetic, 65, 159, 162-4, 249, 259
Mala (= Euphrates), 171-3
Mama, 69
Mansuete, 230
Mari, 122-8, 230
Marduk, 70, 81-4, 99, 109, 115, 118,
    120f., 133, 137f., 258
Marriage, sacred, 113, 145, 243f.
Mattock, 75
Meal, cultic, 181f.
Mediator, 167, 169
    king as, 19
Melitene, 231
Melquart, 228f., 232-4, 243f., 246f.
Melucca, 78
Memphis, 36, 253, 256
Mercy, 32f., 35, 109, 115, 137, 169, 172
Meresger, 44
Meret-seger, 35
Merikare, 8, 44
Mesha, 227, 236-40
Messenger of God, 95, 196, 202-4,
    213-5, 231
Miatanzipa, 163
Milid, 231
Milk, 80
Mockery, 61
Molok sacrifice, 234f., 266
Moon, moon god, 37, 51, 53, 65, 82-4,
    104, 116, 177-9, 234, 243, 247
    cult of, 104, 116
Moriah, 251
Moses, 70, 98
Mother, goddess as, 113, 118
Mountain, 35, 79, 155
    of God, 193, 197f., 200, 202, 204; see
        also Zaphon
    of the north, 187, 193
    Mount Casius, 253
    Mount Knkny, 214
    Mount Nisir, 96f.
    see also Zalinu

Mourning rite, 143f., 215
Mullesh, 258
Mummy, mummifying, 67
Mursilis II, 169-71
Mushdama, 80
Mut (Egyptian goddess), 37-9
Mut (= Mot, Ugaritic god of the
    underworld), 200, 212-4, 217-20,
    267

Nabu, 115, 258
Nahar, 198, 203-5
Name, 46, 232, 243
    bestowed as a creative act, 4, 7, 77, 105
    of God, 5, 20, 23-6, 32-4, 36, 38, 40,
       65f., 82, 110f., 113
Nammu, 69, 76f.
Nanna, 104-6, 116f.; see also Sin, Suen
Narnaka, 233
Nebuchadnezzar I, 121
Nebuchadnezzar II, 115, 253
Nefertiti, 17, 19
Nergal, 258
Nerik, 150, 155, 157f., 164, 177
New Year, 6, 81, 191
Nikkar, 258
Nile, 6f., 18f., 26, 41, 53; see also
    Inundation
Nimrud, 129
Nineveh, 72, 90, 93, 108, 118, 121, 131
Ningal (= Ninkal), 106, 116, 118, 258
Ningirsu, 112, 127
Ninhursanga, 69f., 76f., 85
Ninlil, 107, 120, 130, 154
Ninmah, 69, 76f., 143
Ninshiku-Ea, 94
Ninsikil, 85
Nintu, 69
Ninurta, 94f., 130, 260
Nippur, 69, 75, 78, 97, 99f., 120, 140,
    144, 155
Nisaba, 119
Noah, 8, 88f.
Nudimmud, 84, 86
Nun, 8-10, 12, 14, 21, 26
Nuru, 258
Nusku, 258
Nut, 8, 10

Oath, 130, 139, 168, 171-3, 179, 261f.

Ocean, see Sea
Offering, 7f., 67, 90, 97, 139, 155, 166,
    178, 225, 233f.; see also Sacrifice
Oil, 162f., 219
Omen, 71, 126f., 138, 144, 147, 166, 169,
    174, 176, 178
Omri, 238
Onnophris, 43
Oracle, 24, 59, 147, 166, 171-4, 178, 225
Order in the world, 7, 13, 16, 75, 78, 82,
    93, 145, 153, 156
Osiris, 2, 11f., 42, 63f., 66, 160
Ossuary, 245f.

Palace, 200-3, 208-11, 225; see also
    Temple
Papaia, 163
Paradise, 45, 70, 85
Parallelism, 187, 249
Passover, 254f.
Patriarchs, 88, 225
Peace, 85, 87, 196, 199
    of mind, 12
Penitence, 108, 110
Perjury, 36, 53, 57, 132, 139, 168
Philo of Byblos, 266
Phoenix, 66
Pi (Piankhi), 29
Pidraya, 193, 201, 210, 214
Pidri, 248
Piety, personal, 30ff., 49, 251
Plague, 169-74, 259
    of blood, 98
Plough, 101
Poor (= humble), 32-8, 41, 62
Poseidon, 267
Potter, God as, 56, 61, 77
Prayer, 30, 32, 36, 48, 51, 70, 104, 108-13,
    115, 135, 139, 165-74, 178f., 222
    heard by God, 14, 20, 24, 26f., 30,
       32-8, 41, 48, 55, 103, 109f., 139ff.,
       169, 172-4, 178, 231, 237
    penitential, 108-11, 156f.
Precincts, holy, 197
Priests, 69, 110, 124-6, 131, 155, 166,
    180, 233, 237
Procession, 45, 66, 100, 125, 149, 155
Prophecy, 71, 118-28, 166, 171, 230
Prophets, 153, 169, 247, 251
    lying, 71, 126

Ptah, 4f., 25, 27, 32, 36f., 42, 256
Ptolemy II Philadelphus, 232f.
Purity, 15, 62, 64, 66f., 85, 163, 170,
    180ff., 255; see also Rites of
    purification

Qadesh-Amurru, 202, 204, 207
Qarhoh, 237-9
Qaus, 246
Qorban, 246
Queen of heaven, 80, 152, 255f.

Rain, 19, 84, 102, 119, 131, 152, 155,
    157, 193, 196, 198, 201, 208, 210,
    214, 217, 221, 226, 240, 249f.
Ramesses II, 8, 28
Ramesses III, 8
Ramesses IV, 65
Ramesses VI, 8
Rashap/Resheph, 240, 242
Raven, 85, 97
Re, 8-10, 14, 25, 28-30, 33, 41, 53
Rebellion against gods, 7, 8ff., 46, 57, 91,
    100, 152ff.
    ritual, 66
Recitation, cultic, 192, 199
Remission of debt, 58
Remnant, 8, 10
Renenet, 38
Repentance, 108-11, 113, 133, 176
Responsibility, collective, 170ff., 180f.
Righteous man, righteousness, 35, 43,
    45f., 59, 103-5, 107, 122, 241
Rites, 139, 151, 171-3
    of purification, 80, 109, 131, 162, 176,
    179, 180ff.

Sabbath, 82; see also Seven days
Sacrifice, 17, 30, 46, 63, 65f., 90, 93,
    105-7, 109f., 112, 126, 128, 143,
    150, 166, 171-4, 178-84, 186f., 192,
    216, 219, 222, 224f., 234f., 239, 242,
    244; see also Bread, sacrificial
    human, 167, 239, 267
Salvation, 27, 29, 36, 49, 121, 123, 163,
    167, 230, 242
Sam'al, 231
Sanchuniaton, 266f.
Sanctuary, 105f., 112, 116, 118, 208, 233
Sarcophagus, 245
Sargon, 98f.

Sarpanitu, 258
Sarra, 244f.
Sarruma, 149, 168
Sasm, 233, 248
Scapegoat, 175
Scepticism, 180, 182
Scorpion, 248f., 259
Sea, ocean, 7, 14, 20f., 76f., 81, 94, 103,
    156, 197f., 200, 202, 207; see also
    Apsu, Yam
Seal, 59, 246f.
Seasons, 19, 191
Seer, 169, 231
Sehr, 232
Sekhmet, 38
Self-revelation of God, 5, 101
Serpent, 7, 12, 15, 32, 35, 86, 153, 198,
    259
    primal (= uraeus), 14, 23
Sesostris I, 27
Seth, 6
Seven days, 90, 92f., 96, 143, 210, 255
    years, 219f., 226, 259
Shabaka, 4
Shahar and Shelem, 189, 221
Shai, 38
Shakan, 119
Shamash, Shamsh, 78, 95, 101-3, 106,
    109, 123, 130, 133, 167, 188, 232,
    258
Shapash (Shapsu), 188, 200, 213, 216,
    218-20
Sheol, 213; see Underworld
Shepherd, God as, 13, 15, 26f., 28, 40,
    46, 102, 107
    king as, 137, 143
Shu, 4, 8, 10, 37
Shulgi, 119f.
Shullat, 95
Shurrupak (Shurripak), 69, 89, 94
Sickness, 23, 26, 32, 34-6, 65, 86, 110f.,
    130, 132, 137, 141f., 169, 223-5,
    242, 259
    mental, 61
Sidon, 245
'Silent man', 51-3, 55, 60f.
Silver, 8, 182f., 207, 209f., 234, 245, 254
Sin, 34f., 58f., 64-7, 72, 94, 108f., 111,
    113, 131-3, 141, 148, 161, 166, 169,
    173

Sin (Suen), the moon god, 80, 83, 104f., 112, 116, 130, 145, 258
Sippar, 88, 123
Son of God, *see* King as
Sons of god(s), 207, 240, 243, 248
Son of man, 265
Sorrow, suffering, 24, 72, 133-45, 148, 168f.; *see also* Sickness
Soul, 169
  of gods, 6, 169, 219
Spell, magical, 86
Sphinx, 247-9
Spirit of God, 34; *see also* Ka
Spring, sacred, 202, 208
Stars, 82f., 196, 199, 244
Statue, 52, 110, 121, 126, 178, 240, 243
Stele, 32-5, 225, 228f., 232, 234f., 237, 252, 256ff.
'Strange woman', 48
Substitution, 174-9
Suen, *see* Sin
Sun, sun god, 5, 7, 11-27, 44, 52, 55, 65-7, 78, 90, 95, 101ff., 106, 161, 163-5, 167, 169, 176-9, 188, 232, 243f., 258
Sun boat, 13, 22
Sun goddess, 152, 176, 188, 219
Suppiluliumas I, 167, 170
Swallow, 97
Symbolic actions, 174

Taboo, 57, 65, 245
Talaya, 193, 201, 210, 214, 221
Tammuz, 80, 216
Tannin, 198
Tarhuis, 243
Taru, 159
Tashmetu, 258
Tasmi(su), 154
Tauthos, 267
Tazzuwasi, 158
Tears, of the creator, 4
Tefnut, 4, 8
Telipinu, 159-65
Temple, 21, 28, 43, 46, 48, 52, 65f., 72, 82, 100, 106-8, 112, 116, 121, 126, 144, 147, 171, 180ff., 193, 196ff., 202, 209-11, 216, 224, 244, 255, 263
  of Yahweh, 253f.
  roof of, 23, 224

Terror, 104, 106, 111, 138, 193, 221, 262f.; *see also* Fear
Teshub, 149, 152-4
Thank-offering, 155
Thebes, 32-4, 37, 43, 48
Theodicy, 3, 7, 72f., 133ff., 137ff., 140f., 142ff.
Thoth, 37, 43, 51, 53
Threats, prophetic, 72, 129
Threshing, 115, 218
Throne of God, 9, 36, 44, 105, 154, 198, 202, 204f., 208, 212, 215, 217, 220f.; *see also* Enthronement
Throne name, 246
Thunder (as voice of God), 93, 95, 163, 209, 211
Thunderclouds, 51
Tiamat, 81-3
Tiglath-pileser III, 240, 257
Tigris, 79, 92, 154
Tilmun, 78, 85f.
Time, 22, 83
  primal, 10
Tinnit-in-the-face-of-Baal, 235
Tomb, 12, 46, 65, 251
Tongue, 5, 50, 55-9
Toothache, 77
Treaty, 72, 147, 256ff.
  gods of, 72, 130f., 154, 229, 239, 248, 258-65
Tree goddess, 188
Trinity, Egyptian, 25
  Ugaritic, 206
Trust, 30, 71
Truth, 13, 36f., 64f., 101
Tudhaliyas II, 170
Tudhaliyas IV, 168
Tukultinimurta I, 120
Tutankhamun, 171f.
Tuthmosis II and III, 29
Tuthmosis IV, 40
Tyche, 244
Typhon, 156
Tyre, 229, 245, 247, 255

Ugar, 197, 213, 215
Ugarit, 185-9, 196f., 209, 222-4, 248, 253
Ullikummi, 151-3
Unchastity, 65

Underworld, 20, 22f., 25, 32, 40, 55, 67, 74, 102, 105, 139, 143, 154, 159, 161, 213
  gods of, 148, 163f., 167, 176f., 118, 203, 212-8, 234, 242, 258
  gate of, 164
Unennofer, 65
Upelluri, 151-3
Ur, 69, 78, 88, 104-6, 112, 116-9, 142-5
Urnammu, 88, 142-5
Urninurta, 88
Uruk, 80, 86, 88, 122
Ut-napishtim, 89, 91, 93-5
Utu, 90, 106f.
Uzu-e, 75

Vassal treaties, 72, 129ff.
Vegetation god, 188, 191, 215f.
Vegetation myth, 160, 226
Venus, 131
Victory, prayer for, 115, 165
Virtue, 46
Visions, 71, 122f., 126, 225
Voice of God, 209; see also Thunder
Vows, 30, 32-5, 109, 147, 150, 229f., 234f., 237
Votive offerings, 187, 234
  inscriptions, 32-9, 112, 227, 228-37, 243

Water, 105
  as offering, 112
  primal, 5, 12, 21
  death in, 52
War, 123-8, 148, 171f., 224, 230-2, 238-41, 261
  waged by gods, 81-3, 153ff., 193-5, 198, 203-6, 218-20; see also Rebellion against gods
  goddess of, 193ff., 226, 230

Weapons of gods, 106, 218, 226; see also Battle-axe
Weather god, 79, 93, 149, 152-9, 159ff., 170-4, 177, 205, 211, 220f., 241, 243
Weeping, 46, 118, 126, 216
Wen-amon, 71
Wine, 192f., 208, 219, 224, 226
  as offering, 182
Wisdom, 6, 47, 72, 87, 113, 133, 137, 208
Witchcraft, 66, 132, 150
Witness, false; see Lying, Perjury
Word of God, 4f., 13, 84, 105, 107, 126, 143, 145, 168, 173, 238
Worm, 77f.
Wrath, 38
  cup of, 192
  day of, 263; see also God feeling anger

Yaabdar, 201
Yabamat Limim, 195f., 206, 221
Yagrush, 205
Yahweh, 68f., 72, 154, 170, 187, 194, 202, 209, 238f., 251-4
Yam, 156, 197f., 203-6, 213
Yazilikaya, 149, 168

Zababa, 106
Zakkur, 229f., 231f.
Zalinu, 155, 157f.
Zaphon, 193, 196-9, 207, 209-11, 216f., 221f.
Zashapuna, 158
Zimrilim, 71, 123-8
Zion, 106
Ziusudra, 85, 89f.

INDEX OF BIBLICAL REFERENCES

Genesis

1	4, 26
1.1f.	267
1.2	11, 82
1.3	4
1.4	6, 152
1.6ff.	74, 77
1.6	4, 6, 152
1.7	6, 83, 152, 200
1.14ff.	83
1.14	4, 6, 22, 152
1.18	6, 152
1.21	156f., 198
1.26f.	46
1.30	85
2.2f.	4, 219
2.4f.	6
2.5	82
2.7f.	27, 56
2.7	76, 77
2.15	84
2.19	27
3-11	7
3	267
3.23f.	8
3.24	45
4	6
4.17ff.	88
5.1ff.	88
5.3	46
5.24	88
6-8	8, 91
6.1-4	158
6.2, 4	240
6.5-8.22	94
6.5	7, 173
6.8ff.	8
7.11	19, 83
8.2	19, 83
8.21	7, 108, 141, 173

8.22	19
9.5f.	170
9.6	46
9.12, 16	248
11.1-9	86, 87
12.1ff.	225
12.2f.	232
12.3	42
14.18ff.	258, 268
14.18	171, 245
14.19, 22	240
15	129
15.1	42
15.9-18	260
18.10ff.	225
21.33	243
22	235
22.2	251
22.25ff.	225
26.24	42, 225
28.10-22	223
28.13	225
28.15, 20	43
31.53	225
32.29	5
35.4	248, 249
37-50	240
41.34ff.	240
41.39	240
41.43	241
41.47ff.	240
44.5	166
45.8	241
49.25	225, 258

Exodus

1.16	35, 39
2.1-10	98
3.1	198
3.6	225
3.8	219
3.14	5
3.15	225

3.17	219
6.2	5
7.3	63
7.9f.	198
7.14-25	98
9.3	45
12.1-20	254
12.15-20	254
13.5	219
14.2, 9	254
15.5	11
15.8, 10f.	205
15.11	84, 105
15.17f.	154, 197, 198
15.18	20, 205
15.26	23
20.2	5
20.2-17	131
20.4ff.	45
20.5	173, 180
20.7	5, 24, 66
20.11	219
20.12	45
20.13f., 16f.	132
21.12ff.	132
22.18	46, 132
22.21ff.	62
22.22ff.	45, 225
23.2	132
23.3, 6	225
23.9	62
23.10f.	219, 220
24.13	198
28.38	175
30.1, 27	250
31.17	219
32.1ff.	45
32.3	248, 249
32.4	199
33.3	219
34.7	173, 180
34.10-26	42

(Exodus cont.)

34.13	261
34.19f.	216
39.19	37
35.2	5
36.2	5

Leviticus

2.1	251
2.10	181
2.15	251
3.1	192
3.16f.	181
3.16	192
4-5	175
5.13	181
7.20f.	254
10	180
14.7, 53	175
16.12f.	250
16.20-28	175
17.11	175
18.7ff.	225
18.21	235
18.27, 29	245
19.12	36, 132
19.15	59
19.26	166
19.27f.	215
19.31	166, 216
19.33f.	62
19.35f.	64
20.2-5	235
21f.	180
23.5-8	254
23.14	246
23.15f.	254
24.7	251
25.3ff.	219
25.3-7	220
26	160
26.4	121, 250
26.5	122
26.19	131
26.22	259
26.26	257
26.37	233
27.21, 28	246

Numbers

3.10, 38	171
9.13	246
14.18	173, 180
15.15f.	181
16.2	240

18.14	246
18.22f.	175
19.21	250
21.25	232
21.29	244
21.32	232
24.16	258
28.16-18	254
28.24	192
28.25	254
29.2	234
30.3	34, 132
31.50	246
32.42	232
33.7	254
33.52	240
35.33f.	170

Deuteronomy

2.15	45
4.19	104
4.26	248
4.38	239
5.6-21	131
5.8ff.	45
5.11	24, 66
5.16	45
5.17f., 20f.	132
6	42
7-11	79
7.2	238
7.5	261
8.3	14
9.12	240
10.17	21, 225
11	42
11.11ff.	250
11.11-17	208
12.3	261
12.15	216
13.12-17	238
14.1	215
14.5	216
15.1ff.	219
15.7f.	67
16.11, 14	182
16.19	59
16.21	261
17.3	104
18.9ff.	46, 166
18.10f.	132
18.11	216, 248, 249
19.14	53, 132
20.17	238

23.23	34, 132
24.16	173, 180
24.17	45, 62
24.19ff.	62
25.5f.	232
25.13ff.	64
26.1-11	37
26.11	182
26.13f.	64
27.15ff.	225
27.17	53, 132
27.19	45, 62
28	130, 160, 240
28.1f.	250
28.12	208, 250
28.23f.	259
28.23	131
28.24	208
28.28-34	130
28.38-40	257
28.54, 56	249
28.58	21
29.1	248
29.23	259
30.19	248
31.6ff.	42
31.10f.	219
31.16-18	160
31.28	248, 258
32.1	248, 258
32.8	267
32.20	160
32.40ff.	194
33.3	27
33.5	154
33.8	166
33.10	251
33.26	79, 196, 210

Joshua

1.5	42
3.10	43
3.11, 13	248
6.18-24	238
7	166, 238
7.9	232
7.12	246
7.19	36
7.24f.	180
8.2	238
9.3ff.	170
11.21	251
16.3, 5	249

(*Joshua cont.*)

18.13	249
20.7	251
21.11	251
23.9	239
24	42
24.25-27	263

Judges

2.14f.	160
2.14, 16	238
3.8	160, 238
3.9ff.	238
5.3	26
5.4	208
5.31	42
6.9	239
6.25-30	261
8.21, 26	248, 249
9.3	192
9.6	263
9.13	211
9.15	23
9.45	259
9.46ff.	224
10.7f., 10ff.	238
11.23f.	239
11.24	244
11.27	172
11.30-40	235
13.1	239
13.5, 7	28
13.16	234
13.17f.	5
20.23, 28	238

Ruth

2.12	42
4.5, 10	232

I Samuel

1.3ff.	182
1.9-18	46
1.13	48
1.21	242
2.6f.	61
2.10	139
2.12-17	180, 181
2.19	242
2.22	180
2.28	251
2.29ff.	180, 181
2.29f.	180
2.30	42
6.5	45

7.3	42
7.6	249
7.9	222
7.10	249
8.7	154
9.9ff.	166
9.13f., 19, 25	238
12.3	64
12.12	154
12.16-18	208
14.37	238
14.41ff.	166
15	238
15.8	239
15.12	229
15.22	46
15.33	239
17.26	43
20.6	242
23.2, 4	238
24.20	42
24.22	232
28	166
28.6	166, 174
28.8	216
28.15	166

II Samuel

1.2	215
5.2	28, 107, 137, 143
6.14, 18	171
7	27, 28, 225
7.7	209
7.8ff.	129
7.11f.	225
7.14	19, 29, 30
14.7f.	225
14.7	232
14.17, 20	39
15.10	231
17.8	259
18.18	232
21	160
21.1ff.	166
21.1.1-14	170
21.1	226
21.5ff.	173, 180
21.9f.	226
22.3	42
22.8-15	163
22.11	296, 210
22.32	42
23.3ff.	45
24	160

I Kings

2.2ff.	225
3.4-15	27, 28, 223
3.7	28, 29
3.12f.	29
5.6ff.	210
7.48	251
8.12	210
8.17	5
8.29ff.	46
8.35f.	208
8.52	24
8.64	234
10.28	231
11.5	206
11.7	238, 244
11.33	206, 244
12.28ff.	45
12.28f.	199
14.15, 23	261
15.3, 11	225
15.13	261
16.16ff., 28ff.	238
16.31f.	229
16.33	261
17	160
17-19	208
17.1	208
18	160
18.1	208
18.16-40	229
18.19ff.	247
18.20ff.	71
18.21-46	208
18.27	160
18.41-46	250
19	202
19.1	247
19.8	198
20.1ff.	230
21.1-4	45, 53
22.6, 12, 15	125
22.19ff.	154
22.52ff.	238
22.52	231

II Kings

1.1	238
3.1ff.	238
3.4-27	237, 238
3.15ff.	125
3.26f.	267
3.27	235
6.24ff.	230
10.18-27	229

(II Kings cont.)

10.19	247
13.1	231
13.6	261
14.23	231, 261
15.5	213
15.8	231
16.2	225
16.3	235
16.4	238
17.9f.	238
17.10, 16	261
17.30	252
18.3	225
18.4	261
18.34	231
19.13	231
19.16	24
19.20ff.	123
19.30	233
20.6	24
20.10	252
21.2ff.	72
21.3	261
21.6	235
21.7	261
22f.	171
22.2	225
22.13	171, 172
23.5	104
23.6f.	261
23.10	235
23.12	23
23.13	206, 244
23.14f.	261
23.21-23	171
23.24	248, 249
23.26	72
24.3	72
25.7	260

I Chronicles

11.2	28, 107, 137
16.31ff.	22
17	27, 28
17.6	209
17.13	29, 30
29.14	23

II Chronicles

1.1-12	27, 28
1.12	29
2.2ff.	210
3.1	251
14.2	261

15.16	261
19.3	261
24.18	261
26.16-18	171
28.1	225
28.3	235
29.2	225
30.15-18, 21	254
31.1	261
33.2ff.	72
33.3f.	261
33.6	235
33.7, 19	261
34.2f.	225
35.2, 17	254

Ezra

3.7	210
6.19-22	254

Nehemiah

3.30	245
5.19	42
12.44	245
13.7	245
13.9	251
13.31	42

Job

1f.	222
1.1-2.10	140
1.6ff.	64
1.6	240
1.21	75
2.1	240
2.8	215
3.8	82
4.1-5.27	45
4.7ff.	166
4.8-11	135
4.17	108, 173
5.6ff.	36
5.7	240
5.9ff.	36
5.9-11	45
5.9	20
7.12	83
8.5f.	135
9f.	138
9.11f.	45
9.13	46
10.9	56, 61
10.21f.	11
11.7ff.	140
11.7-9	135

12-14	138
12.24f.	11
15.14-16	141
15.14	108, 173
15.22	11
17.13	11
18.5-21	135
18.13	212
18.18	11
19.13-20	139
20.8	63
21	138
21.6ff.	135
24.2	53
25.4-6	141
26.7ff.	13, 26
26.12f.	46, 83, 156, 198
29-31	138
31	64
31.6	64
31.26ff.	104
33.6	56, 61
34.16	45
34.19	62
34.35-37	135
37.2ff.	13, 209
37.5f.	4
38.4f.	23
38.7	13, 83, 240
38.8	83
38.11, 16f.	200
38.17	11
38.22-30	84
38.39-41	45
39.6	259
42.7-9	140

Psalms

1	52
1.3	52, 134
2	107
2.6	251
2.7	19, 29, 30
3	43
3.3-6	42
4.5	222
5.2	43, 154
5.3	222
5.4ff.	167
6	108, 110
	133
6.3	110, 141
6.5	11
7.3ff.	167

(Psalms cont.)

7.9-11	36	22.22	32	34	32
7.17	110, 115	22.24	27, 32, 41	34.2	32, 43
8	20, 26	22.25	32, 229	34.3f.	32
8.1	20, 26	22.27ff.	32	34.6, 8ff.	32
8.3ff.	26	23.1ff.	26, 40	34.11	32
8.3	83	23.2ff.	43	34.15	24
8.5	46	23.4	42	34.16	45
8.9	20, 26	24.1f.	26	35.9f.	110, 115
9-10	110	24.3	251	35.11	138
9.1ff.	167	24.3-6	43, 64, 108	35.13f.	43
9.11	198	24.4	36	35.16f.	135
9.13	40, 164	25.3	40	35.17	110
10.1-4	180	25.4	50	35.20f.	138
10.3ff.	135	25.16	43	35.27f.	110, 115
10.11	180	26	171	36.7	23
11.1	42	26.3ff.	167	36.9	102
11.6	117	26.4f.	64, 132	37	49, 135
13.1ff.	110	27.1ff.	37, 42, 167	37.1-11	43
13.1f.	141	27.4, 10	43	37.7	48, 180
13.	139	28.8f.	139	37.9f., 13	180
13.5	110, 115	28.9	40, 43, 46,	38	108, 110,
14	180	29	20, 154,		133
14.7	265		187, 205	38.1ff.	36, 166
15	43, 64, 108	29.1-10	220	38.1f.	36
15.2	132	29.1f.	13	38.11	43
16.1f.	42	29.1	222, 240,	38.13ff.	49
16.11	37, 63		248	38.15	43
17.1ff.	167	29.2	20	38.18, 21f.	36
17.2-5	171	29.3ff.	209	39.6	54, 62, 63
17.8	23	29.10	20, 205	40.1-4	32
18	32	30	32	40.4	41
18.3ff., 6ff.	32	30.2f.	32	40.5-11	32
18.7-14	163	30.3	20, 40	40.5	112
18.10	196, 210	30.5, 7	32	40.6	46
18.13f.	209, 220	30.9	167	40.9f.	32
18.15	200	31	43, 133	41	32
18.25ff.	32	31.1	167	41.4	36
18.31	42	31.3	37	42.2	43
18.49	32	31.7f.	110, 115	44.4	26, 154
19.1ff.	26	31.15	44, 58	44.5	24
19.1-6	13	32	32, 36, 108,	44.9ff.	160
19.1	83		110	44.23	162
19.4-6	13, 20, 101	32.3ff.	36	44.24ff.	160
19.5f.	102	32.3f.	32	45	39, 107
20	107	32.4	36	45.6	39
20.1-5	43	32.5	173	46	43
20.3	234	32.6, 10	32	46.7, 11	42
21	107	33	20	47	20, 26
21.4	115	33.6f.	13, 26	47.1f.	20
21.10	233	33.6	4, 13	47.3	107
22.1	138	33.8	20	47.9	20
22.14	259	33.9	4, 13, 26	48	43, 106
22.17	33	33.18f.	110	48.1f.	251
22.22ff.	32	33.18	24	48.2	197
		33.19	20	48.11	251

(Psalms cont.)

49.5ff.	54
49.7ff.	62
49.15	40
49.17	62
50.1	240
50.4	248, 258
50.8ff.	192
50.16ff.	132
51.1f.	36
51.1	222
51.3ff.	36
51.7ff., 13	36
51.16f.	222
52.7	54
52.8	52, 134
53.6	265
54.1	24
55.12ff.	139
56.3f., 11	37
57.1	23, 167
57.2	258
58.6	135
59.9	42
59.10	238
59.16f.	42
60.11	37
61.6f.	43, 108, 115, 139
61.6	240
62	43
62.5-8	42
62.9	64
62.10	54
63.2f.	43
63.7	23
64.5	180
65	20
65.2	20, 26, 41
65.4	43
65.6ff.	5
65.6	13
65.7f., 12f.	20
66.2	110
66.3, 5	20, 26
66.8	20
68.2	259
68.4	110, 196, 210
68.8f.	208
68.8	145, 198
68.17	198, 250
68.33	196
69.30	110
69.33	41, 79, 210

70.1, 5	222
71	41
71.1-6	167
71.4	41
71.19	112
71.20	40
72	43, 107
72.1-4	45, 225
72.7	241
72.12-14	45, 225
72.16f.	226
72.17	243
73.3ff.	135, 180
73.11	180, 258
73.17f.	180
73.20	63
74	160
74.1	40, 46, 170
74.2	198
74.4ff.	170
74.7	241
74.12	26, 154, 198
74.13f.	46, 156
74.13	198
74.14	82, 83
76	43
76.7ff.	45
77.9f.	258
77.16ff.	205
77.17ff.	163
77.17	208
78.35	258
78.55	239
78.65	162
78.71f.	28, 107, 137, 143
79	160
79.11	26
79.13	40, 46
80.1	40, 46, 100
80.3	110
80.4ff.	170
80.7, 19	110
82	154
82.1, 6	222
84	43, 106
84.2-5	43
84.3	154
84.8f.	139
84.10	43
84.12	41
86	41
86.8	105, 112

86.13	40
86.14	41
87	43, 106
87.1f.	198
88.5f.	213
88.5	215
88.6	11
88.10-12	11
88.10	245
88.14	139
88.18	11
89	107
89.5	248
89.6	222, 240, 248
89.7	222, 248
89.9f.	46, 156, 205
89.11ff.	26
89.12	197
89.26f.	19, 29, 30
89.27	29
89.34f.	143
89.38ff.	143, 160
89.46	45
90.2	6
90.10	238
91	37
91.1f.	23
91.1	113
92	32
92.1	32
92.5	99
92.12ff.	52
93	20
93.2	205
93.5	205
94.7	180
94.17	64
95	101
95.3	13, 89, 118, 145, 154, 201, 212
95.4-7	13, 26
95.4f.	26
95.7	15, 40, 46, 102
96.4	84, 118, 145, 154, 201, 212
96.8	20
96.10ff.	20
96.11ff.	22
97.5	248, 259
97.7	154

(*Psalms cont.*)					
97.9	84, 105, 118, 145, 154, 201, 212	118.6	42	148.7	156, 198
		118.7	238	148.13	20, 26, 104, 105
		118.8f.	37		
98.6-8	20	119	43, 134	150	20, 26
99.3f.	20	121.1	251		
101	45, 107, 225	121.3ff.	46	*Proverbs*	
		121.3	15	1.10	47
101.5ff.	107	122	43	1.12	213
101.8	241	122.6-9	43	1.15	47
102	108, 110, 133	123.2f.	173	1.23	264
		126.1	265	2.1	47
		126.5f.	86	2.16-19	48
102.1ff.	43	130.3	108	2.19	37, 50, 63
102.2	110, 139	130.7	36	3.1	47
102.6f.	43	132	106	3.4	44
102.23f.	24	136	101	3.10	242
102.24	238	136.2	201, 212	3.21	47
103-105	100	136.3	20	4.1f., 10, 20	47
103.3	23	136.5ff.	5, 13, 26	5.1-14	48
103.14	61	137	43	5.1	47
103.19	20	138	32	5.6	37, 63
104	13, 16, 26, 79, 101	138.1f.	32	6.6	47
		138.3f., 6	32	6.13	249
104.3f.	79	139.1-4	108	6.16f.	57
104.3	250	139.15f.	77	6.20-35	48
104.5	80	139.15	75	7.1-27	48
104.7	205	140.1, 4	41	7.5-23	48
104.10ff.	13, 16, 26	140.7	37	7.5, 12	48
104.14f.	45, 80	141.2	251	7.19, 21, 23	48
104.20f.	16	142	133	8.17	48
104.21	45	142.5	37	8.24-26	6
104.24-26	16	143	108, 110	10.10	249
104.26	156	143.7	110, 139	10.17	37, 50, 63
104.27f.	13, 26, 45	144.2	42	10.19	47, 48
106.40-43	238	145	20	11.1	64
107	101	145.3, 11ff.	20	11.4	62
107.11	258	145.15f.	45	11.24ff.	67
107.18	164	145.20	42	12.19	47
108.1ff.	167	146	20, 26	14.21	49
108.12	37	146.3f.	37	14.34	43
110	107, 245	146.6-9	26	15.16f.	54
110.1	107	146.6-8	13	15.24	37, 50, 63
110.3	29, 30	146.6	13, 26	16.1	49
110.4	171	146.7ff.	103, 110	16.8	54
111.9	20	146.10	20	16.9	49, 58
112.4	102	147	20, 104	16.15	47
113	20, 101	147.4	4, 82	16.30	249
113.3	240	147.6, 8f.	104	17.1	54, 58
115.17	64	147.9	45	17.12	259
116	32	147.15-18	104	18.4	48
116.1-3, 5f.	32	148	20, 26	18.5	59
116.8	20, 32, 40	148.1ff.	13	18.21	55
116.13ff.	32	148.4	79	19.1	54
116.14ff.	32, 229	148.5	4, 13, 26	19.17	42
116.18	32	148.6	83	19.19	43

(Proverbs cont.)

19.21	49, 58
19.22	54
20.9	108, 141, 173
20.22	49
21.1	28
21.3	46
21.6	54
21.21	43
21.23.	47
21.26	52
22.2	49
22.9	67
22.17–23.11	49
22.17f.	50
22.19	50
22.20	62
22.21	50
22.22f.	225
22.22	51
22.24f.	56
22.24	55, 60
22.28	53, 132
22.29	62
23.1–3	61
23.4f.	54
23.5	55
23.6–8	57
23.9	60
23.10	53
23.12–24.22	47
24.23	59
24.30ff.	47
25.6f.	47
27.1	44, 58
28.15	259
28.21	59
29.8	43
29.13	61
29.14	46
30.16	213
31.1–9	45

Ecclesiastes

3.1ff.	54
3.16	136
5.9ff.	54
7.26f.	48
8.9ff.	135
8.16f.	134, 140
11.2	200, 249
11.5	134, 140

Song of Solomon

4.9	248, 249
7.5	233

Isaiah

1.2	248, 258
1.8	117
1.10–17	46
1.11	239
1.15	160
1.17	45, 225
1.23	225
1.26ff.	121
3.5	120
3.18, 20	248, 249
4.5f.	121
5.14	213
6.8f.	125, 128
6.9–13	63
7.3ff.	123
8.17	45, 160
8.19	216
9.2	102
9.6	246
9.19f.	120
10.5ff.	123
10.9	231
11.1	232
11.6–9	85
11.10	233
13.10	117
13.19	121
13.21f.	259
14.9	245
14.13	197
14.22	121
14.29	233
15.2	215
17.1ff.	123
19.1	196, 210
19.3	248, 249
19.18	87
19.23	233
21.10	218
22.21	241
23.15	238
24–27	119
24.23	231
25.4	23
25.6ff.	192
25.8	86
26.14	245
27.1	82, 156, 198
28.7ff.	123

28.15	212
29.4	216
29.7f.	63
29.14ff.	160
29.16	56, 61
29.17–21	85
29.20f.	86
30.1ff.	42
30.2	23
30.22	240
30.23	121
30.30	259
30.33	235
31.8	121
32.15–20	85
33.14–16	64
34.3	232
34.5ff.	194
34.5	121
34.10ff.	259
34.11–17	129
35.2	233
35.5	47
35.9	85, 86
35.10	86
37.16	26
37.21ff.	123
37.31	233
38.10ff.	24, 32
38.17	32
38.18	11
38.20	229
40.8	20
40.11	40, 46
40.13	99
40.15	64
40.26	4, 82
41.4	4
41.10	42
41.13ff.	232
43.1ff.	232
43.1	47
43.5	..:
43.7	27
43.11	42
43.20	22
44.2ff.	232
44.8	42
44.24	26
44.26f.	4
45.6	240
45.9	27, 56, 61
45.15	45
45.19	160

(Isaiah cont.)

47.9, 12	248, 249
48.13	4
48.16	160
50.2	4
50.9	240
51.8	240
51.9f.	46, 156, 198
51.11	86
51.17, 22	117
53	175
53.2	233
53.4-7, 12	175
54.4ff.	232
54.8	160
55.8f.	134
55.8	49
55.10f.	4
58.7	67
60.4	121
64.2	264
64.8	56, 61
65.25	85
66.22	232

Jeremiah

1.4f.	29
1.5	27, 28
1.7	125, 128
2.12	248
2.16	254
2.21ff.	7
2.31	11
3.15	28
5.2	36
5.23ff.	7
5.31	123
6.14	123
6.15	245
6.20	251
7.5f.	225
7.9	36
7.18	255
7.31ff.	235
8.17	248, 249
9.17ff.	216
9.23f.	43
10.10	43, 145
10.13	208
11.16ff.	52
11.16	134
11.20	49
12.1	135
12.7	160

13.26	260
14.12	222
14.13ff.	123
15.4	72
15.21	41
16.6	215
17.5-8	52
17.6	259
17.8	52, 134
17.11	238
17.12-18	110
18.1ff.	56, 61
19.4f., 11	235
19.13	23
20.13	41
21.11f.	45
22.1ff.	45
22.2f.	225
23.1f.	137
23.5	45, 233
23.9ff.	123
23.13	126
23.16ff.	166
23.16	126
23.20	5
23.23ff.	166
23.23f.	160
25.15ff.	192
26.12, 15	125, 128
27.9f.	123
27.9	46
29.7	43
29.21ff.	123
30.10f.	232
31.10	40, 46
31.29f.	173
31.40	252
32.35	235
32.44	265
33.6	23
33.7, 11	265
33.15	233
34.18	260
39.7	260
41.5	215
43.7ff.	253
43.7-9	254
44.1	255
44.11ff.	254
44.17-19, 25	255
46.14	254
46.18	233
47.5	215
48	244
48.7, 13, 46	244

48.37	215
49.6	265
49.23	231
52.11	260

Lamentations

1-2	116
3.10	259
3.25ff.	43
4.3f.	258
4.21	117
5.7	173, 180
5.20ff.	160

Ezekiel

2.3	125, 128
8-11	126, 127
8.14	216
11.17	121
12.12f.	260
12.13	117, 127
13.11, 13	259
13.19	66
14.15	259
16.20f.	235
16.37	260
17.5ff.	52
17.9	233
17.11-21	172
17.20	127
18	173
18.2	173, 180
18.7, 16	67
20.28f.	238
20.34, 41	121
21.21	166
22.6f.	225
24.17	215
25.13, 16	45
27.9	202
28.1-19	244
29.3	198
30.2	259
30.18	254
32.2	198
32.3	128
34.1-10	137, 143
34.2, 23	28
34.25	85, 86
34.27	121
34.28	85
38.22	259
39.25	265
44.16ff.	180
45.10ff.	64

(*Ezekiel cont.*)

45.23	234

Daniel

1.20	248, 249
2.2	248, 249
5.27	64
8.23–25	119
11.2–45	119
11.4, 6, 8f.	120
12.1	120

Hosea

2.2–13	208
2.3	260
2.20	85
3.1	125
4.10	160, 257
5.6	160
5.10	53
5.12	240
6.2	243f.
6.6	46
7.12	128
8.4ff.	45
8.5	200
9.12	257
9.14	160, 258
9.16	233, 257
10.4	36
10.11	218
12.8	64
13.2	200
13.4	42
13.8	259

Joel

2.20	232
2.28	123

Amos

1.2	160
1.3	218
1.8	45
2.9	233
4.7f.	208
4.10	232
5.11	257
5.18	117
5.21–24	46
7.15	125, 128

8.5	64
8.10	215
9.14f.	121

Jonah

1.2ff.	166
1.7	166
2.2ff.	32
2.2, 6	32
2.9	32, 229

Micah

1.4	259
2.2	45
2.12	121
3	166
3.5ff.	123
3.11	42
4.6	121
4.7	231
4.13	218, 248
5.5	200, 249
5.14	261
6.2	248
6.6f.	239
6.7	267
6.10f.	64
6.14f.	160, 257
7.5f.	120

Nahum

3.5	260

Habakkuk

2.5	213
2.20	48
3.5	205, 240
3.6	200
3.8	205
3.9f.	209
3.10	208
3.15	205

Zephaniah

1.5	23
1.7	48
1.12	180
1.13	257
1.18	62
2.9, 13f.	259
3.4	123

Haggai

1.6	257

Zechariah

1.17	121
2.13	48
3.8	233
4.14	248
5.3	36
6.5	248
6.11–13	245
6.12	233
7.10	225
9.1	230, 231
10.1	208
12.8	39
12.11	216
14.20	248, 249

Malachi

1.6ff.	180
1.11	240
3.5	45
3.13–4.3	42

Wisdom of Solomon

15.7	61

Sirach

9.3	48
33.13	61

II Maccabees

4.18–20	229

Matthew

5.37	132
6.5–7	48
11.5	47
15.5	246
16.18	164
19.30	47

Mark

7.11	246

Luke

7.22	47

Romans

9.21	61